SURROUNDED *by*
BITTERNESS

SURROUNDED *by* BITTERNESS

Image Schemas and Metaphors
for Conceptualizing Distress
in Classical Hebrew

Philip D. King

PICKWICK Publications • Eugene, Oregon

SURROUNDED BY BITTERNESS
Image Schemas and Metaphors for Conceptualizing Distress in Classical Hebrew

Copyright © 2012 Philip D. King. All rights reserved. Except for brief quotations in critical publications or reviews, no part of this book may be reproduced in any manner without prior written permission from the publisher. Write: Permissions, Wipf and Stock Publishers, 199 W. 8th Ave., Suite 3, Eugene, OR 97401.

Pickwick Pubications
An Imprint of Wipf and Stock Publishers
199 W. 8th Ave., Suite 3
Eugene, OR 97401

www.wipfandstock.com

ISBN 13: 978-1-61097-224-6

Cataloging-in-Publication data:

King, Philip D.

    Surrounded by bitterness : image schemas and metaphors for conceptualizing distress in classical Hebrew / Philip D. King.

    xxiv + 420 pp. ; 23 cm — Includes bibliographical references, indexes, and illustrations.

    ISBN 13: 978-1-61097-224-6

    1. Bible—O.T.—Criticism, interpretation, etc. 2. Metaphor in the Bible. 3. Grief—Religious aspects.

BS1199. M45. K50. 2012

Manufactured in the USA

Scripture quotations are from New Revised Standard Version Bible: Anglicized Edition, copyright © 1989, 1995 National Council of the Churches of Christ in the United States of America. Used by permission. All rights reserved.

Figure 2.2 is taken from Foundations of Cognitive Grammar, Volume 1, by Ronald W. Langacker. © 1987 by the Board of Trustees of the Leland Stanford Jr. University. All rights reserved. Used with the permission of Stanford University Press. www.sup.org

Figure 6.2. is taken from Toward a Cognitive Semantics: Concept Structuring Systems, by Leonard Talmy, published by The MIT Press.

For my family

Contents

Abstract / xvii
Acknowledgements / xix
Abbreviations / xxi

1 **Conventional Distress Language / 1**
    1.1. Introduction
    1.2. Approaches to Conventional Language
        1.2.1. Historical Criticism and Idiosyncratic Language
        1.2.2. Form Criticism and Liturgical Language
        1.2.3. Literary Criticism and Intertextual Language
        1.2.4. Psychological Interpretation and the Language of Humanity
        1.2.5. Cultural Linguistic Interpretation and the Language of Conceptual Metaphor
    1.3. Purpose and Outline of the Thesis

2 **Culture, Language, and Thought / 12**
    2.1. Introduction
    2.2. The Tradition of Linguistic Relativity: Humboldt, Boas, Sapir, and Whorf
        2.2.1. Humboldt (1767–1835): Language Determines Characteristic Worldview
        2.2.2. Boas (1858–1942): Language Reflects Unconscious Categories

Contents

- 2.2.3. Sapir (1884–1939): Language Creates Different Worlds
- 2.2.4. Whorf (1897–1941): Language Organizes the "Kaleidoscope Flux" of Impressions
- 2.3. Linguistics and Biblical Studies I: Barr and Sawyer
  - 2.3.1. Barr (1924–2006)
    - a) No Simple Correspondence between Language Structure and Thought Structure
    - b) No Privileged Cultural Mind
    - c) Correct Use of Etymology
    - d) The Root Fallacy
    - e) The Unitary Concept Fallacy
  - 2.3.2. Sawyer
- 2.4. Precursors to Cognitive Linguistics—Wittgenstein, Rosch, Fillmore, Schank, Abelson, and Reddy
  - 2.4.1. Wittgenstein (1889–1951): Family Resemblances
  - 2.4.2. Rosch: Prototypes and Basic Level Categories
  - 2.4.3. Fillmore: Frames
  - 2.4.4. Schank and Abelson: Scripts
  - 2.4.5. Reddy: The Conduit Metaphor
- 2.5. The Cognitive Linguistics Paradigm
  - 2.5.1. Lakoff and Johnson: Conceptual Metaphors and Image Schemas
    - a) Philosophical Basis
    - b) Image Schemas and Gestalt Perception
    - c) Conceptual Metaphor
    - d) Idealized Cognitive Models
    - e) Further Evidence for Conceptual Metaphor
    - f) Linguistic Relativity
  - 2.5.2. Langacker and Taylor: Cognitive Grammar
    - a) Encyclopaedic Knowledge
    - b) Schematic Networks
    - c) Linguistic Relativity
    - d) Taylor's Cognitive Grammar
  - 2.5.3. Talmy: Force Dynamic Patterns
  - 2.5.4. Fauconnier: Mappings and Integration

Contents

- 2.5.5. Wierzbicka: Natural Semantic Metalanguage
- 2.5.6. Gibbs: Psychological Evidence for a Poetic Mind
  - a) No "Literal" Meanings
  - b) Metaphor Comprehension
  - c) Poetic Metaphor
  - d) Idiom Comprehension and Image Schemas
  - e) Metaphor and Culture
- 2.5.7. Kövecses: Emotion and Cultural Variation
  - a) Research Methodology
  - b) Emotion Metaphors
  - c) Conceptual Metonymy
  - d) Metaphor and Culture
  - e) Language and Thought
- 2.5.8. Deignan: Metaphor and Corpus Research
- 2.5.9. Cognitive Linguistics and the Legacy of James Barr
- 2.6. Linguistics and Biblical Studies II: Applications of Cognitive Semantics to Hebrew
  - 2.6.1. Overview
  - 2.6.2. The South African School
  - 2.6.3. The European School
  - 2.6.4. SIL
- 2.7. Position of this Thesis

3 Corpus / 70

- 3.1. Introduction
- 3.2. The General Corpus
  - 3.2.1. Development of the Hebrew Language
  - 3.2.2. A Recognized Corpus
- 3.3. The Specific Corpus
  - 3.3.1. Definition of the Specific Corpus
  - 3.3.2. Context of the Specific Corpus
    - a) Job
    - b) Psalms
    - c) Lamentations
    - d) Confessions of Jeremiah
    - e) Distress Language in Narrative Contexts
    - f) Hodayot

3.4. Summary

4 Methodology / 86
4.1. Introduction
4.2. Metaphor Terminology
4.3. Metaphor Identification
4.4. Collection of Data
4.5. Framework for Presenting Results
    4.5.1. Establishing the Image Schema or Primary Source Domain
    4.5.2. Comparative Data
    4.5.3. Presentation and Analysis of Mappings
    4.5.4. Further Evidence
    4.5.5. Universality and Variation
4.6. Summary

5 Distress and the VERTICALITY Schema / 99
5.1. Introduction
5.2. Establishing the Schema
    5.2.1. Physiological / Universal Factors
    5.2.2. Culture-specific Factors
        a) Spatial Scale
        b) Postural Scale
5.3. Comparative Data on Emotion Language and the VERTICALITY Schema
    5.3.1. Contemporary Cross-Linguistic Comparisons
    5.3.2. Ancient Near Eastern Comparisons
5.4. Presentation and Analysis of Hebrew Mappings
    5.4.1. BEING IN DISTRESS IS BEING DOWN ON THE SPATIAL GEOGRAPHICAL SCALE
    5.4.2. BEING IN DISTRESS IS BEING DOWN ON THE POSTURAL SCALE
5.5. Further Evidence
    5.5.1. Generalizations over Polysemy
    5.5.2. Generalizations over Inference Patterns
    5.5.3. Novel Metaphor

5.5.4. Larger Scale Metaphorical Systems
5.5.5. Non-verbal Realizations
5.6. Universality and Variation
5.6.1. Variation within Source and Target Domain
5.6.2. Variation in Linguistic Expression
5.7. Summary

6 Distress and the CONSTRAINT Schema / 140
6.1. Introduction
6.2. Establishing the Schema
6.2.1. Physiological / Universal Factors
6.2.2. Culture-specific Factors
a) The Root צרר
b) Semantics and Syntax of the Verb
c) Nouns
d) The Root צוק I
e) "Surrounding" Roots: אפף, נקף, סבב
f) Restricting Roots: עטף, סגר, חבל, אסר
g) Evaluation
6.3. Comparative Data on Emotion Language and the CONSTRAINT Schema
6.3.1. Contemporary Cross-Linguistic Comparisons
6.3.2. Ancient Near Eastern Comparisons
6.4. Presentation and Analysis of Hebrew Mappings
6.4.1. EXPERIENCING DISTRESS IS PHYSIOLOGICAL CONSTRICTION
6.4.2. EXPERIENCING DISTRESS IS LACKING SPACE TO MOVE
a) Narrow Places and Blocking Walls
b) Being Shut In
c) צרר and צוק
d) Entailments
6.4.3. EXPERIENCING DISTRESS IS BEING SURROUNDED
a) Surrounding Enemies
b) Surrounding Animals
c) Job Surrounded

- d) Surrounded by Abstract Hostile Entities
- e) Entailments
- 6.4.4. EXPERIENCING DISTRESS IS BEING ENCLOSED BY WATER
  - a) Examples
  - b) Entailments
- 6.4.5. EXPERIENCING DISTRESS IS BEING UNDER SIEGE
  - a) Encyclopaedic Knowledge
  - b) Examples
  - c) Entailments
- 6.4.6. EXPERIENCING DISTRESS IS BEING HELD IN A NET OR TRAP
  - a) Encyclopaedic Knowledge
  - b) Examples
  - c) Entailments
- 6.4.7. EXPERIENCING DISTRESS IS BEING CONFINED IN A PIT
- 6.4.8. EXPERIENCING DISTRESS IS BEING TIED UP WITH CORDS
  - a) Examples
  - b) Entailments
- 6.4.9. EXPERIENCING DISTRESS IS BEING IMPRISONED
- 6.4.10. EXPERIENCING DISTRESS IS BEING GRIPPED BY THE CONTRACTIONS OF LABOR
- 6.4.11. EXPERIENCING DISTRESS IS BEING STUCK IN MUD

6.5. Further Evidence
- 6.5.1. Generalizations over Polysemy
- 6.5.2. Generalizations over Inference Patterns
- 6.5.3. Novel Metaphor
- 6.5.4. Larger Scale Metaphorical Systems
- 6.5.5. Non-verbal Realizations

6.6. Universality and Variation
- 6.6.1. Variation within Source and Target Domain
- 6.6.2. Variation in Linguistic Expression

6.7. Summary

7 **Distress and the Force Schema / 210**
   7.1. Introduction
   7.2. Establishing the Schema
      7.2.1. Physiological / Universal Factors
      7.2.2. Culture-specific Factors
   7.3. Comparative Data on Emotion Language and the Force Schema
      7.3.1. Contemporary Cross-Linguistic Comparisons
      7.3.2. Ancient Near Eastern Comparisons
   7.4. Presentation and Analysis of Hebrew Mappings
      7.4.1. Being in Distress is Experiencing Force Damaging Part of the Body
      7.4.2. Being in Distress is Experiencing Fragmentation
      7.4.3. Being in Distress is Being Forcefully Gripped
      7.4.4. Being in Distress is Encountering a Moving Force
      7.4.5. Being in Distress is Experiencing Enforced Movement
      7.4.6. Being in Distress is Being Attacked by Wild Animals
      7.4.7. Being in Distress is Being Attacked by a Human Opponent
         a) Various Adversaries
         b) Deliberate Preparation
         c) The Enemy's Hand
         d) Other Hand-to-hand Combat
         e) Bows and Arrows
         f) Swords
         g) Military Battle
         h) Summary
      7.4.8. Being in Distress is Experiencing the Forces of Nature
         a) Torrents
         b) Waves
         c) Storms
         d) Wind

Contents

        7.4.11. BEING IN DISTRESS IS EXPOSURE TO HEAT / FIRE
        7.4.12. BEING IN DISTRESS IS BEING TRAMPLED
        7.4.13. BEING IN DISTRESS IS CARRYING A WEIGHT
  7.5. Further Evidence
        7.5.1. Generalizations over Polysemy
        7.5.2. Generalizations over Inference Patterns
        7.5.3. Novel Metaphor
        7.5.4. Larger Scale Metaphorical Systems
        7.5.5. Non-verbal Realizations
  7.6. Universality and Variation
        7.6.1. Variation within Source and Target Domain
        7.6.2. Variation in Linguistic Expression
  7.7. Summary

8 Distress and DARKNESS / 289
  8.1. Introduction
  8.2. Establishing the Source Domain
        8.2.1. Physiological / Universal Factors
        8.2.2. Culture-specific factors
            a) Darkness in the Ancient Near East
            b) Prototypical Associations for Darkness
            c) Intensity of Darkness
  8.3. Comparative data
        8.3.1. Contemporary Cross-Linguistic Comparisons
        8.3.2. Ancient Near Eastern Comparisons
  8.4. Presentation and Analysis of Hebrew Mappings
        8.4.1. BEING IN DISTRESS IS DARKNESS IN PART OF THE BODY
        8.4.2. BEING IN DISTRESS IS PROTOTYPICALLY SUFFERING IN THE DARK
        8.4.3. BEING IN DISTRESS IS BEING IN A DARK PLACE
  8.5. Further Evidence
        8.5.1. Generalizations over Polysemy
        8.5.2. Generalizations over Inference Patterns
        8.5.3. Novel Metaphor
        8.5.4. Larger Scale Metaphorical Systems
        8.5.5. Non-verbal Realizations

8.6. Universality and Variation
       8.6.1. Variation within Source and Target Domain
       8.6.2. Variation in Linguistic Expression
   8.7. Summary

9 Distress and the Bad Taste Primary Metaphor / 322
   9.1. Introduction
   9.2. Establishing the Source Domain
       9.2.1. Physiological / Universal Factors
           a) Physiology
           b) Difference from Other Senses
           c) Linguistic Typology
       9.2.2. Culture-specific Factors
   9.3. Comparative Data on Emotion Language and the Bad Taste Metaphor
       9.3.1. Contemporary Cross-Linguistic Comparisons
       9.3.2. Ancient Near Eastern Comparisons
   9.4. Presentation and Analysis of Hebrew Mappings
       9.4.1. Experiencing Distress is Experiencing Bitterness in the Body
       9.4.2. Experiencing Distress Produces Bitterness
       9.4.3. Experiencing Distress is Ingesting an Unpleasant Substance
       9.4.4. Experiencing Distress is Being Exposed to Poison
       9.4.5. Experiencing Distress is Other Exposure to Something Bitter / Noxious
   9.5. Further Evidence
       9.5.1. Generalizations over Polysemy
       9.5.2. Generalizations over Inference Patterns
       9.5.3. Novel Metaphor
       9.5.4. Larger Scale Metaphorical Systems
       9.5.5. Non-verbal Realizations
   9.6. Universality and Variation
       9.6.1. Variation within Source and Target Domain
       9.6.2. Variation in Linguistic Expression
   9.7. Summary

Contents

    10 Conclusion / 355
        10.1. Introduction
        10.2. Summary of Results
        10.3. Implications
            10.3.1. Implications for Biblical Studies
            10.3.2. Implications for Cognitive Linguistics
            10.3.3. Implications for Translation
        10.4. Future Directions

Appendix / 367

Bibliography / 383

Scripture Index / 405

Subject and Name Index / 415

Preface

THIS VOLUME EXPLORES THE Classical Hebrew concept of "distress" through the Cognitive Linguistic approach of George Lakoff, Mark Johnson, and Zoltán Kövecses. It investigates the conceptual metaphors ancient Hebrew speakers used to conceptualize their distressing experiences through basic embodied experiences. It studies image schemas (recurring patterns of experience) and primary metaphors (such as cognitive links between darkness and distress) which give structure to distressing situations and suggest actions to take. It provides a detailed and descriptive inventory of the main image schemas (VERTICALITY, CONSTRAINT, and FORCE) and primary metaphors (DARKNESS and BAD TASTE) reflected in the conventional Hebrew language of distress found in the Psalms, Lamentations, Job, and the Hodayot.

The first chapter introduces the topic of conventional distress language, arguing that the Cognitive Linguistic approach provides a useful complement to previous studies of the matter. The second chapter describes the theoretical semantic framework, particularly arguing that where it opposes James Barr's lexical semantics it is nevertheless linguistically justified. Chapters three and four identify a specific corpus of Classical Hebrew texts that refer to situations of distress, and show how these texts are classifiable according to image schemas and metaphors. Chapters five, six, and seven present all the examples of conceptualizations of distress based on the VERTICALITY, CONSTRAINT, and FORCE schemas, respectively, and compare them to similar metaphors in other languages. They argue that in Classical Hebrew the FORCE schema is the most significant for conceptualizing negative experience, and that, further, the CONSTRAINT schema is both more entrenched and more linguistically elaborated than the CONSTRAINT schema in English, and than the VERTICALITY schema in Hebrew. These chapters establish that forces and constrained situations are more significant for understanding situations of distress than up or down movement. Chapters eight and nine present conceptualizations of distress based on DARKNESS and BAD TASTE, arguing that the way vision and taste are perceived in Hebrew constrains the way distress is understood through metaphor. The conclusion argues that all these metaphors cohere to create a prototypical conceptualization of distress, whose characteristic features are that it is unexpected by the sufferer, unjustified, and caused by a personal external agent. Moreover, these metaphors highlight that distress is an experience sufferers are unable to relieve by their own means.

Acknowledgments

THIS BOOK ORIGINATED AS a thesis supervised at London School of Theology and submitted for the degree of Doctor of Philosophy at Brunel University in January 2010. The thesis would have been impossible without the help of many people, just some of whom can be thanked here. First and foremost, my supervisor Jean-Marc Heimerdinger has encouraged me throughout, both in person and via Skype to Papua New Guinea. He also first instilled in me a love of the Hebrew Psalms, and it is still his voice I hear in my head as I read them. Other staff at London School of Theology also sowed seeds for this thesis: Deryck Sheriffs first challenged me to probe the emotions of the psalmists; and Peter Riddell first opened my eyes to biblical semantics.

Several colleagues have provided further encouragement and support along the way, listening to ideas and providing feedback. In Northwood, fellow students in the Guthrie Centre shared their lunch and their time, especially Nick Gatzke, Andy Bannister, and Maurice Rubin. In Papua New Guinea, special thanks go to René van den Berg and Anne Henderson for always being willing to discuss Hebrew and linguistics. Other SIL colleagues offered listening ears and thoughtful comments, especially during coffee break times at LCORE. Matt Taylor, Ben Pehrson, Pekka and Maiju Laihia, and Paul Minter all deserve thanks for their help in the last stages, freeing me from other responsibilities and repeatedly encouraging me to keep going.

Financially, I am very grateful to the sponsorship of both SIL International and SIL PNG who contributed significantly to the course fees, and to Emmanuel Church, Northwood, and Holywell Church,

Acknowledgments

Loughborough, as well as other friends and family, who have continued to support us throughout this project. Physically, I am grateful to the physiotherapists who helped me get through the long hours of sitting behind a computer.

Within my family, my parents grounded me in the intellectual disciplines of science and theology and have continued to believe in me throughout the years. My children, Simeon and Joshua, have shared their dad with this project for most of their lives, and I am thankful for their acceptance of this and simple demonstrations of encouragement. However, the biggest thanks are for my wife, Kate, who has sacrificed the most to enable this project to reach completion. Words are not enough to thank her for her continual love and support.

Abbreviations

AB	Anchor Bible
ABD	*The Anchor Bible Dictionary*. 6 vols. Edited by David Noel Freedman. New York: Doubleday, 1992
ABRL	Anchor Bible Reference Library
ANET	*Ancient Near Eastern Texts Relating to the Old Testament*. 3rd ed. Edited by James B. Pritchard Princeton: Princeton University Press, 1969
ASOR	American Schools of Oriental Research
ASTI	*Annual of the Swedish Theological Institute*
BAR	*Biblical Archaeology Review*
BCE	Before the Common Era
BDB	Francis Brown, S. R. Driver, and Charles A. Briggs, *Hebrew and English Lexicon of the Old Testament* Oxford: Oxford University Press, 1906
BETL	Bibliotheca Ephemeridum Theologicarum Lovaniensium
BibInt	*Biblical Interpretation*
BSOAS	*Bulletin of the School of Oriental and African Studies*
BT	*The Bible Translator*
BWANT	Beiträge zur Wissenschaft vom Alten und Neuen Testament
BZ	*Biblische Zeitschrift*
BZAW	Beihefte zur Zeitschrift für die alttestamentliche Wissenschaft
CAD	*The Assyrian Dictionary of the Oriental Institute of the University of Chicago*
CBQ	*Catholic Biblical Quarterly*
CBQMS	Catholic Biblical Quarterly Monograph Series
CE	Common Era

Abbreviations

CLR	Cognitive Linguistics Research
COS	*Context of Scripture*. Edited by W. W. Hallo. 3 vols. Leiden: Brill, 1997–
DBI	*Dictionary of Biblical Imagery*. Edited by Leland Ryken et al. Downers Grove, IL: InterVarsity, 1998
DCH	*Dictionary of Classical Hebrew*. 7 vols. Edited by David J. A. Clines. Sheffield, UK: Sheffield Academic, 1993
ESV	English Standard Version
ET	*Expository Times*
FAT	Forschungen zum Alten Testament
HALOT	Ludwig Köhler and Walter Baumgartner. *The Hebrew and Aramaic Lexicon of the Old Testament*. 4 vols. Leiden: Brill, 1999
HSM	Harvard Semitic Monographs
HvTSt	*Hervormde Teologiese Studies*
ICC	International Critical Commentary
ICM	Idealized Cognitive Model
IDB	*The Interpreter's Dictionary of the Bible*. 4 vols. Edited by George Arthur Buttrick. New York: Abingdon, 1962
ITC	International Theological Commentary
JANESCU	*Journal of the Ancient Near Eastern Society of Columbia University*
JNES	*Journal of Near Eastern Studies*
JNSL	*Journal of Northwest Semitic Languages*
JSOT	*Journal for the Study of the Old Testament*
JSOTSup	Journal for the Study of the Old Testament Supplement Series
JSS	*Journal of Semitic Studies*
KJV	King James Version
KTBH	Key Terms in Biblical Hebrew
LCORE	Language Collaboration Opportunities Resources Encouragement
LXX	Septuagint
MT	Masoretic text
NET	New English Translation
NIDOTTE	*New International Dictionary of Old Testament Theology and Exegesis*. 5 vols. Edited by Willem A. VanGemeren. Carlisle: Paternoster, 1996
NLT	New Living Translation
NRSV	New Revised Standard Version
NSM	Natural Semantic Metalanguage

Abbreviations

OTE	*Old Testament Essays*
OTG	Old Testament Guides
OtSt	Oudtestamentische Studiën
PNG	Papua New Guinea
RB	*Revue Biblique*
RevQ	*Revue de Qumran*
SBL	Society of Biblical Literature
SBLDS	Society of Biblical Literature Dissertation Series
SBT	Studies in Biblical Theology
SDBH	Semantic Dictionary of Biblical Hebrew
SIL	Summer Institute of Linguistics
SJOT	*Scandanavian Journal of the Old Testament*
SJT	*Scottish Journal of Theology*
SSN	Studia Semitica Neerlandica
STDJ	Studies on the Texts of the Desert of Judah
SUNT	Studien zur Umwelt des Neuen Testaments
TDOT	*Theological Dictionary of the Old Testament.* 15 vols. Edited by G. Johannes Botterweck et al. Translated by Geoffrey W. Bromiley et al. Grand Rapids: Eerdmans, 1974–2006
TWOT	*Theological Wordbook of the Old Testament.* 2 vols. Edited by R. Laird Harris and Gleason L. Archer, Jr. Chicago: Moody, 1980
TynBul	*Tyndale Bulletin*
UF	*Ugarit-Forschungen*
VT	*Vetus Testamentum*
WBC	Word Biblical Commentary
ZAH	*Zeitschrift für Althebräistik*
ZAW	*Zeitschrift für die alttestamentliche Wissenschaft*

1

Conventional Distress Language

"You have put me in the depths of the pit, in the regions dark and deep."
—Ps 88:6[7]

1.1. Introduction

HOW CAN PEOPLE COMMUNICATE meaningfully about distressing psychological and emotional experiences? In English, the experience of up-and-down movement offers some possibilities: someone may be *down* or *low*; *nosedive, spiral,* and *crash*; or *hit rock bottom* and have to *climb out again.* All these expressions use the embodied experience of downward movement in relation to gravity to communicate the experience of English *depression.* However, how universal is this way of understanding such experiences? Are other types of embodied experience used in other cultures? This work investigates the embodied experiences used in Hebrew.

The exploration is rooted in the *conventional language of distress* found in Classical Hebrew texts (including biblical and Qumranic material). The Cognitive Linguistics framework of George Lakoff, Mark Johnson, and Zoltán Kövecses then provides a basis to investigate the most significant *image schemas* (recurring patterns of bodily experience) and *primary metaphors* (basic associations between perceptual and other more abstract domains) used to conceptualize distress, mapping structure from experiential domains of containment, force, sight, and taste to the more abstract domain of distress. The first challenge, however, is to identify such conventional language of distress and briefly compare the Cognitive Linguistic approach used in this study with other approaches to it.

1.2. Approaches to Conventional Language

Several images for distressing life experiences (including darkness, nets, "the Pit," or bitter food) recur throughout Classical Hebrew texts. This is unsurprising, since "'originality' of metaphoric invention does not appear to have been a consciously prized poetic value."[1]

Texts using such images sometimes contain near identical clauses, as in Ps 143:3 and Lam 3:6:

הוֹשִׁיבַנִי בְמַחֲשַׁכִּים כְּמֵתֵי עוֹלָם׃

Ps 143:3: Making me sit in darkness like those long dead.[2]

בְּמַחֲשַׁכִּים הוֹשִׁיבַנִי כְּמֵתֵי עוֹלָם׃

Lam 3:6: He has made me sit in darkness like those long dead.[3]

Elsewhere, texts only overlap thematically, with little shared vocabulary, as in Lam 3:2 and Job 30:28:

אוֹתִי נָהַג וַיֹּלַךְ חֹשֶׁךְ וְלֹא־אוֹר׃

Lam 3:2: He has driven and brought me into darkness without any light.

קֹדֵר הִלַּכְתִּי בְּלֹא חַמָּה

---

1. Alter, *Poetry*, 189.
2. English translations are from the NRSV unless otherwise footnoted.
3. Author's translation.

Job 30:28: Darkling I wander, lacking the daystar.[4]

Such recurring images have been studied in various ways. For *historical criticism*, they indicate authorship, date, and provenance, for *form criticism* they represent cultic liturgy, and for *literary criticism* they show intertextual relationships. Alternatively, this language may reflect *universal psychology*. These perspectives will be outlined below, before introducing the complementary *conceptual metaphor* perspective used in this work.

1.2.1. Historical Criticism and Idiosyncratic Language

Specific common images or expressions could be used to place texts historically, though it is often inconclusive for poetry. For example, specific images could date Job to Solomon's time (given affinities to Psalms 88 and 89)[5] through to the post-exilic period (given similarities to Hezekiah's thanksgiving in First Isaiah).[6] Similarly, common authorship of Lamentations and Jeremiah is suggested by the common imagery and language.[7] For others, however, the imprisonment imagery of Lamentations 3 suggests an exilic provenance similar to Second Isaiah.[8] Finally, analysis of common motifs among the Hodayot also suggests common authorship, helping ascertain which (if any) come from the "Teacher of Righteousness."[9]

However, rather than being idiosyncratic, these expressions may actually reflect "a common fund of technical lament terminology which was used in the laments of the Psalter, the book of Job and Lamentations."[10] Conceptual metaphor theory explains this cognitively, suggesting fairly stable mappings between mental domains (such as "bad tastes" and "distressing experiences") giving rise to this conven-

---

4. Wolfers, *Deep*, 354.
5. Delitzsch, *Job*, 22–23.
6. Wolfers, *Deep*, 54–59.
7. Kaiser, *Lamentations*, 29.
8. Middlemas, "Isaiah."
9. Douglas, "Hypothesis."
10. Gottwald, *Studies*, 42–43.

tional "lament terminology," metaphorical mappings exploited by different writers in slightly different ways. As Gibbs claims, "the way creative writers compose is not unlimited" but constrained by "the ways we actually think of our ordinary experiences."[11] Thus, although one author may have a particularly salient mapping between two domains, so that similar phrases may suggest common authorship, the emphasis here will be on the commonalities in linguistic metaphors, and what they reveal concerning common thinking about distress.

1.2.2. Form Criticism and Liturgical Language

Second, form criticism prioritizes the *use* and *transmission* of texts in religious settings over their original historical setting.[12] Thus, conventional depictions of distress in Gunkel's laments and thanksgiving songs are seen as basically liturgical and, to a degree, merely formulaic. For von Rad, then, this language only expresses actual suffering "in a few typical and very faded concepts," severely diminishing the personal element,[13] and the Psalms are "in no sense whatever to be understood as personal outpourings, . . . but as discourses bound to the cult and the liturgy."[14] Kraus is more positive, arguing that while the phraseology is "conventionalized" it is nevertheless "a living language, open to manifold possibilities of application."[15]

In Cognitive Linguistics, expressions that reflect "systematic metaphorical concepts . . . [and] structure our actions and thoughts . . . are 'alive' in the most fundamental sense: they are metaphors we live by. The fact that they are conventionally fixed . . . makes them no less alive."[16] Thus, even if language is "typical," the concepts reflected are not necessarily "very faded," but may significantly influence thought and action. Such typical language perpetuated within the cult defines and consoli-

---

11. Gibbs, *Poetics*, 8.
12. Gunkel, *Einleitung*.
13. Von Rad, *Old Testament Theology* 1:399.
14. Ibid., 399–400.
15. Kraus, *Psalms 1–59*, 49.
16. Lakoff and Johnson, *Metaphors*, 55.

dates participants' conceptualizations of what distress "is" and frames their experiences as problems to be solved.[17]

Form criticism, therefore, usefully emphasizes the conventional nature of distress language, and its use by generations of worshippers in varied settings. However, it prompts the question as to how the entrenchment of these metaphors and prototypical situations in liturgy might have served to structure the life experiences of participants in Israel's religion.

1.2.3. Literary Criticism and Intertextual Language

Third, literary criticism recognizes that texts are not independent entities but "inevitably shot through with references, quotations, and influences of every kind,"[18] so that conventional distress language may allude to other texts. This "intertextuality" can consider influences from just written texts, or experiences of any kind. Biblical research has investigated both the rhetorical use of earlier texts to enrich and authorize claims, and the intentional and unintentional allusions of literary language.[19] For example, Second Isaiah may have deliberately recollected the figure of Lamentations 3 in his writing.[20] Johnston describes intertextuality in the Psalms as conventional images "juxtaposed kaleidoscopically to become alternative and interchangeable images, a common stock of expressions for distress. The distinctiveness of each poem lies not so much in its unique images (though these do occur occasionally) as in its unique blend of the common ones."[21]

The Dead Sea Scrolls provide a supreme instance of intertextuality,[22] revealing a community that interpreted the Scriptures differently from the New Testament authors, using them to give their theology a biblical base and establish the community's self-understanding.[23] For example,

17. As in the conventional use of "heart" in the Swedish hymnal, Nørager, "'Heart.'"
18. Still and Worton, "Introduction," 1.
19. Koptak, "Intertextuality."
20. Willey, *Remember*.
21. Johnston, "Distress," 73.
22. Loader, "Qumran," 898. For a good example, see Jassen, "Intertextual."
23. Ibid., 907.

intertextual practices in a Qumranic Messianic text use biblical texts to "reciprocally contribute to each other's significance by limiting, extending, focusing, and emending what they would mean in isolation" giving the text "meanings that are not otherwise present in the same words."[24]

The more dispersed intertextual relationships of the Hodayot may reflect similar deliberate compositions of texts. Holm-Nielsen concluded that the author bound himself to Old Testament words since "he felt himself to be in the same situation as portrayed in the Old Testament" so the significant issue is "not that these expressions suit in detail his own life, but that the Old Testament portrayals are now fulfilled in his own experience."[25] Holm-Nielsen's method tended to overemphasize correspondences,[26] but it is still usually assumed that the Hodayot's distress imagery refers deliberately to particular scriptural passages.

Qumran's authors undoubtedly knew the Psalms and their conventional language well. The interesting aspect for a conceptual metaphor approach is that authors still use these conventional metaphors to conceptualize their own experience. Previous scholarship presumed that the community simply copied conventional language, but recent comparison of the Cave 1 Hodayot lacunae with Cave 4 documents show several places where the linguistic metaphors vary more significantly than expected from the biblical texts. Such creative elaboration of metaphors suggests the imagery is still "active" in the author's mind, not just dead convention,[27] and so provides a way in to how the authors thought about and acted upon distressing situations.

1.2.4. Psychological Interpretation and the Language of Humanity

The fourth set of approaches are psychological, investigating the common vocabulary and forms of Hebrew distress discourse as a reflection of pan-cultural psychological phenomena, as in Ryken's investigation

---

24. Ibid., 904.
25. Holm-Nielsen, *Hodayot*, 327–28.
26. Kittel, *Hymns*, 14.
27. Taylor, *Grammar*, 500–501.

of archetypes,[28] in Brueggemann's hermeneutical approach to lament psalms[29] and in various cross-cultural studies of distress language.

First, Ryken's *The Dictionary of Biblical Imagery* sees conventional imagery of traps or darkness as *archetypes*, which are images and symbols recurring "not only throughout the Bible, but in literature generally and in life." Archetypes originate in Jungian psychology, where they are universal, primal, and innate. For Ryken, archetypes are a "universal language," understood "simply by virtue of being human," so that "we all know the experiences of hunger and thirst, garden, and wilderness."[30] Whilst Ryken is correct that *hunger* and *thirst* have physiological justification as universal experiences, the latter two do not, as shown by attempts to translate either *garden* or *wilderness* into Papua New Guinean languages. The dictionary articles themselves distinguish more carefully between universal and culture-specific imagery. Similarly, in this volume, certain embodied experiences (such as containment or force) are considered universal and thus "archetypal." Other embodied experiences, such as bird trapping, are more culture-specific, evoking a "limited range of associated commonplaces"[31] when used in metaphor.

Second, Brueggemann uses psychology and linguistics to explore the function of conventional metaphors in lament psalms within the common life of faith.[32] His Freudian approach emphasizes universal experiences, arguing that people in all eras and cultures experience "dislocation and disorientation,"[33] which typically drive people to "the extremities of emotion, integrating capacity, and of language,"[34] so that when an orderly life is lost people can no longer affirm the conventional assertions of blessing and security. The alternative language found should not be "reduced to clichés."[35] Instead, "the rich array of language in which the words tumble out becomes . . . a pastoral opportunity to

28. Ryken et al., *Dictionary*.
29. Brueggemann, "Psalms."
30. Ryken et al., *Dictionary*, xvii.
31. Hillers, "Dust," 105.
32. Brueggemann, "Psalms."
33. Ibid., 8.
34. Ibid.
35. Ibid., 27.

let the impressionistic speech touch the particular circumstance of dislocation."[36] Thus, while Brueggemann acknowledges recurring metaphors of pits, enemies, and snares, he is only interested in the specifics of these metaphors to the extent they reflect timeless human experiences, so that he argues one can say that for today's English-speaking world "to fall into 'the pit' is indeed to lose one's old equilibrium."[37]

Following Brueggemann, Cognitive Linguistics emphasizes that lament language is a way of viewing reality rather than an exegetical problem to be solved in terms of Sitz im Leben or formal structure. However, it sees language, and especially metaphor, as very important for structuring experience itself. Brueggemann's attempts to parallel the negative experiences of his contemporaries and those of the psalmist requires today's conceptual metaphors and image schemas,[38] conceptualizing them as "extremities," "disorientation," "disintegration," "lost equilibrium," "displacement," or "regression." Rather than reflecting Hebrew conceptual metaphors, these show the significance of image schemas of BALANCE[39] ("losing" and "regaining" equilibrium, totally absent from the Hebrew corpus), NEAR-FAR (in "extremity"), and PATH ("orientation / disorientation / reorientation") for structuring contemporary distress metaphors. This work explores how metaphors of pits, snares, enemies, and darkness give structure to negative experiences, and how this differs from a modern American who feels he has "lost his equilibrium."

Third, Dobbs-Allsopp compares conventional language in Lamentations 3 with language of severe trauma elsewhere. Grief-filled Polish texts do not go beyond or disintegrate traditional expressions, suggesting that "in response to horrific situations, people draw on the traditional motifs they know well,"[40] rather than creating novel metaphors. Further, using stereotyped images allows "a multiplicity of identities and

---

36. Ibid., 12.

37. Ibid., 12–13.

38. The plural "schemas" has become convention, rather than "schemata," as in Geeraerts, *Cognitive*.

39. An extended discussion of the BALANCE schema is given in Johnson, *Body*, 74–98.

40. Dobbs-Allsopp, *Lamentations*, 116.

settings,"[41] where they can be fitted "for the saying of the unsayable."[42] Psychological studies by Kübler-Ross[43] and Spiegel[44] also suggest universal patterns in distress. Moore thus argues that the imagery and language of Lamentations enables the nation to do the necessary emotional "grief work."[45] Brueggemann also recognizes the psychological benefit of having existing forms to use in situations of grief.[46] Joyce defends the supposed inconsistencies of Lamentations, arguing that a mixture of hope and despair is typical of the grief processes. Joyce also helpfully acknowledges that an identity of psychological grief processes in Hebrew and Modern Western society cannot be assumed.[47]

Cognitive Linguistics similarly explores universal psychological and emotional phenomena, and investigates the relationship between these and conventional language. However, it also recognizes the different ways universal experiences are structured in specific cultures.

1.2.5. Cultural Linguistic Interpretation and the Language of Conceptual Metaphor

The conceptual metaphor approach adds an extra perspective to conventional language, using cognitive science and linguistic anthropology to investigate how particular metaphors used in distress conceptualize negative experiences, giving them culture-specific structure. This approach is rooted in research by George Lakoff and Mark Johnson,[48] but

---

41. Ibid., 115.
42. Ibid., 116.
43. Kübler-Ross, *Death*.
44. Spiegel, *Grief*.
45. Moore, "Human."
46. Brueggemann, "Typology."
47. Joyce, "Lamentations," 316.
48. For example, Lakoff and Johnson, *Metaphors*; Lakoff, *Women*; Lakoff and Turner, *Reason*; Lakoff, "Contemporary"; Lakoff and Johnson, *Philosophy*.

more recently also by Mark Turner,[49] Raymond Gibbs,[50] and Zoltán Kövecses.[51]

Following historical criticism, this approach recognizes linguistic expressions may be peculiar to a particular time or author. However, it searches for commonalities across different texts to investigate how these unique expressions stem from similar understandings of reality. Following the intertextual approach, it recognizes conventional language may deliberately allude to other texts. However, it focuses on how common embodied experiences and conceptualizations may guide which texts are re-used. The psychological approach has most commonalities, with both approaches recognizing far-reaching psychological influences on language content and form. However, the approach of this work recognizes that psychology itself may be influenced by culture, so that recurring themes reveal a unique set of ethnopsychological contours, not just universal archetypes.

1.3. Purpose and Outline of the Study

This research has three aims. First, from a linguistic perspective, it contributes further to applications of conceptual metaphor theory to Classical Hebrew, testing theses generated from a study of contemporary English on an ancient text. Specifically, it adds a further investigation of conceptual metaphors and metonymies used to structure emotion concepts.[52] Second, from a Biblical Studies perspective, this work provides a comprehensive catalogue of the metaphors used to structure the experience of distress within the specific corpus in consideration, showing its most significant ethnopsychological contours. Third, by performing this

---

49. For example, Lakoff and Turner, *Reason*; Turner, *Literary*; Turner and Fauconnier, "Binding"; Fauconnier and Turner, *Think*.

50. For example, Gibbs, *Poetics*; Gibbs, "Heads"; Gibbs, "Researching."

51. For example, Kövecses, *Pride*; Kövecses, *Concepts*; Kövecses, "Models"; Kövecses, *Emotion*; Kövecses, "Scope"; Kövecses, *Metaphor*; Kövecses, *Culture*; Kövecses, *Language*.

52. Other examples include for Zulu, Taylor and Mbense, "Dogs"; for Polish, Mikołajczuk, "Conceptualisation"; McMullen and Conway, "Depression"; and for Hebrew, Kotzé, "Conceptualisation."

interdisciplinary study, some new insights will be offered concerning the relationship between language and thought in Hebrew linguistics.

The present work is organized in the following way. The next chapter focuses on the relation between culture, language, and thought. Conceptual metaphor theory holds a relatively strong position on cognitive and linguistic relativity. That is, it is foundational to this research that the conventional language different cultures use to speak about experiences of distress reflect different ways of thinking about these experiences. This is not a generally accepted position in Biblical Studies, so the chapter will substantiate this claim more fully, situating it within twentieth-century approaches to semantics and linguistic relativity, particularly dialoguing with James Barr's work in Hebrew linguistics.

Having laid this foundation, the third and fourth chapters introduce the research methodology, focusing first on the corpus of texts to be used and then on the way they will be analyzed and presented.

The following chapters cover the main conceptual metaphors that appear through analyzing the texts. First, basic image schemas will be considered, with chapter five looking at the VERTICALITY schema, chapter six at the CONSTRAINT schema, and chapter seven at the FORCE schema. Chapter eight turns to the primary metaphor of darkness and chapter nine to primary metaphors based on bad taste. Finally, the conclusion summarizes the results and presents the implications of this research.

2

Culture, Language, and Thought

"As soon as evidence from linguistic phenomena is used in the contrast of... ways of thinking, a relation is being established between mental patterns and linguistic structure. What has not been apparent when such evidence has been used in theological discussion... has been the consciousness of how difficult a problem such a relation constitutes and how impossible it is to bypass the discussion of it in philosophy, psychology, and linguistics." —James Barr[1]

"It is all too easy to indulge in imaginative nonsense." —Norman Porteous[2]

2.1. Introduction

This research is about conceptualizing distress, and thus, fundamentally, about how people think. The only evidence of how Classical Hebrew speakers thought is found in the texts they left, a few tokens of their language. Native intuition is inaccessible. So, what can language reveal about how people think? Moreover, how does language affect the way communities perceive and conceptualize the world they live in?

1. Barr, *Semantics*, 25.
2. Porteous, "State," 71.

Culture, Language, and Thought

Clarifying the relationship between language and thought has long exercised philosophers, anthropologists, and linguists. Some focus on universals and the "psychic unity of mankind," others emphasize "linguistic relativity," urging that differences in language across the globe must be reflected in different ways of thinking. Perhaps language reflects, influences, constrains, guides, or even determines thought processes. This chapter will summarize some of the central issues.

The aim of this chapter is threefold. First, it theoretically grounds the cognitive semantics used throughout this book, emphasizing embodied experience and culture-specific conventional knowledge. These emphases began with Humboldt, Boas, Sapir, and Whorf, who are the founders of the linguistic relativity tradition on which cognitive semantics rests. Their approach was developed by Rosch and Fillmore. The concepts of prototypes, scripts, semantic networks, and conceptual metonymies will all be introduced here. Second, this chapter introduces more recent Cognitive Linguists whose contributions frame this research. Third, it discusses significant applications of linguistics to biblical studies against this backdrop. Specifically, it interacts with James Barr, whose forceful critique of carelessly applied Whorfian linguistics has dominated for fifty years. The argument will show how Cognitive Linguistics can be used without suffering the same criticisms as the preceding linguistic models.

A chronological perspective will be presented, surveying linguistics and biblical studies from Boasian linguistics and its Humboldtian heritage (section 2.2) to the biblical semantics of James Barr and John Sawyer (section 2.3), then on to Cognitive Linguistics, both at its foundation (section 2.4) and, most fully, in its more recent development by Lakoff, Johnson, Langacker, Talmy, Taylor, Gibbs, and Kövecses (section 2.5). Finally recent applications to biblical studies will be surveyed (section 2.6).

2.2. The Tradition of Linguistic Relativity: Humboldt, Boas, Sapir, and Whorf

2.2.1. Humboldt (1767–1835): Language Determines Characteristic Worldview

Carl Wilhelm von Humboldt was an influential founding figure for relativist linguistics,[3] beginning to relate the global diversity of linguistic structures to a new post-Kantian philosophy in which an objective world was no longer accessible. He maintained that each language contains a characteristic worldview and "draws a circle around the people to whom it adheres which it is possible for the individual to escape only by stepping into a different one."[4]

However, linguistic features like parts of speech or case are universal, acting as guiding principles within languages even when there is no explicit form to represent them.[5] Since mental capacities are universal, "the form of all languages must be essentially the same."[6] Thus, while new evidence on "exotic" languages directed Humboldt towards relativity, with language somewhat constraining a person's worldview, his anthropological presuppositions precluded much real difference.

2.2.2. Boas (1858–1942): Language Reflects Unconscious Categories

Next, Franz Boas, the founder of American anthropological linguistics, sought to empirically validate Humboldt's ideas.[7] His *Introduction to the Handbook of American Indian Languages* carefully outlines the relationship between language and thought. For example, he doubted Humboldt's contention that grammatical forms of a language permanently constrain its speakers' thoughts. Rather, "generalized" forms would "develop just as soon as needed" for new ideas,[8] since humanity

---

3. Although some of his ideas had a longer heritage, Koerner, "Pedigree," 3.
4. Humboldt, *Werke*, 7:60, cited in Wierzbicka, *Concepts*, 3.
5. Foley, *Anthropological*, 194.
6. Humboldt, *Language*, 214.
7. Foley, *Anthropological*, 194.
8. Boas, *Introduction*, 55.

is psychologically equal. He substantiated this by making a Kwakiutl speaker conceive a meaning for an abstract form which usually required inalienable possession. Thus, "language alone would not prevent a people from advancing to more generalized forms of thinking if the general state of their culture should require expression of such thought; ... under these conditions the language would be moulded rather by the cultural state."[9]

However, Boas was very interested in how languages make accessible unconscious mental processes, without secondary explanations,[10] advocating searching analyzes of linguistic concepts, especially investigating "the grouping of ideas in different languages."[11] For Boas, then, a language does not dictate how its speakers have to think, but, through unconscious categorization, it reflects how speakers habitually think.

2.2.3. Sapir (1884–1939): Language Creates Different Worlds

Edward Sapir studied under Boas and developed his ideas, becoming a key figure in American structuralism. His famous statement on linguistic relativity was first read in 1928:

> Human beings do not live in the objective world alone ... but are very much at the mercy of the particular language which has become the medium of expression for their society ... The fact of the matter is that the "real-world" is to a large extent unconsciously built on the language habits of the group ... The worlds in which different societies live are distinct worlds, not merely the same world with different labels attached ... Even comparatively simple acts of perception are very much more at the mercy of the social patterns called words than we might suppose.[12]

Here language is an oppressive master, holding speakers "at its mercy," whereas for Boas it was more subservient, "moulded ... by the

---

9. Ibid., 54–56.
10. Ibid., 59.
11. Ibid.
12. Sapir, *Culture*, 68–69, italics added.

cultural state."[13] Further, Boas' contention that an Indian could "reach abstract forms strictly corresponding to the abstract forms of our modern languages"[14] still betrayed a Platonic idealism that these concepts exist independently of culture. This universalism is targeted by Sapir's warning that we actually live in different worlds, not the same world with different labels. For example, chapter eight will show how visual perception is influenced by language. Whereas in English *darkness* is a scalar concept related to degrees of light, there is no evidence that the most similar concepts in Hebrew were conceived as gradable, so they are not just *darkness* with another label.

2.2.4. Whorf (1897–1941): Language Organizes the "Kaleidoscope Flux" of Impressions

Next, Benjamin Lee Whorf was a largely self-taught American linguist. His "principle of linguistic relativity" states that:

> The world is presented in a kaleidoscope flux of impressions which has to be organized by our minds—and this means largely by the linguistic systems in our minds. We cut nature up, organize it into concepts, and ascribe significances as we do, largely because we are parties to an agreement to organize it in this way—an agreement that holds throughout our speech community and is codified in the patterns of our language. The agreement is, of course, an implicit and unstated one, but its terms are absolutely obligatory; we cannot talk at all except by subscribing to the organization and classification of data which the agreement decrees.[15]

Whorf sought to empirically demonstrate the relationship between linguistic structure and habitual thought, by comparing English and Hopi. Following Sapir and Boas, Whorf was interested in the unconscious structure of language and the influence this has on thinking, such

---

13. Boas, *Introduction*, 56.
14. Ibid., 54.
15. Whorf, "Science," 213–14.

as the semantic similarities between verbs that can take the prefix *un-* in English. He argued that a language's "constant ways of arranging data"[16] became part of the "habitual thought" of its speakers. Thus, linguistics lights up a community's thought and culture, allowing "a heuristic approach to problems of psychology which hitherto [a researcher] may have shrunk from considering."[17]

For Whorf, these culturally relative influences pervade both grammar and lexicon. For example, there is a "far-reaching compulsion from large-scale patterning of grammatical categories, such as plurality, gender, and similar classifications,"[18] so that things sharing a gender are thought about in similar ways. Further, Whorf operates on a structuralist basis, with language limiting the free plasticity of culture because "language is a system." Whereas culture can change quickly, the language system "can change to something really new only very slowly" and thus language "represents the mass mind."[19]

Whorf also discusses how metaphor reveals differences in thinking between peoples. For example, he found an "almost inexhaustible" set of metaphors from the field of spatial extension to describe duration and intensity in Standard Average European[20] (SAE), contrasted with very few non-metaphorical terms. [21] Thus, speakers "can hardly refer to the simplest nonspatial situation without constant resort to physical metaphors."[22] The extraordinary thing is the lack of such spatialization in Hopi, supporting linguistic relativity.

Nevertheless, Whorf recognized that contemporary linguistic descriptions were insufficient to be categorical about implications from language structure to mentality. He advocated surveying many more languages, including a grammar for each "worked out scientifically and on the basis of the language's own patterns and classes, and as free as possible from any general presuppositions about grammatical logic."[23]

16. Whorf, "Relation," 135.
17. Whorf, "Linguistic," 73.
18. Whorf, "Relation," 137.
19. Ibid., 156.
20. Whorf describes European languages as a whole this way.
21. Ibid., 145.
22. Ibid., 146.
23. Whorf, "Linguistic," 77.

Whorf has been both dismissed outright and uncritically approved, with, until recently, very few attempts to systematically prove or disprove his hypothesis. The Chomskyan emphasis on universal syntax pushed Whorf's views into contempt, but they have resurfaced since the 1990s. John Lucy has particularly attempted to test Whorf's hypothesis.[24] Sydney Lamb has also used neurocognitive research to confirm that "languaging" during infancy influences perception and thought throughout life, since top-down effects operate from conceptual structure to lower perceptual layers in the brain.[25] However, the next step here is to return to Whorf's time and the vigorous critique from James Barr.

2.3. Linguistics and Biblical Studies I: Barr and Sawyer

2.3.1. Barr (1924–2006)

James Barr's work, particularly *The Semantics of Biblical Language* (1961),[26] is important for the prominent position his negative critique of linguistic relativity has gained in biblical studies. Recent treatments of biblical linguistics still devote significant sections to Barr's work, with little or no qualification.[27]

Barr primarily attacks the presuppositions and methodology used in biblical studies to argue for profound differences between Hebrew and Greek minds, claiming that any approach that assumes linguistic structure reflects thought structure is "wholly outmoded."[28] He advocates a "strict and systematic method of discussing the relation between grammatical structures and lexical phenomena on the one hand and the Hebrew or Greek mind or any other national or cultural mind on the

---

24. Lucy, "Scope."
25. Lamb, "Structure."
26. Barr, *Semantics*.
27. Cotterell and Turner devote a chapter to Barr's critique of word studies, and assess negative reviews as misguided (Cotterell and Turner, *Linguistics*, 106–28). Groom has a chapter on Barr's impact on comparative philology, demonstrating the ongoing relevance (Groom, *Analysis*, 45–71).
28. Barr, *Semantics*, 33.

Culture, Language, and Thought

other."²⁹ Further, this method must be integrated with general linguistics and applied to the whole language. Embarking on "demonstrating how the features of Hebrew thought are built into Hebrew language, without giving full thought to these requisites, indicates a serious overconfidence and an ignoring of basic problems."³⁰ As this book is such an embarkation, Barr's arguments need careful examination.

Barr's attacks are rooted in Saussurean structuralism, and where he quotes contemporary linguists they are structuralists like Bloomfield and Ullmann. Thus, insistence that biblical theologians must heed "modern linguistics" means structuralist emphases on synchronic rather than diachronic description, on descriptions of language as a system and not as isolated parts, and on the arbitrary nature of words,³¹ whose meaning is determined by their indication of "an essential difference"³² to other words within the linguistic system, rather than etymology or "inner meaning."

Representing Barr's targets, Snaith argues that the first word of Psalm 1 (אשרי, normally translated *happy* or *blessed*) comes from a root meaning "to go straight ahead," illustrating Hebrew thought, where "a happy man is the man who goes straight ahead."³³ Snaith and others often unquestioningly appropriated information on word meanings in newly discovered cognate languages. Strengthened by popular ethnopsychology and linguistic relativity, they produced many thought-provoking, but not necessarily linguistically well-grounded, claims about Hebrew thought.

Five of Barr's most relevant arguments about the relationship between language, culture, and thought are outlined below, based mainly on *Semantics*, which includes his fiercest critique of the ethnopsychology of Herder, Humboldt, and Whorf.

---

29. Ibid., 24.
30. Ibid., 25.
31. For example, ibid., 204.
32. Ibid., 188.
33. Snaith, "Language," 225.

a) No Simple Correspondence between Language Structure and Thought Structure

First, Barr argues one cannot assume a simple correspondence between language structure and thought structure, whether in grammar or vocabulary,[34] since in fact some peoples have very common worldviews despite radically different languages (such as Finns versus Swedes), whereas others have very similar languages yet different worldviews (such as fourth-century Jews versus Phoenicians).[35] Thus, grammatical structure (such as the verbal system or lack of a copula) cannot show Hebrew thought is more "dynamic" than Greek.[36] Similarly, grammatical gender "cannot be taken to reflect a thought pattern,"[37] since the lack of distinct gender in Turkish does not mean Turks cannot differentiate male and female.[38]

Regarding vocabulary, the absence of distinct words does not imply the absence of distinct mental concepts (such as the "lack" of a Hebrew "body" / "soul" distinction) nor does the existence of more than one word reflect a "need" to distinguish mental concepts.[39] Such arguments fail to appreciate both the often unmotivated historical background for the words available in a given domain and the possibility of thinking about something without having a word to describe it.[40]

Since identity cannot be assumed between linguistic and mental structure, Barr argues any theologian addressing Hebrew thought must explicate his or her assumptions on the relationship between linguistic structures and mental patterns.[41] This chapter fulfils precisely this purpose within this book.

---

34. Barr, *Semantics*, 33.
35. Ibid., 42–43.
36. Ibid., 26–34, 46–106.
37. Ibid., 40.
38. Ibid., 39.
39. Ibid., 34–38.
40. Here, Barr explicitly opposes Whorf's contention that the vocabulary of a language reveals its way of organizing the world (ibid.).
41. Ibid., 26.

b) No Privileged Cultural Mind

Second, presuppositions about the way people think in a culture cannot be used to interpret linguistic evidence.[42] Barr's contemporaries presumed the Hebrew mind viewed the world a certain way (from anthropological claims about "primitive" mentality or theological convictions regarding the peculiarity, and superiority, of the Hebrew mentality), so linguistic evidence supporting this was presented, ignoring other evidence and alternative hypotheses. Barr claimed that his opponents defended the peculiarity of Hebrew psychology on the basis of the peculiarity of linguistic phenomena that were actually very widespread, through ignorance of general linguistics and failure to critically examine their own languages.[43] Instead, they needed a respectable linguistic methodology examining the whole language, one integrated with general linguistics, and "open to relevant data for semantics of any language."[44] It can be said that the Cognitive Linguistic methodology fits these criteria, originating in mainstream linguistics and increasingly well tested cross-linguistically.

c) Correct Use of Etymology

Third, Barr attacks abuses of etymology, stressing that a word's original meaning does not determine its current meaning.[45] Following Saussure, synchronic considerations (how a word fits with other possibilities in a language system at a given point in time) have priority over diachronic considerations (when a word originated). Before Barr, scholars used cognate languages to establish the "exact" meanings of Hebrew words, even when spoken centuries earlier in different settings.[46] However, Barr found English words whose meaning changed beyond recognition even

---

42. Ibid., 22–23.
43. Ibid., 135.
44. Ibid., 25.
45. Barr, "Etymology"; Barr, "Limitations"; Barr, "Scope"; and to a lesser extent in Barr, "Synchronic."
46. For example, Jacob, *Theology*, 94, argues from an Arabic cognate that the "exact" meaning of צדק in Hebrew is "conformity to a norm."

within one language and thus showed the falsity of supposing "that the etymology of a word is necessarily a guide either to its 'proper' meaning in a later period or to its actual meaning in that period."[47] The use of "necessarily" is important: Barr is not saying that a word's etymology is always irrelevant, just that one cannot assume uncritically that etymology is determinative of a word's current meaning. Thus, in Snaith's exegesis of Psalm 1 (introduced at the start of section 3.1) he does not attack the use of etymological evidence, but that "the etymological associations are used without any inquiry whether they existed in the minds of those who used the poem."[48]

d) The Root Fallacy

Fourth, the same Hebrew root for two words is insufficient evidence of associations between them in speakers' minds. Those who assert a "root meaning" commit the "root fallacy." In the case of לֶחֶם (bread) and מִלְחָמָה (war), for example, it is "doubtful whether the influence of their common root is of any importance . . . in the normal usage of the words."[49] Although Boman produces the root meaning of being "closely packed,"[50] he misses Barr's real point, which is whether this meaning influences normal usage.

Barr claims only forms produced by "narrowly grammatical variation," such as the paradigm of forms for different persons as subject, could be influenced by a "root meaning." Conversely, the different conjugations (like the hiphil) are new semantic formations with potentially their own "semantic history."[51] Thus, "to be guided by the 'fundamental meaning' of a 'root' in discussing the various extant forms is to neglect the force of word-formation, which creates, or may create, separate fields of significance for what are independent forms."[52] Later, Barr is more constructive, affirming "a 'root' is semantically significant, in a

47. Barr, *Semantics*, 109.
48. Ibid., 116.
49. Ibid., 102.
50 Boman, "Review."
51. Barr, *Semantics*, 102.
52. Ibid., 165.

synchronic sense, usually only where the root morpheme is active and productive, usually as a rather basic verb or noun, in the Hebrew of biblical times."[53]

e) The Unitary Concept Fallacy

Fifth, Barr argues that the same form in multiple contexts is insufficient evidence to argue a meaning overlap in these contexts. He calls this the *unitary concept fallacy*. Theologians must avoid illegitimately carrying the entire situated meaning of a word in one context to another context, as when "good" used eschatologically in one context is taken to imply that "good" always has an eschatological meaning.[54]

This issue relates to polysemy and homonymy, which are important in Cognitive Linguistics,[55] so Barr's views need consideration. Polysemy is usually defined as a word having more than one sense, whereas homonymy is two distinct words that have developed the same form. The difference is historical: for polysemy the senses originated in some motivated way from an original meaning, whereas in homonymy the "accidental" coming together of two forms produces multiple senses. As Barr acknowledges, history may not effect the perceived links between words for current speakers, since many English speakers assume a polysemous relationship between a human "ear" and an "ear" of corn, despite originating from distinct roots.

Polysemy deriving from metaphorical transference is especially significant for this work. Consider the English example "seethe." Although the first dictionary definition usually describes a bubbling liquid, contemporary English uses it much more commonly with an angry human subject, potentially still evoking the "bubbling liquid" meaning. Such metaphorical transference is central to conceptual metaphor theory. Barr's synchronic emphasis means that he allows only minimal impact of such possible metaphorical transference on semantics, so that

---

53. Barr, "Factors," 35.
54. Barr, *Semantics*, 219–20.
55. Geeraerts describes modelling the "polysemic architecture of expressions" as one of four specific characteristics of Cognitive Linguistics (Geeraerts, "Introduction," 9).

senses for a word derived this way should not be assumed to activate links to a possible original more literal sense. For example, discussing חטא, usually translated "sin" in English, but also used to describe how the Benjaminites could throw a stone at a single hair and not "miss" (Judges 20:16), Barr dismisses the idea that "missing a target" is accessible in every use of the word, saying it is "more likely" that the meaning is "do wrongly." The Benjaminites' success is then an extension of not "doing wrongly." More generally, Barr criticizes "the overemphasizing of 'concrete' or physical meanings in the presentation of lexical material."[56] Similarly, Barr dismisses the proposed link between "belief" and "established," arguably visible through the common consonants אמן.[57] Cognitive Linguistics prioritizes the "concrete," perceptual, and "embodied" for understanding more abstract domains,[58] so there is potential conflict with Barr here.

Despite Barr's polemicism and tendency towards criticism rather than constructing his own linguistic methodology,[59] *Semantics* was widely acclaimed, as a "trumpet blast against the monstrous regiment of shoddy linguistics."[60] Subsequent authors hesitated to relate Hebrew language and thought. John Sawyer, however, did successfully challenge some of Barr's assertions.

2.3.2. Sawyer

Sawyer differs from Barr over which words may be mentally linked, and in his approach to root meanings. Further, he began constructing a methodology for deciding whether an etymological connection still has current force in the minds of users.

First, whereas Barr would not assume words are semantically associated unless provable through sound linguistics, Sawyer's approach is more generous, defining an *associative field* including "all the words

---

56. Barr, "Scope," 8.
57. Barr, *Semantics*, 161–205.
58. Geeraerts, "Introduction," 1.
59. Tångberg, "Linguistics," 310.
60. Silva, *Words*, 18.

Culture, Language, and Thought

associated in any way with a term."⁶¹ These may share a "root," be antonyms or synonyms, or even share similar letters or sounds. This associative field links many more words in a Hebrew speaker's mind than Barr allowed.

Second, regarding root-meanings, Sawyer is cautiously optimistic, claiming "a recurring group of consonants common to several words carries with it some common semantic element into words and contexts in which it occurs."⁶² Comparison should not be made with Indo-European roots because of three Semitic distinctives: first, compounds are not natural; second, the root of a Hebrew word is particularly obtrusive; and third, the data is written, so the root can be seen, not just heard. These create "transparency," with semantic components visible in a word's form, meaning that "the root of a Semitic word is of particular importance in communicating information."⁶³

Finally, concerning metaphorically transferred senses (like "seethe"), Sawyer's methodology investigates generalizations over polysemy, central to Lakoff's later theory. Multiple words having meanings in two distinct domains suggest an active semantic link between the domains. Whilst Barr claimed that the play on words in Isaiah 7:9 (תַאֲמִינוּ 'you will believe' / תֵּאָמֵנוּ 'you will be established') could not be explained through root meanings, Sawyer considered semantic fields in Hebrew connected to both belief or truth (words that collocate with people) and firmness or fixedness (words that collocate with things). Comparison of the fields produces "at least four words that can occur both in *truth*-contexts and in *firmness*-contexts."⁶⁴

Further, Sawyer stresses transfer from concrete to abstract in metaphor, showing that source domains for salvation covered "almost every sphere of human experience: light, space, height . . . and others."⁶⁵ Such transfers likely occurred when the source domain was emotionally charged, so that spatial terminology may have transferred to salvation during territorial expansion.⁶⁶ Cognitive Linguistics also prioritizes

61. Sawyer, *Semantics*, 30.
62. Sawyer, "Root-Meanings," 41.
63. Ibid., 39–40.
64. Ibid., 45.
65. Sawyer, *Semantics*, 54.
66. Sawyer, "Spaciousness"; Sawyer, *Semantics*, 41–43, 54.

motivation, though it prioritizes embodied motivation in infanthood above a culture's historical development.[67]

Sawyer allows a return from Barr back towards using roots, polysemy, and metaphorical transference in semantic description, an increasingly necessary move as linguists began studying language systems less abstractly and more as they are used by individuals. Linguists started investigating how people learn word-meanings and create categories to fit their experiences, integrating developing emphases in other disciplines, including philosophy of language (Wittgenstein), artificial intelligence (Schank), and cognitive psychology (Abelson) to create "Cognitive Science." This research showed that structuralist attempts to define words via oppositions or componential analysis without considering the experiential world of speakers or the scenarios to which such words typically applied, omitted a large area of meaning. The next section introduces some of this research, before turning to the development of Cognitive Linguistics.

2.4. Precursors to Cognitive Linguistics—Wittgenstein, Rosch, Fillmore, Schank, Abelson, and Reddy

2.4.1. Wittgenstein (1889-1951): Family Resemblances

Wittgenstein's later philosophy made the first step towards a new type of semantics (prototype semantics), emphasizing that speakers do not mentally check off a list of attributes when using a word, so necessary and sufficient conditions cannot accurately describe semantics. Wittgenstein took the word *game* and showed there are no common features for all games. Some involve competition, others skill, others just amusement. Instead, games share *family resemblances,* certain parameters (such as skill) that parallel shared features among family members. The same characteristics are not expected in each family member. Similarly, identical properties should not be expected in all *games.*[68] For semantic theory, a central sense for a word covering all contextual instantiations should not be expected, but rather networks of possible

---

67. See for example Gibbs, "Heads"; or Kövecses, *Culture*, 231–43.
68. Wittgenstein, *Investigations*, 66–67.

instantiations sharing various attributes. This emphasis is clearly in line with Barr's "unitary concept fallacy."

2.4.2. Rosch: Prototypes and Basic Level Categories

Eleanor Rosch developed prototype semantics further,[69] using cognitive psychology to discover "prototype effects" and the "basic level" of categorization, delivering the fatal blow to prevailing semantic models using necessary and sufficient features.

First, the feature model suggests every entity with the correct features should be rated equally. Thus, if *bird* is defined by features like "has feathers" and "lays eggs," then every such creature should be an equally good example. However, Rosch found in several psychological experiments that robins were considered "better" examples than penguins. These asymmetries are called *prototype effects*, showing certain members of a category considered more representative, or prototypical, than others.

Second, certain categories are at the *basic level* and thus especially privileged, a foundational empirical discovery for cognitive science.[70] For example, when shown a card with a terrier, people normally identify *a dog* rather than *an animal* or *an Airedale*. The category "dog" is thus at the basic-level,[71] with the super-ordinate level (*animal*) and subordinates (*terrier, Airedale*) less psychologically basic. This is the highest level with a coherent mental image, the level at which entities are related to in similar functional ways, and has names children learn first.

Both results demonstrate gradations in psychological processes, which must be prominent in any cognitively realistic lexical semantics, focusing more on what is typical and salient than necessary or sufficient.

---

69. For example in Rosch, "Categories"; Rosch et al., "Objects"; and Rosch, "Principles," cited and discussed in Lakoff, *Women*, 39–57.

70. Lakoff and Johnson, *Philosophy*, 90.

71. For alternative definitions, see Taylor, *Categorization*, 53–55.

2.4.3. Fillmore: Frames

Charles Fillmore's frame semantics[72] further challenged existing semantic descriptions, to account for meaning that relies on the whole scene, or *frame* for an utterance. Specifically, frames are "unified frameworks of knowledge, or cultural schematizations of experience."[73] Thus, the word *breakfast*[74] relies on a sociocultural frame with typically three meals a day and typical foodstuffs consumed at each. This frame allows *breakfast* to be used when only the food is in focus ("all day breakfasts") or when something different (salad, for example) is eaten in the morning. Words then *evoke* frames (like the three-meal-a-day frame evoked by *breakfast*) that need retrieving to understand an utterance.[75]

2.4.4. Schank and Abelson: Scripts

Roger Schank and Robert Abelson were developing a computer program to understand natural language when they discovered that much implicit information needed to understand texts came not from words but from knowledge structures arising from life experiences.[76] On hearing "John likes apples," we presume he likes *eating* apples, because this is the typical relationship humans have with apples. The computer needed these knowledge structures, not just a lexicon and a grammar.

Much of this is structured in *scripts*, "a predetermined, stereotyped sequence of actions that defines a well-known situation."[77] Scripts may be activated by individual words, allowing much information to be left implicit. English speakers can process "*the* waitress" after the word "restaurant" has been used in a discourse because the script has been activated.[78]

---

72. Fillmore, "Frame"; and Fillmore, "Understanding."
73. Fillmore, "Understanding," 223.
74. Fillmore, "Frame," 380.
75. Ibid.
76. Schank and Abelson, *Scripts*.
77. Ibid., 41.
78. Ibid., 47–50.

Scripts mean embodied experience is crucial. Words do not just provide access to isolated prototypical contexts, but to conventionalized sequences of events in scripts. This work will show how "hunting" and "lion attack" scripts are used to understand distressing situations in Hebrew.

2.4.5. Reddy: The Conduit Metaphor

In 1979, Michael Reddy demonstrated even more conceptual structure implicit in various words by showing how the conduit metaphors used to problematize communication difficulties fail to reflect actual communication.[79] The way we conventionally discuss communication both reveals how we habitually think about communication and constrains our inferences when it fails. Thus, conventional language does influence thought.

Using the conduit metaphor, communication is understood as a conduit carrying mental material (thoughts, ideas, or meanings) in containers (words or other media) from one person to another. Linguistic expressions include: *I couldn't get much from Max's paper; the paragraph was overloaded with meaning; Steve's ideas don't come across clearly in his writing.* This fundamental metaphor constrains inferences regarding miscommunication. A prototypical conduit should work efficiently, so communication failures must be the communicator's failure when loading their mental stuff into the container. A more accurate metaphor should acknowledge that miscommunications are "tendencies inherent in the system, which can only be counteracted by continuous effort and by large amounts of verbal interaction."

Reddy showed that systematic metaphorical structuring in language could influence thinking. He is the direct precursor to Lakoff and Johnson's conceptual metaphors, and the beginning of Cognitive Linguistics.[80]

---

79. Reddy, "Conduit."

80. Cognitive Linguistics (capitalized) is conventionally used for Lakoff and Johnson's strand of cognitive linguistics, Geeraerts, "Introduction," 3.

2.5. The Cognitive Linguistics Paradigm

2.5.1. Lakoff and Johnson: Conceptual Metaphors and Image Schemas

George Lakoff's conceptual metaphors were introduced in his 1980 work with Mark Johnson, *Metaphors We Live By*. They acknowledge the influence of Sapir, Whorf, Wittgenstein, Schank, Fillmore, and Rosch,[81] creating a theory of language and thought that prioritizes categorization and metaphor.

a) Philosophical Basis

Understanding Lakoff and Johnson requires comprehending their claims about metaphor,[82] that "the essence of metaphor is understanding and experiencing one kind of thing in terms of another."[83] Thus, metaphor is located in *thought* and concerned with conceptualization (hence conceptual metaphor) and how metaphors are expressed in *language* is less important for them. "Understanding" here does not mean rational beliefs, but rather "our bodily, cultural, linguistic, historical situatedness in, and toward, our world."[84]

Lakoff and Johnson then develop their framework upon three results of cognitive science.[85] First, the mind is inherently embodied, so our thought processes are a result of our experiences of living in the world. Second, thought is largely unconscious, operating "too quickly to be focused on."[86] Lakoff and Johnson suggest 95% of thought is un-

---

81. Lakoff and Johnson, *Metaphors*, xi–xii. Reddy is recognized in Lakoff, "Contemporary," 186–87.

82. Lakoff claims his view of metaphor differs radically from the classical tradition since Aristotle, which viewed metaphor as special language. More accurately, it challenges the prevailing approaches of the mid-twentieth century. For Aristotle's actual view of metaphor, see Mahon, "Sources."

83. Lakoff and Johnson, *Metaphors*, 5.

84. Johnson, *Body*, 138.

85. Lakoff and Johnson, *Philosophy*, 3–93.

86. Ibid., 10.

Culture, Language, and Thought

conscious, and this shapes conscious thought.[87] Meaning, then, is no longer just about conscious associations. This fits with Boasian emphases on unconscious categorization in language, but also reopens the gate for irresponsible linguistics.[88] If thought, and thus meaning, is largely unconscious, the analyst must avoid unchecked flights of fancy. Third, abstract thought is largely metaphorical. Not only is thought the locus for metaphor, but "metaphorical thought is unavoidable, ubiquitous, and mostly unconscious."[89] A person may thus "understand" certain domains metaphorically through other domains without being consciously aware of it. These three results create a philosophical position Lakoff and Johnson term "experiential realism,"[90] or more recently, "embodied realism."[91]

b) Image Schemas and Gestalt Perception

If thought is largely metaphorical, what are these metaphors based on? Lakoff and Johnson's solution lies in embodied experience, with two kinds of pre-conceptual (non-metaphorical) structures forming the basis for thought, specifically *image schemas* and *gestalt perception*.

First, image schemas are directly meaningful preconceptual structures emerging from our embodied experience of movement, perception, and manipulation of objects.[92] They have a basic internal structure, as in the CONTAINER schema (structured with a boundary, interior, and exterior) or the SOURCE-PATH-GOAL schema, deriving from bodily movement.[93] Mark Johnson defined an image schema as "a recurring, dynamic pattern of our perceptual interactions and motor

---

87. Ibid., 13.

88. This difficulty is acknowledged by several Cognitive Linguists, as in Fauconnier, *Mappings*, 1–13; Gibbs, "Researching."

89. Lakoff and Johnson, *Metaphors*, 272.

90. Lakoff, *Women*, 269–303.

91. Lakoff and Johnson, *Philosophy*, 74–93.

92. Hampe, "Schemas," 1.

93. These prototypical schemas are often used in place of a definition. However, schemas are still a useful and central concept in Cognitive Linguistics. See Grady, "Definition."

programs that gives coherence and structure to our experience."[94] Thus, the CONTAINER schema derives its existence and structure from experiencing our bodies as containers and moving our bodies in and out of other containers. They exist "*beneath* conscious awareness, prior to and independently of other concepts,"[95] generalizing individual mental images and integrating information from multiple modalities. Johnson represents schemas through line drawings, as in Figure 2.1, although realizing this implies an unwarranted similarity between image schemas and rich images.[96]

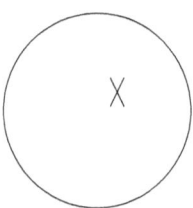

FIGURE 2.1: A Representation of the CONTAINMENT Image Schema

The internal structure of such schemas constrains meaning. For example, in FORCE schemas, the internal structure of source, intensity, movement, and barriers is used to "understand" modal verbs. Thus, *may* as root modal (*you may go to town*) and as epistemic modal (*he may have gone to town*) both use an image schema with no barrier blocking forceful movement, whether in the physical domain or more abstractly where the movement is from premise to conclusion.[97] Here, embodied experiences of forces constrain our inferences in non-physical domains.

Second, *gestalt perception* provides more preconceptual structure for Lakoff's semantics, integrating frames and scripts, and being used

---

94. Johnson, *Body*, xiv. Despite moves to extend or alter this definition, recent literature affirms Johnson's original emphases on fundamental units of sensory experience, Grady, "Definition."

95. Hampe, "Schemas," 2.

96. Johnson, *Body*, 23.

97. Ibid., 41–64. Full discussion in Sweetser, *Etymology*.

for objects at Rosch's basic level (section 2.4.2).[98] Thus, recognizing a *dog* rather than a *cat* is based on gestalt perception, psychologically recognizing the whole object, rather than a complex sum of different features. *Experiential gestalts* are then "ways of organizing experiences into structured wholes,"[99] with dimensions that emerge naturally in experience. Thus, a CONVERSATION is an experiential gestalt, and image schemas themselves are highly schematic gestalts.[100] Experiential gestalts tend to have structural elements including: participants; parts combining to form a whole; stages; linear sequence; causation; and purpose.

Lakoff and Johnson illustrate experiential gestalts with CONVERSATION, ARGUMENT and WAR, each perceived as a structured whole with participants acting in prototypical ways through a sequence of stages to achieve their purposes. Actual experience is perceived relative to these gestalts. Demonstrating how metaphor uses these gestalts, they discuss two people talking. They may impose the CONVERSATION gestalt on their experience, but if through the words used some dimensions begin to fit the STRUGGLE gestalt (such as seeing the participants as opponents, or the interaction as verbal aggression), and they hold the conceptual metaphor ARGUMENT IS STRUGGLE, the experience may begin to be perceived as fitting the ARGUMENT gestalt instead, so that they see themselves as having an "argument."[101] This work shows, for example, how an experiential gestalt of SIEGE structures experiences of DISTRESS, mapping onto the purpose, participants (the self, God, and "enemies"), and sequence of events, when someone holds the metaphor BEING IN DISTRESS IS BEING UNDER SIEGE.

c) Conceptual Metaphor

It has been established that image schemas and perceptual gestalts have *structure*. Structure is then mapped through metaphor from these two types of *source domains* onto experiences (*target domains*) lacking their

---

98. Lakoff, *Women*, 46.
99. Lakoff and Johnson, *Metaphors*, 81.
100. Hampe, "Schemas," 1.
101. Lakoff and Johnson, *Metaphors*, 77–86.

own discernible preconceptual structure.[102] Thus, the simply structured SOURCE-PATH-GOAL schema is mapped to the "journey" of life to evaluate "progress," where some "get ahead" while others are "left behind." Similarly, THE MIND IS A MACHINE metaphor maps structure from our gestalt perception of machines (movement, efficiency, component parts) to question whether someone is "functioning" properly or has "a screw loose."

A basic way of importing structure is through *primary metaphor*, where distinct domains (such as "affection" and "warmth") are conflated during a person's infancy through repeated correlation in experience, creating co-activation patterns in different parts of the brain's neural network, "wiring together" the two domains. Primary metaphors include MORE IS UP, SEEING IS KNOWING, DIFFICULTIES ARE BURDENS and HAPPY IS UP. These metaphors form unconsciously and automatically, so are as universally acquired as the embodied experiences they reflect are universal experiences.[103]

Lakoff and Johnson contend that metaphorical mappings primarily *create* similarities, rather than reflecting pre-existing similarities (as in comparison theories).[104] Correlations in experience do not require any intrinsic similarity between two domains; the similarities are created by mapping structure from one domain to another. Thus, a complex concept is usually partially structured by different metaphors that are somewhat inconsistent with each other, each *highlighting* certain aspects of the target domain and *hiding* others, as in the English metaphors AN ARGUMENT IS A CONTAINER (that can be "empty") and AN ARGUMENT IS A JOURNEY (that can "lose its way").[105]

d) Idealized Cognitive Models

These structures and processes produce a cognitive semantics resulting in *idealized cognitive models* (ICMs) through which we organize knowledge, handle concepts and construct categories. Each ICM is a gestalt

102. Lakoff, *Women*, 303.
103. Lakoff and Johnson, *Philosophy*, 45–58.
104. Lakoff and Johnson, *Metaphors*, 147–55.
105. Ibid., 87–96.

and produces various prototype effects, as when their idealized structure fits experience to varying degrees. Thus, a *bachelor* is not defined simply through necessary and sufficient conditions (unmarried, adult, male), but relative to an ICM including a society with heterosexual marriage occurring at a typical age. Whether Tarzan or the Pope is a bachelor then becomes a problem of how well this ICM fits the world. The worse the fit, the less appropriate it is to apply the concept.[106]

An ICM may have intrinsic structure (propositional or image-schematic) or receive structure from metaphoric or metonymic mappings.[107] First, metaphoric mappings map structure from propositional or image-schematic models to other domains. For example, the BALANCE image schema (from maintaining bodily equilibriums) maps structure to emotions and psychology. A *well-balanced* individual is *stable* and keeps emotions *on an even keel*.[108] Similarly, the source domain of STRUGGLE structures arguments, with claims "defended," positions "surrendered," and participants as "opponents." These structured, metaphorical mappings exist in thought, producing systematic conventional metaphors in language. Therefore, analysis of conventional linguistic metaphors reveals the mental mappings. As with communication "conduits," the entailments of these mappings constrain the way the target domain is thought about, problematized, and acted upon. Second, *metonymic* mappings map structure from one element of an ICM to another within the same ICM. Traditionally, metonymy refers to linguistic expressions where a word is substituted by an associated one, as in *10 Downing Street has yet to respond*, where *10 Downing Street* stands for the Prime Minister. However, just as locating metaphor in thought redefines linguistic metaphor, so does locating metonymy in the mind. Cognitive Linguistics links metaphor and metonymy in a simple formulation: whereas metaphor maps between different domains, metonymy maps within the same domain.[109] Metonymic mappings are used when

106. Lakoff, *Women*, 69–71.
107. Ibid., 68, 113–14.
108. Johnson, *Body*, 74–100.
109. This unification of metaphor and metonymy is a significant strength of Cognitive Linguistics (Geeraerts, "Introduction," 13). Important collections on metonymy include Panther and Radden, *Metonymy*; and Barcelona, *Metaphor*.

a concept is understood through a particular instantiation, and produce many prototype effects, as seen in the different uses of social stereotypes, typical examples, ideal examples, and salient examples.[110]

e) Further Evidence for Conceptual Metaphor

Lakoff advocated empirical research to support his hypotheses about metaphorical thought. The strands of evidence increased from two in 1980 to nine by 2003.[111]

First, Lakoff stresses *generalizations over polysemy*, where several words have senses in two domains. Thus, *seethe, fume, explode*, and *simmer* all describe heated fluids, but also human anger. This systematic polysemy demonstrates a conceptual link between anger and heated fluids, a link rarely mentioned in dictionaries. In *Metaphors We Live By* this was the primary evidence, with conceptual metaphors being "proved" by a few sentences incorporating such systematic polysemy.

Second, *inference patterns* show reasoning in abstract domains based on inferences from more concrete domains, implying a conceptual mapping between them. For example, if someone *explodes*, they may have been *simmering* for a long time, but *keeping a lid on it*. These inference patterns offer generalizations when reasoning in one domain (heating a fluid in a container) is systematically used for reasoning in another domain (anger).

Third, extensions to *novel* examples show conceptual metaphors are indeed "alive," though entrenched in conventional vocabulary. *More Than Cool Reason* claims poets extend, elaborate, question, or conflate conventional metaphors, rather than creating totally new ones,[112] as when Hamlet extends DEATH IS SLEEP to include dreaming, by asking, "What dreams may come?"

Fourth, generalizations over historical *semantic change* provide evidence, as in perception verbs which developed figurative meanings with remarkable consistency across Indo-European languages and

---

110. Lakoff, *Women*, 84–90.
111. Lakoff and Johnson, *Metaphors*, 246–49.
112. Lakoff and Turner, *Reason*, 67–72.

beyond.[113] Verbs of seeing became metaphors for knowledge, verbs of hearing for internal receptivity, verbs of touch for emotions, and verbs of taste for personal preference.[114]

Fifth, *psychological* evidence comes from Ray Gibbs' experiments, detailed in section 2.5.6 below.

Sixth, *gestures* "often trace out images from the source domains of conceptual metaphors,"[115] as when moving hands like scales when talking about choices, reflecting a CHOOSING IS WEIGHING conceptual metaphor.

Seventh, *discourse* studies show conceptual metaphors needed to make coherent sense of connected utterances.

Eighth, *sign languages* may reflect conceptual metaphors. For example, the sign for *past* may indicate the area behind a speaker, reflecting the metaphor that the past is behind.[116]

Finally, childhood *language acquisition* shows children learn conceptual metaphors in a conflated form when source and target domains appear together, and only later differentiate. For example, they learn SEEING IS KNOWING when they "see" and "know" something simultaneously (as in "See, Daddy's home") and only later use "see" without a visible stimulus (as in "See what I mean?"). Significantly, this suggests humans acquire more abstract senses of polysemous words later than physical senses, contrary to Barr's contention that physical senses should not be privileged.

f) Linguistic Relativity

For Lakoff, relativity in thought, and therefore also in language, arises from two areas. First, varying basic experience produces varying preconceptual structures. Bodily experiences of "containing" food may be universal, but other experiences depend on geography and culture. Thus, for the mountain-dwelling Cora people basic hill shape is a "fun-

---

113. Sweetser, *Etymology*.
114. Ibarretxe-Antuñano also investigates smell (Ibarretxe-Antuñano, "Mappings").
115. Lakoff and Johnson, *Philosophy*, 85.
116. Other gesture research supports the existence of image schemas and conceptual metaphors, as in Cienki, "Schemas."

damental aspect of their constant experience."[117] As a result, rather than culture giving a conceptual overlay to experience, "we experience our 'world' in such a way that our culture is already present in the very experience itself."[118]

Second, basic experiences may overlap but motivate different conceptual systems. For example, orientations like up-down may be universal image schemas, but which concepts are oriented which way varies across cultures.[119]

Thus, Lakoff substantially agrees with Whorf, but places more emphasis on metaphor, dissolving Whorf's distinction between habitual thought and metaphor, and claiming metaphorical thought is universal, so that Whorf's analysis of Hopi needs re-evaluation.

2.5.2. Langacker and Taylor: Cognitive Grammar

Ronald Langacker developed a new "cognitive" grammar, again utilizing Wittgenstein, Rosch, Fillmore, and Schank's ideas, prioritizing psychologically real processes (particularly imagery) over his contemporaries' mathematical formalism. Langacker's *Foundations of Cognitive Grammar* is still the core text for Cognitive Linguistics, focusing on appropriate methodology, principles, and assumptions, to create an "open" text to be filled out by others.[120] Langacker and Lakoff (with Leonard Talmy) are the most influential Cognitive Linguists,[121] but form two schools: the "Berkeley" school following Lakoff (concentrating on the centrality of metaphor to thought) and the "San Diego" school around Langacker (investigating the interface between thought and grammar in every area of linguistics).[122]

For Langacker, metaphor results from the foundational cognitive process of establishing correspondences,[123] and is thus constitutive of

---

117. Lakoff, *Women*, 310.
118. Lakoff and Johnson, *Metaphors*, 57.
119. Ibid., 24.
120. Taylor, *Grammar*, 40.
121. Geeraerts, "Introduction," 24.
122. Werth, *Worlds*, 42.
123. Langacker, *Foundations (I)*, 90–96.

mental life, not peripheral to it.[124] In mental categorization, such correspondences may reflect *schematicity* (the ability to conceive an entity at various levels, such as being a *tree*, an *oak*, and a *sessile oak*), or *comparison with a prototype* (such as recognizing a *palm* as a *tree*). The mind continually makes comparisons and this ability "underlies the detection of regularity and imposition of structure on cognitive activity."[125]

Thus, Langacker's lexical semantics complements *Metaphors* and can be used in this work. It emphasizes an *encyclopedic* approach to meaning and *schematic networks*, to which linguistic expressions provide points of access.

a) Encyclopedic Knowledge

First, Langacker advocates an *encyclopedic* view of semantics, with all the information a speaker knows about an entity legitimately belonging to the meaning of a lexeme referring to it.[126] Further, there is a graded scale, with certain specifications more entrenched through conventional usage, and thus more accessible in a usage event. Which specifications are salient depends on the speaker's individual exposure to language and on an utterance's context. As an example, Langacker explains how "the cat is on the mat" could be easily understood at the climax of a tiger-wrestling competition: "It is not that the expression intrinsically *holds* or *conveys* the contextual meaning, but rather, that conventional units *sanction* this meaning as falling within the open-ended class of conceptualizations they *motivate* through judgments of full or partial schematicity. These conceptualizations may draw on any facet of a speaker's conceptual universe."[127]

This conceptual universe is modeled (simplistically) as a knowledge system consisting of a network of nodes (corresponding to different domains) and arcs representing relationships between them. Lexical units afford points of access to these knowledge networks.

---

124. Ibid., 5.
125. Ibid., 100.
126. Ibid., 154–65.
127. Ibid., 158.

b) Schematic Networks

Second, this encyclopedic approach links Langacker's *schematic networks* to lexical semantics,[128] describing polysemy and homonymy through the complex category created by using the same word for a network of different conceptualizations. Schematic networks demonstrate, in an ideal situation, both prototypical specifications for a word and the highest level abstract schematization covering all instantiations. For example, a (British) child may first acquire the concept [TREE] through generalizing typical deciduous trees, such as oaks or sycamores, forming a prototypical sense for the category *tree*. Later, discovering pine *trees* with different leaves, the child creates [TREE′], an abstract schematization allowing both pines and deciduous trees as elaborations. Later still, the schematic concept [TREE″] is formed when the child discovers palms are also *trees*. As the category grows by extension from the prototype, an abstraction process forms increasingly "fuzzy" schemas compatible with the new category, containing only sufficient detail to cover the various elaborations. This schematic network is represented in Figure 2.2:[129]

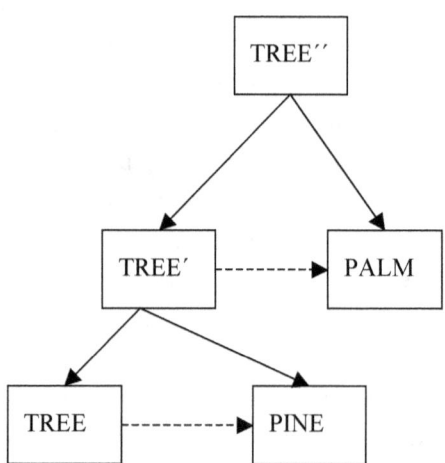

Figure 2.2: Schematic Network for the Category *tree*

---

128. Ibid., 369–408. Langacker uses schematic networks across the grammar, including phonology and morphology.
129. Ibid., 374.

In general, the nodes in a lexical network provide alternate "windows" on a knowledge system. In a specific usage, a speaker "activates a particular node that approximates the notion he wishes to convey,"[130] which also facilitates the activation of linked nodes. The nodes and links vary in cognitive salience, with prominent domains (such as visual and spatial), or particularly entrenched senses, being most salient.

c) Linguistic Relativity

Langacker agrees with Whorf that we impose structure on the flux of impressions in the world, and that "it is our conception of reality (not the real world per se) that is relevant to linguistic semantics."[131] Still, Langacker thinks cognitive grammar is useful for describing universals. However, rather than seeking universal syntactic features to deduce universal mental properties (as Chomsky had done), Langacker uses universal mental processes (such as acquiring categories through lived experience, by extensions from prototypes and generalizations to form schemas) to formulate potential language universals.

d) Taylor's *Cognitive Grammar*

Taylor's *Cognitive Grammar* (2002) mostly restates Langacker's theory, supporting Langacker's encyclopedic conception of knowledge, and incorporating conceptual metaphor theory.

First, Taylor experimentally supports Langacker's claim that words are highly flexible points of access to multiple domains, variously activated in different contexts. For example, *the young man lifted the piano* was recalled when cued with *heavy*, whereas *the young man played the piano* was not. Both were recalled when cued with *music*, showing the music domain is more central to conventional conceptions of a piano than its weight, which is only activated in certain contexts.[132] Other psychological research confirms that a word's senses are not "things" but creative processes accessing various domains in different contexts.

130. Ibid., 382.
131. Ibid., 114.
132. Taylor, *Grammar*, 442–44.

Meanings only seem stable because "most uses of the word will serve to highlight a recurring configuration of conceptual knowledge,"[133] entrenching these uses and making the domains they activate more salient. Thus, for example, the Hebrew word צָרָה may provide varying access to domains of enclosing and constraining in different contexts.

Second, Taylor integrates conceptual metaphors with schematic networks,[134] suggesting conceptual metaphors like CONCLUSIONS ARE DESTINATIONS are schematic for linguistic expressions like "we reached a conclusion," abstracting the commonalities of two domains. Johnson's image schemas and Talmy's force dynamics are also then schematic notions.[135]

Understanding conceptual metaphors as schemas provides a framework for discussing a metaphor's productivity. Schemas are salient to the extent they are entrenched through a large number of instances. Similarly, a conceptual metaphor's productivity can be categorized by speakers' abilities "to create a large (and open-ended) set of expressions which instantiate the metaphor,"[136] revealed in the number of differently worded linguistic expressions. Further, comparing with the schema and instance treatment of complex morphology, Taylor contends that "if we find that a metaphor can be creatively elaborated, by bringing in various aspects from the source domain, we can be confident that the source domain is active in the expression's use."[137] In this book, variety in syntactic expression will be investigated to demonstrate the productivity of conceptual metaphors like DISTRESS IS CONSTRAINT, and extra elements introduced from the source domain will be taken as evidence of active cognitive links.

---

133. Ibid., 445.
134. Ibid., 487–504.
135. Ibid., 519–28.
136. Ibid., 497.
137. Taylor, 499–501.

2.5.3. Talmy: Force Dynamic Patterns

Leonard Talmy's force dynamics[138] parallels Johnson's image schemas, and provides a potential universal structure for analyzing emotion.[139] Force dynamic patterns concern how entities forcefully interact, including "the exertion of force, resistance to such a force, the overcoming of such a resistance, blockage of the expression of force, removal of such blockage, and the like."[140] They offer a significant generalizing principle for understanding language structure,[141] especially causation, but also psychological and social interactions, modals,[142] and argumentation within discourse.[143]

Talmy argues that we frequently frame situations linguistically by attributing forces to the entities involved, even though not scientifically justified. For example, saying "the ball *kept on* rolling" gives the ball a force tendency to movement, overcoming some other force seeking to stop it. Here, "one force-exerting entity is singled out for focal attention—the salient issue in the interaction is whether this entity is able to manifest its force tendency or, on the contrary, is overcome."[144] The focal entity is the *Agonist*, having a tendency to either movement or rest; the entity seeking to overcome it is the *Antagonist*.

In the interaction, either may prove stronger. This gives four scenarios: the Antagonist overcomes the Agonist's tendency, making it move or rest (against its tendency), or, conversely, the Agonist prevails against the Antagonist and manifests its tendency, to move or rest. For causation, these reflect the English difference between "making" something happen (when the Antagonist prevails) and "letting" something happen (when the Antagonist fails). Although these four basic situations can be made more complex, Talmy identifies a prototypical force-dynamic interaction that limits the linguistic system, of "a stronger force

---

138. Talmy, "Dynamics," revised and republished in Talmy, *Semantics*, 409–70.
139. Kövecses, *Emotion*.
140. Talmy, *Semantics*, 409.
141. Ibid., 410.
142. Sweetser, *Etymology*.
143. Oakley, "Dimensions."
144. Talmy, *Semantics*, 413.

opposing a weaker force head on, with all-or-none conditions."[145] Thus force interactions in language involve two forces rather than three or more, a constant Agonist force, rather than one that varies, a tendency in the Agonist only to rest or movement, and a two-valued resultant state for the Agonist, either action or rest.

As with image schemas, force dynamics are grounded in an "understanding system" underlying commonsense conceptions and sophisticated reasoning, but diverging from the results of contemporary science. For example, privileging one entity within an interaction, or ascribing to it a force tendency, have no counterpart in physical theory, nor do the notions of blocking, letting, resistance, or overcoming. This discrepancy between science and naïve models leaves linguistic relativity open. If the ascription of force to entities is a matter of folk rather than scientific theory, and much of our conception of causality is based on such attribution, there is the possibility of different conceptualizations across languages. Since Talmy only considers English data, this avenue is not explored.

2.5.4. Fauconnier: Mappings and Integration

Gilles Fauconnier contributes a theory of "mental spaces" and mappings between them.[146] He contends that "mappings between domains are at the heart of the unique human cognitive faculty of producing, transferring, and processing meaning,"[147] so that "the simplest meanings are not simple at all. They rely on remarkable cognitive mapping capacities, immense arrays of intricately pre-structured knowledge, and exceptional on-line creativity."[148]

Writing on *conceptual integration,* the evolution of conceptual systems that include cross-domain (metaphorical) mappings, he concludes

---

145. Ibid., 467.

146. Including "conceptual blending," analysing source and target domains interacting to create a new, blended space, Turner and Fauconnier, "Binding"; Fauconnier and Turner, "Integration"; Fauconnier and Turner, *Think*. This is most relevant to novel metaphor, thus outside the scope of this volume.

147. Fauconnier, *Mappings*, 1.

148. Ibid., 187.

that the source domain remains accessible "at any time to provide further vocabulary and, more important, new ideas for dealing with the target" as long as a word continues to be used in both domains, so the mapping is "linguistically transparent." [149] This holds from the start of conceptual integration when an analogy is first made, through to cases of motivated polysemy (where source and target domains become increasingly distinguished). A word apparently applying directly in both domains (like a computer *virus*) "does not sever the link between the original source domain and the target or diminish the importance of the source as an archetype for some abstract properties of the target."[150] Rather, the synchronic conception of the vocabulary changes, so that speakers feel they are not talking about target domain entities "as if" they were in the source domain, but that terms from the source domain can be used to speak of them (as possibly in the Hebrew description of other participants in distress as "enemies"). By now, the mapping may be less consciously noticeable, but "more available than ever for reasoning, inference transfers, and conceptual elaborations."[151] Conceptual links only disappear when the source domain changes vocabulary, so that, for example, "idea" no longer has conceptual links to sight because the Greek *idein* 'see' is no longer used in the domain of vision.

2.5.5. Wierzbicka: Natural Semantic Metalanguage

Although critical of Lakoff,[152] Anna Wierzbicka works within a broadly Cognitive Linguistic paradigm, recognizing the profound impact of language on thought, but also claiming meaningful universalism. Her approach is summarized as "Universal Human Concepts in Culture-Specific Configurations"[153] and derives from Cartesian foundationalism, assuming certain unanalyzable, basic concepts (or *semantic primitives*) that are, moreover, "universal words" present in all languages. Thus "universal words stand for universal human concepts, that is,

149. Ibid., 18–25.
150. Ibid., 21.
151. Ibid., 22.
152 Wierzbicka, "Linguists."
153. The subtitle for Wierzbicka, *Concepts*.

the universal building blocks of human thought,"[154] and can be used to paraphrase more complex concepts, permitting translation and cross-cultural communication.

Wierzbicka has sought to elucidate these primitives, constructing a "Natural Semantic Metalanguage" for cross-linguistic comparisons. In 1992, it contained around 30 words: I, you, someone, something, this, say, want, no, feel, think, know, where, good, when, can, like, the same, kind of, after, do, happen, bad, all, because, if, two, part, become, imagine, and world.[155] By 2002, the list contained some 60 items.[156] Importantly, these primitives are not metaphorical, since "the meaning of metaphors . . . can be explained in non-metaphorical language."[157] This clearly opposes Lakoff and Johnson, who claim the mind is inherently and foundationally metaphorical.[158]

Wierzbicka emphasizes prototypes in semantic description, with word "definitions" written in her semantic metalanguage being cultural prototypes rather than necessary and sufficient conditions. These prototypes enable comparison of concepts like friendship, understanding of the self, or emotions across different cultures. She prioritizes individual words (rather than sentences) as access points to concepts, focusing on key words in different languages.[159] Thus, although the absence of a word does not mean a speaker cannot form a concept, "the *presence* of a word proves the presence of the concept, and, moreover, its salience in a given culture."[160] She has been criticized for having too monolithic a view of language and culture here,[161] but replies that "language—and in particular, vocabulary—is the best evidence of the reality of 'culture',

---

154. Wierzbicka, *Sermon*, 8.

155. Wierzbicka, *Concepts*, 10.

156. Wierzbicka, "Parable," 86.

157. Ibid.

158. Lakoff's approach is preferred. Wierzbicka actually unconsciously uses her primitives metaphorically, as when she uses "something" to refer to an event ("do something bad"), not a concrete entity (Wierzbicka, *Sermon*, 6–7).

159. Wierzbicka, *Understanding*.

160. Wierzbicka, *Concepts*, 21.

161. Mondry and Taylor, "Dynamics," 30.

in the sense of a historically transmitted system of 'conceptions' and attitudes."[162]

For emotion language specifically, words are important since "the way people interpret their own emotions depends, to some extent at least, on the lexical grid provided by their native language... whether or not two feelings are interpreted as two different instances of, essentially, 'the same emotion' or as instances of 'two different emotions' depends largely on the language through the prism of which these emotions are interpreted."[163]

Whilst this is undoubtedly valid, it excludes almost all the data in this work, since it "ignores the important fact that talk about the emotions does not require that the emotions be named."[164] It is possible to express depression without explicitly saying, "I am depressed," and it is this discourse the present work investigates. Thus, this research follows Wierzbicka in taking vocabulary seriously, but uses biblical form criticism to define a wider set of linguistic expressions (discussed in 3.3.1 and 3.3.2.b), where the experience may not be explicitly named, that can be used to study the conceptualization of distress.

2.5.6. Gibbs: Psychological Evidence for a Poetic Mind

Raymond Gibbs contributes through experimental psycholinguistics, questioning the distinction between literal and figurative meaning and demonstrating "how common metaphorical knowledge motivates people's use and understanding of ordinary and literary language."[165]

Gibbs desires to clarify the role of metaphor within thought and language, offering four hypotheses as to how figurative thought may influence ordinary language use and understanding:

> Hypothesis one: Metaphoric thought might play some role in changing the meanings of words and expressions over time, but

---

162. Wierzbicka, "Character," 52.
163. Wierzbicka, "Non-universality," 5.
164. Taylor and Mbense, "Dogs," 193.
165. Gibbs, *Poetics*, 18.

does not motivate contemporary speakers' use and understanding of language.

Hypothesis two: Metaphoric thought might motivate the linguistic meanings that have currency within linguistic communities, or may have some role in an idealized speaker/hearer's understanding of language. But metaphoric thought does not actually play any part in individual speakers' ability to make sense of, or process, language.

Hypothesis three: Metaphoric thought might motivate individual speakers' use and understanding of why various words and expressions mean what they do, but does not play any role in people's ordinary on-line production or comprehension of everyday language.

Hypothesis four: Metaphoric thought might function automatically and interactively in people's on-line use and understanding of linguistic meaning.[166]

James Barr's emphasis on separate semantic histories following metaphorical transference suggests he assumed hypothesis one, so that metaphoric thought does not occur when a polysemous word is used with a figurative sense. By contrast, Lakoff risks uncritically assuming hypothesis four, with linguistic metaphors providing direct access to "on-line" metaphoric thought. For Gibbs, his psycholinguistic evidence confirms at least hypothesis three, and possibly (though not conclusively) hypothesis four.

a) No "Literal" Meanings

First, Gibbs attacks "literal" meanings,[167] concluding "there is no stable account of literality for either concepts or language."[168] If "literality" cannot be defined, the mind cannot process information in a predomi-

---

166. Gibbs, "Researching," 42–43; Gibbs, *Poetics*, 18.
167. See also Rumelhart, "Problems."
168. Gibbs, *Poetics*, 19–20.

nantly "literal" way, and handling of "literal" versus "figurative" language cannot be contrasted. Rather, the mind works in an inherently poetic way. Following Reddy, words are not containers of meaning but ways of accessing highly interconnected networks, requiring an encyclopedic approach to knowledge, and suggesting that concepts are "temporary constructions in working memory constructed on the spot from generic and episodic information in long-term memory rather than . . . stable structures stored in long-term memory."[169]

Next, Gibbs investigates any special process for understanding figurative language. Reaction times for comprehension of "figurative" or "literal" language show no differences, given an adequate contextual background, suggesting the mind processes both similarly, constructing meaning against the conceptual background and common knowledge of speaker and hearer. All the evidence contradicts the idea that figurative language requires a three stage process of understanding (literal processing, recognition of anomaly, and figurative processing).

b) Metaphor Comprehension

Gibbs clarifies what does happen in understanding figurative language. At different time scales, it may involve *comprehension*, *recognition* that an utterance is an example of figurative language, *interpretation* of the utterance, and *appreciation* as to whether it is a good or bad example. Comprehension comes first and relates to the *process* of understanding, the other three relate to the *product* of this process. Many theories of understanding figurative language confuse these stages of understanding. Any metaphor theory has to accept no difference between "literal" and metaphorical language for the time taken in the earliest stages of comprehension. This rules out comparison, substitution, "loose talk," anomaly, speech act, and most interaction views of metaphor in their handling of this stage of understanding, as all require extra processing for the early comprehension of figurative language, whether in identifying that communicative norms have been broken, creating new interactions between source and target domains, or substituting literal

---

169. Ibid., 54, a development of Barsalou, "Instability."

meanings.[170] The only solution is the *conceptual structure* view, with both figurative and "literal" language relying on similar pre-existing structures, so that there must be a pre-existing "constrained set of conceptual mappings, itself metaphorical, that structures our thinking, reasoning, and understanding."[171] Only this approach allows us to understand metaphorical utterances before we even realize they are metaphorical.

c) Poetic Metaphor

Gibbs sees literary metaphors as special instantiations of shared conceptual metaphors. For example, when subjects shared their thoughts as they read love poetry, they used the same conventional figurative expressions (based on conceptual metaphors) identified in another experiment where participants defined love and described their experiences of it. Thus, the interpretation of poetic literature is constrained by ordinary metaphorical mappings, rather than creating novel ones. Gibbs concludes that "the vast majority of novel metaphors in poetry and literature reflect fixed patterns of metaphorical mappings between dissimilar source and target domains."[172] This is a significant empirical result for this project, which analyzes literary texts.

d) Idiom Comprehension and Image Schemas

Idioms show further that conceptual metaphors constrain thought. People's mental images for the conventional expressions "blow your stack," "hit the ceiling," and "flip your lid" shared many similarities, whereas images for "blow your tire," "hit the wall," and "flip your hat" were more varied. This suggests a constraining conceptual metaphor, in which internal pressure causes a substance to move upwards in a violent manner, linking the idioms to their figurative meanings. Elsewhere, Gibbs showed that *cognitive topology* (relationships within a domain) transferred from source to target domain for idioms. When questioned about causation, intentionality and manner when a sealed container ex-

---

170. Ibid., 208–48.
171. Ibid., 250.
172. Ibid., 255.

plodes, most participants agreed it was due to internal pressure, was not the intention of the container, and would be violent. Other participants considered anger idioms like "blow your stack" and again understood the cause to be internal pressure, resulting in violent and unintentional behavior. Thus, non-trivial aspects of the source domain may be preserved in idioms.[173]

Other research supports the psychological reality of image schemas as "the essential glue that binds embodied experience, thought, and language,"[174] demonstrated by studies on how the mind represents momentum, on childhood development, and on the relationship between stimuli in different modalities. In each area the mind apparently uses image schemas deriving from recurring bodily experience.[175]

e) Metaphor and Culture

Gibbs argues cognition is not just located in the head, but distributed into the wider cultural system. Thus, image-schemas and basic body experiences are themselves complex (and diverse) social and cultural constructions. Although containment, for example, is universal, "scholars should look extensively at people's social / cultural experiences of embodied containment, such as what causes people to move in and out of containers [and] how the escape of fluids from different containers is socially understood."[176] Here, this means Hebrew embodied experiences of containment are significant for metaphor comprehension.

2.5.7. Kövecses: Emotion and Cultural Variation

Zoltán Kövecses makes several relevant contributions. First, he has empirically investigated conceptual metaphors behind linguistic expressions found in various corpora, offering practical methodologies for this investigation. Second, he has researched emotions and relationships,[177]

173. Gibbs, "Heads," 148–51.
174. Gibbs, "Status," 113.
175. Gibbs and Colston, "Reality."
176. Gibbs, "Heads," 161.
177. Kövecses, *Pride*; Lakoff and Kövecses, "Model"; Kövecses, *Concepts*; Kövecses, *Emotion*.

similar domains to Hebrew distress language, so he offers some of the best comparative examples. Third, Kövecses relates conceptual metaphors to conceptual metonymies. Fourth, he has increasingly considered cultural influences on conceptual metaphor,[178] investigating cross-cultural variation.[179]

a) Research Methodology

First, Kövecses' methodology typically involves collecting linguistic metaphors from specific corpora, classifying into groups according to source domains and then quantifying which conceptual metaphors are instantiated most frequently. For example, one project used a selection of romantic novels to discover metaphoric conceptualizations for "lust" and then tabulated results. In another, magazine articles in Hungarian and English were read to find out how emotions were conceptualized in both languages. These methods provide prototypes for this book.

Kövecses has also developed analytical tools to describe how source domains are used to conceptualize target domains. These include the *scope* of a metaphor and its *main meaning focus*.[180] The scope of a metaphor is the full range of target domains, to which a specific source concept applies.[181] Across this range, there are often main meaning foci for the source domain, being culturally predetermined conceptual materials that are contributed to the target domains.[182] For example, building metaphors used to structure arguments, relationships, theories, or careers all focus on the creation and stability of the target domain's complex system. Similarly, fire and heat in English focus particularly on "intensity," whichever target domain they conceptualize.

---

178. Kövecses, "Models."
179. Kövecses, *Culture*.
180. Kövecses, "Scope."
181. Ibid., 80.
182. Ibid., 82.

b) Emotion Metaphors

Kövecses' best-known study concerns the English conceptualization of anger,[183] using conventional expressions to identify the main conceptual metaphors, such as ANGER IS AN OPPONENT, ANGER IS A DANGEROUS ANIMAL, and (most significantly) ANGER IS A HEATED FLUID IN A CONTAINER. The different parts of the experience which these domains highlight create a prototypical *scenario*[184] for anger in American culture, involving five stages: offending event; anger; attempted control; loss of control; and act of retribution. ANGER IS A DANGEROUS ANIMAL, for example, highlights the stages of "loss of control" and "act of retribution" (as in "he unleashed his anger," "she bit his head off"). Against this prototypical scenario, non-prototypical cases stand out, such as successful control, or insatiable anger (where anger remains despite retribution). This work will investigate the prototypical scenario for Hebrew distress.

Kövecses also investigated other basic-level emotions, including happiness, love, and sadness, discovering some source domains only used for certain emotions (such as FEAR IS A HIDDEN ENEMY or SHAME IS A DECREASE IN SIZE). However, many applied to most emotion concepts: containers; natural and physical forces; social superiors; opponents; or captive animals; a divided self; burdens; and illness. Other domains associated with more than one emotion included heat, light-dark, up-down, economic value, nutrient, war, hunger, and physical damage.[185] Many of these metaphors can be considered as instantiations of the master (more schematic) metaphor that EMOTIONS ARE FORCES.[186]

Kövecses suspects that conceptualizing emotions as forces is a language universal arising from physiological experiences. Cultural variation arises from such general schemas being "filled out in diverse ways with specific cultural material."[187] By contrast, those who concentrate on

---

183. Kövecses, *Pride*; then Lakoff and Kövecses, "Model," included in Lakoff, *Women*, 380–415.

184. Emotional "scenarios" overlap with scripts, both having a chronological sequence of conventional actions or events.

185. Kövecses, *Emotion*, 36–40.

186. Ibid., 61–86.

187. Ibid., 185.

lexical items at the expense of conventional figurative language (as in Wierzbicka's work[188]) miss these bodily based universals.[189]

c) Conceptual Metonymy

Following Lakoff, Kövecses sees conceptual metonymy as "a cognitive process in which one conceptual entity, the vehicle, provides mental access to another conceptual entity, the target, within the *same* idealized cognitive model."[190] Focusing on emotions, this allows for conceptual metonymies like THE PHYSIOLOGICAL AND EXPRESSIVE RESPONSES OF AN EMOTION STAND FOR THE EMOTION,[191] a schematic metonymy encompassing instances such as BODY HEAT STANDS FOR ANGER seen in linguistic expressions like *Billy's a hothead*.[192] Kövecses argues that such conceptual metonymies motivate more elaborate conceptual metaphors, like ANGER IS A HEATED FLUID IN A CONTAINER.[193] Others show that a metonymic basis for metaphor accounts for the experiential basis of many metaphors, suggesting a universal phenomenon,[194] thus this work investigates possible Hebrew metonymic motivations for metaphor.

d) Metaphor and Culture

In *Metaphor in Culture*, Kövecses analyzes universality and variation in conceptual metaphors. Specifically, Kövecses compares American English, Hungarian, Chinese, Japanese, and to a lesser extent Wolof (spoken in West Africa), Zulu (spoken in South Africa), Polish, the language of the Ifaluk (spoken in Micronesia[195]), and Chagga (spoken in Tanzania). In the first seven languages, pressurized containers map onto

---

188. Wierzbicka, *Concepts*; Wierzbicka, *Emotions*.
189. Kövecses, "Constructionism."
190. Radden and Kövecses, "Theory," 21, italics added.
191. Kövecses, *Emotion*, 134.
192. Ibid., 156.
193. Kövecses, "Anger"; Kövecses, *Emotion*, 156–61.
194. Radden, "Metonymic"; Barcelona, "Plausibility."
195. Studied in Lutz, "Ethnopsychology"; and Lutz, "Goals."

the domain of anger. Usually, heat is the source of the pressure.[196] This universal conceptualization across such varied languages suggests universal embodied experiences (presumably increase in skin temperature and blood pressure) rather than linguistic borrowing. Thus, there may be several potentially universal conceptual metaphors (including anger as pressure).

However, when these generic metaphors are culturally instantiated, variation emerges. First, some variation relates to understanding of the source and target domains, and of the mapping between them. Source domains may have a different scope in different cultures (mapping onto a different set of target domains) or target domains may have a different "range" (a different set of source domains used for conceptualization). Sometimes the range is very similar, but certain domains are preferred in different cultures.[197] For example, although Americans and Hungarians both use the metaphors LIFE IS WAR and LIFE IS A GAME, the former was most commonly used by Hungarians and the latter by Americans, with the alternative conceptualization much less frequent.

Even where the same source domain is used, variation may result from the source domain's *construal* (as in spatial motion, where English verbs like *march* or *run* encode manner whereas Turkish do not) or *cultural prototypes* (as in the metaphor SOCIETY IS A FAMILY, where it matters whether the prototypical family is dominated by a "strict father" or is a place for "nurturing" one another).[198] Metaphors may also map different elements from source to target, or produce different entailments. For example, pouring water on someone's anger to "extinguish" it is a conventional entailment of ANGER IS FIRE in Zulu, but not in English.

Second, linguistic expressions for a shared conceptual metaphor may vary across cultures: in the degree of elaboration (the variety of expressions instantiating a particular conceptual metaphor); the kinds of linguistic expression used (whether words, multiword phrases, or more complex syntactic constructions); the degree of conventionalization; and the degree of transparency.[199] These variations stem from either

196. Kövecses, *Culture*, 39–43.
197. Ibid., 85.
198. Ibid., 118–19.
199. Ibid., 151–55.

differential experience or differential cognitive preferences or styles.[200] Different experience may come from a different physical, social, or cultural context, or from a different cultural memory. Different cognitive preferences may be seen in different cultures focusing on different aspects of universal physiological experience (for example pressure or heat in the experience of anger), in the cultural prototypes for specific domains, or in a preference for metonymic over metaphoric conceptualization (or vice versa).

e) Language and Thought

Kövecses distinguishes conventionalized metaphors within a language (the "supraindividual" level) from those activated within the heads of individual speakers (the "individual" level). Thus, "it is not the case that all the mappings arrived at by cognitive linguists at the supraindividual level are activated by individual speakers in the course of on-line thinking and communication in the real world."[201] However, he remains positive about using language to discover how the mind works, noting that the main patterns that "emerge from the study of language characterize . . . other (non-linguistic) types of manifestation of the mind as well" suggesting that "language can be taken to be a fairly reliable instrument in identifying general conceptual patterns and that the general conceptual patterns that we find give us a fairly good clue to what is going on in the mind."[202] However, the emphasis on individual experience within a culture puts Kövecses a long way from Whorf's determinism. Alternative conceptualizations are possible and ubiquitous.

2.5.8. Deignan: Metaphor and Corpus Research

Finally for this survey, Alice Deignan investigates metaphors in large corpora,[203] demonstrating that figurative uses of a word may still evoke a physical mental image, even though never used in a physical sense

> 200. Ibid., 231.
> 201. Kövecses, *Metaphor*, 243.
> 202. Kövecses, *Culture*, 169–70.
> 203. Deignan, "Corpus-based."

within the corpus. Thus, lack of a concrete usage within the biblical corpus does not necessarily mean a word no longer generated an image from the physical domain.

For example, of 1,000 random instances of *shoulder*, Deignan found 47 were verbal, 39 of which suggested responsibility, as in *shouldering a wide variety of risks*. This evokes "an image of a person carrying a heavy load on their shoulders; the load is the metaphor for their responsibility, and the verb **shoulder** is a metaphor for taking on or coping with this responsibility."[204] However, only two uses described a physical situation, and those described pushing through a crowd. Thus, although the mental image of physically lifting a heavy weight onto the shoulders seems a perfectly reasonable background for the metaphorical use, such physical usage did not occur. For the noun *shoulder*, the physical sense far outweighed the "responsibility" sense (828 to 31), so the form *shoulder* still primarily evokes a physical entity. However, lack of a physical context amongst the occurrences in one part of speech (here, verbs) does not preclude a physical mental image, especially if physical usage is still current in another part of speech. Thus, even if the Bible only shows a root having a physical sense in one part of speech and only more abstract senses in another, the physical mental image may still be evoked by both. Specifically, although the nominal צרה is only found for abstract "trouble," this is insufficient evidence to preclude a mental image of constraint, as found in the physical contexts for the verb צרר.

2.5.9. Cognitive Linguistics and the Legacy of James Barr

So, does Cognitive Linguistics face Barr's critique any better than its Whorfian predecessors? This section applies Barr's concerns in *Semantics* to Cognitive Linguistics.

First, Barr warned against simply correlating language structure and thought structure, pleading for an approach from general linguistics. Cognitive Linguistics has developed within mainstream linguistics and moves beyond the simplicity of identifying linguistic structure and thought structure. However, it *is* optimistic that language provides generally reliable access to cognitive processes, based on convergent

204. Ibid., 186.

cross-linguistic research across psychology, linguistics, and anthropology, contrasting with Barr's emphasis on the unmotivated link between language and thought structures. Correlated language structure and thought structure *is* assumed, with many Cognitive Linguists adopting the "Cognitive Wager," that linguistic constraints are most likely general to other cognitive processes, and others should prove otherwise.[205] The difference between Barr and Cognitive Linguistics is partly one of emphasis. For Barr, since some linguistic structure derives from purely form-related phenomena (like Indo-European gender arising from an accent system[206]), semantic explanations should not be privileged. For Cognitive Linguistics, since much linguistic structure is explainable through general cognitive processes (such as comparison and salience), explanations in terms of "thought structure" should be considered first.

For example, Lakoff's discussion of the Japanese noun classifier *hon*[207] and Barr's discussion of grammatical gender both examine those nouns united by a common grammatical structure. For Barr, gender "cannot be taken to reflect a thought pattern" because gender determination "is not . . . made by distinctions in thought or by distinctions in the actual objects named but by matters of linguistic form and type."[208] Lakoff, conversely, emphasizes that such classifiers do create cognitive categories, and thus require consideration in any model of thought. Moreover, such categories exhibit expected properties for thought categories: central and peripheral members; basic-level prioritization; conventional mental images; metonymy applied to these images; and metaphor.[209]

Polysemy further exemplifies this conflict. Barr seeks the earliest stage where Hebrew senses established by metaphorical transference have a non-concrete sense, allowing an individual semantic history separate from the physical sense.[210] His concern is when a physical sense

---

205. Gibbs, *Poetics*, 15.
206. Barr, *Semantics*, 40.
207. Lakoff, *Women*, 104–9.
208. Barr, *Semantics*, 40.
209. Lakoff, *Women*, 109–10.
210. See discussion of "faith" and "truth" in Barr, *Semantics*, 161–205.

"ceased to be active and productive,"[211] no longer being relevant for speakers' cognitive processes. For Cognitive Linguistics, conversely, using a word in an "abstract" target domain, even if no longer commonly used in the source domain, is insufficient evidence to preclude reasoning from the physical domain. The domains may still be conceptually integrated, especially if structural patterns in conventional language (generalizations over polysemy, generalizations over inference patterns, and novel extensions) support this. Thus, evidence for whether a polysemous word may still activate a physical domain comes more from comparison with other words suggesting the same link than from detailed analysis of that word's semantic development.

Finally, although Cognitive Linguists do assume language reflects thought, the thought structures reflected are more carefully articulated and restricted than by Barr's contemporaries, only allowing relationships consistent with research in cognitive science on thought processes.[212] Perceptual abilities to recognize similarities (and thus create categories) and identify certain entities as salient, are fundamental to human thought. Thus, mental categories are organized around prototypes and have varying salience, with the basic-level being prioritized. Language categories share these properties, with grammatical and lexical structure reflecting these same psychological phenomena. In this sense, language and thought are similarly structured.

Second, Barr argued one cannot use presuppositions about a cultural mind to interpret linguistic evidence. Cognitive Linguistics assumes no peculiarity for the Hebrew, or any other, mind. Universal psychological phenomena are emphasized, though producing differing linguistic phenomena in different contexts. However, Cognitive Linguistics does sometimes privilege an Anglo-American ethnopsychology, using English terms (such as ANGER) to state universal conceptual phenomena, although several scholars try to minimize this.

Using image schemas and primary metaphors reflecting near universal experience provides a relatively neutral basis for analyzing any given language. Common cultural experiences and linguistic conventions do produce typical and salient mental categories that may be

211. Barr, *Semantics*, 186.
212. Lakoff, "Contemporary," 234.

widespread within a speech community. Only in this sense does a "cultural mind" have any meaning.

Third, Barr contended that etymology is insufficient evidence for current cognitive associations in speakers' minds. Cognitive Linguists do sometimes carelessly use historical metaphorical transference to prove current conceptual metaphors.[213] A proposed conceptual metaphor argued only from etymological evidence, even if across several words, is less likely to influence on-line processing of language than when words continue to be used in both domains (as Fauconnier argues). Kövecses therefore no longer uses linguistic examples to assert how a domain is "understood," but to make hypotheses that could be tested by cognitive psychologists.[214] However, Gibbs' work on idiom comprehension does show that coherent mental images may still be evoked by "dead" figurative language, particularly for a well-elaborated conceptual metaphor, and as Deignan discovered, this mental image may still be accessible even if a word is not used in its non-figurative sense in contemporary culture.

Fourth, Barr argued against root meanings, claiming the same root form for two words is insufficient evidence of cognitive associations between them. Here the schematic networks of Langacker, Lakoff, and Taylor provide a potential descriptive framework. A common morpheme like a Hebrew root creates a category, providing a point of access to a network of domains linked by a degree of shared symbolization. Graded salience of the different links in the network enables description of the relationship between different forms. The transparency of a root in different forms (as noted by Sawyer, section 2.3.2) increases the salience of the link between such senses, as does the salience of a schematic, generalizing, link between the set of senses for two forms. Thus the dispute over the schematic link between מלחמה and לחם suggests a low salience for this link. However, more generally, the links between forms of a root in the qal and hiphil conjugations would be much more salient, and the most salient links would join forms within the same paradigm.

---

213. Criticized by Cameron, "Identifying."
214. Kövecses, *Culture*, 28–29.

Psycholinguistic studies also support the distinct mental representation of the consonantal root of Hebrew words, separate from the template in which it is found.[215] Berman affirms that "the consonantal root has definite psychological reality as both the structural and the semantic basis for new-word formation," even for pre-literate children who have not yet been taught orthography or grammar.[216] Other studies found Hebrew speakers sensitive to the consonantal root in word recognition, with priming effects discovered for words after seeing one based morphologically on the same root.[217] Although biblical and modern Hebrew differ, the mental representation of words is potentially very similar, especially for children who have not yet been formally educated in grammar, suggesting the root has more cognitive significance than Barr recognized.

Fifth, Barr argued that the same form in different contexts is insufficient evidence for an overlap in meaning. Here Cognitive Linguistics potentially has much to contribute, through its treatment of polysemy. The flexibility of concepts in different contexts fundamentally agrees with Barr, but the modeling of structural links between senses, and the existence of image schemas and conceptual metaphors, provides a way of describing "nodules"[218] of meaning that are more stable across contexts. A schematic network accessed by the use of a lexical form, incorporating extensions from prototypes and schematic generalizations, provides a good descriptive framework. Different nodes and related domains are accessed in different contexts, with links to other domains differing in salience, and thus accessibility. Within this framework, "illegitimate totality transfer" is not the problem of suggesting a word always contains the same bundle of semantic features, but the recognition that different contexts provide different points of access to the network, so that different aspects of knowledge are accessible. Adopting encyclopedic rather than logical semantic structures makes concepts even more flexible than for Barr, but emphasizing schematic generalizations and prioritizing perceptual experience in cognitive development, makes

215. Shimron, *Processing*.
216. Berman, "Innovations," 244–45.
217. Shimron, "Languages," 18.
218. Cruse, "Micro-structure."

cognitive links to physical and prototypical senses much more salient than Barr suggested.

In summary, although Cognitive Linguistics follows the relativist tradition Barr so strongly criticized, especially with its mentalist assumptions about the reflection of psychology in language, it has descriptive frameworks and systematic approaches to face most of Barr's criticisms. In particular, the psychological reality of prototypes, categories and conceptual metaphor provides a justified framework for arguing the priority of "concrete" senses over "abstract" ones, and the schematic network model provides a systematic method for describing the relationship between language and thought.

2.6. Linguistics and Biblical Studies II: Applications of Cognitive Semantics to Hebrew

2.6.1. Overview

Scholars have begun applying Cognitive Linguistics to biblical texts. Many are unaware of Barr's concerns. Others mention him, but there has been little dialogue regarding the fundamental differences in linguistic approach, necessitating the preceding discussion.

Some Cognitive Linguists use biblical texts to test hypotheses in a non-Indo-European language. Thus, Sweetser cites the Hebrew metaphorical transfer from "hear" to "obey" as showing common semantic development of perceptual verbs,[219] and Gibbs uses biblical evidence to show the prevalence of the "journey" metaphor.[220] Jäkel's investigation of the biblical metaphor LIFE IS A JOURNEY is more thorough,[221] investigating the conceptual metaphor LEADING A MORAL LIFE IS MAKING A JOURNEY ON GOD'S WAY. Comparing with English, he notes similarities (such as difficulties in life being impediments to travel) and differences (such as whether the path itself is crooked or straight). Most significant is the lack of elaboration of the "path." In English, journey stages correspond to life stages, but this is absent in the Bible. Jäkel's work considers seriously the way a biblical conceptual metaphor is instantiated,

219. Sweetser, *Etymology*, 42–43.
220. Gibbs, *Poetics*, 190–91.
221. Jäkel, "Hypotheses."

Culture, Language, and Thought

but suffers from using an English translation rather than the Hebrew original, and from imposing his own interpretative logic on the text, as when he claims the "path to life" in Proverbs 10:17 must refer to eternal life in God, since the earthly lifespan is already conceptualized as the journey, not the goal,[222] This logic is at odds with the focus in wisdom instruction on maintaining a wise life in this world, not some after death experience.

More sensitive applications of Cognitive Linguistics to the Hebrew text come from biblical scholars. Three significant groups can be identified.

2.6.2. The South African School

Several scholars associated with the University of Stellenbosch have applied Cognitive Linguistics to the Hebrew Bible. First, within lexicography, Reinier de Blois has started creating a "Semantic Dictionary of Biblical Hebrew" (SDBH)[223] to remedy the failure of previous lexicons to show semantic structure, the very relations between word meanings prioritized in Cognitive Linguistics. It aims to represent "as much as possible the ways of thinking of the speaker of the language, and do justice to his / her organization of experience."[224] Specifically, it shows prototypical meanings, represents encyclopedic knowledge in different domains and highlights metaphorical transfer.

Elsewhere, Rechenmacher investigates prototypes and basic-level categorization for Hebrew lion terminology,[225] whilst Foster cognitively analyzes בְּרִית 'covenant', arguing biblical words must be understood against the ancient Near Eastern prototypical assumptions.[226] Christo van der Merwe praises SDBH for representing encyclopedic knowledge and cognitive categories,[227] setting it above Clines' *Dictionary of*

---

222. Jäkel, "Hypotheses," 27.
223. De Blois, "Dictionary."
224. De Blois, "Lexicography."
225. Rechenmacher, "Kognitive."
226. Foster, "Prototypical."
227. Van der Merwe, "Towards."

Classical Hebrew, which only lists syntactic frames.[228] His own lexicographic application of Cognitive Linguistics[229] investigates the *meaning potential* of Hebrew words related to strength. Meaning potential is "all the information that a word has been used to convey either by a single individual or, on the social level, by the language community,"[230] a potential partially activated in any given context. Elsewhere, van der Merwe investigates Hebrew conceptual metaphors, and explores the translation implications.[231]

Second, several works utilize Kövecses' emotion research, noting that the conventional language approach fits better with contemporary psychological studies of emotion than approaches focused on theological implications or Hebrew anthropology.[232] Kruger seeks Hebrew evidence for Kövecses' conceptual metaphors for anger[233] and fear,[234] though restricting himself to evidence of the English metaphors, rather than investigating specific Hebrew conceptual metaphors. He has also investigated depression[235] and the face and emotions,[236] and summarized Hebrew emotion research.[237] Kotzé's approach is more sensitive, utilizing Kövecses' "scope of metaphor" by first finding the source domains for a given target, then investigating the scope of these source domains within the Hebrew corpus in an attempt to deduce their main meaning foci.[238] For example, the main meaning focus for "fire" in Hebrew is "destruction," compared with "intensity" in English. Kotzé then studies target domains of sex, lust and rape, showing the use of fire in lust metaphors evokes resulting destruction

---

228. A similar criticism is given in Muraoka, "Dictionary."
229. Van der Merwe, "Lexical."
230. Allwood, "Potential," 43.
231. Van der Merwe and Hendriks, "Metaphors."
232. Kotzé, "Approach."
233. Kruger, "Anger."
234. Kruger, "Fear."
235. Kruger, "Depression."
236. Kruger, "Face."
237. Kruger, "Emotions."
238. Kotzé, "Methodology."

more than the intensity of passion.²³⁹ However, Kotzé's main focus is the conceptualization of anger,²⁴⁰ enumerating the source domains conceptualizing anger in Hebrew, showing particularly the significance of breathing through the nose.

Elsewhere, Basson analyzes metaphors in lament psalms, noting the significance of the up-down schema,²⁴¹ and the conceptual metaphor PEOPLE ARE PLANTS, which demonstrates structural mappings, such as blossoming corresponding to a person's prosperity.²⁴² Pohlig also uses conceptual metaphor theory and surveys the methodological difficulties in applying Cognitive Linguistics to the Bible: the tendency to treat biblical culture as monolithic; the reliance on texts rather than native speaker intuition; and the theoretical difficulties at the heart of conceptual metaphor theory that this chapter has sought to partly address.²⁴³

2.6.3. The European School

The European Association of Biblical Studies' research program on "Metaphor in the Hebrew Bible" uses the Cognitive Linguistic approach as one strand in a multifaceted approach intending "to fully grasp the phenomenon of religious metaphor."²⁴⁴ Encyclopedic knowledge and conceptual metaphor have been explored in relation to images of enemy and self,²⁴⁵ animals,²⁴⁶ fire,²⁴⁷ walls,²⁴⁸ restricted space,²⁴⁹ and bitterness²⁵⁰

---

239. Kotzé, "Women."
240. Kotzé, "Conceptualisation."
241. Basson, *Divine*.
242. Basson, "People."
243. Pohlig, "Cognition."
244. European Association of Biblical Studies, "Metaphor."
245. Riede, "Sprache"; Eidevall, "Images."
246. Labahn, "Wild."
247. Labahn, "Fire."
248. Baumann, "Weg."
249. Eidevall, "Spatial."
250. Labahn, "Bitterkeit."

in lament Psalms and Lamentations. These studies are referred to as necessary within the present work.

2.6.4. SIL

SIL is also producing a Cognitive Linguistic lexicon, called "Key Terms in Biblical Hebrew" (KTBH). This assumes "our experience, knowledge, and beliefs are structured in cognitive or conceptual networks which may be activated by language."[251] The documentation is based on Langacker and Taylor, using Fillmorean "frames" for networks that interrelate all information that a speech community typically associate with a given term, and Langacker's "domains" for a coherent body of background information. Thus, frames link domains together, and words provide points of access to the domains. Further, the SIL approach distinguishes core domains that are accessed in nearly every use of a word from non-core domains that are more peripheral, accessed only in certain contexts.

Second, Ken McElhanon uses conceptual metaphor theory to investigate "truth" in the New Testament, finding the ancient conceptual metaphor TRUTH IS A ROAD.[252] Elsewhere, he applies image schemas and human physiological universals to Old Testament metaphors.[253] He considers VERTICALITY, CONTAINMENT, and NEAR-FAR schemas, concluding that heaven, holy, strength, honor, security, prosperity, pride, arrogance, and intelligence are all UP, and their opposites DOWN. Whilst the entailments McElhanon deduces are helpful ("being accepted is being allowed to approach," "being uninvolved is being distant," "rejecting is being absent"), his attempt to apply logic to conceptualizations found in poetic works written by different authors at different times often ignores the possibility of people holding alternate, potentially conflicting conceptual metaphors for the same target. Conceptual metaphor theory relies on the existence of structural and systematic conventional links between domains. However, since metaphors highlight different

---

251. Summer Institute of Linguistics, "Guide," 10.

252. McElhanon, "Word."

253. McElhanon, "Metaphors." Unfortunately, McElhanon's work is limited by being based predominantly on English rather than Hebrew.

aspects of experiences, they typically cohere, but only rarely will they be consistent.[254]

All these approaches help to shape the research here through their methodologies and the pitfalls they highlight, as well as through their specific results.

2.7. Position of this Work

In conclusion, the following claims of cognitive semantics are assumed in this thesis.

1. Language and thought: The cognitive processes governing language use are in principle the same as other cognitive abilities. Thus, language structure does provide access to thought structure.
2. Encyclopedic knowledge: Understanding language requires networks that link many different domains of knowledge. There is no arbitrary cut-off point between linguistic and encyclopedic knowledge.
3. Prototype categories: Categories in the mind are structured around prototypical examples, so that particular experiences may be better or worse examples of a category depending on their proximity to prototypical examples.
4. Basic-level categories: Some categories in the mind are more salient than others. The most salient are basic level categories.
5. Language Universals: There is a strong universal component in the relation between human thought and language. These universals are rooted in embodiment. Cognitive, and thus linguistic, universals arise from common experiences of life within a human body, particularly through image schemas such as CONTAINMENT, SOURCE-PATH-GOAL, or UP-DOWN.
6. Linguistic Relativity: Linguistic relativity is significant, as recognized by Humboldt, Sapir, and Whorf. The schemas chosen and elaborated within cultures, and the way different geographical

---

254. Lakoff and Johnson, *Metaphors*, 96.

7. Thought mappings: Conceptual structures are characterized by mappings, whether metaphorical mappings between domains or metonymic mappings within domains.

8. Priority of the concrete: In contrast to Barr, abstract domains are normally understood through more concrete ones, which, as more experientially basic, are taken to be more prototypical.

9. Polysemy: Senses are not isolated meanings. Rather sense networks are accessed by a given word, with certain clusters of meaning being more stable than others. Polysemy reflects links between domains, particularly from prototypical instances to other domains, which are entrenched to varying degree and are reflected in overarching schemas of varying salience. Thus, whilst heeding Barr's warnings that polysemy does not necessarily show any current relation in the mind of readers or hearers, nevertheless, polysemy is a significant *potential* source for investigating what domains a culture may see as corresponding with each other.

This chapter has introduced this theoretical framework and refuted the claim that such an approach is "outmoded." Naturally, several difficulties remain when applying this approach to the restricted corpus of an ancient language, without access to native intuition. However, the growing literature relating cognitive semantics to Hebrew texts shows some potential options.

The body of this work investigates Hebrew conceptual metaphors for distress in a specific corpus. Following the methodology of Kövecses and Kotzé, the source domains for "distress" (image schemas of VERTICALITY, CONSTRAINT, and FORCE, and primary metaphors from vision and taste) will be examined to find how they constrain inferences about distress.

However, first, the corpus needs clarification. If encyclopedic knowledge is crucial to semantics, it is important to investigate the geographical, cultural, and social milieu of the texts, including ascertaining whether it is that of post-exilic Judea or the early Israelite monarchy. Defining a coherent target domain also requires a systematic methodology: how can one argue that a particular metaphor relates to the target domain of "distress" in a way that is intersubjectively testable, and does not import Anglo-centric categories? The next chapter considers these two issues, firstly identifying a coherent general corpus of Classical Hebrew and clarifying the cultures that gave rise to it, and then arguing for a specific corpus of personal distress discourse for detailed study, with the target domain justified on extra-linguistic form critical grounds in order to reduce the subjective element.

3

Corpus

"A first task for any study of meaning in Classical Hebrew is to define the corpus under investigation." —Sue Groom[1]

3.1. Introduction

This chapter clarifies the texts to be investigated and the situations that produced them. Cognitive Linguistics assumes conceptual metaphors depend on embodied experiences within culture, so it is necessary to know which cultures they arise from, a controversial issue for Hebrew texts. First, Classical Hebrew is identified, a period of Hebrew language development (incorporating biblical and Qumranic material) sufficiently homogeneous in language and cultural background for a cognitive investigation. Second, a specific sub-corpus of texts referring to first person situations of distress is identified, forming the basis for the subsequent research.

---

1. Groom, *Analysis*, 3.

3.2. The General Corpus

Hebrew has over three thousand years of literary history,[2] exhibiting a surprising "fundamental unity" of language.[3] For some, this unity dates everything to Persian times or later, reflecting no earlier culture or language.[4] However, it is more likely that authors accessed "quite substantial Judean oral and written sources that had originated between the eighth and sixth centuries B.C.E.," even if they tuned it to Persian contexts.[5] Substantial archaeological evidence from the Iron Age (and only then) also converges with biblical texts. These cannot have been invented by writers in Persian times, so they must have had access to very substantial early and authentic witness to this period.[6]

If the biblical text reflects sources from at least the Iron Age, what other sources are relevant for a linguistic study of comparable texts? Pragmatically, texts considered must be limited to some *general corpus*. This general corpus excludes Ugaritic texts and the Mishnah, but includes all significant Hebrew texts from the intervening era, whether biblical or Qumranic. The justification for this general corpus is given below.

3.2.1. Development of the Hebrew Language

Hebrew is a North-West Semitic language and by the earliest biblical texts was sufficiently distinct from Ugaritic, Aramaic, and other Canaanite dialects to qualify as a separate language.[7] Even so, Ugaritic texts might have significant relevance to this work, revealing the "source of Hebrew mythopoeic thought and expression."[8] However, the gulf in theological worldview diminishes the relevance of these texts, as does

---

2. More if Ugaritic texts are included, Dahood, *Psalms 1–50*, xxix.
3. Sáenz-Badillos, *History*, 50.
4. Davies, *Search*; Davies, "Society"; Naudé, "Perspective."
5. Deist, *Culture*, 77.
6. Dever, *Writers*.
7. Hebrew possibly separated from Ugaritic around 1900 BCE, Rabin, "Lexicostatistics."
8. Dahood, *Psalms 1–50*, xxvii.

the ongoing debate over the relationship between the two languages. Alongside the pragmatic inability to do justice to the literature in Ugaritic studies, there are sufficient reasons to exclude Ugaritic texts from the general corpus.

The first distinctively Hebrew texts to which we have access[9] are biblical poetry such as Judges 5 or Exodus 15, possibly dating to the twelfth century BCE.[10] The Hebrew of these texts has been termed *Archaic Hebrew*,[11] and may exemplify a literary language, "clearly distinguished from the everyday spoken language."[12] Most biblical texts, however, preserve a relatively homogeneous stage of Hebrew language development, mostly deriving from pre-exilic times, termed *Classical* or *Standard Biblical Hebrew*. This was perhaps "an 'official' language . . . used at court and in educated circles in Jerusalem."[13]

The social impact of exile undoubtedly affected language, especially through contact with Aramaic. *Late Biblical Hebrew* is used for a third distinctive stage, preserved in uncontroversially post-exilic texts such as Chronicles, Ezra-Nehemiah, and Esther.[14] Sáenz-Badillos claims this is now an artificial language, venerating and imitating traditional formula and vocabulary, but thoroughly divorced from the spoken language of the Judean community.[15]

This is significant since separation between written text and everyday language suggests it less straightforwardly reflects mental categorizations. Sáenz-Badillos uses Kutscher's study of 1QIsa^a to argue that during the last centuries BCE ordinary people "could barely understand [Biblical Hebrew (BH)] or even read it correctly."[16] Such claims exag-

---

9. Some scholars argue that the language of the current text has no direct relationship with the language used at the time of the composition (Naudé, "Perspective"). Epigraphic parallels, however, show that biblical Hebrew is more similar to pre-exilic inscriptions than later external sources.

10. Sáenz-Badillos, *History*, 43.

11. Ibid., 52.

12. Ibid., 62.

13. Ibid., 68.

14. Alternatively, these texts come from a different geographical setting, Naudé, "Perspective," 96–98.

15. Sáenz-Badillos, *History*, 105–29.

16. Ibid., 134.

gerate Kutscher's work, which argued "Hebrew was still more or less generally understood,"[17] stressing that though Hebrew was declining in its domains of use, it was precisely amongst the "ordinary" semi-literate people that Hebrew was spoken longest.[18]

Archaic, Standard, and Late Biblical Hebrew traditionally comprised "Classical Hebrew," seen as distinct from Mishnaic Hebrew.[19] Qumran texts, however, incorporate features of both Late Biblical Hebrew and Mishnaic Hebrew, blurring the boundaries between these two previously distinct domains.

The Qumran scrolls date from the final two centuries BCE and the first century CE, and exhibit such a variety of idiolects, dialects, styles, and registers that the term "Qumran Hebrew" suggests a false unity.[20] It is unclear whether the texts demonstrate a substandard language to make Biblical Hebrew easier to understand by the semi-illiterate masses,[21] or a struggle between living Aramaic, spoken Late Biblical Hebrew, and a liturgical Classical Hebrew, or whether they reflect a stable language between biblical and Mishnaic Hebrew.[22] It is agreed, though, that the Hebrew represents "a fundamentally biblical form of language,"[23] and second, that the differences from Late Biblical Hebrew reflect a spoken, rather than solely literary, language.[24] These make Qumran Hebrew appropriate for the general corpus.

The social upheaval of 70 CE, and even more following the Bar Kokhba revolt (132–135 CE), finally ended Hebrew's use as a living dialect.[25] Thus, texts from this era (the Tannaitic phase of the Mishnah) are the last texts to consider including in the general corpus, if it is to reflect a period when at least some form of Hebrew was still spoken. When the

17. Kutscher, *Language*, 73.
18. Ibid., 11–13.
19. Or "Rabbinic Hebrew."
20. Naudé, "Perspective," 97.
21. Kutscher, *Language*, 61–73.
22. Waldman, *Study*, 100.
23. Sáenz-Badillos, *History*, 133.
24. Based on phonological changes, Morag, "Typological."
25. Kutscher, *History*, 115–16.

Mishnah was first written (around 200 CE) the language it was written in was already "dead."

Although initial analysis of the Mishnah's language concluded it was an artificial literary creation, since Segal[26] most scholars agree that Mishnaic Hebrew was actually a living language (albeit possibly a syntactically limited version of the spoken language),[27] particularly following discovery of the Bar Kochba letters at Qumran, non-religious material written in essentially Mishnaic Hebrew.[28] Now, many see "vital links between biblical Hebrew and Mishnaic Hebrew,"[29] so semantic study of Classical Hebrew should include the Mishnah. However, as the Mishnah lacks poetic depictions of distress, it would not contribute greatly to this volume, and so can be reasonably excluded from the general corpus.

3.2.2. A Recognized Corpus

This definition of Classical Hebrew concurs with several recent semantic projects. The *Dictionary of Classical Hebrew* considers "all kinds of Hebrew from the period prior to about 200 CE, that is, earlier than the Hebrew of the Mishnah,"[30] as does the *Theological Dictionary of the Old Testament*. "Classical Hebrew" was also used for this selected corpus by the Oxford Hebrew Lexicon project.[31] Elsewhere, the European Science Foundation database project chose "the language of the Hebrew Bible, . . . ancient Hebrew epigraphical material, Ben Sira, and the Hebrew Qumran texts."[32] This convergence validates the general corpus of Classical Hebrew outlined above.

---

26. Segal, *Grammar*.
27. Neusner, *Introduction*, 12–13.
28. Waldman, *Study*, 109–11.
29. Muraoka, "Dictionary," 89.
30. Clines, *DCH*, 14.
31. Barr, "Lexicography," 138.
32. Hoftijzer, "History," 80.

3.3. The Specific Corpus

3.3.1. Definition of the Specific Corpus

Within this general corpus, a *specific corpus* will be exhaustively analyzed to show how significant each metaphor for distress is.[33] This corpus is defined as comprising all *first person singular texts that refer to a situation of distress*. The three elements here are elucidated below.

First, *first-person-singular* texts provide best access to individual emotional and psychological perceptions, potentially differing from third person perspectives,[34] and echoing an anthropological trend towards personal subjective experience.[35]

Second, choosing texts *referring* to a situation of distress means it may be portrayed as present, as in Job, or past as in the Hodayot. This also avoids the difficulties of time reference for Hebrew verbs in poetry.

The final aspect, a *situation of distress,* is most controversial. What classifies something as a distress situation? This work claims there is a gestalt concept of "distress" structured by various metaphorical and metonymical mappings that surface in the linguistic expressions used in distress situations.[36] To investigate these expressions, a way of identifying pertinent texts is needed, even when lexical items for "distress" (such as צָרָה) are absent.[37] This difficulty is common to any metaphorical research investigating the vehicles for a given conceptual topic (which may well be implicit), versus investigating the scope of an image, which must be explicitly present. Subjectivity is thus unavoidable, but can be minimized by identifying tokens using formal and structural elements common to "distress" discourse (as identified by form criticism) alongside characteristic contents. More detail is provided in section 3.3.2.b.

Language expressing distress is, broadly speaking, emotional language, even if "distress" is not considered a basic universal emotion, so

---

33. This is common in applications of conceptual metaphor theory. For example, taking editorials to the *Economist* in Boers, "Joy," or interviews with teachers in Cortazzi and Jin, "Bridges."
34. Kövecses, *Culture*, 244.
35. For example: Rosaldo, "Grief"; Rosaldo, "Anthropology."
36. See section 2.5.1.
37. Recalling the weakness of Wierzbicka's lexical approach, see section 2.5.5.

this study fits alongside recent cognitive studies of emotion language.[38] Defining emotion has become controversial, especially as linguists have become involved in the debate.[39] One definition is a "spontaneous human reaction to reality,"[40] making the Hebrew descriptions of distress "emotional" to the extent they verbalize spontaneous reactions to negative situations. Psychologists and philosophers have traditionally studied universal physiological aspects, including quickened pulses or widened eyes, defining a few universal emotions, such as sadness, happiness, anger, fear, disgust, and shame. However, humans can express emotions verbally, and linguists have discovered substantial variation in how different cultures conceptualize emotions, consolidating different physiological and social aspects within linguistic convention.[41] Thus, "whereas feelings may be universal, humankind's conceptualization of segments of the emotional continuum may strongly depend on cultural norms and beliefs,"[42] with languages offering several conventionalized ways of expressing emotion, both in poetic and "normal" discourse. Athanasiadou claims further that correspondences or universals "are to be found on the level of image schemas rather than on the level of translation equivalents."[43]

Thus, this work cannot single out one particular emotion of, say, "fear," against "sadness," or even "anger." The metaphorical language of "distress" overlaps with each of these specific emotions expressed in English, and yet has a conceptual unity seen in the conventional forms of literature in which it is expressed and the conventional metaphors themselves used to articulate these experiences. This broad target domain, avoiding the terms of Anglo[44] ethnopsychology, distinguishes

38. As in Niemeier and Dirven, *Language*; and Athanasiadou and Tabakowska, *Emotions*.

39. Wierzbicka, *Emotions*; Kövecses, *Emotion*.

40. Kryk-Kastovsky, "Surprise," 155.

41. Wierzbicka claims even the concept of "emotion" is culture specific. "Feelings" are universal, but the particular interaction of "thinking" and "feeling" implied by *emotion* is particular to Anglo culture (Wierzbicka, *Emotions*, 1–7).

42. Athanasiadou and Tabakowska, "Introduction," xxi.

43. Ibid., xi–xii.

44. This term is used by Wierzbicka to refer to the culture of English speakers in the United States, United Kingdom, and Australia.

this work from Kruger's and Kotzé's previous cognitive treatments of Hebrew emotion.[45]

Explicitly then, the specific corpus contains Job's laments, individual laments and thanksgivings of the Psalter, Lamentations 3, Isa 38:10–20, Jon 2:2–9[3–10], the "confessions" of Jeremiah, and the Hodayot from Qumran. All contain either Standard Biblical Hebrew or the variety of Qumran Hebrew most closely resembling it.

The "distress" target domain can now be somewhat clarified by investigating the cultures and situations these texts reflect, although the texts were mostly preserved for their broad applicability.[46]

3.3.2. Context of the Specific Corpus

a) Job

Job is difficult to situate, as its language is difficult and historical details did not serve the author's purpose.[47] Unusual names for God suggest the speeches are early, whereas Aramaisms[48] or the possibility that Job represents a post-exilic crisis in Jewish thinking suggest a late date.[49] The second century BCE Targum at Qumran dates Job earlier than this, probably between the seventh and third centuries BCE.[50] Similarities to Isaiah and Jeremiah suggest an early post-exilic date, but absence of clear reference to exile or Jerusalem's destruction suggests a pre-exilic composition.[51] Wolfers specifically dates Job between Sennacherib's siege of Jerusalem in 701 and the destruction of 586, since, although Job suffers, like Jerusalem, his life is spared.[52] Certainly a pre-exilic date cannot be dismissed.

45. Kruger, "Anger"; Kruger, "Fear"; Kruger, "Depression"; Kotzé, "Conceptualisation."
46. Gerstenberger, "Life."
47. Bullock, *Introduction*, 66.
48. However, Job also juxtaposes these with elements considered archaic (Sáenz-Badillos, *History*, 115).
49. Janzen, *Job*, 5.
50. Lucas, *Exploring*, 129.
51. Pope, *Job*.
52. Wolfers, *Deep*, 51–59.

Regarding the situation occasioning the conventional metaphors of distress, the narrative context is one of great loss (of wealth and family) and illness. Even if they should be "metaphorically processed"[53] as representing the Fall of Jerusalem or the siege of Sennacherib,[54] the narrative context has priority for this work.

b) Psalms

Psalms referring to a "situation of distress" provide the broadest set of metaphors for this work. This section provides the form critical argument, then surveys potential historical and social backgrounds.

Gunkel identified three major Psalm types including first person reference to a distressing experience: individual lament, individual thanksgiving psalm, and communal lament.[55] His categories derived from form and content: common literary form, a common life-setting within a specific occasion of worship, and a common treasury of thoughts and moods.[56] He saw these all originating as early liturgical poetry composed by priests[57] to be used in the sanctuary at times of illness,[58] although the extant psalms have become spiritual poems[59] with only the figurative presupposition of sickness remaining.[60] Most scholars accept Gunkel's typology,[61] but see a cultic setting for many more Psalms (in contrast to the more pietistic Hodayot), whether in the temple[62] or in post-exilic local community worship.[63] Most likely, then,

---

53. Gibbs distinguishes this as a later stage of interpretation than online processing of language, Gibbs, "Researching," 40–41.
54. Wolfers, *Deep*.
55. Gunkel, *Psalms*; Gunkel, *Einleitung*, 140–71.
56. Gunkel, *Psalms*, 10.
57. Ibid., 25.
58. Ibid., 20.
59. Ibid., 26.
60. Ibid., 34.
61. Day, *Psalms*, 13.
62. Since Mowinckel, *Worship*.
63. Gerstenberger, *Cultic*.

the biblical texts contain "a large number of both pre- and post-exilic psalms."[64]

Kraus[65] and Brueggemann[66] challenged Gunkel's typology. First, Kraus criticized Gunkel for mixing form and content in classification, and for naming genres with words external to the texts. Kraus himself used headings from the Psalms to distinguish songs of praise (תהלת), songs of prayer (תפלה), royal psalms (מעשי למלך), and songs of Zion (שיר ציון). "Songs of prayer" embrace Gunkel's Communal Laments, Individual Laments, and Individual Thanksgivings, emphasizing the strong content similarities between Gunkel's "Thanksgivings" and "Laments," with the only objective difference sometimes being the order of elements. Thus, Williamson argues both types were intended for use *after* a period of distress.[67] Second, Brueggemann distinguishes three functional groups, classified via orientation, disorientation, and re-orientation. Psalms of disorientation and re-orientation refer to distress, with those of disorientation arising from periods of psychological imbalance and those of re-orientation from a time of return to equilibrium, but referring to the previous experiences.[68]

These approaches show a coherent group of psalms referring to a situation of distress, whether through Gunkel's form criticism, through thematic links native to the text (Kraus' "songs of prayer") or through psychological conditions suggested by their content (Brueggemann's disorientation and re-orientation). The convergence of all these interpretative strands gives credibility to this research. Given this coherent category of psalms, it is legitimate to hypothesize correlated mental categories for life experiences that might "fit" their use.

What experiences occasioned these Psalms? Three settings are typically suggested: illness, battle, and accusation.[69] Illness is suggested for various psalms referring to body parts in abnormal states. Seybold's thorough treatment (especially of vocabulary) argues that Psalms 38

64. Day, *Psalms*, 16.
65. Kraus, *Psalms 1–59*.
66. Brueggemann, "Psalms."
67. Williamson, "Reading," 10–13.
68. Brueggemann, "Psalms."
69. Lucas, *Exploring*, 4.

and 88 certainly reflect illness, probably also 6, 13, and 51, and possibly 31, 35, and 71.

The language of armed conflict is also frequent, and sometimes the "enemies" are foreigners, suggesting the king offered these psalms, representing the people.[70] However, sometimes the enemies are explicitly within the psalmist's community. These texts exemplify the final suggested setting, that of trial. First Kings 8:30–31 provides a possible background, with an accused man appealing to God as judge in the temple. Although Schmidt assigned most lament psalms to this life setting,[71] there is really insufficient evidence to substantiate any kind of cultic trial.[72]

Thus, there is no consensus on the precise situations, the psalms being "couched in such vague and general terms they were probably capable of being employed in a wide range of types of distress."[73] For this work, the significant result is that the language of illness, armed conflict, and trial provide salient examples, functioning as prototypes to metonymically structure the experience of a much wider range of distressing situations.

c) Lamentations

Lamentations' five poems date from after Jerusalem's destruction in 586 BCE, and probably before 538 BCE. Most likely they come from lay people speaking "the language of ordinary discourse, not that of a specialized group, school or profession," shown by the analogies used,[74] and the faith they reflect.[75] The acrostic form may be a later overlay,[76] or come from the temple-singers finding a new form of prayer.[77] Several

---

70. Lucas, *Exploring*, 4.
71. Schmidt, *Angeklagten*.
72. Day, *Psalms*, 28.
73. Day, *Psalms*, 29–30.
74. Westermann, *Lamentations*, 57.
75. Gordis, *Song*, 126.
76. Westermann, *Lamentations*, 62–63.
77. Renkema, *Lamentations*, 44–45.

scholars stress the essential unity throughout the book,⁷⁸ with Shea arguing the poems have been together since their composition based on the macrostructure of three long and two short poems, as in *qinah* meter.⁷⁹

Chapter 3 is in the specific corpus, and differs from other chapters. References to Jerusalem's destruction are much less obvious here.⁸⁰ Correspondingly, this chapter draws most on the conventional language of distress (as in Job and Psalms), perhaps being a later attempt to typify the historical situation for use in liturgy,⁸¹ or reflecting an exilic perspective to correct the other poems' theology.⁸² Further, only chapter 3 uses the first person singular, recounting the voice of the גֶּבֶר, a typical figure "who represents what any man may feel when it seems that God is against him."⁸³

Lamentations 3 is significant in the corpus because we have a fixed date and context. The degree of unity ties all the poems inescapably to the experiences of 587–586 BCE in Jerusalem. Further, the authors were undoubtedly aware of earlier lament psalms, so the conventional language may draw deliberately on their phrases and motifs. A direct intertextual relationship with Job is harder to substantiate, despite the linguistic affinities. Rather, this chapter suggests the existence of "a common fund of . . . lament vocabulary which was used in the laments of the Psalter, the book of Job, and Lamentations."⁸⁴

d) Confessions of Jeremiah

Several of Jeremiah's "confessions" were form-critically identified by Gunkel as individual laments.⁸⁵ The texts include 8:18–23; 10:19–25;

---

78. Dobbs-Allsopp, *Lamentations*, 5; Gordis, *Song*, 126; Martin-Achard and Re'emi, *God's People in Crisis*, 75–76.
79. Shea, "Structure."
80. Westermann, *Lamentations*, 71.
81. Childs, *Introduction*, 596.
82. Middlemas, "Isaiah."
83. Hillers, *Lamentations*, 64.
84. Gottwald, *Studies*, 42.
85. Gunkel, *Einleitung*, 172.

11:18–23; 12:1–6; 14:2—15:21; 17:9–18; 18:18–23; and 20:7–18,[86] which Baumgartner claimed couched Jeremiah's inner struggles in the conventional language of lament Psalms.[87] Such material is unparalleled in the prophets, perhaps being transmitted orally by Jeremiah to his friends (rather than publicly proclaimed) and eventually becoming part of the present text.[88] Although they give access to Jeremiah's personal anguish, this anguish is all the more real as "it did not arise from his personal suffering alone, but was a reflection of the suffering of his people and the suffering of God."[89]

e) Distress Language in Narrative Contexts

There are two lament-type psalms in narrative contexts referring to a distress situation, specifically Jonah's (Jonah 2) and Hezekiah's prayers (Isaiah 38).

The book of Jonah has been variously dated linguistically from the eighth to third centuries BCE. Further, the psalm itself could faithfully reflect Jonah's words,[90] or be a later scribal addition.[91] Whichever holds, it is a good, structured example of a thanksgiving psalm by all the form-critical criteria, containing conventional psalm imagery, albeit particularly apposite imagery for Jonah's narrative situation. Stuart describes it as "the closest one can get to a psalm composed specifically for the events Jonah experienced while still remaining a true psalm, i.e. general and pan-temporal,"[92] whereas Sawyer more skeptically "wonders whether the situation, of Jonah inside a big fish, was not invented just to provide points of reference for details in the psalm."[93] Usefully

---

86. A compilation of the texts identified in McKane, *Jeremiah*, xcii; and McConville, *Prophets*, 56.
87. Baumgartner, *Poems*.
88. Bright, *Jeremiah*, lxix.
89. Craigie et al., *Jeremiah 1–25*, 173.
90. Stuart, *Hosea-Jonah*, 473–74.
91. Salters, *Jonah*, 38–39.
92. Stuart, *Hosea-Jonah*, 439.
93. Sawyer, *Semantics*, 13.

for this work, it shows conventional imagery and forms being applied to a specific narrative situation of distress, that of drowning in the sea.

Second, Hezekiah's prayer in Isa 38:10–20 uses conventional imagery in the context of Hezekiah's illness, placed after Hezekiah had recovered, despite appearing formally closer to a lament than a thanksgiving. Thus, Hezekiah's "lament" is located after recovery and Jonah's "thanksgiving" from the midst of distress, further demonstrating the similarity of individual thanksgivings and laments, and cautioning against jumping too quickly from form to life-setting.

f) Hodayot

The limited redactional activity for the Hodayot simplifies identification of authorship, date, and provenance. However, fragmented manuscripts make it harder to ascertain the original text.[94]

The first scroll found, 1QH^a, has been dated palaeographically after 50 BCE. However, the handwriting of 1QH^b suggests it is a copy from between 100 and 50 BCE.[95] Thus, they may come from the early years of the Qumran community (second century BCE), with at least some possibly penned by the Teacher of Righteousness himself.

Holm-Nielsen first suggested the Hodayot were a collection (rather than a literary unity), originating "possibly from different authors and from different times."[96] He divided them into Thanksgiving Psalms and Hymns. The former center on first person reference to distress situations and correspond to the following columns and verses of 1QH^a: 10:1–19; 10:20–30; 10:31—11:4; 11:5–18; 11:19–36; 11:37—12:4; 12:5—13:4; 13:5–19; 13:20–end; 14:1—15:5; 15:6–25; 16:4–end, and 17:1–36.[97]

Several scholars divided this collection further into those from the Teacher of Righteousness versus other anonymous members of the community.[98] However, most recently, Michael Douglas argues linguis-

---

94. This study relies on the reconstruction provided in Martínez and Tigchelaar, *Scrolls*.
95. Schuller, "Thanksgiving," 1217.
96. Holm-Nielsen, *Hodayot*, 131.
97. Following labelling in Martínez and Tigchelaar, *Scrolls*.
98. This position is articulated by both Jeremias, *Lehrer*, and Becker, *Heil*.

tically (using a signature phrase) that "1QH cols 10–17 are substantially the work of a single author,"[99] probably the "Teacher of Righteousness" describing his experience of conflict in Jerusalem and culminating in his exile from the land (ידיחני מארצי, 1QH[a] 12:8).

The relation to the biblical psalms is also debated, given many similar images and metaphors. Licht claimed the Hodayot made "rather awkward use of a great many biblical phrases" and were "on the whole rather humdrum . . . [and] repetitive, to the point of monotony."[100] Conversely, Kittel argued they stand alongside other great poems of the ancient world.[101] Newsom also speaks positively, seeing a "first-class piece of rhetoric," partly resulting from the traditional quality of the imagery.[102] Further, the unanticipated ways Cave 4 copies fill lacunae in Cave 1 manuscripts shows that "the vocabulary of these hymns seems to have been less stereotypical and standardized than has sometimes been assumed,"[103] where "biblical words and phrases are reworked and reconfigured in a style that is quite different from earlier biblical poetry."[104] Such activity, bringing in extra aspects of the source domain, is evidence that the source domain continues to be active in the minds of the authors,[105] rather than being just a humdrum repetition of tradition. The copying and use of these hymns for more than a hundred years must have also consolidated these ways of viewing distress, becoming "an important factor in shaping the self-identity and worldview of the community members."[106] Indeed, while one cannot be sure of the original *Sitz im Leben*, one can be sure that "the repetition of the various forms and images, and even the emotional patterns of the Hodayot, served to shape the beliefs and religious emotions of those who read them."[107]

99. Douglas, "Hypothesis," 256.
100. Licht, *Scroll*, cited in Kittel, *Hymns*, 6.
101. Kittel, *Hymns*, 6.
102. Newsom, "Burke," 121.
103. Schuller, "Contributions."
104. Schuller, "Thanksgiving," 1216.
105. Taylor, *Grammar*, 500–501, see section 2.5.2.d.
106. Schuller, "Thanksgiving," 1218.
107. Newsom, "Burke," 122.

3.4. Summary

This chapter has presented a general corpus of Classical Hebrew texts and a specific corpus for analysis of first person texts that refer to a situation of distress. The origin and character of these specific texts has been discussed. The next chapter describes the methodology used to analyze the conceptualizations of distress in this specific corpus.

4

Methodology

"Any research project needs to include overt discussion of the extent to which the reader can be confident about the nature of the data which has been selected or omitted from the study, about the techniques of analysis and categorization used, and about the extent to which the data support the conclusions."
—Graham Low[1]

4.1. Introduction

Having introduced Cognitive Linguistics and identified a corpus of texts to investigate, the next step is to outline the methodology for investigating the conceptualizations within this corpus.

First, to operationalize this research, two areas need clarification: the terminology for describing metaphors; and a method to identify and categorize them. Taking metaphors as fundamentally conceptual, the focus is on investigating conceptual entities (cognitive models, image schemas, prototypes, metaphoric, and metonymic mappings) structuring distress experiences. However, since these are only accessible

---

1. Low, "Validating," 48.

through linguistic expressions, a framework is necessary for analyzing linguistic metaphors. Unfortunately, this receives little consideration in standard works on conceptual metaphor theory,[2] so other works are used here.[3]

4.2. Metaphor Terminology

Following cognitive semantics, prototypes can be used to describe metaphorical language. First, *topic* and *vehicle* are easily seen in an "ideal" linguistic metaphor: "A is B," where A and B are both nouns. The topic, A, is ideally a literal referent in the world of the text. B is the vehicle. Consider Psalm 84:11[12]:

כִּי שֶׁמֶשׁ וּמָגֵן יְהוָה אֱלֹהִים׃

For the LORD God (is) a sun and shield.

Here, "the LORD God" is the topic and "a sun and a shield" are vehicles. The topic is explicit and the vehicle predicates something of it that creates tension. It is literally inapplicable: God is not a shield in the most experientially basic way.

Such ideal prototypes are rare in the specific "distress" corpus, although Lam 3:10 gives one example.

דֹּב אֹרֵב הוּא לִי

He (is) a bear lying in wait for me.

Much more commonly within linguistic corpora,[4] the linguistic vehicle is a verb, as in Lam 3:9.

גָּדַר דְּרָכַי בְּגָזִית

He has blocked my way with hewn stones.

Here, the verb phrase is the vehicle. Identifying the topic is problematic, however, because of terminological confusion between using *topic* in surface language description and description of conceptual

---

2. For example, there is no discussion in Kövecses, *Metaphor*.
3. Principally, Cameron and Low, *Researching*.
4. Cameron, "Operationalising," 15.

phenomenon.⁵ In 3:10 ("he is a bear . . ."), "he" (God) was both the pragmatic topic of the sentence and the metaphorical topic, the entity conceptualized in terms of the vehicle. In Lam 3:9, "he" (God) is still the pragmatic topic, but the vehicle conceptualizes some unexpressed activity, the metaphorical topic. This *conceptual topic* could be paraphrased as "the distress he caused me," suggesting the implicit metaphor "(the distress he caused me is) he has blocked my way with hewn stones."

This terminological conflict is avoided by distinguishing *surface topic* from *conceptual topic*.⁶ Whereas the surface topic is usually easily discernible, the conceptual topic is often only inferable through knowledge of the discourse situation,⁷ with the metaphor being *implicit*. These include *co-textual* implicit metaphors (where the conceptual topic is explicitly present elsewhere in the discourse) and *contextual* implicit metaphors (where the conceptual topic is not mentioned anywhere in the context).⁸

Thus, the request to be saved from "dogs" in Ps 22:20[21] is a co-textual implicit metaphor, since dogs and evildoers are equated in 22:16[17]. Conversely, the waves and breakers in Ps 42:7[8] create a contextual implicit metaphor. The genre implies the conceptual topic is the psalmist's distressing experience, but the co-text gives few clues to any more precise identification.

Finally a *conceptual vehicle* can be identified,⁹ clarifying which conceptual source domain(s) the surface vehicle provides access to and what prototypical knowledge about this domain is being mapped. Consider, for example, Lam 3:5a:

בָּנָה עָלַי׃

He builds against me.

---

5. Ibid., 14.

6. Ibid. Steen has a more comprehensive framework, distinguishing three layers in metaphorical discourse (linguistic, conceptual, and communicative) with different terminology for each layer (Steen, "Discourse").

7. Steen, "Discourse."

8. Ibid., 82–91.

9. Extra steps are given in Steen, "Steps."

Methodology

Here the surface topic is God (anaphorically), and the surface vehicle is "building against" someone. The conceptual topic is being in distress, identifiable from the discourse context. Establishing the conceptual vehicle is harder, especially at such a distance in time and culture, requiring knowledge of prototypical "builders," what they would be building, and why. Here, the consensus view is that "siege" is the conceptual vehicle, so that the NRSV translates "he has besieged (me)." Elsewhere the conceptual vehicle is more debatable.

4.3. Metaphor Identification

With this terminology, what linguistic expressions should be used to investigate conceptual topics and vehicles? Linguistic cues might include a literal inapplicability of the vehicle[10] (as when discussing God's "arrows" in Job 6:4) or a lack of congruence of the vehicle with the non-verbal setting[11] (as when attack with bow and arrow is used in Ps 11:2[3], but for a context of non-physical attack). However, again, a prototypical approach is more helpful than necessary and sufficient criteria,[12] since "every criterion for a metaphor's presence, however plausible, is defeasible in certain circumstances."[13] With a prototype approach to the category of metaphors, linguistic examples match the prototype to greater or lesser degree.[14]

The most stereotypical linguistic metaphors resemble Lam 3:15:

הִשְׂבִּיעַנִי בַמְּרוֹרִים הִרְוַנִי לַעֲנָה׃

He has filled me with bitterness; he has sated me with wormwood.

Here, the author describes his distress with vehicles that are unlikely to be physically applicable, referring to bitterness and wormwood to access the quite different domain of consuming something poisonous. Thus, in this prototype, the conceptual topic is clear ("distress"),

---

10. As in Pearsall, *Dictionary*, 1163.
11. Black, "More," 34.
12. See Cameron, "Identifying."
13. Black, "More," 35.
14. Cameron, "Identifying," 105.

and there is a linguistic vehicle accessing a distinct domain, incongruous both to the rest of the co-text and the non-verbal setting. Other linguistic expressions may be better or worse examples by comparison to this prototype.

In less ideal cases, the only point of access to an incongruent source domain may be the etymology of the linguistic vehicle. For example, in Ps 4:1[2], it is the etymological relationship between צַר and situations of physical constraint that reveals a conceptual metaphor, although made more prominent by the following word. Elsewhere, the etymology of one word alone may be a potential vehicle.

בַּצָּר הִרְחַבְתָּ לִּי׃

Ps 4:1[2]: You gave me room when I was in distress.

Such examples, where the incongruity is just at the etymological level, are included in the list of potential data, although their relevance for conceptualization must be substantiated by other evidence, rather than just presuming that such incongruity would be noticed by a hearer,[15] as outlined in chapter two.[16] Etymological incongruity generates a broad base of metaphors to include in the database; the existence of systematic generalizations over different examples can then provide the evidence whether such incongruity is indeed significant.

4.4. Collection of Data

With this broad prototypical definition of relevant data, the following method was used to collect data. First, the specific corpus was read, noting descriptions of the subject's distressing circumstances (where "distress" was the conceptual topic) and comparing them to the metaphor prototype. Where these could potentially be viewed as vehicles describing the conceptual topic in terms of a more basic experiential domain, they were included as tokens in a database. Tokens included vehicles consisting of a single lexical item (like צַר־לִי) through to images sustained in a whole verse (or even collection of verses), as in the

---

15. Cameron, "Identifying," 114–15.
16. Especially section 2.5.9.

metaphor of being trapped in the cords of death that runs through Ps 18:4–5[5–6].

The word "potentially" provides a broad data set, but also an unavoidable subjective element: who decides whether a particular phrase is potentially related to a more basic domain? The main curb came from established lexicons. For example, when deciding if particular lexical items should be considered as potentially relating to a more basic experiential domain, several standard lexicons were consulted (including BDB, *TWOT*, *TDOT*, and *NIDOTTE*) to see if a meaning was given in a more basic domain. If the standard lexicons did not refer to any more basic experiential domain, or only did so in discussion of possible etymologies from cognate languages, these examples were excluded. Thus, for example, every lexicon gives examples where words derived from צרר would be glossed as "narrow" or "tight," so there is a potential basic source domain here. Conversely, roots like עמל are not discussed in the context of any more basic experiential domain. In between, rarer roots, like צוק, are more difficult. Although there are no examples of words derived from צוק being used for "literal" pressure or squeezing within the biblical corpus, all the lexicons mention this domain early in their discussion of meaning, so descriptions using this root are included in the database.

Second, after collecting all the possibly relevant linguistic data, the examples were classified according to the experiential domains they accessed. This involved comparison with "canonical" image schemas of CONTAINMENT, FORCE, SOURCE-PATH-GOAL, NEAR-FAR, BALANCE, and UP-DOWN,[17] as well as perceptual source domains including TASTE and VISION. Since poetic metaphors often conflate different schemas, linguistic metaphors frequently accessed more than one domain. For example, using a "pit" as a vehicle conflates schemas of being down and contained, as well as the perceptual experience of being in darkness. Such tokens were recorded as accessing each domain.

Third, the tokens were counted to estimate the significance of each domain for the conceptualization of distress. There is some vagueness

---

17. As in Lakoff, *Women*; Johnson, *Body*; and more recently in Hampe, *Perception*. For example, Hampe, "Schemas," 2–3; Kimmel, "Culture," 287; Grady, "Definition," 37.

here since some tokens reflect just one word in a verse, whereas others consist of several verses maintaining the same vehicle. However, this gives a fair picture of the relative prominence of these source domains. Out of 489 tokens within the specific corpus, the following table shows the relative frequencies.[18]

Source Domain / Image Schema	Number of Tokens
FORCE	207
CONSTRAINT	129
VERTICALITY	81
DARKNESS	48
TASTE	36
SOURCE-PATH-GOAL	34
NEAR-FAR	16
BALANCE	0

Fourth, the five most significant source domains (image schemas of FORCE, VERTICALITY, AND CONSTRAINT, primary metaphors of DARKNESS and TASTE)[19] were analyzed in greater detail, to see what elements of the source domain are highlighted, what inferences are drawn from these domains to create entailments in the target domain of distress, and how these differ from similar conceptualizations in other cultures. The results are presented in the main body of this book as explained below.

4.5. Framework for Presenting Results

The results are presented identically for each of the image schemas and primary metaphors. First, the image schema or primary source domain is clarified. Second, a selection of cross-linguistic comparisons is offered. Third, the main metaphorical and metonymical mappings from the image schema or primary source domain to the target domain of

---

18. The tokens and their classifications are listed in the appendix.
19. These five alone where chosen because of the limited space in this study.

distress are presented and analyzed. Fourth, evidence is presented that these are indeed significant conceptual mappings. Fifth, comparison is made with other languages. Finally, the import of each image schema or primary source domain for the Hebrew ICM of distress is summarized.

4.5.1. Establishing the Image Schema or Primary Source Domain

The first task is clarifying the image schema or source domain being considered. For image schemas, according to assumptions five and six (section 2.7), this means considering both universal and culture-specific factors. Image schemas derive from recurring patterns of perceptual interaction or motor programs,[20] the most significant of which often derive from common human embodied experience. These universal factors will be considered first.

However, the cultural elaboration of such schemas is not universal,[21] so particular Hebrew instantiations require investigation. Kimmel calls a culturally augmented image schema a *situated schema*, often compounding more primitive schemas, and acquired through culture-specific formative practices, the general cultural environment, and especially through language itself.[22] Further, culture-specific words "reflect a society's past experience of doing and thinking about things in certain ways; and they help to perpetuate these ways."[23] The presentation of cultural influences will thus focus on language, studying the experiential range for Hebrew lexical items to establish recurring patterns. Following assumption 8 of section 2.7, this lexical analysis will prioritize concrete situations. For example, the use of the Hebrew root צרר for sieges, cloth wrappings, and cramped spaces unites basic bodily schemas of containment and constraining forces to create a situated schema in which an Agonist with a desire to move is surrounded by a restrictive Antagonist.

---

20. Johnson, *Body*, xiv.

21. The tension between universal and culturally situated image schemas is still an unresolved theoretical issue, Hampe, "Schemas," 3–6.

22. Kimmel, "Culture," 297–99.

23. Wierzbicka, *Understanding*, 5.

Considering primary source domains, universal and cultural factors again interact. For example, the perception of "taste" is constrained by the universal physiological arrangement of taste buds, but which tastes are salient varies between cultures, so that both universal and culture-specific elements need exploration.

4.5.2. Comparative Data

In this section of each chapter, cross-linguistic comparisons will be given, where the image schema or source domain conceptualizes similar emotional, physical, or psychological target domains. Comparisons come from contemporary languages and from other languages of the ancient Near East. Such comparisons highlight potentially significant aspects of the Hebrew mappings, as well as allowing analysis of both universal and culturally varying aspects of the conceptualization of distress.

4.5.3. Presentation and Analysis of Mappings

The heart of each chapter presents the thought mappings that link the schema or primary source domain to distress. Following assumption one, language structure provides a "way in" to thought structure, so this section provides examples of linguistic metaphors instantiating the specific conceptual metaphors. Hebrew examples have an English translation, usually from the NRSV or Martínez and Tigchelaar,[24] where satisfactory. Where a particular scholar offers a better translation, this is used, and where no satisfactory translation was found, the author's own translation is used.

First, this section investigates encyclopedic, prototypical knowledge relating to the domain, including any prototypical scripts (such as siege, or being hunted by a lion), derived from the Hebrew text or archaeological evidence.[25] Thus, a prototypical "siege" script can be collated from biblical information, archaeological remains at Lachish, and

---

24. Martínez and Tigchelaar, *Scrolls*.

25. At least from the tenth century onwards, archaeology and biblical texts give a coherent picture, see Dever, *Writers*.

from Sennacherib's report of his Judean campaign and the reliefs in his palace in Nineveh.

Then, mappings will be presented showing which parts of source domain gestalts map on to parts of the distress gestalt.[26] These include *participants* (especially agents), *stages, purposes, causes,* and *results*. Thus, where God is conceptualized as "besieging" someone, hostile purpose, and fatal results map onto the distress experience. Since distress is an emotional experience, some elements may map onto elements of prototypical emotional scenarios, such as the cause of the emotion, physiological reactions caused by the emotion,[27] and the emotion itself, including its duration and intensity. Thus, "my enemies set a net for my feet" maps being a hunted animal onto the psalmist's distress experience and maps the "enemies" onto the cause.

Next, entailments of these mappings for understanding the distress situation are presented. For example, if the psalmist's predicament is problematized as a net, what possible solutions are there? Finally, this section investigates source domain elements that are highlighted, to see how these elements highlight or hide aspects of distress experience.

For image schemas, this section enumerates the different source domains exhibiting the schemas recurring pattern. For example, the cluster of vehicles comprising nets, siege, drowning, and prison all exemplify the enclosing CONSTRAINT schema. Since compound image schemas are often acquired through "exposure to culture-specific scenes that create situation-bound knowledge packages,"[28] such culture-specific scenes are used to group the analysis of image schemas.

4.5.4. Further Evidence

Section 2.5.1.e, above, listed several forms of evidence for conceptual metaphors. Unfortunately, the best (psycholinguistic evidence) is inaccessible for Classical Hebrew. However, this section documents other

---

26. See 2.5.1.b.

27. The cause of emotions in English can be found in the spatial prepositions used (as in "Bill was angry at Hillary's remark" versus "Bill was angry over Hillary's remark"), Dirven, "Emotions"; Radden, "Conceptualisation."

28. Kimmel, "Culture," 299.

evidence for the conceptual reality of the mappings suggested by the linguistic expressions presented.

First, generalizations over polysemy will be offered, where several words are used in each of two distinct domains. This demonstrates *elaboration* of the metaphorical mapping and suggests a productive link between the domains. For example, using several roots related to being encircled (אפף, סבב, and נקף) in distress suggests an ongoing conceptual association between being surrounded and distress experiences.

Second, generalizations over inference patterns will show mapping of *inferential structure* from one domain to another. For example, along with several texts describing distress as being somewhere down, other texts infer that relief from distress must be movement upwards. This is a generalized inference, whether moving up to an upright position or moving up to a geographically higher position, revealing a conceptual structure.

Third, extensions from conventional expressions to novel poetic usages are evidence of *active* conceptual metaphors, which are sufficiently *entrenched* in the language to be reflected and developed in different registers. Since the specific corpus contains only poetic texts, this section will show how the more creative expressions reflect the same conceptual metaphors as more conventional poetic expressions, and also as conventional distress language in prose parts of the general corpus. Although there is no surviving biblical language that could be called "everyday" Hebrew,[29] expressions found within narrative are likely more conventional than those within poetry.

Within the poetry, imagery can be broadly distinguished as *conventional imagery*, found in the stock images of the psalms; *intensive imagery*, building on conventional metaphors and similes over several lines, found in Job and especially the prophets; and (most rarely) *innovative imagery*, found in highest concentration in Job.[30] Thus, this section shows how the same conceptual metaphors surface across the spectrum of conventionality, from idioms of prose narrative, through

---

29. The surviving texts are explicitly of a high literary calibre. Some even doubt whether Biblical Hebrew was ever a language of common parlance, Ullendorf, "Biblical."

30. Alter, *Poetry*, 189–90.

the Psalms' stock images, to the intensive structures of the prophets and the heights of Joban innovation. The Hodayot generally use stock images similarly to the biblical psalms, but sometimes use intensifying structures, as in 1QH 10:7–18 where a simple simile comparing distress to labor pains becomes an involved exposition on childbirth, bringing in imagery of the sea, pit, and death.

Fourth, the existence of a conceptual metaphor is supported by its *coherence* with larger-scale metaphorical systems. Conceptual metaphor theory claims that metaphors fit within larger hierarchies, so these will be investigated. For example, the metaphor EXPERIENCING DISTRESS IS TASTING BITTER FOOD fits with the higher-level (more schematic) conceptual metaphor LIFE EVENTS ARE INGESTED SUBSTANCES.

Fifth, any available non-linguistic expressions for the suggested conceptual metaphors will be presented, demonstrating its entrenchment throughout the linguistic and non-linguistic system. Conceptual metaphor research needs to recognize aspects "offloaded" into the cultural world, not just those in the brains of individuals.[31] Kövecses lists possible non-linguistic realizations of conceptual metaphor, including: drawings, sculptures, and buildings; symbols; myths; dream interpretation; interpretation of history; social institutions; and social practices.[32] For example, eating bitter herbs at Passover to remember the Israelites' suffering powerfully consolidates the conceptual metaphor EXPERIENCING DISTRESS IS EATING BITTER FOOD.

4.5.5. Universality and Variation

Finally, this section of each chapter will demonstrate how Hebrew metaphorical conceptualizations compare to the cross-linguistic examples, using Kövecses' parameters for variation described in section 2.5.7.d. This includes, first, presenting differences related to the conceptualization of the source and target domains, their prototypical instantiations, and the inferences when used in metaphor. Second, variation in linguistic expressions will be presented, including different parts of experience highlighted by the linguistic expressions in different cultures, differ-

---

31. Gibbs, "Heads."
32. Kövecses, *Metaphor*, 57–66.

ences in conventionality of expressions, and differences in syntactic form. For example, dark weather is used to conceptualize negative emotional experience in English and in Hebrew (being "gloomy" or קדר), but whereas in English this maps an intensity structure onto the target domain of emotion (one can be "very" gloomy), in Hebrew it does not.

4.6. Summary

This chapter has described how the data was collected for use in this study, and introduced some terminology for describing that data, as well as outlining the format for presentation in the remainder of this thesis. It is now possible to present research results, beginning with the VERTICALITY image schema.

5

Distress and the VERTICALITY Schema

"You have put me in the depths of the pit, in the regions dark and deep."
—Ps 88:6[7]

5.1. Introduction

This chapter first establishes the VERTICALITY image schema, considering universal factors (like gravity) and more cultural-specific factors, like the vertical conception of the cosmos. Second, a brief cross-linguistic exploration shows how this schema conceptualizes distress in other languages. Third, mappings within the specific corpus are given. Fourth, additional support for these mappings is presented. Finally, Hebrew and English mappings are compared, before summarizing how the VERTICALITY schema in Hebrew distress discourse helps make sense of life experiences.

5.2. Establishing the Schema

5.2.1. Physiological / Universal Factors

The VERTICALITY schema is potentially universal since all humans experience gravity and, from infancy, unconsciously employ numerous processes to stay upright against it. More specifically, "the VERTICALITY schema . . . emerges from our tendency to employ an UP-DOWN orientation in picking out meaningful structures of our experience. We grasp this structure of verticality repeatedly in thousands of perceptions and activities we experience every day, such as perceiving a tree, our felt sense of standing upright, the activity of climbing stairs, forming a mental image of a flagpole, measuring our children's heights, and experiencing the level of water rising in the bathtub. The VERTICALITY schema is the abstract structure of these verticality experiences, images, and perceptions."[1]

Although standing upright is universal, other examples here are culture-specific (bathtub water or flagpoles), underlining how culture and cognition both shape image schemas. Other examples would fit an ancient setting: drawing water from a well; building a wall; or forming a mental image of a tent pole.

Cognitive Linguistics emphasizes embodiment, so the upright human body is seen as prototypically giving structure to the VERTICALITY schema, alongside STRAIGHT and BALANCE schemas. As Cienki writes, "There is a significant relation between our bodies being straight, up, and in control; resisting the force of gravity, standing up straight, involves a specific kind of muscular tension. Contrast this with the relation between being bent, down, and a lack of control; when submitting to a force or influencing factor (e.g., fatigue), the body is bent over, slouched. The qualities of straightness, control, and being up, strong, and firm, therefore, commonly *group together in our experience* given how our bodies function, with a *contrasting grouping* being bent/curved, lack of control, down, weak, and soft."[2]

---

1. Johnson, *Body*, xiv.
2. Cienki, "Straight," 111.

Thus, data fitting the STRAIGHT schema (including being "bowed down") has been included with the VERTICALITY schema, as their co-occurrence in experience makes them difficult to distinguish.

The VERTICALITY schema is often structurally linked to the SCALE schema, allowing degrees of "up" and "down." The SCALE schema arises from experiencing our world as "a massive expanse of quantitative amount and qualitative degree or intensity . . . We can have more, less, or the same *number* of objects, *amount* of substance, *degree* of force, or *intensity* of sensation."[3] Scales tend to be, first, directional, and oriented upwards. Second, they are typically normative, so that, typically, more is good. Finally, scales may or may not have fixed limits (in contrast to paths which generally terminate at definite points).[4] Johnson concludes that "this experientially basic, value-laden structure of our grasp of both concrete and abstract entities is one of the most pervasive image-schematic structures in our understanding."[5] This value-laden structure maps to English emotion language, as in conventional metaphors for depression, where being *down* is culturally "associated with all of what we strive to avoid—for example, being 'not normal,' devalued, of low status, lacking in power and control, morally bad, inferior, inadequate, and less than others."[6]

In fact, Krzeszowski argues several spatial image schemas have such values attached, such as CONTAINER, BALANCE, FRONT-BACK, CENTER-PERIPHERY, LINK, AND VERTICALITY. In each, a plus pole contrasts with a minus pole, the plus pole aligning with the canonical state: being linked; central; in; in front; or up.[7] Although Hampe questions whether values inhere in the primitive VERTICALITY image schema or just in specific embodied instantiations of it,[8] this chapter shows further contexts (the Hebrew conception of the universe and discourse of distress) in which "up" is viewed positively and "down" negatively.

---

3. Johnson, *Body*, 122.
4. Ibid., 122–23.
5. Ibid., 123.
6. McMullen and Conway, "Depression," 177.
7. Krzeszowski, "Parameter," 325.
8. Hampe, "Down," 106.

5.2.2. Culture-Specific Factors

For Hebrew, the absence of particles paralleling English *up* or *down* complicates comparison with conceptual metaphors like MORE IS UP or GOOD IS UP. The English word *up* in *he went up* and *he stood up* cognitively links erect posture and spatial upward movement. There is no comparable word in Hebrew, with only derivatives of רוּם 'to be high' used in both spatial and postural domains.[9] Therefore, these two VERTICALITY schemas (the spatial and postural) will be first considered separately.

a) Spatial Scale

The vertical spatial scale encompasses the whole cosmos, from heaven to Sheol. This section examines first the tangible environment, including mountains, pits, and graves, before considering more fluidly conceptualized extremities.

Hills (הָרִים) and valleys (עֲמָקִים) were salient phenomena for ancient Israelites due to the hilly terrain ranging from the Judean hills (up to 1000m) down to the Dead Sea (down to 400 meters below sea level).[10] Nowhere exceeded the mountains further north (including Hermon at 2,840 meters), but it was certainly more mountainous than the Egyptian or Mesopotamian civilizations situated on river plains.[11]

The summits of hills were the highest humanly accessible points, and were often associated with divine encounter in Hebrew narrative (as in the case of Moses or Elijah) and in poetic theophanies. Similarly, in Ugaritic texts, El's council meets at his mountain dwelling, the entrance to both heaven and the underworld.[12] Mountains thus connect heaven and earth.[13] With roots in the deepest seas and summits in the heavens, they unite the whole vertical cosmological scale.[14] Even on

---

9. Firmage et al., "רוּם."
10. Rogerson, *Chronicles*, 58–60.
11. Walton, *Thought*, 175.
12. Mullen, *Assembly*.
13. Keel, *Symbolism*, 29.
14. Talmon, "Har," 132.

the Mesopotamian plains, ziggurats created artificial mountaintops on which to meet the gods.[15] Associating high places with gods even in Mesopotamia warns against claiming too deterministic a relationship between geography and culture.[16]

Aside from idolatrous worship, mountaintops are generally viewed positively in the Hebrew Scriptures expressing "affirmed, positive, socio-religious values."[17] Valleys (עֲמָקִים) conversely, are more multivalent. They are praised as agricultural land (Ps 65:13[14]), but negatively viewed as sites of battles, as places of stoning, or filled with dead bodies and ashes around Jerusalem. Verbs derived from עמק describe making things deep, such as pits, with Semitic cognates also evoking "depth."[18] The related noun מַעֲמַקִּים describes deep places, especially the deep subterranean waters.

Using wells and cisterns (to provide water in a dry climate), pits and graves required descending further, below the earth's surface. Sometimes natural underground water supplies were accessed using buckets at wells (usually בְּאֵר), like the ancient forty-meter deep shaft at Beersheba.[19] Elsewhere, cisterns (usually בּוֹר[20]) were dug to store rainwater. Some people had individual cisterns,[21] with a narrow shaft leading to a wider chamber some 10–15 meters below ground,[22] but elsewhere towns shared collective cisterns, sometimes very impressive engineering feats,[23] with spiral steps around the walls of the shaft wide enough for pack animals to descend and bring up the water.[24] Some towns had similar storage pits for dry produce, like the eleven-meter-

---

15. Roaf, *Atlas*, 104.
16. As in Smith, "Differences."
17. Talmon, "Har," 125.
18. Beyse, "עֶמֶק," 202.
19. Thompson, *Handbook*, 113.
20. The use of בְּאֵר in 2 Sam 23:15 and בּוֹר in the parallel verse in 1 Chron 11:17 suggests the Hebrew distinctions may not be totally clear cut. Perhaps in later Hebrew בּוֹר came to mean both wells and cisterns (BDB 92).
21. According to the Moabite Stone, King Mesha told each of the inhabitants of Qarhoh to dig their own cistern, Arnold and Beyer, *Readings*, 162.
22. Thompson, *Handbook*, 115.
23. Mazar, *Archaeology*, 478.
24. Ibid., 478–83.

wide, seven-meter-deep pit at Megiddo.²⁵ These constructions provided an embodied experience where people could "descend into the pit" together. When the psalmists describe being in the בּוֹר, this variety of cisterns and pits were cognitively accessible, alongside Sheol itself as an underground "pit."

שַׁחַת also prototypically describes a pit or cistern,²⁶ particularly for trapping animals.²⁷ Although lions or donkeys may also fall into a similarly shaped בּוֹר (as attested in Torah legislation and in Benaiah's exploits of 2 Sam 23:20), the main difference is that a שַׁחַת was dug deliberately for catching animals. It also frequently describes the underworld, often paralleling שְׁאֹל, especially in the sectarian Qumran writings.

Burial practices also required going below the ground. A קֶבֶר was "a grave, excavated hole, or corresponding stone structure."²⁸ Surviving graves²⁹ are hewn from rock caves, comprising a square room with a narrow sealable entrance passage. Bodies and artifacts were first respectfully laid on benches, then unceremoniously swept aside when the bench was needed for another body.³⁰ A typical tomb (at Tell Dothan) has a 3.3-meter-deep vertical shaft leading down into a 5.5-meter-tall central chamber.³¹ Thus, entering such a grave to bury family members certainly involved descent into the ground.

Beyond the tangible environment, the cosmos extends upwards into the heavens (שָׁמַיִם) and downwards expects watery depths (תְהוֹם), and, somewhere, the netherworld destiny of the dead (שְׁאֹל). Some Hebrew evidence suggests a tripartite cosmological division into heaven, earth (אֶרֶץ) and (potentially underground) seas (תְהוֹם, or more commonly, יַמִּים).³² A tripartite division is represented in Egypt

25. Ussishkin, "Gate," 425.
26. The Moabite cognate is used on the Moabite stone passage referred to above.
27. Wächter, "שַׁחַת."
28. Koch, "קֶבֶר," 492.
29. Koch argues that earthen graves were more common for most people, but have left no trace (ibid., 496).
30. Cooley and Pratico, "People," 89.
31. Ibid., 75–78.
32. Keel, *Symbolism*, 35.

and Mesopotamia,[33] although often in Egypt it is heaven, earth, and realm of the dead (Duat). In Mesopotamia, the third place is most commonly the primeval ocean (Apsu).[34] However, since Ps 135:6 mentions four locations (listing seas and depths separately), and given frequent bipartite descriptions of heaven (שָׁמַיִם) and earth (אֶרֶץ), any Hebrew tripartite division is not rigid.

Typically for the ancient Near East, the subterranean regions are somewhat fluidly conceptualized, always including water but varying as to how the inhabited earth stayed afloat (suggesting pillars, beams, or more direct divine action).[35] In Hebrew, watery depths are also a very consistent element of the conceptualization, though totally alien to twenty-first-century understanding. In Sumerian texts, this water is "sweet," supplying the springs needed for agriculture.[36] In Hebrew, the subterranean water is יַמִּים (Ps 24:2) or מַיִם (Exod 20:3), neither specifying salt or fresh water.[37] The phrase מַיִם רַבִּים also occurs, encompassing subterranean waters and the world-embracing oceans.[38] However, passages describing their proximity to Sheol show they are prototypically "low."

Similarly, מְצוּלָה describes "something which is 'sunken down, deep,'"[39] or at "an extreme distance."[40] It occurs most frequently with water, so may prototypically refer to deep water, and be appropriate cosmologically for the deep parts of subterranean water. Fabry claims it does not "necessarily evoke some sort of vertical dimension,"[41] but its occurrence in a semantic domain with many other "low" places suggests vertical dimension may indeed be evoked.

---

33. Cornelius, "Representation."
34. Keel, *Symbolism*, 35.
35. Ibid., 39.
36. Lambert, "Cosmology," 47.
37. Fabry and Clements, "מַיִם," 269.
38. Ibid., 275.
39. Fabry, "מְצוּלָה," 514–15.
40. Tromp, *Conceptions*, 56.
41. Fabry, "מְצוּלָה," 516.

Next, שְׁאֹל was the final destiny of all, but especially the ungodly or those who died an untimely death.[42] Although appearing more in the context of personal emotional engagement than in cosmology,[43] and associated with destruction, desert, and ocean as well as depths,[44] the abode of the dead is nevertheless "down" on the cosmological scale,[45] probably "a great space in the depths."[46] Across the ancient Near East, "the movement downwards was universally associated with death."[47] However, שְׁאֹל is distinctively Hebrew, with major attributes including silence, darkness, dust, decay, and subterranean depth, all also characteristic of graves. Thus, possibly, "every grave is a little 'Sheol.'"[48] However, קֶבֶר occurs very rarely in the Psalms or Job (despite common reference to the underworld), and only very rarely are those in their graves linked to שְׁאֹל.[49]

The relative locations of Sheol and watery deep are debated. In Mesopotamian literature, where distinct levels are given, the realm of the dead is below the (positive) Apsu,[50] so that "the furthest realm in the direction downward was 'the netherworld.'"[51] Cornelius, conversely, portrays Hebrew שְׁאֹל as a cavern within the solid earth, above the bottomless subterranean waters.[52] Frymer-Kemsky argues that Sheol is "perhaps on the bottom of the sea" since the way to get there is always through water,[53] assuming the underground seas do indeed have a "bottom." Certainly, Ps 139:8 puts שָׁמַיִם and שְׁאֹל as vertically opposite

---

42. Johnston, *Shades*, 79–83.

43. Ibid., 72.

44. Barth thus argued that Sheol was not a particular locality (Barth, *Errettung*, 80–89, cited in Knibb, "Life," 405).

45. Tromp, *Conceptions*, 133; Johnston, *Shades*; 75, Wächter, "שְׁאוֹל."

46. Wächter, "שְׁאוֹל," 241–42.

47. Wyatt, *Space*, 40.

48. Keel, *Symbolism*, 63. This is more restrained than Pedersen's contention that "Sheol is the totality into which all graves are merged," Pedersen, *Israel*, 462.

49. Koch, "קֶבֶר," 494, 497.

50. Lambert, "Cosmology," 48.

51. Rochberg, "Cosmology," 325.

52. Cornelius, "Representation," 218.

53. Frymer-Kemsky, "Cosmology," 233.

Distress and the Verticality Schema

extremities. At least, שְׁאוֹל is unequivocally down cosmologically, as are the subterranean waters. Further, the lowest point on the cosmological scale is the depths of Sheol.

Did the Israelites, then, actually think you passed through water when descending to Sheol?[54] Probably not. Since the Israelites' cosmic conception included subterranean water, being in this water is being cosmologically "down," being very low is being down in Sheol, being the lowest possible is down in the depths at the very bottom of Sheol. But this does not mean a literal path through water is followed to get to Sheol at death.

This suggests the following spatial vertical scale, with positions indicating the depth of prototypical referents:

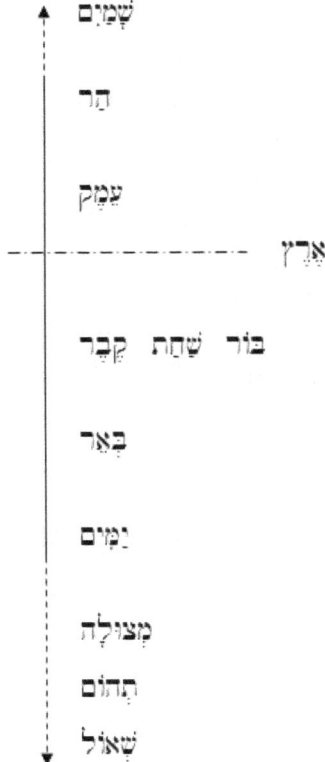

Figure 5.1

54. See Rudman, "Imagery."

The basic-level verbs for movement on this scale are עלה (upwards) and ירד (downwards).⁵⁵ ירד describes descending into a pit or moving to lower ground.⁵⁵ People descend to coastal cities or to the Philistines, and most typically, to Egypt. Perhaps traveling from north to south is seen as descent,⁵⁶ somewhat fitting the topography and the flow of the Jordan.⁵⁷ However, the simplest explanation is to recognize an instantiation of the conceptual metaphor DOWN IS BAD.

Going up, עלה basically means "move to a higher place."⁵⁸ Figuratively, it describes one country becoming greater than another (Deut 28:43) or a wife surpassing others (Prov 31:29), both showing positive evaluation of the UP pole.

b) Postural Scale

The postural VERTICALITY schema extends from an erect posture to lying prone on the ground. Universally, "as physical bodies we are usually oriented upright when we are healthy, awake, and alive; and we are often prone when we are ill, sleeping or dead."⁵⁹ There are also culture-specific reasons for standing or prostrating oneself.

The basic verb for becoming more erect is קום, typically describing a human achieving an erect posture, but extending to other objects or concepts (such as the Davidic dynasty) to emphasize their solidity and stability, or the readiness to act.⁶⁰ Basson argues from the psalmists' use to entreat God to act that the up-down schema is the most common orientational metaphor in lament psalms.⁶¹

Conversely, שכב describes becoming horizontal, sanctioning all three prototypical scenarios: sleeping, sexual intercourse, and, most frequently, dying, perhaps motivated by burial customs.⁶² שכב also

55. Mayer, "יָרַד," 316–19.
56. Ibid., 318.
57. Wyatt, *Space*, 40.
58. Fuhs, "עָלָה," 81.
59. McMullen and Conway, "Depression," 174.
60. Gamberoni, "קוּם."
61. Basson, *Divine*, 243.
62. Beuken, "שָׁכַב," 661.

describes the horizontal posture of sickness, grief, or petition, as when David hears of Bathsheba's son's sickness (2 Sam 12:16) or that Absalom has killed all his sons (2 Sam 13:31).

Next, נפל describes involuntary movement down the postural scale ("falling"). Similarly, the noun דְּחִי is used for stumbling, the root צלע for both limping (as Jacob following Peniel) and stumbling, and the verb טול (in the hophal) for being thrown down.

חוה (in the ishtaphal[63]) focuses posturally on bending over at the waist,[64] prostrating oneself before gods in worship, before kings, or to show respect. Only a few cases (as in Gen 22:5) evoke more general worship without a postural focus.[65] The Black Obelisk of Shalmeneser III shows Jehu adopting this posture before his Assyrian overlord.[66] Sometimes texts emphasize noses or faces touching the ground, possibly only temporarily, expecting the invitation to rise.[67] Egyptian and Mesopotamian iconography show a specific prototypical posture with one knee forward, hands level with the shoulders, and chin on the ground.[68] Although חוה is not associated with any verbs in the specific corpus, the phonological similarity to שחה allows some cognitive links, as in Sawyer's associative fields (section 2.3.2).

Other roots relate to this posture. קדד often occurs with חוה, and specifically with אַפַּיִם (nostrils), potentially highlighting putting the head to the ground, within the posture described above.[69] כרע, by contrast, highlights the lower limbs, covering "kneeling" and "crouching,"[70] and perhaps evoking a posture "sitting on the lower leg."[71] A posture with shins in front of one another on the ground and arms upraised

---

63. This way of explaining the form found in the Hebrew scriptures is preferred over a hithpael of שחה because it explains the otherwise intrusive vav, and is paralleled in Ugaritic texts, Preuss, "חוה," 249.

64. Gruber, *Aspects*, 91–92.

65. Ibid., 123.

66. Shown in Unger, *Archaeology*, 250.

67. Preuss, "חוה," 251.

68. Keel, *Symbolism*, 268 (Assyrian), 304–5, 309–10 (Egyptian).

69. Gruber, *Aspects*, 123–31.

70. Eising, "כרע."

71. Gruber, *Aspects*, 171–72.

is shown in Egyptian reliefs,[72] from which it would be easy to drop to the more fully prostrate form described above, explaining the formula כֹּרְעִים וּמִשְׁתַּחֲוִים used in Esther 3:2. כפף also evokes a bowed posture, maybe with just the upper torso bent over, as in a bulrush bending its head (Isa 58:5).

Forms from שחח and שׁיח are also relevant,[73] describing crouching lions (Job 38:40), and evil people bowing before the good (Prov 14:19). However, שחח also describes bringing down inhabitants of the heights (Isa 26:5), or city walls (Isa 25:12), schematically describing making something erect become low, rather than a particular posture. The hithpolel form תִּשְׁתּוֹחֲחִי (Ps 43:5[6]) is often translated "downcast" or "bowed down," deriving it from שחח.[74] Elsewhere, this form is attributed to שׁיח 'dissolve,'[75] so that the psalmist's נֶפֶשׁ is dissolving rather than being "down." However, melting, flowing, or spreading is potentially linked to being down, in that something that spreads out also decreases in height.

Thus, several roots indicate specific low postures in the Classical Hebrew cognitive environment.

5.3. Comparative Data on Emotion Language and the VERTICALITY Schema

5.3.1. Contemporary Cross-Linguistic Comparisons

This section reviews three articles studying the VERTICALITY schema in contemporary emotion language, first for English depression, second, for Russian emotional states entered using verbs of downward movement, and third for Punjabi "sinking" hearts.

First, McMullen and Conway studied metaphors used by depressed English speakers, finding 90 percent instantiated the conceptual

---

72. Keel, *Symbolism*, 304, 305, 309.

73. Ruppert lists שׁיח, שׁוּח, and שׁחה all as 'secondary forms' of שחח, Ruppert, "שׁחח," 559.

74. As in Long, "שׁחח."

75. As in Ruppert, "שׁחח," 559, and Wolf and Holmstedt, "שׁיח" (inconsistent when compared to Long's article elsewhere in *NIDOTTE*, Long, "שׁחח").

metaphor DEPRESSION IS DESCENT.⁷⁶ This metaphor is entrenched in both conventional and novel expressions, and has several entailments. Feeling *low*, *down*, or *depressed* are normal ways of expressing depression, as are the more creative *being down in the dumps*, *hitting rock bottom*, or *being in a slump*. Novel expressions included *being down in my catacombs* and *wallowing in a dreary, dismal pit*, easily comprehensible through familiarity with more conventional expressions.

An obvious entailment links depth to emotional intensity, descending from feeling *a bit low* to being *in the depths*. Second, easy downward movement (because of gravity) contrasts with difficulty moving upwards, so that verbs for entering depression like *spiraling down*, *crashing*, *nose-diving*, *sliding*, and *slipping* show that "depression is conceptualized as a downward progression that, once begun, is difficult, if not impossible, to stop."⁷⁷ Third, since conscious bodily control is unnecessary for descent, the metaphor highlights external causality and the lack of control sufferers experience in depression.⁷⁸ Fourth, experiences of physical descent imply that the further one descends, the harder it is to come back up; that if one goes too far, one goes beyond reach; and that once one begins to fall, one normally has to hit the bottom before any attempt to climb out is possible. Thus, this metaphor highlights failure, loss of control, and the difficulty returning to "normality."⁷⁹

Second, in Russian, verbs for entering different emotional states use the VERTICALITY schema. Thus, *on pogruzit'sja v X* 'he sank / plunged into X' is acceptable where X is *strax* (fear), *užas* (terror), *pečal* (sadness), *otčajanie* (despair), *gore* (grief), *skorb'* (sorrow), *blaženstvo* (bliss), or *ljubov'* (love), but not *ispug* (fright), *panika* (panic), *ogorčenie* (distress), *radost'* (joy), *vostorg* (delight), or any words relating to anger, disgust, or surprise. Conversely, *vpal v X* 'he fell into X' is acceptable where X is *trevoga* (anxiety), *panika* (panic), *otčajanie* (despair), or any words related to anger. It is unacceptable for surprise, disgust, or love.⁸⁰

76. McMullen and Conway, "Depression."
77. Ibid., 172.
78. Ibid., 178.
79. Ibid., 172–79.
80. Mostovaja, "Emotions," 299.

Pogruzit'sja refers to "gradually getting deeper and deeper into a substance until an object is fully covered with this substance (normally a liquid),"[81] so only appropriate if entering something deep. Depth on the VERTICALITY scale then maps to the emotion's duration, so that "the longer the emotion lasts, the deeper it is. On the other hand emotions which pass quickly are not 'deep' at all."[82] Conversely, *vpal* focuses on falling into something bad. Thus, "since real falling into something which happens in physical space is normally an undesirable event, it makes it easy to understand why words referring to positive emotions cannot occur in slot X in the construction *on vpal v X* 'he fell into X.'" Rather, words here "always denote inner states which are thought of as bad for the experiencer."[83]

Third, Punjabi speakers use a "sinking heart," *dil ghirda hai*, to describe a cluster of negative emotional and physical symptoms brought on by hunger, sunstroke, excessive anger, unhappiness, pride or shame, heart attacks, children leaving home, or loss of family members.[84] *Ghirna* evokes falling, sinking, dropping or stumbling,[85] explainable in the idiom as "when the heart moves downwards or decreases in strength."[86] Krause observes that "Punjabis label their experience 'sinking heart' when feelings of anxiety are combined with physical sensations in the heart or chest."[87] The importance here is the VERTICALITY schema collocating with the most important body part (the heart is the source of life in Punjabi) to express a salient negative experience, combining social, physical, and emotional components. It also warns against overusing universals in describing emotional and physical conditions. The cluster of causes and symptoms of a "sinking heart" do not match any salient diagnosis in Western medicine, though salient in the Punjabi community.

81. Ibid., 300.
82. Ibid., 304.
83. Ibid., 324.
84. Krause, "Heart," 568–71.
85. Ibid., 566.
86. Ibid., 564.
87. Ibid., 567.

Distress and the Verticality Schema

Thus, in English, Russian and Punjabi, the DOWN pole of the VERTICALITY scale helps conceptualize negative emotional (and physical) experience. These studies also suggest entailments potentially present in Hebrew. Does Hebrew map depth to duration (as in Russian), so that the longer the state of distress the farther the scale is descended? Do they allow the entailment (as in English) that the farther one has descended, the more difficult it is to return? Comparing with Punjabi, do salient idioms use a VERTICALITY schema, and if so, do they evoke a culture-specific constellation of causes and symptoms?

5.3.2. Ancient Near Eastern Comparisons

Next, two illustrative ancient Near Eastern examples show the antiquity of conceptualizing negative experience through the VERTICALITY schema. First, lines in the Akkadian *Ludlul Bel Nemeqi* demonstrate this mapping:

> *ina ṭa-a-bi i-ta-ma-a i-li šá-ma-'i*
> *ú-taš-šá-šá-ma i-dab-bu-ba a-rad ir-kal-la*
> (Column II, lines 46–47)
>
> In prosperity (happiness) they speak of scaling heaven,
>
> Under adversity (sadness) they complain of going down to hell.[88]

Significantly, this describes a contemporary conventional idiom, not just the poet's own expression, and shows that conceptualizing distressing experiences as a descent to the netherworld is not unique to Hebrew.

A few lines later, the sufferer's symptoms are summarized, with his[89] low position on the postural VERTICALITY schema (at the hands of demons) symptomatic of his troubles.

---

88. Akkadian transliteration and English translation from Lambert, *Wisdom*, 40–41. Alternative translation from Fuhs, "עָלָה," 80.

89. Throughout this study, authors of biblical and ancient Near Eastern texts are generally assumed to be male, so that male pronouns are used to describe them and their situations. Gender-neutral pronouns are used for later users of the texts.

Surrounded by Bitterness

> *la-na zaq-ru i-bu-tú i-ga-ri-iš*
>
> *gat-ti rap-šat ú-ru-ba-iš uš-ni-i-la*
>
> *ki-i ú-lil-te an-na-bi-uk bu-pa-niš an-na-di*
> (Column II, lines 68–70)
>
> My lofty stature they destroyed like a wall,
>
> My robust figure they laid down like a bulrush,
>
> I am thrown down like a bog plant and cast on my face.[90]

Although the most significant schema here is FORCE, each line highlights something typically erect (wall, bulrush, and bog plant) being brought down from its normative status.

A second illustrative Akkadian usage is the idiom *libbi šapil* "low heart." In Assyrian medical texts *libbu* usually more generally references the intestines in the abdomen, contrasting with lungs and organs higher in the chest,[91] and the idiom is associated with depression or worry, such as the inability to speak or sadness over a child.[92]

These comparisons again raise questions. What is the significance of the descent to the underworld motif in Hebrew distress discourse? How does the postural scale describe the lamenter's troubles? Are internal body parts described as "low"? Some of these are answered below.

5.4. Presentation and Analysis of Hebrew Mappings

5.4.1. Being in Distress is Being Down on the Spatial Geographical Scale

The most fundamental mapping here is that EMOTIONAL EXPERIENCE IS BEING IN A SPATIAL LOCATION, as in English being *down in the dumps*, or *in heaven*. Psalm 130 is an obvious initial example:

> מִמַּעֲמַקִּים קְרָאתִיךָ יְהוָה:
>
> Ps 130:1: Out of the depths I cry to you, O LORD.

---

90. Lambert, *Wisdom*, 43.
91. Stol, *Epilepsy*, 27.
92 Reiner, *CAD (Š)*, 424.

This supports the general mapping, but also the value-laden mapping that negative experience is being in a spatial location low on the VERTICALITY scale. Several low locations are used for the distressed person, most commonly a בּוֹר or שַׁחַת.

קָרָאתִי שִׁמְךָ יְהוָה מִבּוֹר תַּחְתִּיּוֹת׃

Lam 3:55: I called on your name, O LORD, from the depths of the pit (בּוֹר).

שַׁתַּנִי בְּבוֹר תַּחְתִּיּוֹת בְּמַחֲשַׁכִּים בִּמְצֹלוֹת׃

Ps 88:6[7]: You have put me in the depths of the pit (בּוֹר), in the regions dark and deep.

[...] מה עלי כיורדי שאול ועם 29 מתים יחפש רוחי כי הגיעו לשחת

1QH 16:28–29:[93] [...] over me like those who go down to Sheol, and with the dead my spirit hides because [my] li[fe] has drawn near to the pit (שחת).

Elsewhere, the lamenter sinks (טבע) into mud, a root describing the stone "sinking" into Goliath's head, Jeremiah sinking into mud (טיט) at the bottom of a cistern, and the Egyptian army in the Yam Suph (Exod 15:4). All describe an entity embedding into something soft,[94] especially if the Egyptians in Exod 15:4 were stuck in the mud before the waters returned and the deeps covered them in 15:5, rather than actually sinking through the water itself. Thus, whereas *sink* in English is prototypically framed against a medium of water, טבע is framed against mud and does not evoke the same unbounded downward trajectory.

---

93. The references, Hebrew transcription, and English translations of Qumran texts are based on Martínez and Tigchelaar, *Scrolls*, unless otherwise stated. *Hodayot* citations use 1QH[a], although lacunae may be filled by other versions. 1QH[a] likely had a privileged position within the Qumran community, being, together with 1QS and 1QM, "venerated copies of earlier authoritative models of the major sectarian works" (Dimant, "Character").

94. Also suggested by the Hebrew cognate noun טַבַּעַת 'signet ring' (BDB 371).

Surrounded by Bitterness

Psalm 69:2[3] (and similarly 69:14[15]) has an intensification structure[95] between the two parallel lines, the psalmist being first stuck in the mud, but by the second line being in deep water. 1QH 15:2 parallels Jer 38:22, with the noun בִּיץ suggesting the petitioner's feet are stuck in swampy ground, a less dramatic image than the psalmist's יְוֵן מְצוּלָה. Psalm 40:2[3] has no "sinking" verb, but the psalmist is rescued from a "miry bog" (טִיט הַיָּוֵן), another place of boggy danger.

טָבַעְתִּי בִּיוֵן מְצוּלָה וְאֵין מָעֳמָד בָּאתִי בְמַעֲמַקֵּי־מַיִם וְשִׁבֹּלֶת שְׁטָפָתְנִי׃

Ps 69:2[3]: I sink in deep mire, where there is no foothold; I have come into deep waters, and the flood sweeps over me.

הַצִּילֵנִי מִטִּיט וְאַל־אֶטְבָּעָה אִנָּצְלָה מִשֹּׂנְאַי וּמִמַּעֲמַקֵּי־מָיִם׃

Ps 69:14 [15]: Rescue me from the mire, do not let me sink—let me be delivered from those who hate me, even from watery depths.[96]

ותטבע ‹ב›בביץ רגלי

1QH 15:2: My feet sink in the mud.

וַיַּעֲלֵנִי מִבּוֹר שָׁאוֹן מִטִּיט הַיָּוֵן

Ps 40:2[3]: He drew me up from the pit of tumult, out of the miry bog.

Other lamenters locate themselves in deep (subterranean) waters. Sometimes מַיִם רַבִּים is used, elsewhere it is more specifically the subterranean waters, evoked by תְהוֹם or מְצוּלוֹת יָם. Psalm 71 refers to the earth's depths, without referring to water.

יִשְׁלַח מִמָּרוֹם יִקָּחֵנִי יַמְשֵׁנִי מִמַּיִם רַבִּים׃

Ps 18:16[17]: He reached down from on high, he took me; he drew me out from the deep waters.[97]

---

95. Alter, *Poetry*, 62–84.
96. Tate, *Psalms*, 187.
97. Craigie, *Psalms 1–50*, 167.

Distress and the Verticality Schema

וישימו נפש[י] כאניה ב[מ]צולות ים

1QH 11:6: They have set [my] soul like a boat in the [de]pths of the sea.⁹⁸

[כ]לאי עם תהום נחשב לאין [. . .]

1QH 13:38: My [ga]ol is comparable to the deep without there being [. . .]

בָּאתִי בְמַעֲמַקֵּי־מַיִם וְשִׁבֹּלֶת שְׁטָפָתְנִי׃

Ps 69:2[3]: I have come into deep waters, and the flood sweeps over me.

וּמִתְּהֹמוֹת הָאָרֶץ תָּשׁוּב תַּעֲלֵנִי׃

Ps 71:20: From the depths of the earth you will bring me up again.

Finally, sometimes the lamenter apparently locates himself in Sheol, more frequently in thanksgivings than laments.⁹⁹ In Ps 86:13, the psalmist may only have been destined for Sheol when rescued, since **נצל מן** in Gen 32:11 is used for Jacob's deliverance from a distress that has not yet fully arrived. The following two examples, however, more clearly place the petitioner in Sheol. The four final examples portray Sheol more as a person than a place, who can tie the petitioner up, buy him, or be on his bed with him. However, these are included here since Sheol prototypically refers to an underground location, even if personified in these texts.

וְהִצַּלְתָּ נַפְשִׁי מִשְּׁאוֹל תַּחְתִּיָּה׃

Ps 86:13: You have delivered my soul from the depths of Sheol.

יְהוָה הֶעֱלִיתָ מִן־שְׁאוֹל נַפְשִׁי חִיִּיתַנִי מִיָּרְדִי־בוֹר׃¹⁰⁰

Ps 30:3[4]: O LORD, you brought up my soul from Sheol, restored me to life that I should not go down to the Pit.¹⁰¹

---

98. Martínez and Tigchelaar, *Scrolls*, 165.
99. Johnston, *Shades*, 89.
100. Here, and elsewhere with a Ketiv-Qere distinction, the Qere is written.
101. The Qere translation, footnoted in the NRSV.

Surrounded by Bitterness

וַיֹּאמֶר קָרָאתִי מִצָּרָה לִי אֶל־יְהוָה וַיַּעֲנֵנִי מִבֶּטֶן שְׁאוֹל שִׁוַּעְתִּי שָׁמַעְתָּ קוֹלִי:

Jon 2:2[3]: And he said, "I called to the LORD out of my distress, and he answered me; out of the belly of Sheol I cried, and you heard my voice."

אֲפָפוּנִי חֶבְלֵי־מָוֶת וּמְצָרֵי שְׁאוֹל מְצָאוּנִי צָרָה וְיָגוֹן אֶמְצָא:

Ps 116:3: Death's cords were all around me, Sheol's nooses had seized me, I encountered distress and anguish.[102]

חֶבְלֵי שְׁאוֹל סְבָבוּנִי קִדְּמוּנִי מוֹקְשֵׁי מָוֶת:

Ps 18:5[6]: The cords of Sheol have surrounded me, the snares of Death have confronted me.[103]

למות 10 הייתי בחטאי ועוונותי לשאול מכרוני ותצילני 11 יהוה

11Q6 19:9–11: I was near to death because of my sins, and my iniquities have sold me to Sheol, but you YHWH, saved me.

[. . .אפפוני] 4 משברי מות ושאול על יצועי

1QH 17:3–4: The breakers of death [surround me], Sheol is upon my bed.

All these verses conceptualize distress as being located low on the VERTICALITY scale, mapping both the low position to the distressing situation, and the person there to the petitioner. Other dimensions of the experiential gestalt of "being in a low place" are also mapped onto the target domain of distress, potentially including: participants; parts; stages; linear sequence; causation; and purpose.[104] For example, the person in a low position is a *participant* in the gestalt. Four further elements are considered below.

First, regarding *causation*, embodied experiences of becoming low are often non-volitional. Sinking into mud results from the external

---

102. Allen, *Psalms 101–150*, 111.

103. Craigie, *Psalms 1–50*, 166.

104. Lakoff and Johnson, *Metaphors*, 77–86, see section 2.5.1.b.

Distress and the Verticality Schema

force of gravity. Alternatively, someone may fall into a trap or be imprisoned in an underground pit. These images map the external cause of being low onto the external cause of distress, whether unspecified (like gravity, Ps 69:1–2[2–3], cited above), or a deliberate, hostile agent: either God (Ps 88:6[7], putting the psalmist in a pit, cited above), or the "enemies" (Pss 119:85; 57:6[7]; 35:7–8). The petitioner neither desires nor has any control over his low position, highlighting external causes and hiding the lamenter's own part in the situation.

כָּרוּ־לִי זֵדִים שִׁיחוֹת אֲשֶׁר לֹא כְתוֹרָתֶךָ׃

Ps 119:85: The arrogant have dug pitfalls for me; they flout your law.

כָּרוּ לְפָנַי שִׁיחָה נָפְלוּ בְתוֹכָהּ׃

Ps 57:6[7]: They dug a pit in my path, but they have fallen into it themselves.

כִּי־חִנָּם טָמְנוּ־לִי שַׁחַת רִשְׁתָּם חִנָּם חָפְרוּ לְנַפְשִׁי׃ תְּבוֹאֵהוּ שׁוֹאָה לֹא־יֵדָע וְרִשְׁתּוֹ אֲשֶׁר־טָמַן תִּלְכְּדוֹ בְּשׁוֹאָה יִפָּל־בָּהּ׃

Psalm 35:7–8: For without cause they hid their net for me; without cause they dug a pit for my life. Let ruin come on them unawares. And let the net that they hid ensnare them; let them fall in it—to their ruin.[105]

In some (mainly Qumranic) texts, the cause comes from the deep place itself (that may swallow up the petitioner, have traps to catch him, or shoot arrows out upwards).

אַל־תִּשְׁטְפֵנִי שִׁבֹּלֶת מַיִם וְאַל־תִּבְלָעֵנִי מְצוּלָה וְאַל־תֶּאְטַר־עָלַי בְּאֵר פִּיהָ׃

Ps 69:15[16]: Do not let the flood sweep over me, or the deep swallow me up, or the Pit close its mouth over me.

ותשוך בעדי מכול מוקשי שחת

1QH 10:21: You have protected me from all the traps of the pit.

---

105. The NRSV translation reverses the order of pit and net, to make sense of the pit being dug rather than the net.

Surrounded by Bitterness

בהתעופף כול חצי שחת לאין השב ויודו לאין תקוה

> 1QH 11:17: When all the arrows of the pit fly forth without return. Then they rend beyond hope.[106]

Second, returning to the *parts* of the low scenario, several texts highlight the depth of the low places through a descriptive adjective. Thus, the petitioner is in the "lowest" pit (בּוֹר תַּחְתִּיּוֹת, Lam 3:55; Ps 88:6[7]), the "depths" of Sheol (שְׁאוֹל תַּחְתִּיָּה, Ps 86:13), and "deep" mud and deep water (יְוֵן מְצוּלָה, מַעֲמַקֵּי־מָיִם, Psalm 69:2[3]). In Ps 88:6[7], the psalmist explicitly mentions the depth again (מְצֹלוֹת), after positioning himself in the lowest pit, to emphasize his plight. This syntax suggests depth is explicitly mapped onto the intensity of distress, and also demonstrates active use of the source domain.[107]

Third, the perceptual experience of low places (both in hearing and vision) is another *part* mapped onto the perceptual experience of the petitioner. The tumultuous noise of deep waters is highlighted (Ps 42:7[8]), sometimes specifically mapped onto the noise of opponents, as in 1QH 10:27. Similarly, Psalm 69 also maps the perceptual experience of being in the water to the effect of the speech of the enemies so that "like the relentless pounding of waves, slander, insult, and false accusation crush the psalmist."[108] Visually, the location's darkness may be highlighted, as in Ps 88:6[7], cited above.

תְּהוֹם־אֶל־תְּהוֹם קוֹרֵא לְקוֹל צִנּוֹרֶיךָ

> Ps 42:7[8]: Deep calls to deep at the thunder of your cataracts.

וכהמון מים רבים שאון קולם נפץ זרם להשחית רבים

> 1QH 10:27: And like the roar of the deep waters is the sound of their voice, torrents of rain for the destruction of many.[109]

Considering *stages* and *linear sequence*, some evidence suggests that stages of downward cosmological descent, and vertical closeness to the lowest point, Sheol, are mapped to a sequence of worsening distress

---

106. Kittel, *Hymns*, 59.
107. See section 2.5.2.d.
108. Brown, *Seeing*, 114.
109. Translation based on Kittel, *Hymns*, 35.

Distress and the Verticality Schema

and "closeness" to the final stage, death. For example, the writer positions himself with those "descending" to the pit or Sheol (יוֹרְדֵי בוֹר in Pss 28:1; 88:4[5]; and 30:3[4], cited above; יורדי שאול in 1QH 16:28, cited above). A trajectory towards Sheol is also visible where the petitioner is "near" ("touching," נגע) Sheol or death (Ps 88:3[4]; 1QH 14:24). In Isa 38:10, Hezekiah considers himself "deposited" by God in the "gates of Sheol," marking "the threshold between life and death. Once one has crossed this ultimate bourne there is no returning to the land of the living."[110] Using this image allows the inference that Hezekiah is as near as he could be, yet not quite locked in for good.

פֶּן־תֶּחֱשֶׁה מִמֶּנִּי וְנִמְשַׁלְתִּי עִם־יוֹרְדֵי בוֹר׃

Ps 28:1: For if you are silent to me, I shall be like those who go down to the Pit.

נֶחְשַׁבְתִּי עִם־יוֹרְדֵי בוֹר הָיִיתִי כְּגֶבֶר אֵין־אֱיָל׃

Ps 88:4[5]: I am counted among those who go down to the Pit; I am like those who have no help.

כִּי־שָׂבְעָה בְרָעוֹת נַפְשִׁי וְחַיַּי לִשְׁאוֹל הִגִּיעוּ׃

Ps 88:3[4]: For my soul is full of troubles, and my life draws near to Sheol.

תהום לאנחתי ונ[פשי תגיע] עד שערי מות

1QH 14:24 The deep thunders at my sigh, [my] so[ul nears] the gates of death.

בְּשַׁעֲרֵי שְׁאוֹל פֻּקַּדְתִּי יֶתֶר שְׁנוֹתָי׃

Isa 38:10: I am consigned to the gates of Sheol for the rest of my years.

However, since the only indication of a downward trajectory occurs in the fixed idiom יוֹרְדֵי בוֹר, the "path" part of the mapping is not as elaborated as in English, where verbs like *spiraling, nose-diving,*

---

110. Barré, *Lord*, 75.

crashing, sinking, going downhill, and *plunging* elaborate the manner of worsening emotional distress.

These mappings can be summarized as follows:

Position low on geographical scale (pit, Sheol, mighty waters)	→	Situation of distress (sickness, opposition)
Person in low position	→	Person in distress
(Agentive) cause of being low (God, hunters)	→	(Agentive) cause of distress (God, opponents)
Perceptual experience in low place (crashing waters, darkness)	→	Perceptual experience of distress (taunts of opponents)
(Vertical) proximity to Sheol	→	Likelihood of distress situation resulting in death

These mappings also have several explicit entailments. First, if distress is being low, *relief* becomes movement upwards. Psalms 40:2[3] and 30:3[4] (cited above), and 1QH 11:20 use עלה. Psalm 9:13[14] uses רום, another general root, whereas Ps 18:16[17] uses משׁה (only used elsewhere for drawing Moses up from the water), and Ps 30:1[2] uses דלה, prototypically used for drawing water from a well.

וַיַּעֲלֵנִי מִבּוֹר שָׁאוֹן מִטִּיט הַיָּוֵן

Ps 40:2[3]: He drew me up from the pit of tumult, out of the miry bog.

אודכה אדוני כי פדיתה נפשי משחת ומשאול אבדון 20
העליתני לרום עולם

1QH 11:19–20: I thank you, Lord, because you have saved my life from the pit, and from the Sheol of Abaddon have lifted me up to an everlasting height.

מְרוֹמְמִי מִשַּׁעֲרֵי מָוֶת׃

Ps 9:13[14]: You are the one who lifts me up from the gates of death.

יִשְׁלַח מִמָּרוֹם יִקָּחֵנִי יַמְשֵׁנִי מִמַּיִם רַבִּים:

Ps 18:16[17]: He reached down from on high, he took me; he drew me out of mighty waters.

אֲרוֹמִמְךָ יְהוָה כִּי דִלִּיתָנִי

Ps 30:1[2]: I will extol you, O LORD, for you have drawn me up.

Further, any help in distress comes from above, as in Ps 144:7 and Isa 38:14.

שְׁלַח יָדֶיךָ מִמָּרוֹם פְּצֵנִי וְהַצִּילֵנִי מִמַּיִם רַבִּים מִיַּד בְּנֵי נֵכָר:

Ps 144:7: Stretch out your hand from on high; set me free and rescue me from the deep[111] waters, from the hand of aliens.

דַּלּוּ עֵינַי לַמָּרוֹם

Isa 38:14: My eyes are weary with looking upwards.

Second, gravity means descending bodies continue falling if nothing supports them and no one pulls them up. This entailment is used when writers seek help to prevent them descending to the pit. In Ps 28:1 and 143:7, God must answer (quickly) otherwise the psalmist will descend, whereas in Ps 88:4[5] the lack of help means the psalmist is descending.

פֶּן־תֶּחֱשֶׁה מִמֶּנִּי וְנִמְשַׁלְתִּי עִם־יוֹרְדֵי בוֹר:

Ps 28:1: If you are silent to me, I shall be like those who go down to the Pit.

מַהֵר עֲנֵנִי יְהוָה כָּלְתָה רוּחִי אַל־תַּסְתֵּר פָּנֶיךָ מִמֶּנִּי וְנִמְשַׁלְתִּי עִם־יוֹרְדֵי בוֹר:

Ps 143:7: Answer me quickly, O LORD; my spirit fails. Do not hide your face from me, or I shall be like those who go down to the Pit.

נֶחְשַׁבְתִּי עִם־יוֹרְדֵי בוֹר הָיִיתִי כְּגֶבֶר אֵין־אֱיָל:

---

111. NRSV has "mighty" here.

> Ps 88:4[5]: I am counted among those who go down to the Pit; I am like those who have no help.

Third, pleading for quick action uses experiences where the longer the time spent descending, the deeper something becomes. Thus, the distance down highlights the duration of distress. Combined with the above mapping from depth to intensity of distress, the longer a situation goes on without God's involvement, the deeper a person goes, and thus the more serious the situation.

The most sustained descent metaphor is in Jonah 2, fitting neatly with the unique narrative context. Many of the conventional mappings and entailments mentioned above are apparent: existence in a variety of low positions (הָאָרֶץ, קִצְבֵי הָרִים, לְבַב יַמִּים, מְצוּלָה, בֶּטֶן שְׁאוֹל, בְּרִחֶיהָ בַעֲדִי לְעוֹלָם) describes the distressing situation; the agent causing lowness on the scale (God) is the agent causing distress; and movement upward is relief from distress (עלה). Further, descent to deeper locations represents an increasingly intense situation, so that "the narrator made use of the fish episode and the spatial dimensions attached to it to depict the nature and depth of the experience Jonah suffered."[112] That so many conventional mappings and entailments are present shows the narrative artistry here, integrating conventional mappings of distress with Jonah's personal plight.

קָרָאתִי מִצָּרָה לִי אֶל־יְהוָה וַיַּעֲנֵנִי מִבֶּטֶן שְׁאוֹל שִׁוַּעְתִּי שָׁמַעְתָּ קוֹלִי: וַתַּשְׁלִיכֵנִי מְצוּלָה בִּלְבַב יַמִּים וְנָהָר יְסֹבְבֵנִי כָּל־מִשְׁבָּרֶיךָ וְגַלֶּיךָ עָלַי עָבָרוּ: אֲפָפוּנִי מַיִם עַד־נֶפֶשׁ תְּהוֹם יְסֹבְבֵנִי סוּף חָבוּשׁ לְרֹאשִׁי: לְקִצְבֵי הָרִים יָרַדְתִּי הָאָרֶץ בְּרִחֶיהָ בַעֲדִי לְעוֹלָם וַתַּעַל מִשַּׁחַת חַיַּי יְהוָה אֱלֹהָי:

> Jon 2:2–5[3–6]: I called to the LORD out of my distress, and he answered me; out of the belly of Sheol I cried, and you heard my voice. You cast me into the deep, into the heart of the seas, and the flood surrounded me; all your waves and your billows passed over me. The waters closed in over me; the deep surrounded me; weeds were wrapped around my head at the roots of the mountains. I went down to the land whose bars closed upon me forever; yet you brought up my life from the Pit, O LORD my God.

112. Nel, "Symbolism," 222.

Distress and the Verticality Schema

To conclude this section, the relation to previous studies needs brief consideration. Several scholars (including Pedersen,[113] Barth,[114] Tromp,[115] and Johnston[116]) use the verses considered in this section to relate distressing experiences and death experiences. Knibb summarizes Pedersen, Barth, and Tromp as arguing that "any impairment, or threat to, life is a form of death."[117] These scholars generally took as many linguistic metaphors as possible as describing death experiences, whether being surrounded by water, sinking in mud, or being in the earth's depths. Debate has focused on how "real" the experience of death was. Pedersen's ideas about "totalities" meant such language implied a real and total experience of death, since it is not life.[118] Barth similarly thought it mistaken to interpret lament language as metaphorical. Rather, the experience of death for the distressed individual is real. Even proximity to death is "counted as a real experience of death."[119] However, it is only partial, because he still has hope whereas the dead man does not.[120] For Tromp, such language reflects real experience of death, so that "deadly peril is experienced as real death, partial death as total death."[121] Johnston is more balanced, agreeing that "any illness or misfortune is a partial experience of death's power and of underworld conditions,"[122] but arguing such restriction of life cannot be considered "real death," and that such expressions should not be taken literally.

This analysis differs by not conflating all subterranean localities into references to death, assuming that the VERTICALITY schema is more psychologically basic (an embodied experience from birth) than the complex concept of death (which itself needs conceptual metaphors to be understood). These verses then instantiate the conceptual

---

113. Pedersen, *Israel*.
114. Barth, *Errettung*.
115. Tromp, *Conceptions*.
116. Johnston, *Shades*.
117. Knibb, "Life," 400.
118. Pedersen, *Israel*, 466.
119. Barth, *Errettung*, 111, cited in Johnston, *Shades*, 91.
120. Barth's views cited in Knibb, "Life," 407.
121. Tromp, *Conceptions*, 138.
122. Johnston, *Shades*, 97.

metaphor BEING IN DISTRESS IS BEING IN A LOW PLACE, being a useful, structured metaphor for understanding distressing experiences. Thus, it is not "mere" metaphor or poetic ornamentation. The conceptualization is "real" in constraining inferences about the situation, but, as Johnston notes, to insist on the dichotomy "that Israelites were either fully alive or actually experiencing Sheol is to deny the wide range of human experience, or at least deny Israelite awareness of it."[123]

Rather, descent provides a way to understand distressing experiences, and draw meaningful inferences. For example, understanding distress as a cosmological descent away from God to deep places, increasing the separation between the sufferer and God, provides a way for understanding situations where God does not appear to be acting as he should to preserve life. Further, this problematization of the situation directs the psalmist to particular actions.[124] For example, conceptualizing distress as involuntarily succumbing to the force of gravity highlights the inability to do anything oneself and directs the psalmist to look "upward," to God who can "rescue" him, and hence the writing of the psalm itself.

5.4.2. BEING IN DISTRESS IS BEING DOWN ON THE POSTURAL SCALE

Posturally, the basic mapping is BEING IN DISTRESS IS BEING LOW ON THE POSTURAL SCALE. There is potentially a physiological metonymic motivation here, in the involuntary "downward" position of head, face, shoulders, and hands characteristic of sadness, listlessness, or depression.[125] However, postures adopted for prayer complement this downward movement, complicating the separation of linguistic expressions describing the psalmist's actual posture in prayer from idiomatic expressions no longer having physical ties. For example, דָּבְקָה לָאָרֶץ בִּטְנֵנוּ (Ps 44:25[26]) could describe a lament ritual, ly-

---

123. Johnston, *Shades*, 97.

124. See Reddy, "Conduit," for the way conceptual metaphors problematize situations and suggest solutions.

125. Kruger, "Depression," 187.

ing on the ground "to manifest distress in order to establish a request."[126] Alternatively, it could be idiomatic, understood as "our body is stuck in the netherworld."[127] However, given that a physical act still instantiates a conceptual metaphor (albeit non-verbally), all such expressions were included as potential data.

Most generally, a person (or part of a person) in low posture maps onto the person in distress, demonstrated first using forms from שחח, שוח, or שיח. In Ps 38:6[7], the initial verb derives from עוה, prototypically referencing something bent or twisted,[128] showing some elaboration of this schema.

מַה־תִּשְׁתּוֹחֲחִי נַפְשִׁי וַתֶּהֱמִי עָלָי הוֹחִילִי לֵאלֹהִים כִּי־עוֹד אוֹדֶנּוּ יְשׁוּעוֹת פָּנָיו: אֱלֹהַי עָלַי נַפְשִׁי תִשְׁתּוֹחָח

Ps 42:5–6[6–7]: Why are you cast down, O my soul, and why are you disquieted within me? Hope in God; for I shall again praise him, my help and my God. My soul is cast down within me . . .

זָכוֹר תִּזְכּוֹר וְתָשׁוֹחַ עָלַי נַפְשִׁי:

Lam 3:20: My soul continually thinks of it and is bowed down within me.

כִּי שָׁחָה לֶעָפָר נַפְשֵׁנוּ דָּבְקָה לָאָרֶץ בִּטְנֵנוּ:

Ps 44:25[26]: For we have been prostrated in the dust, our belly clings to the earth.[129]

נַעֲוֵיתִי שַׁחֹתִי עַד־מְאֹד כָּל־הַיּוֹם קֹדֵר הִלָּכְתִּי:

Ps 38:6[7]: I am utterly bowed down and prostrate; all day long I go around mourning.

Mostly, the petitioner's נֶפֶשׁ is in low posture, best understood here as a person's "vitality."[130] Further, use of נֶפֶשׁ frequently suggests

---

126. Keel, *Symbolism*, 319–20.
127. Tromp, *Conceptions*, 36.
128. Schultz, "עוה."
129. Craigie, *Psalms 1–50*, 330.
130. Johnson, *Vitality*, 8–11.

that "humans have a relationship with themselves,"[131] as in Psalm 42, where the petitioner addresses his נֶפֶשׁ, but also uses עָלַי. Elsewhere, individuals lift up (נשׂא) their נֶפֶשׁ, again distinguishing the נֶפֶשׁ from other volitional parts of the self, and reflecting a positive emotional and volitional attitude toward something.[132] This demonstrates a positive emotional state for the up-pole for the נֶפֶשׁ, contrasting with the negative state for the down-pole.

Sometimes, more specific roots for "low" posture occur. כפף (prototypically describing a bowed head) describes the נֶפֶשׁ in Ps 57:6[7], whereas in Pss 119:25 and 44:25[26] (cited above) the verb דבק evokes a much lower posture, "stuck" to the ground.

כָּפַף נַפְשִׁי

Ps 57:6[7]: My soul was bowed down.

דָּבְקָה לֶעָפָר נַפְשִׁי

Ps 119:25: My soul clings to the dust.

These examples, alongside Cain's face falling and Elijah putting his face between his knees on Carmel, lead Kruger to conclude that "the feeling of depression most often finds expression in the Hebrew Bible in a definite "downward" bodily posture."[133] Certainly these examples associate negative emotional experience with the down pole on the postural scale, but such experience is not necessarily best understood as "depression" (particularly with the narrative examples cited), nor is this necessarily the schema used "most often" to conceptualize such experiences.

Forms from דלל also possibly belong here. Fabry argues the verb "essentially reflects its original, etymological meaning, 'to be/become lowly, small,'"[134] being used for the diminishing streams of Egypt in Isa 19:5.

131. Seebass, "נֶפֶשׁ," 510.
132. Ibid., 507.
133. Kruger, "Face," 660.
134. Fabry, "דַּל," 229.

Distress and the Verticality Schema

שָׁמֵר פְּתָאיִם יְהוָה דַּלּוֹתִי וְלִי יְהוֹשִׁיעַ׃

Ps 116:6: The LORD protects the simple; when I was brought low, he saved me.

הַקְשִׁיבָה אֶל־רִנָּתִי כִּי־דַלּוֹתִי מְאֹד

Ps 142:6[7]: Give heed to my cry, for I am brought very low.

מַהֵר יְקַדְּמוּנוּ רַחֲמֶיךָ כִּי דַלּוֹנוּ מְאֹד׃

Ps 79:8: Let your compassion come speedily to meet us, for we are brought very low.

These verses also demonstrate lower physical posture entailing greater distress. First, the modifier מְאֹד deepens the low posture to strengthen the cry of distress, with דלה in Ps 142:6[7], and שחח in Ps 38:6[7]. Second, the variety of verbs suggests this entailment, with כָּפַף נַפְשִׁי in Ps 57:6[7] reflecting less intense distress than דָּבְקָה לָאָרֶץ בִּטְנֵנוּ in Ps 44:25[26].

Other verses map non-volitional downward movement onto entering a state of distress.

כִּי הִצַּלְתָּ נַפְשִׁי מִמָּוֶת הֲלֹא רַגְלַי מִדֶּחִי

Ps 56:13[14]: For you have delivered my soul from death, and my feet from falling.

כִּי־אָמַרְתִּי פֶּן־יִשְׂמְחוּ־לִי בְּמוֹט רַגְלִי עָלַי הִגְדִּילוּ׃ כִּי־אֲנִי לְצֶלַע נָכוֹן וּמַכְאוֹבִי נֶגְדִּי תָמִיד׃

Ps 38:16–17[17–18]: For I pray, "Only do not let them rejoice over me, those who boast against me when my foot slips." For I am ready to fall, and my pain is ever with me.

This mapping also allows the entailment (shown in Ps 37:24) that the further one falls, the greater the distress, so that stumbling is less severe than falling flat on the ground.

כִּי־יִפֹּל לֹא־יוּטָל כִּי־יְהוָה סוֹמֵךְ יָדוֹ׃

Ps 37:24: If he falls, he won't fall flat on his face, for the LORD is holding his hand.[135]

---

135. Craigie, *Psalms 1–50*, 295.

As with the spatial scale, the *agent* causing a low position maps to the agent causing distress, whether God (Lam 3:16; Job 30:19; Ps 22:15[16]) or human "enemies" (Pss 143:3; 7:5[6]; 17:11; and 1QH 17:8–9).

וַיַּגְרֵס בֶּחָצָץ שִׁנָּי הִכְפִּישַׁנִי בָּאֵפֶר׃

Lam 3:16: He has made my teeth grind on gravel, and made me cower in ashes;

הֹרָנִי לַחֹמֶר

Job 30:19: He has cast me into the mire.

וְלַעֲפַר־מָוֶת תִּשְׁפְּתֵנִי׃

Ps 22:15[16]: You lay me in the dust of death.

כִּי רָדַף אוֹיֵב נַפְשִׁי דִּכָּא לָאָרֶץ חַיָּתִי

Ps 143:3: For the enemy has pursued me, crushing my life to the ground.

יִרַדֹּף אוֹיֵב נַפְשִׁי וְיַשֵּׂג וְיִרְמֹס לָאָרֶץ חַיָּי וּכְבוֹדִי לֶעָפָר יַשְׁכֵּן׃

Ps 7:5[6]: Then let the enemy pursue and overtake me, trample my life to the ground, and lay my soul in the dust.

עֵינֵיהֶם יָשִׁיתוּ לִנְטוֹת בָּאָרֶץ׃

Ps 17:11: They set their eyes to cast me to the ground.[136]

ואשיבה למבלעי דבר 9 ולמשתוחיחי בי תוכחת

1QH 17:8–9: I can give a reply to those who wish to devour me and a rebuke to those who wish to cast me down.

Restoration to an erect posture then describes rescue from distress, or the ability to withstand it, although more common in third person references (God raising those who are bowed down) than in the spe-

---

136. Basson, *Divine*, 88.

cific corpus. Psalm 119:28 is a rare individual example, and Ps 20:8[9] is communal.

דָּלְפָה נַפְשִׁי מִתּוּגָה קַיְּמֵנִי כִּדְבָרֶךָ:

Ps 119:28: I have collapsed with intense sorrow: make me stand upright as your word promises.[137]

הֵמָּה כָּרְעוּ וְנָפָלוּ וַאֲנַחְנוּ קַּמְנוּ וַנִּתְעוֹדָד:

Ps 20:8[9] They will collapse and fall, but we shall rise and stand upright.

The third-person references use a wider range of verbs for God's action in keeping someone erect, including סָמַךְ (support), זָקַף (lift up), עוֹד (restore[138]), רוּם (raise) and קוּם (make erect).

סוֹמֵךְ יְהוָה לְכָל־הַנֹּפְלִים וְזוֹקֵף לְכָל־הַכְּפוּפִים:

Ps 145:14: The LORD upholds all who are falling, and raises up all who are bowed down.

יְהוָה זֹקֵף כְּפוּפִים:

Ps 146:8: The LORD lifts up those who are bowed down.

מְעוֹדֵד עֲנָוִים יְהוָה מַשְׁפִּיל רְשָׁעִים עֲדֵי־אָרֶץ:

Ps 147:6: The LORD lifts up the downtrodden; he casts the wicked to the ground.

מְקִימִי מֵעָפָר דָּל מֵאַשְׁפֹּת יָרִים אֶבְיוֹן:

Ps 113:7: He raises the poor from the dust, and lifts the needy from the ash heap.

---

137. Allen, *Psalms 101–150*, 127.

138. This verb does not necessarily imply erect posture (BDB 729), but the contrast with לְפֹשׁ in the second colon brings the up-down orientation into focus.

ונותן לנמוגי ברכים חזוק מעמד 7 ואמוץ מתנים לשכם מכים

1QM 14:6–7: Those with knocking knees he gives strength to stand upright, and vigor of loins to broken backs.

These mappings and entailments can be summarized as follows:

Position low on postural scale (bowed, prostrate, low)	→	Situation of distress
Person in low posture	→	Person in distress
Agentive cause of low posture (God, enemies)	→	Agentive cause of distress (God, opponents)
Adopting low posture (falling, stumbling, being pushed)	→	Entering state of distress
Returning to upright posture	→	Relief from distress

Entailments:
The lower the posture the more intense the distress.

5.5. Further Evidence

Having presented these texts, what evidence suggests they indeed represent significant conceptual metaphors? Lakoff and Johnson's criteria (section 2.5.1.e) are investigated below.

5.5.1. Generalizations over Polysemy

Generalizations over polysemy show how well elaborated a conceptual metaphor is by different expressions, with several words being used in the same two distinct domains suggesting significant conceptual integration. The best examples here are words describing relief from distress. All the following roots describe an upward trajectory, whether spatial-geographic or postural, and also describe relief from distress: עלה ('go up,' Ps 40:2[3]), רום ('raise,' Ps 9:13[14]), משה ('draw up,' Ps 18:16[17]), דלה ('pull up,' Ps 30:1[2]), קום ('make erect,' Ps 119:28). This variety demonstrates an entrenched mapping from upward movement to relief from distress, and thus also from being low to being in distress.

Distress and the Verticality Schema

By comparison, the downward trajectory is less elaborated. Only ירד indicates a significant downward trajectory on the spatial scale, and this only in fixed expressions. The postural scale is more elaborated, with נפל 'fall,' צלע 'stumble,' דכא 'press down,' and נטה 'thrust down'—all describing downward trajectories, whether forced or unforced.

Nouns used for low locations form a larger set than verbs of descent, including בּוֹר, שַׁחַת, מַעֲמַקִּים, מְצוּלָה, מַיִם רַבִּים, and שְׁאוֹל. Similarly, many roots for low postural states are used, including שׁחח, דלה, דבק, כרע, כפף.

This variety of verbs and nouns demonstrates the entrenchment and conventionality of BEING IN DISTRESS IS BEING DOWN ON THE VERTICAL SCALE. Different writers can utilize this metaphor in different ways and still be understood. Further, it guides the problematization of distress and thus the inferences for how to resolve it. In this sense, the composers of these petitions "thought of" distress as being in a low place from which they desired to be raised up.

5.5.2. Generalizations over Inference Patterns

Next, generalizations over inference patterns, here generalizing over both sub-schemas, demonstrate common inferential structure. First, on both scales, mapping low position to distress leads to the inference that relief is movement upwards, whether spatially from water, from a well, or to higher ground, or posturally, being raised up, or made to stand erect.

Second, both scales develop the inference that greater "depth" implies more intense distress. For the spatial scale, adjectives denoting depth added to the petitioner's description of his locality intensified his plight. Posturally, the modifier מְאֹד was added to a low postural state. Both of these show the source domain being actively used, as well as demonstrating a common entailment.

5.5.3. Novel Metaphor

The third kind of evidence comes from the common use of conceptual metaphors in both conventional idioms and novel metaphors, showing active use of the source domain. Two idioms of emotional distress from prose contexts are given below, showing that the VERTICALITY schema is used in both conventional and more novel language.

First, when Cain saw God's response to his offering, Gen 4:5 says וַיִּחַר לְקַיִן מְאֹד וַיִּפְּלוּ פָּנָיו (literally, 'it was very hot to Cain and his face fell'), describing his emotional response. Whether this is more accurately a state of anger, depression,[139] or some more general hot, negative emotion, the use of the verb נפל for entering a state of physical and emotional distress links this idiom to the VERTICALITY schema.

Second, in Josh 2:11, Rahab explains the emotional impact of the Israelites' progress as וְלֹא־קָמָה עוֹד רוּחַ בְּאִישׁ מִפְּנֵיכֶם, describing spirits that no longer "stood." Here, קום, associated with the postural VERTICALITY scale, is used with רוּחַ, describing an emotion something like fear, given the collocation with hearts melting in the previous phrase. Again this conventional idiom associates the VERTICALITY schema, and particularly the down pole, with a negative emotion.

Neither of these idioms is explicitly developed in the specific corpus, though they cohere together. The most conventional collocations within the specific corpus are the association of שחח with נֶפֶשׁ and the idiom יוֹרְדֵי בוֹר, both occurring several times. Conversely, the description in Ps 40:2[3] is more novel, using several unusual collocations (בּוֹר שָׁאוֹן, טִיט הַיָּוֵן) to create a vivid image, yet it too describes a situation of physical and emotional distress using the VERTICALITY schema. There are very few uses in Job, but the one occurrence in Job 30:19 (הֹרָנִי לַחֹמֶר) uses two words found nowhere else in the specific corpus, suggesting novelty.

Thus, the VERTICALITY schema was used in conventional idioms and more novel poetry, suggesting authors could actively utilize the conventional source domain to create new expressions in distress.

5.5.4. Larger Scale Metaphorical Systems

Further evidence comes from coherent larger scale metaphorical systems. First, the most obvious such system is the conceptualization of

---

139. According to Kruger, "Depression," 190; and Gruber, "Cain," but the characteristic lethargy and inaction of English depression certainly does not fit here.

death, which is also "down." Since death is the ultimate distress, it being down coheres with metaphors that place any distress down on the VERTICAL scale.

Second, Egypt is consistently "down." Egyptian bondage and subsequent salvation is the most stereotypical relief from distress within the biblical cultural memory, and is framed as upward movement in Exod 3:17; 13:18; 32:7; Deut 20:1; Judg 6:8; 1 Sam 10:18; 1 Kgs 12:28; 2 Kgs 17:7; Neh 9:18; Ps 81:11; Jer 2:6; Hos 2:17; Amos 2:10; and Mic 6:4. For example, 2 Kgs 17:7 has הַמַּעֲלֶה אֹתָם מֵאֶרֶץ מִצְרַיִם מִתַּחַת יַד פַּרְעֹה מֶלֶךְ־מִצְרָיִם ('who brought them up from the land of Egypt, from under the hand of Pharaoh, king of Egypt'). Such examples cohere with conceptualizing any relief from distress as upward movement.

The exiles' return is also sometimes framed this way, again mapping distress to being down, relief to movement upwards, in the wider conceptual system. For example, Neh 7:6 has אֵלֶּה בְּנֵי הַמְּדִינָה הָעֹלִים מִשְּׁבִי הַגּוֹלָה, 'these are the people of the province who came up out of the captivity of the exiles'.

Thus, both conceptualizing death as "down," and the cultural memory of "upward" rescue from Egypt provide larger metaphorical systems that cohere with, and help consolidate, the metaphor that being in distress is being "down," relief is movement upwards.

5.5.5. Non-verbal Realizations

Finally, non-verbal realizations may reflect conceptual metaphors, accessible through written records of non-verbal communication, particularly here of "low" postures in distress.

For example, Kruger takes Elijah's posture on Mount Carmel as "expressive of a mood of depression."[140] First Kings 18:42 reads וַיִּגְהַר אַרְצָה וַיָּשֶׂם פָּנָיו בֵּין בִּרְכָּיו 'he bowed himself down upon the earth and put his face between his knees.' Also, in the Ugaritic Baal Cycle, the emotional response to Yammu's threat is that "the gods lower their heads onto their knees, upon their princely thrones" (i.22).[141] Both times, a low posture of the head reflects emotional distress, whichever

140. Kruger, "Depression," 190.
141. Hallo and Younger, *COS* I, 246.

precise emotion it signifies. A final non-verbal example comes from people "sitting" in distress. Kruger particularly identifies references to people "sitting" in Lamentations, both figuratively and literally, arguing that "in almost every chapter this rings like a refrain."[142] Thus, in addition to postures mentioned earlier, various non-verbal communicative acts associated with the "down" pole of the VERTICALITY schema signal emotional distress.

These five strands of evidence strongly support the cognitive reality of a conceptual map between experiences of being down and experiences of emotional and physical distress.

5.6. Universality and Variation

Finally, the way this schema conceptualizes negative emotional states in Hebrew can be contrasted with English (using Kövecses' parameters, section 2.5.7.d), to demonstrate both universality and variation across cultural conceptualizations.

5.6.1. Variation within Source and Target Domain

First, both English and Classical Hebrew conceptualize negative experiences with the VERTICALITY schema. However, as Kövecses noted, cultures may prefer different conceptualizations for similar experiences. Whereas for English the VERTICALITY scale subsumes 90% of the linguistic expressions of depression, in Hebrew, FORCE schemas are much more significant. Out of 489 tokens in the database, 81 reflected the VERTICALITY schema, whereas 207 used the FORCE schema.

Second, the target domains differ somewhat for the conceptual metaphors compared here. English metaphors for "depression" can be compared with Hebrew metaphors of "distress" as both cover situations of negative emotion. However, the overlap is incomplete. In English, depression relates to sadness, lasts a long time, easily gets worse, and is hard to recover from. The Hebrew "distress" domain includes physical conditions alongside emotion, and includes elements of both fear and

---

142. Kruger, "Depression," 191.

Distress and the Verticality Schema

activity (such as calling out to God) typically absent from "depression." Yet the VERTICALITY schema means this target domain is also construed as something that goes on a long time, worsens as it does so, and is hard (if not impossible) for the sufferer to recover from alone.

Considering the source domain, the cultural prototypes for being low also differ between English and Hebrew. The prototypical Hebrew low place is the בּוֹר, salient for inhabitants of ancient Israel, yet totally alien to most English people. The real danger of falling into a cistern and the impossibility of getting out on one's own creates different entailments from the prototypical "pit" for most English speakers, from which one may be able to climb out.[143] Further, although English conceptualizations include "catacombs," or "going through hell," the shadowy subterranean world of the dead and turbulent waters are not accessible. In Hebrew, the presumed noise of the subterranean waters is available to highlight the mocking of companions more than in typical English expressions.

Sheol as a prototypical low place also makes the Hebrew metaphors more appropriate for life-threatening situations. In English, someone *plunging into the depths, spiraling down* or *in the pits* rarely describes a threat to their existence, just some kind of depressive emotion. In Hebrew, descent metaphors indicate closeness to Sheol, suggesting death is a distinct possibility, also seen from contextual parallels with מות.

Third, entailments of mappings may differ. Greater depth reflects greater intensity of distress in English and Hebrew. However, the "relief" entailments differ. In English, the entailment that moving upwards is harder than moving downwards means sufferers have to hit *rock bottom* and then try to *climb out*, or *get back up again* after being *knocked down*. That is, prototypically, relief requires the individual making their own, difficult ascent. Conversely, the Hebrew corpus never refers to making one's own ascent, on either the postural or spatial scale. Rather, God always raises the petitioner, and the verbs never suggest difficulty. This is entailed by the different cultural prototypes for low places. In Hebrew, people cannot rescue themselves from the prototypes of cistern or sea. This difference is also symptomatic of the difference in worldview from

---

143. Although the concept of a "pit" is probably not very well defined.

a largely secular Western ethnopsychology, and a Hebrew worldview in which the activity of God was unquestioned.

5.6.2. Variation in Linguistic Expression

Considering linguistic expressions, first, Kövecses notes that certain *parts* of a conceptual metaphor may be more elaborated linguistically in one language than another. Here, the downward trajectory is elaborated in English whereas the place that is down is elaborated in Hebrew. Thus, English uses many verbs evoking downward trajectories to conceptualize increasing emotional distress. All of these, like *plunging, plummeting, spiraling,* and *nose-diving,* imply an external uncontrollable force, and elaborate different manners (such as speed) of descent. The sole Hebrew word (ירד) does not imply an external force, and has no implications for the manner of descent. Conversely, the various Hebrew words for low places, like שַׁחַת, בּוֹר, שְׁאוֹל, תְּהוֹם, or מַיִם רַבִּים show significant elaboration of this part of the mapping in Hebrew, allowing inferences about danger and deliberate causation.

Second, *degree of conventionalization* of linguistic expressions may vary. As the VERTICALITY schema rarely expresses distress in narrative Hebrew texts, it is presumably a less conventional mapping than in English. This is further supported by their being few identical phrases within this corpus. The next chapter contrasts this with the more conventionalized CONSTRAINT schema, with common lexical items in narrative texts accessing this schema.

Finally, syntactic expression may vary. In English, many single words access this VERTICALITY schema when used in situations of emotional distress, such as "down," "low," "collapse," "spiral," or "nosedive." In Hebrew, conversely, it is more common for the schema to be referenced through multiword phrases, as in מִבּוֹר תַּחְתִּיּוֹת or תִּשְׁתּוֹחֲחִי נַפְשִׁי, or more complex syntactic constructions as in דָּבְקָה לֶעָפָר נַפְשִׁי, or וּמִתְּהֹמוֹת הָאָרֶץ תָּשׁוּב תַּעֲלֵנִי.

5.7. Summary

In summary, negative experience is partially understood within this corpus as movement up and down, or position upon, a vertical scale. Perceptual bodily experiences of being low are certainly used to help understand distressing experiences. The most highlighted parts of this mapping are that the experience of distress is being in a place or posture low on the VERTICALITY scale, and that relief from such a situation is therefore being raised up on the scale.

Further, "up is good" and "down is bad" is the prevalent valuation for the VERTICALITY schema in Hebrew, at least for this corpus of distress language. However, this VERTICALITY schema is less significant for conceptualizing feelings of distress than in English. It mainly surfaces in conceptualizations of distressing experiences as part of the descent into the underworld and in descriptions that can be tied to bodily posture. Actual movement up and down is not as significant in Hebrew as other schemas for understanding distress.

Our prioritization of the VERTICALITY schema in English makes some examples appear more salient than they warrant, whilst at other times the use of particular English translations makes the schema appear more significant. For example, metaphors translated as "sinking in the mud" are likely more about being "stuck" than a downward trajectory. Similarly, the main meaning focus in references to pits and water may be more the inability to escape than their low position. It is precisely such metaphors of constraint and confinement that the next chapter considers.

6

Distress and the CONSTRAINT Schema

"You, my God, have opened a broad space in my heart,
but they have increased the narrowness and have wrapped me in darkness."
—1QH 13:32–33

6.1. Introduction

This chapter starts investigating how FORCE schemas conceptualize situations of distress. FORCE schemas are very significant, subsuming over 50 percent of the database examples, and are therefore split into two categories. This chapter investigates the first category: a CONSTRAINT schema where the petitioner sees himself as an Agonist with a force tendency toward movement, surrounded by an Antagonist restricting that freedom, instantiated as ropes, waves, bars, mud, nets, or traps. This chapter argues that this schema forms a natural cognitive category for Classical Hebrew speakers, shown in the way Hebrew lexicalizes this schema and the variety of images it schematizes.

Goldingay notes the importance for distress discourse, writing that "a negative event is often experienced as one of constraint and confine-

Distress and the Constraint Schema

ment, like imprisonment,"[1] as does Fabry, observing that all uses of צַר "involve situations of being in unpleasant "straits," a sense of having no saving access to "expanse," of stricture necessarily implying anxiety and oppressiveness prompted by a hopeless situation."[2] Similarly, Eidevall notes that "width, or open space, stands for health and freedom // narrowness, or confinement, means suffering and oppression."[3] This chapter expands these statements, showing the frequency and variety of images instantiating this schema.

The first step is to establish the existence and nature of the CONSTRAINT schema, then some cross-cultural comparisons will be offered, before presenting and analyzing the mappings from this schema to situations of distress. Following this, supporting evidence for the conceptual metaphor is offered, before, finally, both universal and culturally varying aspects of the metaphor are suggested.

6.2. Establishing the Schema

6.2.1. Physiological / Universal Factors

This CONSTRAINT schema is very culturally constrained, being a recurring pattern of experience that is made salient in Hebrew through the lexicon (for example, the variety of senses of the root צרר). It is striking that no English gloss highlights the same pattern. *Enclosure, containment,* or *constraint* come closest. Nevertheless, FORCE and CONTAINMENT schemas offer potentially universal comparisons to this schema from the Cognitive Linguistic literature, which includes both being forcefully held and contained. These universal schemas are considered in turn.

First, Talmy argues that experiencing FORCE is a fundamental human universal. His linguistic "force dynamics" were introduced in section 2.5.3. This schema represents the scenario where the "Agonist has a tendency toward motion, the Antagonist is . . . stronger and so effectively *blocks* it," and "the Agonist is kept in place."[4] This FORCE schema

---

1. Goldingay, *Psalms I*, 267.
2. Fabry, "צַר I," 459.
3. Eidevall, "Spatial," 134.
4. Talmy, *Semantics*, 415.

is represented below. The circle represents the Agonist, the arrow shows its force tendency to movement, and the plus sign that the Antagonist is stronger. The line and circle underneath show the resultant state of rest.

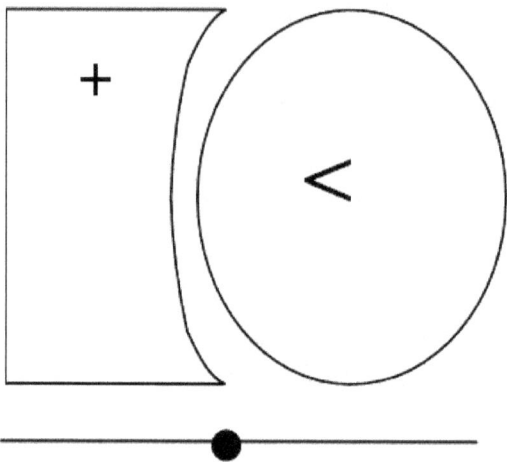

Figure 6.1: Taken from *Toward a Cognitive Semantics: Concept Structuring Systems*, by Leonard Talmy (Cambridge, MA: MIT Press)

For Johnson, this "blockage" schema is a common experiential FORCE structure, grounded in everyday encounters with obstacles that block our way, and learned from early infancy onwards.[5]

Second, the CONTAINMENT schema is also frequently discussed. Johnson writes that

> Our encounter with containment and boundedness is one of the most pervasive features of our bodily experience. We are intimately aware of our bodies as three-dimensional containers into which we put certain things (food, water, air) and out of which other things emerge (food and water wastes, air, blood, etc.). From the beginning, we experience constant physical containment in our surroundings (those things that envelop us). We move in and out of rooms, clothes, vehicles, and numerous kinds of bounded

---

5. Johnson, *Body*, 45.

spaces. We manipulate objects, placing them in containers (cups, boxes, cans, bags, etc.). In each of these cases there are repeatable spatial and temporal organizations.[6]

The most "experientially salient" of these examples are those of three-dimensional containment, where someone is restricted in an enclosure.[7] Such situations typically have at least three entailments, available for reasoning based on this schema. First, containment involves resistance to external forces or protection from them. Second, containment restricts forces within the container. Third, containment fixes the locality of the entity being contained.[8] The use of these entailments to reason about distress will be explored later.

Gibbs adds a cultural component, arguing that the containment experiences giving rise to the schema affect the way other experiences are understood and valued. Thus, for example, our experience of containment is influenced by our feelings as we go in and out of different "containers" or put things in and out of our body.[9] The way cultural examples of containment affect the evaluation of the CONSTRAINT schema for the Classical Hebrew texts will be examined below.

The salient Hebrew CONSTRAINT schema conflates this CONTAINMENT schema with Talmy's FORCE schema (above), and can be diagrammed as follows, modifying Talmy's picture to represent the Antagonist completely surrounding the Agonist (the circle). The Antagonist is still stronger (shown by the plus sign), holding the Agonist in one place.

---

6. Ibid., 21.
7. Ibid., 22.
8. Ibid.
9. Gibbs, "Heads," 154.

Surrounded by Bitterness

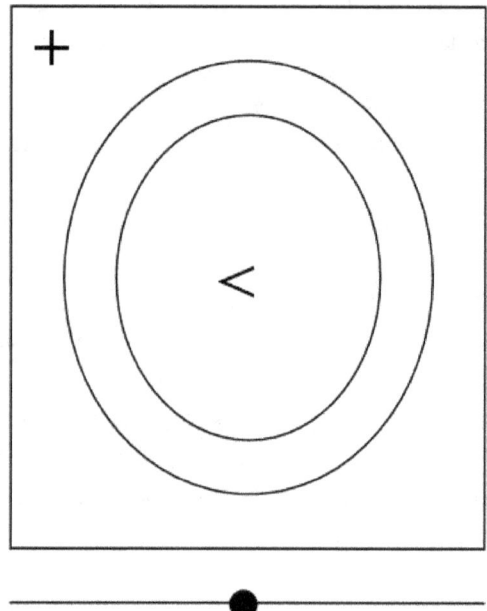

Figure 6.2.

6.2.2. Culture-Specific Factors

The clearest example of, and best evidence for, this specific Hebrew CONSTRAINT schema comes from the semantic network for the root צרר, used for physical situations and more emotional experiences of distress. The physical uses, as when the Israelites' kneading troughs are "wrapped up" in Exod 12:34, imply the root may be "semantically significant,"[10] with the physical source domains accessible even when the root is used in psychological contexts.

The semantics of צרר can be described through both the prototypical scenario of contents held within a cloth, and through the high-level sanctioning schema of an Agonist with a tendency to move being

---

10. Barr, "Factors," 35.

enclosed and restricted. This claim will be substantiated by considering Classical Hebrew usage of צרר.

a) The Root צרר

The major lexicons split צרר into three homonymous senses, supported by Arabic cognates with different initial consonants.[11] Still, there may be cognitive links between the first two roots, glossed for the verb in BDB as "bind, tie up, be restricted, narrow, scant, cramped" versus "shew hostility toward, vex," and for the nouns (צַר,צָרָה) as "straits, distress" versus "adversary, rival wife."[12] Sometimes it is difficult to specifically attribute one of these senses, as in Ps 138:7, אִם־אֵלֵךְ בְּקֶרֶב צָרָה 'if I walk in the midst of enemies / trouble'.[13] However, the first homonym is of most interest here, especially the links between being "restricted" and being "in distress."

b) Semantics and Syntax of the Verb

Starting with the verb, the physical uses of צרר need examination to clarify what entailments may carry over to less concrete situations. Fabry focuses on the linguistic realization of subjects and objects, to distinguish nine transitive uses ("wrap up," "envelop") from thirty-three intransitive uses ("be cramped for space, restricted").[14] However, a semantic analysis of the arguments is more helpful.

In every scenario there is an Agonist that is in some way restricted, and, usually, an Antagonist restricting it. Although the verb (in the qal) usually agrees with the Antagonist, the Agonist is actually more in focus, since it is always present as a core argument (without a preposition, as in Isa 8:16, צוֹר תְּעוּדָה, "seal the testimony") or in a prepositional phrase (as in Gen 32:7[8], וַיִּירָא יַעֲקֹב מְאֹד וַיֵּצֶר לוֹ 'Jacob was very afraid and distressed'), whereas the Antagonist may just be an impersonal third person agreement on the verb (as in Gen 32:7[8] again).

11. Snaith, "Language," 221.
12. BDB 864–866.
13. Ringgren, "צַר II," 467.
14. Fabry, "צַר I."

Specifically, there are four syntactic frames for the qal. First, there are transitive examples where the Agonist is a core argument and the Antagonist is either a core argument or implicit in a passive construction. Secondly, there are intransitive examples where the Agonist is a core argument and the Antagonist is implicit. Third, sometimes the Agonist is in a prepositional phrase headed by מִן and the Antagonist is a core argument. Finally, the Agonist is frequently in a prepositional phrase headed by לְ and the Antagonist is an impersonal third person, following the pattern of other verbs for which לְ is used "to denote the subj[ect] of a sensation or emotion,"[15] such as חָרָה לְ. The hiphil fits with this last frame as the Agonist is always in a prepositional phrase headed by לְ.

i) Transitive Examples

First, for transitive cases, the most experientially basic use is something wrapped, or held tightly, within material. The Israelites carried their kneading troughs wrapped in their cloaks (מִשְׁאֲרֹתָם צְרֻרֹת בְּשִׂמְלֹתָם, Exod 12:34), and a stone in a sling is tightly held (Prov 26:8). Proverbs 30:4 imagines water restrained in a cloak (מִי צָרַר־מַיִם בַּשִּׂמְלָה 'who can wrap/hold[16] water in a cloak?'). In Job 26:8 (צֹרֵר־מַיִם בְּעָבָיו 'wrapping/holding water in his clouds'), water is again restrained. In Isa 8:16 (צוֹר תְּעוּדָה 'wrap/hold the testimony') the verb may suggest wrapping written testimony in cloth to preserve it. Hosea 13:12 (צָרוּר עֲוֹן אֶפְרָיִם 'Ephraim's iniquity is wrapped up') again preserves something by wrapping. In Josh 9:4, a pual participle describes the Gibeonites' wineskins as בָּלִים וּמְבֻקָּעִים וּמְצֹרָרִים 'worn out', 'ripped', and 'wrapped/held', with material restraining the wine. More metaphorically, in 1 Sam 25:29, Abigail says וְהָיְתָה נֶפֶשׁ אֲדֹנִי צְרוּרָה בִּצְרוֹר הַחַיִּים 'may the life of my Lord be wrapped/held in the bag of the living', rather than thrown out as from a sling. Finally, Hos 4:19, describes Ephraim via צָרַר רוּחַ אוֹתָהּ בִּכְנָפֶיהָ 'a wind has wrapped/held her in its wings.' This is the clearest transitive example, as both core arguments (wind, her) are visible. In every case, something with a tendency to move is wrapped and

---

15. BDB 511.

16. The gloss "wrap/hold" conflates CONTAINMENT and FORCE in English.

Distress and the Constraint Schema

held in place (by material), whether wine, water, the testimony that may otherwise decay, stones and kneading troughs (acted on by gravity), or Ephraim who might otherwise go out to serve Yahweh.

Extending this prototype, in 2 Sam 20:3 David imprisons his concubines so that 'they were shut up until the day of their death', וַתִּהְיֶינָה צְרֻרוֹת עַד־יוֹם מֻתָן. This restriction under guard again uses צרר for an entity desiring to be free being surrounded and unable to go out.

ii) Intransitive Examples

In the second syntactic frame, the verb is intransitive and the Agonist governs verb agreement. It is used twice of legs restricted in movement, in Job 18:7, יֵצְרוּ צַעֲדֵי אוֹנוֹ 'his strong steps will be restricted'; and Prov 4:12, בְּלֶכְתְּךָ לֹא־יֵצַר צַעֲדֶךָ 'your step will not be restricted as you walk'. In Isa 28:20, וְהַמַּסֵּכָה צָרָה כְּהִתְכַּנֵּס 'the blanket is too narrow to cover oneself', something (the blanket) is again restricted. Here, the surrounding Antagonist has receded into the background, and the verb just focuses on restriction to an Agonist, which would normatively be bigger or longer.

The third (again intransitive) frame describes the residence of the prophets in 2 Kgs 6:1 as צַר מִמֶּנּוּ 'cramped for us', and addresses Zion in Isa 49:19 as תֵּצְרִי מִיּוֹשֵׁב 'too crowded for (your) inhabitants'. Here, the verb agrees with the place, which acts as a restrictive Antagonist to the Agonist of those living there, appearing in a מִן prepositional phrase.

The fourth frame (classified by Fabry as intransitive) has the Agonist in a prepositional phrase with לְ, as in Judg 2:15, וַיֵּצֶר לָהֶם מְאֹד 'it was great distress/constraint to them.' In the qal, in Gen 32:7[8]; Judg 2:15; 10:9; 11:7; 1 Sam 13:6; 28:15; 30:6; 2 Sam 1:26; 13:2; 24:14; Job 20:22; Ps 31:9[10]; 59:16[17]; 69:17[18]; 102:2[3]; Isa 49:20; and Lam 1:20, the English translation normally has someone "in distress." The verb agrees with an impersonal third person, usually masculine but occasionally feminine, showing that the Antagonist has not totally disappeared. This syntax conceptualizes distress as an Agonist desiring freedom but being restricted by something external.

In the syntactically related hiphil examples, the external restricting force is caused by an agent, prototypically in siege, as in Deut 28:52,

וְהֵצַר לְךָ בְּכָל־שְׁעָרֶיךָ 'he will cause restriction (besiege) to you in all your gates,' or 1 Kgs 8:37 / 2 Chr 6:28, כִּי יָצַר־לוֹ אֹיְבוֹ בְּאֶרֶץ שְׁעָרָיו 'if his enemy causes restriction (besieges) to him in the land of his gates.' Again, an entity that desires to come out (the city's population) is held in place. This restriction of movement is highlighted through the use of שַׁעַר (gate) as a metonym for the city.

Finally, the hiphil refers to the experience of labor, picturing warriors' hearts in Jer 48:41 and 49:22 as כְּלֵב אִשָּׁה מְצֵרָה 'as the heart of a constraining (laboring) woman.' Here, the Hebrew language perhaps conceptualized the contractions of labor as something (the woman's interior) holding tight around another entity (the baby in her womb) that has a tendency to come out.

iii) Semantic Network

These uses can be summarized in a semantic network.[17] Here, prototypical or sanctioning senses are in bold, solid arrows indicate a schematic extension from a prototype, and dashed lines indicate only partial schematicity. That is, solid arrows show where the extension from the prototype is fully sanctioned by the overarching sanctioning sense, completely fitting the schema. Dashed lines show extensions from the prototype that differ in some way from the overarching schema, and thus are only partially sanctioned by it.

---

17. Based on Langacker and Taylor as in section 2.5.2.b, and developed in Brugman and Lakoff, "Topology," Fillmore and Atkins, "Polysemy," and Tuggy, "kisa."

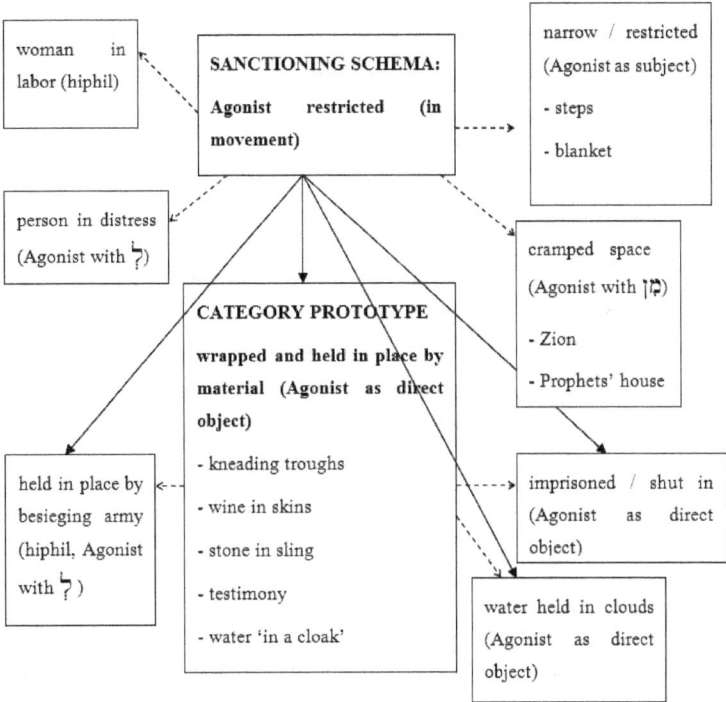

Figure 6.3

c) Nouns

For nouns, Fabry concludes that "restriction in the sense of 'having no space,'" still inheres in both צַר and צָרָה, based on parallel terms and verbs combined with them.[18] Specifically, Ps 4:1[2], בַּצָּר הִרְחַבְתָּ לִּי 'in distress/constraint you gave me space', solves a situation of distress problematized with צַר using רחב, indicating space or width, as also in Pss 31:7[8] and 25:17 Although Goldingay sees this as abnormal awareness of the root meaning, so that normally צַר "means 'distress' more generally,"[19] Cognitive Linguistics argues that even where spatial words do not co-occur with צַר or צָרָה, the spatial domain may nevertheless have been cognitively accessible and constrained some inferences about the distressing situation. *NIDOTTE* agrees that for nouns and adjectives,

18. Fabry, "צַר I," 456–57.
19. Goldingay, "Ambiguity," 162.

as well as verbs, צרר applies "either literally to physical dimensions or metaphorically to human experience in contexts of physical danger, psychological anxiety, or spiritual distress... The forms derived from צרר are applied to any kind of restricting, claustrophobic experience."[20]

Thus, using צרה in distress situations provides cognitive access to networks related to restricted movement. To see this, compare with the English lexeme *stress*, used to describe physical, emotional, and social experience. Although *stress* is used in contexts without any other reference to forces, the very use of this lexeme allows a wealth of inferences based on usage in physical domains. Just as physical stress is scalable, so is psychosomatic stress. Further, after experiencing a little stress, return to normality is possible, but if the stress increases, a person may eventually (and irreparably) snap. In a similar way, the use of צרה potentially makes inferences from the physical domain possible.

d) The Root צוק I

Several other Hebrew roots link to the same schema as צרר. The closest is צוק I. In Akkadian, the cognate root means "narrow" or "tight," both for material things (such as clothes) and for psychological conditions.[21] Lamberty-Zielinski argues that Hebrew is more specialized, meaning "'drive into a corner, press in on, distress, badger' in the sense of a psychologically stressful and even terrifying condition brought about by external circumstances,"[22] as in Delilah's badgering in Judg 14:17. Thus, this word implies more of a force directed at the Agonist in distress contexts than the wrapping implied by צרר.

e) "Surrounding" Roots: סבב, נקף, אפף

Several roots also highlight the "surrounding" aspect, with סבב being most common. Its use prototypically "involves an external circular

---

20. Swart and Wakely, "צרר," 854.
21. Lamberty-Zielinski, "צוק," 301.
22. Ibid., 303.

movement."²³ Within the corpus, it always evokes being encircled and is sometimes translated as "on every side." A prototypical scenario is given by city walls surrounding a city, encompassing everything within, as in 2 Kgs 3:1. Although סבב is used negatively for being surrounded by enemies or war (as in 1 Kgs 5:3[17]), it also fits positive situations such as the protective armies encamped around the king in 1 Sam 26:5.

נקף (in the hiphil) and אפף have similar "surrounding" meanings. Of fifteen occurrences of נקף, eleven occur with סבב, showing very close links. נקף frequently amplifies or complements סבב,²⁴ as in 2 Kgs 11:8, וְהִקִּפְתֶּם עַל־הַמֶּלֶךְ סָבִיב 'they will surround the king, all around'. The fundamental meaning is "to surround," with only context again giving a positive (2 Kgs 11:8) or negative (2 Kgs 6:14) evaluation in different cases.²⁵ Other verses focus on completing a full cycle, whether around the rim of the bronze sea (1 Kgs 7:24), a journey through the land of Moab (Isa 15:8), days of festival (Job 1:5), or annual feasts (Isa 29:1).

Third, אפף also describes the "surrounding" Antagonist and occurs five times, all within the specific corpus. In each case there is a negative evaluation of the situation. Thus, סבב, נקף, and to a lesser extent אפף, all evoke an entity completely encircling or surrounding another entity.

f) Restricting Roots: עטף, סגר, חבל, אסר

Other roots fit the schema by evoking restriction, by being wrapped, shut in, tied, or bound. First, אסר is used for animals that have been tethered (2 Kgs 7:10) and people bound as prisoners (as in Judges 16).

Second, forms from the root חבל also relate to binding. *TDOT* finds four homonyms here: first, related to חֶבֶל 'rope'; second, meaning to 'take in pledge'; thirdly, 'violence' or 'damage'; and fourth, related to pregnancy and labor. Ropes (חֹבְלִים) were used for drawing water, tying animals, and in hunting, alongside snares, nets, and traps (as in

---

23. Garcia-López, "סבב," 130.
24. Ibid., 129.
25. Reiterer, "נָקַף," 10.

Ps 140:5[6]).[26] This last usage is most significant in the corpus, where the noun is used with death or Sheol, illustrating "the tight constraint exercised by the powers of the underworld."[27] This image of being tied is also used where the cords are sin (חֵטְא, Prov 5:22), or affliction (עֳנִי, Job 36:8).

The third homonym accesses the domain of physical, physiological, or social violence. Gamberoni links the unusual pual form רוּחִי חֻבָּלָה (Job 17:1) with this homonym, explaining it as "profound emotional depression."[28] However, he also notes this sense converging with others, arguing that even in the biblical period the "rope" image was associated with this third homonym.[29]

For the fourth homonym, related to pregnancy, חבל does not evoke labor pains (צִירִים) so much as "the state of incipient, continuing, or culminating pregnancy, ... the anxious uncertainty with which the expectant mother awaits the approaching birth."[30] Rabbinic interpretation linked this with being tied by ropes, explaining that ropes hold the baby in the womb until the start of labor.[31] Using cognitive semantics, the basic-level prototype of something tied by ropes (sense I) extends to being bound in a pledge (sense II) and the "binding" of an unborn child (sense IV). Cognitive links between the third homonym ("violence") and this prototype are less salient, but still accessible in some contexts.

Third, the root סגר, when used in the niphal, describes being shut in, fitting the schema of צרר as used with David's concubines. Prototypically, the qal describes shutting doors or city gates. The hiphil usually means to "hand someone over," but can also mean "imprison." The related nouns מִסְגֶּרֶת and מַסְגֵּר are used for prisons, a place of being shut in, although מִסְגֶּרֶת may alternatively be a hiding place, reflecting voluntary rather than forced confinement.[32]

---

26. Fabry, "חבל I," 174.
27. Ibid., 176.
28. Gamberoni, "חָבַל III," 186.
29. Ibid., 188.
30. Fabry, "חבל IV," 189.
31. Ibid.
32. Ringgren, "סָגַר."

Fourth, the root עטף, found several times in the specific corpus in the hithpael, may also link to a prototypical scenario of something that is wrapped. BDB lists three homonyms: "turn aside"; "envelop oneself"; and "be feeble" or "faint."[33] In the qal, the second sense describes being clothed in a garment of violence (Ps 73:6), and in Ps 65:13[14] describes valleys clothed in grain. A derived noun מַעֲטָפָה denotes an "overtunic" in Isa 3:22. Waldman argues that the third homonym, "be feeble" or "faint," actually reflects the more literal "clothing" prototype, since Akkadian texts describe sickness as being covered or wrapped. Thus, Ps 143:4, וַתִּתְעַטֵּף עָלַי רוּחִי, has the petitioner's spirit "wrapped," and Jon 2:8 בְּהִתְעַטֵּף עָלַי נַפְשִׁי is "when my soul is wrapped upon / within me,"[34] so that in both texts part of the person is emotionally and psychologically wrapped and held tight by another part. The significance of the wrapping prototype for understanding צַר־לִי strengthens Waldman's argument, showing a generalization over polysemy, as both צַר and עטף access a physical domain of wrapping and the domain of psychophysical distress.

Finally, the root בלע 'swallow' is also cognitively linked to this schema, since what is swallowed is an Agonist held within another entity. However, what is ingested is also almost certainly destroyed (Jonah being a notable exception), so that בלע becomes a metaphor for destruction,[35] rather than just being held with the potential to escape, as in Ps 124:3, אֲזַי חַיִּים בְּלָעוּנוּ 'then they would have swallowed us alive.'

All these roots link with the schematic network for צרר in some way, whether emphasizing the surrounding Antagonist, the pressure on the Agonist, or its restricted position. The number of roots demonstrates the richness of this domain, justifying this schema as a significant feature of Classical Hebrew language and, potentially, thought. Domains linked by one or more of these roots further demonstrate this. For example, the experience of labor and childbirth is described using the roots צרר, חבל and צוק (1QH 11:7–12; Jer 6:24), all of which have been discussed above. This shows conceptual unity for at least these

---

33. BDB 742.
34. Waldman, "Imagery," 168–69.
35. Schüpphaus, "בָּלַע."

g) Evaluation

Finally, is there a constant value judgment when this CONSTRAINT schema is accessed? סבב, נקף, and צרר can all be used with a positive value, as shown above. In the specific corpus, further examples show surrounding schemas used with both positive and negative evaluation. In Job 1:10 and Job 3:23, the same root (סוּךְ / שׂוּךְ) firstly describes God's protection as a hedge around Job and later describes Job's misfortune. In Ps 32:6–7, distress is conceptualized as being reached by flooding waters, but protection is conceptualized as being "surrounded" (סבב) with shouts of deliverance. These examples reinforce the importance of this "surrounding" schema for Classical Hebrew speakers, but also show that it is not consistently evaluated. Whereas the verticality schema was unified by the evaluation "up is good" and "down is bad," being surrounded may be good or bad, depending on the context.

6.3. Comparative Data on Emotion Language and the CONSTRAINT Schema

6.3.1. Contemporary Cross-Linguistic Comparisons

The only data available for contemporary cross-linguistic comparison comes from McMullen and Conway's study of depression. Although 90 percent of the metaphors fitted DEPRESSION IS DESCENT, there were a small number of examples in which "clients communicated a sense of restriction," such as feeling "trapped," wanting to "break out" or wanting to be "free."[36] The authors postulate DEPRESSION IS CAPTOR to account for these linguistic metaphors. However, these examples would also fit well with the image schema here of a surrounding barrier. The significant thing from this comparison is the infrequency of such metaphors in these psychotherapy sessions compared with other schemas. By contrast, the idea of being constrained pervades the Hebrew corpus.

36. McMullen and Conway, "Depression," 171.

6.3.2. Ancient Near Eastern Comparisons

Looking instead at ancient Near Eastern comparisons, this schema is paralleled in Akkadian. First, several (non-cognate) roots exhibit the same patterns of senses as צרר, showing the conceptual significance of the link between distress and being surrounded. In particular, the root *ašāšu*, found in the line from *Ludlul Bel Nemeqi* cited in the previous chapter, ú-taš-šá-šá-ma i-dab-bu-ba a-rad ir-kal-la, 'under adversity they complain of going down to hell' (Column II, line 47),[37] has a similar semantic network. CAD lists the meanings "to be worried, disturbed, in despair" or "to be in continual distress" (some referring particularly to pregnant women) alongside being "caught in a net," "engulfed," or "overwhelmed."[38] As for צרר, this polysemy links the scenario of an Agonist being surrounded (as in the material of a net) with being in distress. Similarly, the Akkadian root *pašāqu*, is glossed as either "to become narrow, constricted" or "to suffer difficulties, to be anguished." It is used for narrow roads, potentially fatal illness, and for difficult labor during childbirth.[39]

Second, some Akkadian roots related to being wrapped in a garment are used both for physical scenarios and for illness as being "clothed" or "overpowered" by demons. The root *katāmu* 'cover (like a cloak)' is used in examples like *alû lemnu ša kīma ṣubāti ikattamu* 'the evil *alû*—ghost who envelops [his victim] like a garment' or *amēla muttalika kīma ṣubāti iktatam* 'he [the asakku-demon] enveloped the miserable man like a garment.'[40] The verbs *edēqu* 'wrap', and *labāšu* 'wear', also describe "wearing" a disease as one wears clothes.[41] In all of these examples a demon or disease is the Antagonist, enveloping the afflicted sufferer, as the Agonist. These Akkadian examples show illness being conceived as being wrapped or restricted by an external force, prompting a search as to whether there are explicit entities seen as wrapping the person in Hebrew.

---

37. Akkadian transliteration and English translation from Lambert, *Wisdom*, 40–41.

38. Oppenheim, *CAD A/2*, 422–25.

39. Roth, *CAD A/2*, 235–36.

40. Akkadian examples cited in Waldman, "Imagery," 161.

41. Ibid., 163.

6.4. Presentation and Analysis of Hebrew Mappings

In this section, each image utilizing the CONSTRAINT schema is considered separately, clarifying the Agonist and Antagonist and showing how the metaphor maps this structure onto experiences of distress. Utilizing the structure of experiential gestalts,[42] each image is considered with respect to *participants*, *causation*, which *parts* of the image are mapped, whether there is any mapping of *intensity* and the inferable *result* of the situation, since, as Gibbs' showed for English anger idioms, the implicit results of a metaphorically conceptualized situation are frequently accessible for reasoning. For example, people reasoned that someone who has been "simmering" for a long time may eventually "explode" in a violent way.[43] Similarly, possible outcomes for a situation of distress conceptualized as constraint will be considered, to see if generalizations over inference patterns can be observed.

6.4.1. EXPERIENCING DISTRESS IS PHYSIOLOGICAL CONSTRICTION

Sometimes, verbs or adjectives relating to the CONSTRAINT schema are used with physiological aspects of the person. These are often conceptual metonymies rather than conceptual metaphors, highlighting a physiological aspect of the distress experience to "stand for" the whole experience. As noted in section 2.5.7.c, Kövecses sees such conceptual metonymies (like THE PHYSIOLOGICAL AND EXPRESSIVE RESPONSES OF AN EMOTION STAND FOR THE EMOTION) as potential motivations for more elaborate conceptual metaphors, just as BODY HEAT STANDS FOR ANGER motivates metaphors of anger as fire.[44]

The physiological aspects here include the רוּחַ, נֶפֶשׁ, and לֵב, all of which have been described as psychophysical,[45] referencing not just physiological elements of the body (breath, throat, heart) but more psychological functions, such as thinking, feeling, and desiring. For exam-

---

42. Section 2.5.1.b.
43. Gibbs et al., "Idiom."
44. For example, Kövecses, *Metaphor*, 156–57.
45. Lauha, *Psychophysicher*, cited in Warren-Rothlin, "Idioms," 204.

ple, the נֶפֶשׁ physically evokes the throat, but is also used for "vitality," and, idiomatically, for desire,[46] whereas the לֵב describes the "internal organs of cognition and control."[47] However, grouping these examples may reveal some physical symptoms understood in terms of CONSTRAINT that could motivate some of the other metaphorical mappings.

Most clearly, Ps 25:17 uses צָרָה in a construct with לְבָבִי. The solution is framed with רחב, showing that constraint or restriction is cognitively accessible in this use of צָרָה. This spatial conceptualization is maintained in the second colon, with the problematization framed spatially as מְצוּקָה, and the solution then being spatially "brought out."

צָרוֹת לְבָבִי הִרְחִיבוּ מִמְּצוּקוֹתַי הוֹצִיאֵנִי׃

> Ps 25:17: Enlarge my heart's constraint, and bring me out of my distress.[48]

The heart (לְבַב) is also spatially conceptualized in 1QH 13:32–33, contrasting God "opening space" in the petitioner's inner being with the opponents adding to the constricting pressure on him. The use of צוקה allows a rare mapping of scalarity for the CONSTRAINT schema, as it includes pressure inwards as well as being surrounded.

ואת אלי 33 מרחב פתחתה בלבבי ויוספוה לצוקה

> 1QH 13:32–33: And you, my God, have opened a broad space in my heart but they have increased the narrowness.

1 QM 11:9 (outside the specific corpus) also shows relief from physiological distress as God "opening" the heart.

ולב נמס לפתח תקוה

> The melting heart you open to hope.[49]

Jeremiah 4:19 refers to קִירוֹת לִבִּי 'walls of the heart', which, despite interpretative difficulties, again potentially expresses distress through constrained internal parts, here by walls. This verse gives the

---

46. See previous chapter.
47. North, "Brain," 595.
48. Revocalizing to an imperative, following NRSV and Craigie, *Psalms 1–50*, 217.
49. Martínez, *Scrolls*, 104.

best argument for a metonymic grounding for these distress metaphors, since if one aspect of the internal bodily experience of distress is understood as the "walls of the heart" constricting, there is a potential physical basis for other metaphors that understand distress as constriction.

מֵעַי מֵעַי אוֹחִילָה קִירוֹת לִבִּי הֹמֶה־לִּי לִבִּי

> Jer 4:19: My anguish, my anguish! I writhe in pain! Oh, the walls of my heart! My heart is beating wildly.

נֶפֶשׁ is also used with צָרָה, in Pss 31:7[8]; 143:11; 1QH 17:27–28; 7:19; and 13:12. In Ps 31:7[8] the distress conceptualized as צָרוֹת נַפְשִׁי is resolved in verse 8[9] by a wide space for the author's feet. In Ps 143:11, relief is sought from צָרָה by the נֶפֶשׁ being "brought out" (יצא with מִן).

אָגִילָה וְאֶשְׂמְחָה בְּחַסְדֶּךָ אֲשֶׁר רָאִיתָ אֶת־עָנְיִי יָדַעְתָּ בְּצָרוֹת נַפְשִׁי:

> Ps 31:7[8]: I will exult and I will rejoice in your loving-kindness, you who have seen my affliction; you knew about the constraint of my soul.[50]

לְמַעַן־שִׁמְךָ יְהוָה תְּחַיֵּנִי בְּצִדְקָתְךָ תּוֹצִיא מִצָּרָה נַפְשִׁי:

> Ps 143:11: For your name's sake, O LORD, preserve my life. In your righteousness bring my soul out from constraint.[51]

In 1QH 17:27–28, parallels with "wound" and "weakness" suggests a "constricted soul" is a metaphor for the petitioner's physical distress, and again the solution is framed as "width," through the use of רחב. In 1QH 7:19, פתח together with צרת נפשו frames a problem and views its solution in terms of opening a restricted space for the petitioner's נֶפֶשׁ.[52] Although no particular troubles are mentioned in the context, the contrastive themes of "eternal salvation," "endless peace," and lack of "want," suggest צרת נפש refers to the opposite, negative life expe-

---

50. Based on Craigie, *Psalms 1–50*, 256.

51. Author's translation.

52. Although this verse is in the third person, it is in a description of the righteous man, with whom the petitioner identifies himself.

riences. Finally, צרת נפשי occurs in 1QH 13:12, though not solved spatially here.

. . . מח[ץ מכתי ולמכשולי גבורת פלא ורחוב 28 עולם בצרת נפש]י

1QH 17:27–28: . . . the wou]nd inflicted on me, my weakness to wonderful force, the constriction of [my] soul to everlasting expanse.

ולפתוח כול צרת נפשו לישועת עולם ושלם עד ואין מחסור

1QH 7:19: . . . to open all the narrowness of his soul to eternal salvation and endless peace, without want.

כי בצרת נפשי לא עזבתני

1QH 13:12: For in the distress of my soul you did not desert me.

Other examples of physiological parts being "wrapped" may come from עטף, if it indeed provides a cognitive access point to domains of wrapping and covering. In Ps 61:2[3], the psalmist's לֵב is "wrapped," whereas in Ps 77:3[4] it is his רוּחַ. In Ps 142:3[4], 143:4 and Jonah 2:7[8], the use of עָלַי brings the petitioner himself in as a further argument, emphasizing that he feels the emotional situation "acting *upon* him,"[53] again with his רוּחַ wrapped in the first two verses, and his נֶפֶשׁ in Jonah. Perhaps the image here is that the רוּחַ, נֶפֶשׁ, and לֵב are wrapped up and thus restricted within the person.

מִקְצֵה הָאָרֶץ אֵלֶיךָ אֶקְרָא בַּעֲטֹף לִבִּי

Ps 61:2[3]: From the end of the earth I call to you, when my heart is faint (wrapped).

אֶזְכְּרָה אֱלֹהִים וְאֶהֱמָיָה אָשִׂיחָה וְתִתְעַטֵּף רוּחִי׃

Ps 77:3[4]: I think of God and I moan; I meditate, and my spirit faints (is wrapped).

---

53. BDB 753.

Surrounded by Bitterness

בְּהִתְעַטֵּף עָלַי רוּחִי וְאַתָּה יָדַעְתָּ נְתִיבָתִי

Ps 142:3[4]: When my spirit is faint (wraps upon me), you know my way.

וַתִּתְעַטֵּף עָלַי רוּחִי

Ps 143:4: Therefore my spirit faints within me (wraps upon me).

בְּהִתְעַטֵּף עָלַי נַפְשִׁי אֶת־יְהוָה זָכָרְתִּי

Jon 2:7[8]: As my life was ebbing away (was wrapped upon me), I remembered the LORD.

In addition, the unusual form חֻבָּלָה in Job 17:1, although usually derived from the sense of חבל meaning "destroy,"[54] may potentially link to the meaning of being "bound,"[55] paralleling this verse with Job 7:11, where צַר is used in construction with רוּחַ.

רוּחִי חֻבָּלָה יָמַי נִזְעָכוּ קְבָרִים לִי׃

Job 17:1: My spirit is bound,[56] my days are extinct, the grave is ready for me.

גַּם־אֲנִי לֹא אֶחֱשָׂךְ פִּי אֲדַבְּרָה בְּצַר רוּחִי

Job 7:11: Therefore I will not restrain my mouth; I will speak in the constraint[57] of my spirit.

All these examples show a mapping from physiological constraint to a situation of distress. That is, the cognitive model of distress is understood partly in terms of the רוּחַ, נֶפֶשׁ, or לֵב being constrained, a constraint on the vitality, life, and mind of the individual in distress. As a corollary, relief from distress is seen as these parts being "given space" (רחב) or "opened" (פתח). The physiological feeling of "tightness" in the chest (possibly referenced in Jer 4:19) gives a biological grounding for this conceptual metonymy.

54. For example, Clines, *Job 1–20*, 392.
55. Argued by Wolfers, *Deep*, 338.
56. Author's translation.
57. Author's translation.

Distress and the Constraint Schema

The following sections consider the variety of conceptual metaphors that use this schema and that cohere with this metonymy, being potentially conceptually motivated by it.

6.4.2. Experiencing Distress is Lacking Space to Move

In the first group of examples, the petitioner sees himself as restricted when in distress, or conceptualizes relief as a broad place. The basic mapping here is from a person who is an Agonist hemmed in a tight spot and unable to move (possibly in a narrow valley, or between walls) to the person in distress.

a) Narrow Places and Blocking Walls

In 1QH 13:29–30 "narrow places" (מצרים) are symptomatic of the troubles the petitioner faces. These are metaphorical (referring to some sort of trial) as the following verse makes clear, complaining about the charges his enemies bring. The main inference is that in a narrow place there is no escape, the petitioner is totally at the mercy of his enemies.

וישיגוני במצרים לאין מנוס

> 1QH 13:29–30: They have overtaken me in narrow places where there is no escape.

In Job 19:8, Job accuses God of building a wall in his path to restrain him. This image does not fit any normal scenario, as a גָּדֵר normally surrounds a vineyard or sheepfold, rather than blocking a path, but still reflects a hindrance to Job following the normal "course of life" he desires.[58] Lamentations 3:9 again uses גדר with relation to the petitioner's path (דֶּרֶךְ). The assertion that these are particularly "hewn stones" (גָזִית) has perplexed interpreters, maybe reflecting Zion theology,[59] but most likely that it is a very deliberate, premeditated action. These references to paths and blockages instantiate what Lakoff terms the "event structure" metaphor, a potentially universal conceptual

---

58. Clines, *Job 1–20*, 442.
59. Baumann, "Weg."

Surrounded by Bitterness

metaphor. Within this metaphor, purposes are destinations, means are paths to these destinations and difficulties are impediments to motion,[60] so that the petitioners' purposes are being thwarted. Earlier, in Lam 3:7, God is also portrayed as building a wall to block the lamenter, here all around him and stopping him leaving.

אָרְחִי גָדַר וְלֹא אֶעֱבוֹר

Job 19:8: He has walled up my way so that I cannot pass.

גָּדַר דְּרָכַי בְּגָזִית נְתִיבֹתַי עִוָּה׃

Lam 3:9: He has blocked my ways with hewn stones, he has made my paths crooked.

גָּדַר בַּעֲדִי וְלֹא אֵצֵא

Lam 3:7: He has walled me about so that I cannot escape.

In Job 3:23, Job uses the hiphil of סוּךְ, which prototypically means building a hedge or fence.[61] Although used in Job 1:10 to positively portray God's protection on Job's family, here it is used with irony to show Job surrounded by disaster. A final reference to blocking walls is seen in Ps 18:29[30], where leaping over a wall is used to understand getting out of a distressing situation.[62]

לְגֶבֶר אֲשֶׁר־דַּרְכּוֹ נִסְתָּרָה וַיָּסֶךְ אֱלוֹהַּ בַּעֲדוֹ׃

Job 3:23: . . . to the man whose way is hidden, and whom God has hedged about?[63]

---

60. Lakoff, "Contemporary," 204.

61. Patterson, "סוּךְ."

62. Craigie interprets this as scaling enemy walls to capture them (Craigie, *Psalms 1–50*, 175). However, since the psalm focuses on relief from distress, it is preferable to seek an interpretation within that scenario (Goldingay, *Psalms* 1:271).

63. Wolfers, *Deep*, 320.

Distress and the Constraint Schema

$$\text{כִּי־בְךָ אָרֻץ גְּדוּד וּבֵאלֹהַי אֲדַלֶּג־שׁוּר:}$$

Ps 18:29[30]: For through you I rushed a barricade; through my God I leaped a wall.[64]

b) Being Shut In

In several of these examples, the inability of the Agonist to manifest his force tendency to move was explicit. In Job 19:8, עבר is used, showing Job cannot pass the blockage and "move on" in his life. In Lam 3:7, the restriction to the author's force tendency is an inability to "go out" (יצא). The same entailment is explicit in Ps 88:8[9], whereas the restriction is framed using כלא, a general root for spatial restraint or imprisonment (as a noun).[65]

$$\text{כָּלֻא וְלֹא אֵצֵא:}$$

Ps 88:8[9]: I am shut in so that I cannot escape.

Elsewhere in Job, his plight is conceptualized as somewhere lacking in space. In Job 12:14, Job talks about God's power, and uses the example of someone "shut in" (סגר), possibly comparing to his own situation. Later, in Job 36:16, Elihu contrasts Job's distress (conceptualized as constraint using צַר) with רַחַב לֹא־מוּצָק תַּחְתֶּיהָ, a "broad place without constraint." Whilst this difficult verse could be picturing Sheol as the "broad place" Job desires to go to,[66] the rest of the book consistently values width positively and constriction negatively, and never suggests Sheol is "wide." Rather, this verse likely expresses how Job's life before disaster struck was not one of distress but of expanse.[67]

$$\text{יִסְגֹּר עַל־אִישׁ וְלֹא יִפָּתֵחַ:}$$

Job 12:14: If he shuts someone in, no one can open up.

---

64. Goldingay, *Psalms* 1:271.
65. Hausmann, "כָּלֻא."
66. Wolfers, *Deep*, 364.
67. Clines, *Job 21–37*, 863.

וְאַף הֲסִיתְךָ מִפִּי־צָר רַחַב לֹא־מוּצָק תַּחְתֶּיהָ וְנַחַת שֻׁלְחָנְךָ מָלֵא
דָשֶׁן׃

> Job 36:16: He also allured you out of distress into a broad place where there was no constraint, and what was set on your table was full of fatness.

c) צרר and צוק

In many verses, reference to constraint is made through צרר or צוק without any other spatial words used in the context. However, the lack of such words does not preclude spatial inferences being cognitively accessible to users of the poem. Psalm 119:143, for example, uses both צַר and מָצוֹק to describe the distressing situation, both allowing spatial, constraining inferences. Other verses using צרר include Pss 22:11[12]; 31:9[10]; 34:6[7]; 69:17[18]; 71:20; 77:2[3]; 86:7; and 102:2[3]; Jer 15:11; and 1QH 19:31–32, too many to cite in full here.

צַר־וּמָצוֹק מְצָאוּנִי מִצְוֹתֶיךָ שַׁעֲשֻׁעָי׃

> Ps 119:143: Constraint and pressure have come upon me, but your commandments are my delight.[68]

d) Entailments

This mapping allows various inferences with regard to *causation* of distress. It is possible to hide an agentive cause by just describing a narrow place (as in 1QH 13:29) or being shut in (Ps 88:8[9]), or by using the phrase צַר־לִי, where the syntactic form emphasizes the restriction felt by the Agonist, but does not mention a personal agent.

However, images with an *agent* are also fairly common, mapping the agent causing the restriction to the agent causing distress. In Lam 3:7 and 9 and Job 19:8, the author did not just say there are walls surrounding him and blocking his path, but that God built them. In Job 12:14, God is the agent shutting someone in.

---

68. Author's translation.

Distress and the Constraint Schema

As for the *result* mapped in this image, narrow spaces themselves do not lead to increasing distress or difficulty, the person in them is merely contained in one place. Rather, they are appropriate for distress, then, because the fixity of location makes the petitioner especially vulnerable. Enemies can overtake him (1QH 13:29–30) and walls mean there is no escape possible under attack (Lam 3:7; Ps 88:8[9]).

With distress as a lack of space to move, a natural entailment is that *relief* from distress is being brought to a wide space. Psalms 18:19[20] and 36[37] both explicitly describe relief this way, first generally and then specifically for the feet to move freely, for a situation conceptualized in verse 6[7] as בַּצַּר־לִי. Similarly, מֶרְחָב in Ps 118:5 relieves a cry from הַמֵּצַר. Whether this is a prison or desert citadel,[69] it is a place where the force tendency to movement is restricted. Psalm 31 conceptualizes distress using צָרָה in verse 7[8], then in verse 8[9] as being "handed over" to the enemy (סגר, hiphil, suggesting being "shut in"). The second half of the verse conceptualizes relief as a wide space for the psalmist's feet. Psalm 4:1[2] also links together distress conceptualized as צַר and relief as space (רחב). A final example comes in Ps 119:45, where the image of walking in wide spaces evokes a life free of trouble. Briggs and Briggs' comment on Psalm 4 holds true for all these examples, that "distress is here a being constrained into narrow limits; pressed from rightful freedom and shut in on every side. The antith[esis] is the removal of such restraint and pressure, giving room and freedom."[70] In a related way, 1QH 14:30–31 frames relief from the individual's current distress as an eschatological breakthrough into a broad place.

וַיּוֹצִיאֵנִי לַמֶּרְחָב

Ps 18:19[20]: He brought me out into a broad place.

תַּרְחִיב צַעֲדִי תַחְתָּי וְלֹא מָעֲדוּ קַרְסֻלָּי׃

Ps 18:36[37]: You gave me a wide place for my steps under me, and my feet did not slip.

---

69. Allen, *Psalms 101–150*, 120.
70. Briggs and Briggs, *Psalms*, 30.

Surrounded by Bitterness

מִן־הַמֵּצַר קָרָאתִי יָּהּ עָנָנִי בַמֶּרְחָב יָהּ:

Ps 118:5: From my narrow straits I called Yah(weh): Yah(weh) answered me with spaciousness.[71]

וְלֹא הִסְגַּרְתַּנִי בְּיַד־אוֹיֵב הֶעֱמַדְתָּ בַמֶּרְחָב רַגְלָי:

Ps 31:8[9]: [You] have not delivered me into the hand of the enemy; you have set my feet in a broad place.

בַּצָּר הִרְחַבְתָּ לִּי

Ps 4:1[2]: You gave me room when I was constrained.[72]

וְאֶתְהַלְּכָה בָרְחָבָה כִּי פִקֻּדֶיךָ דָרָשְׁתִּי:

Ps 119:45: Thus I will walk on a broad path, for I investigate your ordinances.[73]

וידרוך גבור קשתו ויפתח מצור 31 [...] למרחב אין קץ

1QH 14:30–31: The hero will draw his bow and break open the encirclement [...] into an endless broad place.

Brown notes how open vistas here stand in contrast to the "sore straits of the journey," explaining this as a conceptual metaphor in which "the psalmist's 'pathway' has broadened into a 'refuge.'"[74] However, the idea of a refuge being a wide-open space seems unusual. Rather, these examples all reflect a removal of restrictions. The psalmist becomes an Agonist with plenty of space, able thus to exert his force tendency as desired.

---

71. Based on Allen, *Psalms 101–150*, 119.
72. Author's translation.
73. Kraus, *Psalms 60–150*, 404.
74. Brown, *Seeing*, 45.

Distress and the Constraint Schema

A summary of these mappings is given in the following table:[75]

Domain	Agonist's Force Tendency	Antagonist's Force Tendency	Causation	Resultant Action
Source	*Free person (often on a journey) to move along path to a desired destination*	*Walls or other blockages to prevent movement in a particular direction*	Potentially deliberate action of wall-builder	Person is held in one spot, vulnerable to attack and unable to travel freely or reach destination
Target	*Self to achieve purposes*	*Distressing experiences prevent achievement of purposes*	Potentially deliberate action of others to hinder achievement of purposes	Self is vulnerable to worse disaster, and may never be able to achieve purposes
Other Entailments: Removal of blocking obstacles, coming to wide space → Relief from situation of distress				

6.4.3. Experiencing Distress is Being Surrounded

Another general aspect of the CONSTRAINT schema is focused on when the distressing situation is conceptualized as an Antagonist encompassing or surrounding the petitioner as Agonist, especially using סבב, אפף, and נקף (in the hiphil).

a) Surrounding Enemies

Sometimes, phrases may reflect the writer's actual original situation, since encampments or cities could be surrounded by enemy forces (as in Gideon's attack on the Midianites in Judg 7:18 or Samson in Judg 16:2), or houses by angry men (Gen 19:5; Judg 19:22; or 20:5). In each situation, סבב describes a literally confined Agonist. However, it is notable that the "surrounding" aspect of the situation is highlighted, and doing this in psalms repeated over time by a community solidifies the salience of this spatial situation for understanding other distressing situations.

---

75. Based on the tables for summarizing force metaphors in emotion language found in Kövecses, *Emotion*, 61–86, but adding space for causation and entailments.

Surrounded by Bitterness

The clearest examples are in Pss 140:9[10]; 12:8[9]; 17:9, 11; and 3:6[7], where the enemies are conceived particularly as surrounding the petitioner, whatever their actual original spatial situation.

רֹאשׁ מְסִבָּי עֲמַל שְׂפָתֵימוֹ יְכַסֵּמוֹ׃

Ps 140:9[10]: The heads of those who surround me—may the harm done by their lips overwhelm them.[76]

סָבִיב רְשָׁעִים יִתְהַלָּכוּן

Ps 12:8[9]: On every side the wicked prowl.

אַשֻּׁרֵינוּ עַתָּה סְבָבוּנוּ

Ps 17:11: They track me down;[77] now they surround me.

אֹיְבַי בְּנֶפֶשׁ יַקִּיפוּ עָלָי׃

Ps 17:9: My mortal enemies encompass me![78]

לֹא־אִירָא מֵרִבְבוֹת עָם אֲשֶׁר סָבִיב שָׁתוּ עָלָי׃

Ps 3:6[7]: I am not afraid of ten thousands of people who have set themselves against me all around.

b) Surrounding Animals

Elsewhere, adversaries are conceptualized as surrounding animals. In Ps 118:10–12 they are compared to bees. Repeating סבב in each line and the intensification in verse 11 (גַם־סְבָבוּנִי) shows the significance of "surrounding" for conceptualizing this distress.

כָּל־גּוֹיִם סְבָבוּנִי בְּשֵׁם יְהוָה כִּי אֲמִילַם׃ סַבּוּנִי גַם־סְבָבוּנִי בְּשֵׁם יְהוָה כִּי אֲמִילַם׃ סַבּוּנִי כִדְבוֹרִים דֹּעֲכוּ כְּאֵשׁ קוֹצִים בְּשֵׁם יְהוָה כִּי אֲמִילַם׃

---

76. Allen, *Psalms 101–150*, 264.

77. The Masoretic Text reads "our steps," but NRSV amends to אִישְׁרוּנִי, "they track me down."

78. Craigie, *Psalms 1–50*, 159.

Ps 118:10–12: All nations surrounded me; in the name of the LORD I cut them off! They surrounded me, surrounded me on every side; in the name of the LORD I cut them off! They surrounded me like bees; they blazed[79] like a fire of thorns; in the name of the LORD I cut them off!

In Psalm 22 the situation is understood as both being surrounded by bulls and dogs. Three different roots are used, סבב, כתר, and נקף. Eidevall notes a "concentric" type of spatial metaphor here, with metaphors evoking feelings of "almost suffocating closeness," and the author, throughout the poem, "placed at the very centre of some circular entity, in a position which entails being the focus of everyone's attention (whether hostile or benign)."[80] In Ps 59:6[7], enemies are again conceptualized as dogs, this time surrounding the city.

סְבָבוּנִי פָּרִים רַבִּים אַבִּירֵי בָשָׁן כִּתְּרוּנִי׃

Ps 22:12 [13]: Many bulls encircle me, strong bulls of Bashan surround me;

כִּי סְבָבוּנִי כְּלָבִים עֲדַת מְרֵעִים הִקִּיפוּנִי

Ps 22:16[17]: For dogs are all around me; a company of evildoers encircles me.

יָשׁוּבוּ לָעֶרֶב יֶהֱמוּ כַכָּלֶב וִיסוֹבְבוּ עִיר׃

Ps 59:6[7]: They return at evening, they growl like dogs, and they surround the city.[81]

c) Job Surrounded

Three places in Job describe God's hostility using the root סבב. In Job 16:13, God's archers surround him. In Job 19:10, נתץ describes God's aggression, tearing him down as one might a house or wall, but modified by סָבִיב, linking FORCE and "surrounding."

---

79. NRSV follows the Septuagint here.
80. Eidevall, "Images," 57.
81. Basson, *Divine*, 188.

Surrounded by Bitterness

יָסֹבּוּ עָלַי רַבָּיו

Job 16:13: His archers surround me.

יִתְּצֵנִי סָבִיב וָאֵלַךְ

Job 19:10: He breaks me down on every side, and I am gone.

The second half of Job 10:8 also uses סָבִיב, although difficult to interpret. Possibly, סָבִיב means that Job was fashioned completely by God (as in KJV), but both the MT and LXX include it with the second colon, where it could literally read "together around, you swallow me" showing how completely God has attacked Job (as in ESV and NLT). This interpretation is supported by using בלע, since "swallowing" also entails surrounding with a constrictive presence, which is also used in Ps 124:3, a verse followed by other descriptions of the enemy as a flood surrounding those in distress.

יָדֶיךָ עִצְּבוּנִי וַיַּעֲשׂוּנִי יַחַד סָבִיב וַתְּבַלְּעֵנִי׃

Job 10:8: Your hands fashioned and made me, and now you have engulfed me altogether.[82]

אֲזַי חַיִּים בְּלָעוּנוּ

Ps 124:3: Then they would have swallowed us up alive.

Many metaphors have the petitioner surrounded by watery elements, as in 1QH 13:39, but these are significant enough to warrant their own section below.

[נחלי ב]ל[י]על אפפו נפשי

1QH 13:39: [The streams of Be]l[i]al surround my soul.

d) Surrounded by Abstract Hostile Entities

Sometimes, the words of the petitioner's adversaries surround him. In Ps 140:9[10] (cited above) the surrounding heads are linked to harmful

---

82. Author's translation, based on Wolfers, *Deep*, 329 and ESV.

lips, and in 59:6[7] (cited above) the surrounding dogs "growl" and their words are given in v. 7[8]. The mapping is explicit in Ps 109:2–3, where "words of hate" surround, mapping the abstract entity causing suffering onto a surrounding Antagonist.

כִּי פִי רָשָׁע וּפִי־מִרְמָה עָלַי פָּתָחוּ דִּבְּרוּ אִתִּי לְשׁוֹן שָׁקֶר׃ וְדִבְרֵי שִׂנְאָה סְבָבוּנִי וַיִּלָּחֲמוּנִי חִנָּם׃

Ps 109:2–3: For wicked mouths, deceitful mouths have they opened against me, they have spoken to me with lying tongues, and surrounded me with hateful talk and attacked me without reason.[83]

More abstract still, the idiom "terror surrounds" occurs in the corpus. In Ps 31:13[14] and Jer 20:10,[84] מָגוֹר is used, whereas in Job 18:11 בַּלָּהוֹת terrify on every side. Both of these words reference emotions related to fear, but metaphorically conceptualized, and thus experienced, through a "surrounding" schema.

כִּי שָׁמַעְתִּי דִּבַּת רַבִּים מָגוֹר מִסָּבִיב בְּהִוָּסְדָם יַחַד עָלַי לָקַחַת נַפְשִׁי זָמָמוּ׃

Ps 31:13[14]: For I hear the whispering of many—terror all around!—as they scheme together against me, as they plot to take my life.

כִּי שָׁמַעְתִּי דִּבַּת רַבִּים מָגוֹר מִסָּבִיב הַגִּידוּ וְנַגִּידֶנּוּ

Jer 20:10: For I hear many whispering: "Terror is all around! Denounce him! Let us denounce him!"

סָבִיב בִּעֲתֻהוּ בַלָּהוֹת וֶהֱפִיצֻהוּ לְרַגְלָיו׃

Job 18:11: Terrors frighten them on every side, and chase them at their heels.

Several other abstract entities take the Antagonist position in this conceptualization, this variety demonstrating the conventionality of the surrounding schema for understanding distress. These Antagonists

83. Allen, *Psalms 101–150*, 70.

84. This phrase also occurs in Jer 6:25; 20:3; 46:5; and 49:29, but only 20:10 is in the specific corpus.

include "poison and hardship" (רֹאשׁ וּתְלָאָה, Lam 3:5), "calamity" of the enemies' hearts (הוות לבם, 1QH 13:31), "darkness" (צלמות, 1QH 13:33, but with ישוכו בעדי rather than סבב), "agony and pain" (אנחה ויגון, 1QH 13:34), "evils without number" (רָעוֹת עַד־אֵין מִסְפָּר, Ps 40:12[13]), and the iniquity of the petitioner's persecutors (עֲוֺן עֲקֵבַי, Ps 49:5[6])

וַיַּקַּף רֹאשׁ וּתְלָאָה:

Lam 3:5: He surrounds me with poison and hardship.[85]

וסבבוני בהוות לבם

1QH 13:31: They surrounded me with the calamity of their heart.

ויוספוה לצוקה וישוכו בעדי בצלמות

1QH 13:33: They have increased the narrowness and have wrapped me in darkness.

אנחה ויגון 35 יסובבוני

1QH 13:34–35: Agony and pain surround me.

כִּי אָפְפוּ־עָלַי רָעוֹת עַד־אֵין מִסְפָּר

Ps 40:12[13]: For evils have encompassed me without number.

לָמָּה אִירָא בִּימֵי רָע עֲוֺן עֲקֵבַי יְסוּבֵּנִי:

Ps 49:5[6]: Why should I fear in times of trouble, when the iniquity of my persecutors surrounds me?

e) Entailments

Turning to entailments, first, the surrounding Antagonist often deliberately surrounds the petitioner, mapping the *cause* of the distress to the deliberate action of those surrounding. This holds where people and

---

85. Author's translation.

Distress and the Constraint Schema

animals are the Antagonists, and sometimes where an agent causes the surrounding with something else, as in God's placing the poison of Lam 3:5 around the petitioner. However, sometimes no deliberate agent is necessary as in 1QH 13:34–35, where the reason for the surrounding elements is not explicit.

Another potential entailment could relate to *intensity*, with more complete surrounding evoking more severe distress. However, there is little evidence of this in the texts (which could be shown by repetition, modifying phrases or infinitive absolutes, for example), unless using סָבִיב itself indicates more severe distress than examples without it.

Third, the *result* of such surrounding is also potentially mapped. In most of these verses, the context suggests an imminent threat. The dogs surrounding the city are growling, ready to take their prey (Ps 59:6–7[7–8]), the talk that surrounds is intended to bring down the petitioner (Pss 109:2–3; 31:13[14]), or their eyes are set to bring him down (Ps 17:11). Thus, just as the result in the source domain would be an imminent attack, the result in the target domain is impending serious disaster, which the petitioner, fixed in one place, is unable to escape.

The following table summarizes this mapping:

Domain	Agonist's Force Tendency	Antagonist's Force Tendency	Causation	Resultant Action
Source	*Free person to move without restraint*	*Surrounding people, or animals to threaten, restrict or capture*	Often deliberate action of those surrounding	Person is held captive by the surrounding forces, which are now ready to attack.
Target	*Self To act freely without hindrance*	*Distressing experiences threaten well-being and life of self so that cannot act freely*	Often deliberate action of those causing distress	Self is threatened and unable to avoid worse distress
Other Entailments: Being fixed and vulnerable to attack → being vulnerable to those causing distress				

6.4.4. Experiencing Distress is Being Enclosed by Water

More specifically, several verses describe petitioners surrounded by water. Water is a significant symbolic threat in the ancient Near East. In the Babylonian *Enuma Elish,* the primeval watery elements Apsu (representing freshwater lakes and marshes) and Tiamat (representing marine water) are killed by Ea and Marduk respectively while creating the cosmos.[86] The Ugaritic texts recount Baal fighting against watery elements named Yam (Sea) and Nahar (River).[87] In both contexts, watery elements are enemies to the rightful god. Reading these anthropologically, "the sea represented everything that the civilized world was not and everything it feared. It had no boundaries, no shape. It was vast, open, and unformed."[88]

Genesis 1 also has water, darkness, and "the deep" (תְהוֹם) present "in the beginning," although there is no indication of intrinsic power, nor that God needed to "fight" them. He simply divides and orders the watery mass. However, in Job and the Psalms, God sometimes more dramatically subdues the waters, as in Ps 74:12–15 or Job 38:8–11, showing they are at times considered as hostile forces even in Israel. Thus, water references in the Psalms may fit a creation context, linking together God's first act of imposing order on the primeval waters with his ongoing ability to create order for individuals in threatening circumstances.[89]

Common embodied experience is also significant. The proximity of the Mediterranean Sea, Dead Sea, and Sea of Galilee suggest the experience of helplessness when surrounded by water may be fairly common, and that people may have heard of others who had drowned. Further, the fluid ability of water to completely surround a person makes it a very natural element to be used with the CONSTRAINT schema.

---

86. Dalley, *Myths*, 233–77.
87. Hallo and Younger, *COS I*, 241–74.
88. Armstrong, *Jerusalem*, 15.
89. Anderson, *Creation*, 93–99.

Distress and the Constraint Schema

a) Examples

Ps 88:17[18] is a prototypical example, using both סבב and נקף in conjunction with watery elements.

סַבּוּנִי כַמַּיִם כָּל־הַיּוֹם הִקִּיפוּ עָלַי יָחַד׃

Ps. 88:17[18]: They surround me all day like water; they close in on me together.[90]

Explicit verbs of surrounding also occur in 1QH 13:39; 17:3–4; and Jon 2:3[4] and 5[6]. Jonah 2 gives a concrete situation for the language used more metaphorically in the Hodayot. Interestingly, the verbs describing Jonah's distress use the CONSTRAINT schema more frequently than the VERTICALITY schema, which is only accessed by a verb in verse 6[7], although the VERTICALITY schema is used throughout the book of Jonah as a significant structural element.[91]

[נחלי ב]ל[י]על אפפו נפשי

1QH 13:39: [The streams of Be]l[i]al surround my throat/soul.

[אפפוני] 4 משברי מות

1QH 17:3–4: The breakers of death [surround me].

וַתַּשְׁלִיכֵנִי מְצוּלָה בִּלְבַב יַמִּים וְנָהָר יְסֹבְבֵנִי כָּל־מִשְׁבָּרֶיךָ וְגַלֶּיךָ עָלַי עָבָרוּ׃

Jon 2:3[4]: You cast me into the deep, into the heart of the seas, and the flood surrounded me; all your waves and your billows passed over me.

אֲפָפוּנִי מַיִם עַד־נֶפֶשׁ תְּהוֹם יְסֹבְבֵנִי סוּף חָבוּשׁ לְרֹאשִׁי׃

Jon 2:5[6]: The waters closed in up to my throat; the deep surrounded me; weeds were wrapped around my head.[92]

---

90. Author's translation.
91. Nel, "Symbolism."
92. Author's translation.

Elsewhere, other verbs situate the petitioner in the midst of water. Lamentations 3:54 uses צוּף, "overflow." שטף also evokes overflowing floodwaters, used in other contexts for invading armies (Isa 8:8, Jer 47:2). In the corpus, this verb is used in Ps 69:1–2[2–3] and communally in Ps 124:3–5. In Ps 32:6 the same root describes the overflowing flood that will not touch the faithful. Verse 7 then conceptualizes distress using צַר, contrasted with being surrounded (סבב) by songs of deliverance, showing the surrounding part of the schema being used with both positive and negative evaluations. In Ps 69:15[16] the root שטף is repeated, but in parallel with two other "surrounding" roots, בלע 'swallow' and אטר 'close', prototypically for the mouth of a well closing over the petitioner. Eliphaz summarizes Job's plight in Job 22:11 with כסה, situating him "covered" by a flood of water (שִׁפְעַת־מַיִם), a verb used prototypically for covering something with a garment. Finally, 1QH 14:22–23 has water "roaring over" (המו על) the petitioner, less directly instantiating the schema, but nevertheless implying that he is covered in water. In all of these texts the person in distress is positioned as an Agonist surrounded on all sides by watery elements.

צָפוּ־מַיִם עַל־רֹאשִׁי אָמַרְתִּי נִגְזָרְתִּי׃

Lam 3:54: Water closed over my head; I said, "I am lost."

הוֹשִׁיעֵנִי אֱלֹהִים כִּי בָאוּ מַיִם עַד־נָפֶשׁ׃ טָבַעְתִּי בִּיוֵן מְצוּלָה וְאֵין מָעֳמָד בָּאתִי בְמַעֲמַקֵּי־מַיִם וְשִׁבֹּלֶת שְׁטָפָתְנִי׃

Ps 69:1–2[2–3]: Save me, O God, for the waters have come up to my neck. I sink in deep mire, where there is no foothold; I have come into deep waters, and the flood sweeps over me.

אֲזַי חַיִּים בְּלָעוּנוּ בַּחֲרוֹת אַפָּם בָּנוּ׃ אֲזַי הַמַּיִם שְׁטָפוּנוּ נַחְלָה עָבַר עַל־נַפְשֵׁנוּ׃ אֲזַי עָבַר עַל־נַפְשֵׁנוּ הַמַּיִם הַזֵּידוֹנִים׃

Ps 124:3–5: Then they would have swallowed us alive, so furious was their anger against us. Then the waters would have overwhelmed us, the torrent would have gone above our necks, then it would have gone above our throats—those raging waters.[93]

---

93. Based on Allen, *Psalms 101–150*, 163.

עַל־זֹאת יִתְפַּלֵּל כָּל־חָסִיד אֵלֶיךָ לְעֵת מְצֹא רַק לְשֵׁטֶף מַיִם
רַבִּים אֵלָיו לֹא יַגִּיעוּ׃
אַתָּה סֵתֶר לִי מִצַּר תִּצְּרֵנִי רָנֵּי פַלֵּט תְּסוֹבְבֵנִי׃

Ps 32:6–7: Therefore let every godly one pray to you at a time of stress, at the flood of mighty waters, they shall not reach him. You are a hiding place for me: you will protect me from trouble, you will surround me with shouts of deliverance.[94]

אַל־תִּשְׁטְפֵנִי שִׁבֹּלֶת מַיִם וְאַל־תִּבְלָעֵנִי מְצוּלָה וְאַל־תֶּאְטַר־עָלַי
בְּאֵר פִּיהָ׃

Ps 69:15[16]: Rescue me from sinking in the mire; let me be delivered from my enemies and from the deep waters. Do not let the flood sweep over me, or the deep swallow me up, or the well[95] close its mouth over me.

וְשִׁפְעַת־מַיִם תְּכַסֶּךָּ׃

Job 22:11: A flood of water covers you.

והיי|תי כמלח באוניה 23 ימים גליהם וכול משבריהם עלי המו
בזעף

1QH 14:22–23: I [have become] like a sailor in a ship in the raging seas: their waves and all their breakers roar over me.

b) Entailments

These images map *intensity* onto distressing experiences. The embodied experience of drowning entails that the more of the body covered in water, the more serious the situation. If the water reaches head-level, the predicament is very severe. This entailment is mapped onto general situations of distress here. In Ps 69:1[2] and Jon 2:5[6], waters reach the level of the petitioner's neck (נֶפֶשׁ), signaling the severity of the situation, whereas in Ps 124:4–5 the author offers thanks that the water did not exceed this level (עָבַר עַל־נַפְשֵׁנוּ). Lamentations 3:54 has the

---

94. Craigie, *Psalms 1–50*, 264.
95. NRSV has "the Pit" here.

most serious predicament, with the water already above the head (עַל־רֹאשִׁי), so that the petitioner is indeed "lost." The *result* is also clear. If the petitioner is not helped out he will drown, the ultimate threat of terminal, uncreating disaster.

In terms of *causation*, it is possible here to hide personal agency, since sometimes water alone is mentioned, without any other human or divine agent. This Antagonist can be used for impersonal forces constraining the person, without attributing distress to any particular personal agent.

The mappings and entailments here are summarized in the following table:

Domain	Agonist's Force Tendency	Antagonist's Force Tendency	Causation	Resultant Action
Source	Person in water To carry on breathing	Water To surround the person, preventing him from breathing	Non-agentive "natural" forces	Water finally overwhelms person and he drowns
Target	Self To carry on living	Distressing experiences To destroy the person	Non-specific agents	Increasingly severe distress ends in death
Other Entailments: More complete covering by water → More severe situation of distress				

6.4.5. Experiencing Distress is Being Under Siege

Another "surrounding" image relates to being besieged, linked specifically to the CONSTRAINT schema through the use of צרר in the hiphil for this scenario.

a) Encyclopedic Knowledge

Archaeological, textual, and pictorial evidence reveal much about the experience of siege in Ancient Israel. Archaeological evidence suggests walled cities became the normal dwelling from the tenth century

BCE, whether residential, or with various administrative and military functions.⁹⁶ Still, most inhabitants were farmers, so men spent morning to evening outside the city walls. Fields, olive groves, vineyards, and enclosures for flocks and herds were all outside the city walls, as were threshing floors, winepresses, places for slaughtering animals, and probably potters' and smiths' workshops.⁹⁷ Being under siege prevented all these activities, particularly prohibiting food collection, resulting eventually in starvation. Whilst undoubtedly many Israelite cities experienced siege conditions (for example, according to Assyrian records, Sennacherib laid siege to forty-six Israelite strong cities and walled forts in 701 BCE),⁹⁸ Sennacherib's siege of Lachish has left most evidence, in Assyrian reliefs and archaeological remains,⁹⁹ revealing the siege ramp built by the Assyrians, on which to wheel battering rams, while defenders threw torches or stones or fired arrows from the walls (leaving remains still found at the site).¹⁰⁰ The reliefs and excavations also depict the siege's consequences: exiles are led away and others impaled on spears, the scale of the massacre indicated by some 1,500 skeletons found in a water shaft near the city.¹⁰¹ Although this was an atypical siege (Lachish was probably Judah's second city,¹⁰² and the Assyrian siege ramp has no parallels),¹⁰³ the attention devoted to this particular conquest in Assyria shows its salience there. It may have been salient for Israel's general populace too, despite the minimal discussion in the Bible's official history. The Assyrian record of Sennacherib's campaign also suggests the salient aspects of besieging a city:

> I laid siege to 46 of [Hezekiah's] strong cities, walled forts, and to countless small villages in their vicinity, and conquered (them) by means of well-stamped (earth-) ramps, and battering-rams brought (thus) near (to the walls)

---

96. Fritz, *City*, 117–18.
97. Ibid., 176–89.
98. Pritchard, *ANET*, 288.
99. Dever, *Writers*, 167–72.
100. Mazar, *Archaeology*, 430–34.
101. Dever, *Writers*, 169.
102. Ibid., 171.
103. Mazar, *Archaeology*, 432.

> (combined with) the attack of foot soldiers, (using) mines, breaches as well as sapper work. I drove out (of them) 200,150 people, young and old, male and female, horses, mules, donkeys, camels, big and small cattle beyond counting, and considered (them) booty. Himself I made a prisoner, in Jerusalem, his royal residence, like a bird in a cage. I surrounded him with earthwork in order to molest those who were leaving his city's gate.[104]

Yadin identifies the siege as the most protracted way of conquering a city, and the one least dangerous to the attacker, noting that "its aim was to encircle the city and so prevent supplies from reaching the defenders within . . . it became, in great measure, a passive force."[105]

b) Examples

In the corpus, then, the distressed petitioner is sometimes pictured as an Agonist in a besieged city, with the Antagonist as the besieging army (complete with accompanying siege works), as in Ps 31:21[22] and in 1QH 11:7.

בָּרוּךְ יְהוָה כִּי הִפְלִיא חַסְדּוֹ לִי בְּעִיר מָצוֹר׃

> Ps. 31:21[22]: Blessed be the LORD, for he has wondrously shown his steadfast love to me when I was beset as a city[106] under siege.

וכעיר מבצר מלפני | אויביה | אהיה בצוקה

> 1QH 11:7: Like a fortified city positioned opposite [its enemies], I was in distress . . .

In Job 19, different parts of the siege scenario are mapped onto his distress. In verse 6, the siege works surrounding (הִקִּיף) the city are highlighted. In verse 12, סבב evokes "surrounding" again, now by a

---

104. Pritchard, *ANET*, 288.
105. Yadin, *Warfare*, 18.
106. Literally, "in a besieged city." Craigie, *Psalms 1–50*, 258 emends the MT to עֵת 'time,' but this is unnecessary given the other examples where the siege source domain is explicitly exploited.

multiplicity of troops (perhaps mapped onto the multiplicity of sufferings Job was experiencing). There is also reference to the enemy paving an assault ramp (וַיָּסֹלּוּ עָלַי דַּרְכָּם) against Job, maybe comparable to that at Lachish.[107] Such siege works also likely complete the verb בנה in Lam 3:5, where God "builds against" the author. Indeed, the construction בנה על is used for constructing siege works in Deut 20:20 and Ezek 4:2,[108] albeit with the object explicit there.

דְּעוּ־אֵפוֹ כִּי־אֱלוֹהַּ עִוְּתָנִי וּמְצוּדוֹ עָלַי הִקִּיף׃

Job 19:6: Know then that God has subverted my cause and surrounded me with his siege works.[109]

יַחַד יָבֹאוּ גְדוּדָיו וַיָּסֹלּוּ עָלַי דַּרְכָּם וַיַּחֲנוּ סָבִיב לְאָהֳלִי׃

Job 19:12: His troops come forth all together; they have paved their road against me and have encamped around my tent.[110]

בָּנָה עָלַי וַיַּקַּף רֹאשׁ וּתְלָאָה׃

Lam 3:5: He builds a rampart against me and surrounds me with poison and hardship.[111]

A final example is 1QH 10:25–26, referring to the camps of the enemies and using סבב with weapons of war (כלי מלחמותם).

ואני אמרת חנו עלי גבורים סבבים בכל 26 כלי מלחמותם

---

107. Wolfers sees so much siege imagery in Job as to suggest the book should be read as a metaphor for the sufferings of Israel during Sennacherib's campaign of 702 BCE (Wolfers, *Deep*). However, in the text itself, these images conceptualize Job's personal distress, which according to the prologue is a result of the loss of his family and possessions and the impact of physical illness.

108. Eidevall, "Spatial," 135.

109. The NRSV reads מְצוּדוֹ as "his net." However, the military context suggest it is rather a "temporary wall that besiegers built around a city they were attacking" (Gordis, *Job*, 196, 201).

110. Translation from Gordis, *Job*, 196. The NRSV corrects the text to make "siege works" explicit instead of "their way." In either case, however, the siege metaphor is clear.

111. Author's translation.

Surrounded by Bitterness

> 1QH 10:25–26: And I, I said, mighty men have encamped against me, surrounding <me> with all their weapons of war.[112]

c) Entailments

Turning to entailments, first, understanding distress via the siege mapping allows an explicit *agent* of distress. The commander of the besieging army in the target domain becomes God (in Job and Lamentations), or the petitioner's adversaries (Ps 31:21[22] and 1QH 11:7). Second, the *result* is clear. A siege is designed to wear down resistance and finally defeat the town when it has been suitably weakened. Rescue is not possible without external help. Similarly, where distressing symptoms "besiege" someone, the inference is that if this continues without external help the person will finally be weakened to the point he will not be able to resist anymore, and will finally be ultimately defeated.

The table below summarizes this mapping:

Domain	Agonist's Force Tendency	Antagonist's Force Tendency	Causation	Resultant Action
Source	Inhabitants of city to freely leave the city to harvest food and trade	Besieging army to prohibit exit from the city and destroy defenses	Deliberate action of attacking commander	Inhabitants are unable to break the siege to get food and, ultimately, surrender or die
Target	Self to be able to look after self and freely act to provide for needs	Distressing experiences prohibit self from providing for needs, destroy the self's protection	Deliberate action of God or adversaries	Self is unable to end the distressing experiences and, ultimately, dies

---

112. Kittel, *Hymns*, 35.

6.4.6. Experiencing Distress is Being Held in a Net or Trap

Returning from the "surrounding" aspect of the CONSTRAINT schema to that of being held, one of the most elaborated images is that of being caught in a net or a trap. In this scenario the petitioner maps onto a hunted animal Agonist (whether bird, fish or land animal), and the Antagonist is the trap that closes around it.

a) Encyclopedic Knowledge

The Bible rarely refers to hunting in Israel in narrative contexts (although frequent in poetic texts), and never glorifies it, in contrast to other ancient Near Eastern cultures where the king's hunting prowess is celebrated as a sign of his power.[113] In these cultures, nets and traps were significant for hunting, since the ancient Sumerian sign for hunting originally meant "to surround," making it "evident that the hunt was originally conducted by entrapment in nets or pits."[114] However, depictions of Assyrian royal hunts show other hunting methods, with the king and his companions on foot, on horseback and in chariots armed with bows and arrows and chasing lions, elephants, cattle, or goats across the plains.[115] However, in the psalms the hunting metaphors all relate to pits, traps, nets, and snares. This may reflect the different geography and methods of hunting in Palestine, but also emphasizes a particular kind of hunting. Whereas the enemy is visible and the animal may fight back in the open field, the use of pits and nets relies on concealment and surprise, leading to inescapable disaster. Once caught, the animal has no chance of survival.[116]

Various words signify different nets and traps. A פַּח is prototypically for catching birds, since only they are mentioned in conjunction with the word. The description in Amos 3:5 suggests a triggered snare (shown in Egyptian art) made from two curved frames attached to nets which are set half open. When a bird attempts to take bait from the

---

113. Oeming, "צוד," 272–73.
114. Keel, *Symbolism*, 89.
115. Roaf, *Atlas*, 154–55.
116. Keel, *Symbolism*, 89.

trigger, the snare closes around the bird and it is trapped in the net.[117] מוֹקֵשׁ often occurs with פַּח, probably referring to the trigger or its bait.[118] Kellermann suggests the main meaning focus of פַּח is "trickery and ruin,"[119] however, suddenness and concealment seem to be equally, if not more, important in this corpus.

A רֶשֶׁת is a more general word for nets to catch birds and larger animals. Some could be pulled shut when a bird entered it, others were camouflaged in the ground to catch small animals, or were stretched out so that large animals (such as lions) could be driven in. A רֶשֶׁת never refers to a fishing net, these being most often referred to as מְצוֹדָה.[120] Very occasionally צַמִּים is used, but no precise identification is possible. Cognates suggest at best something drawn together,[121] and translations include "noose"[122] or "web."[123]

These different traps have different scripts, mapped metaphorically to distress situations. For the פַּח (bird snare), the trap is baited and left by the hunter. When a bird takes the bait, the jaws snap shut. If the bird is quick enough, it could potentially escape, otherwise it is trapped in the net, in which case the end is inevitable unless it can manage to break the trap. There is no escaping death on the hunter's return. The רֶשֶׁת script is more general. As a concealed net in the ground, an animal may get its legs caught so that it is, at least temporarily, held fast. It may be possible to break free before the hunter finds the animal, or the animal may be helped out of the net in this time. In other kinds of רֶשֶׁת the hunter stayed close to the net, though concealed, to draw it together as the animal is captured. Parts of these scripts are used metaphorically, and the knowledge of concealment, surprise, suddenness, and inevitability of disaster once caught are all used to draw inferences about distress.

---

117. Kellermann, "פַּח," 514.
118. Keel, *Symbolism*, 91, Ringgren, "יָקַשׁ," 288.
119. Kellermann, "פַּח," 514.
120. Mommer, "רֶשֶׁת," 17.
121. BDB 855.
122. Gordis, *Job*, 188.
123. Wolfers, *Deep*, 339.

b) Examples

One of the clearest examples of the mapping from being in a net to being in distress is found in Eccl 9:12, although outside the specific corpus.

כִּי גַּם לֹא־יֵדַע הָאָדָם אֶת־עִתּוֹ כַּדָּגִים שֶׁנֶּאֱחָזִים בִּמְצוֹדָה רָעָה וְכַצִּפֳּרִים הָאֲחֻזוֹת בַּפָּח כָּהֵם יוּקָשִׁים בְּנֵי הָאָדָם לְעֵת רָעָה כְּשֶׁ־תִּפּוֹל עֲלֵיהֶם פִּתְאֹם׃

> Ecclesiastes 9:12: For no one can anticipate the time of disaster. Like fish taken in a cruel net, and like birds caught in a snare, so mortals are snared at a time of calamity, when it suddenly falls upon them.

Here the sufferer is understood as a bird or a fish that has been trapped, explicitly emphasizing suddenness (פִּתְאֹם) and unexpectedness (לֹא־יֵדַע הָאָדָם אֶת־עִתּוֹ), although also allowing the inference that such calamity, once it falls, is inescapable.

Within the specific corpus, the petitioner is not usually positioned inside the net. However, Ps 31:4[5] and 1QH 16:34 give two such examples, first using the larger רֶשֶׁת, so the trapped animal could conceivably be released before the hunter returns. In the latter, the noun כֶּבֶל 'snare' is only used twice in the Bible, for prisoners' iron fetters. However, here, from Qumran and in conjunction with לכד, it likely refers to a kind of snare. The petitioner is never located inside a פַּח, perhaps because of the finality of such a plight. Psalm 66:11 gives a final example of actually being in a net, from a communal lament.

תּוֹצִיאֵנִי מֵרֶשֶׁת זוּ טָמְנוּ לִי כִּי־אַתָּה מָעוּזִּי׃

> Ps. 31:4[5]: Take me out of the net they hid[124] for me, for you are my refuge.

רג[ל]י נלכדה בכבל וילכו כמים ברכי ואין לשלוח פעם ולא מצעד לקול רגלי

> 1QH 16:34: My [fo]ot has been caught in the snare, my knees slide like water, and it is impossible to move one step forward, there is no sound to the tread of my feet.

---

124. NRSV has "is hidden," but the form here is an active third person.

הֲבֵאתָנוּ בַמְּצוּדָה

Ps 66:11: You brought us into the net.

More commonly, traps have been set and the petitioner fears being caught in them, as in Ps 38:12[13]; 1QH 21:8; Ps 119:110; Lam 1:13; and Ps 141:9–10. The phrase יְדֵי פַח in Ps 141:9 suggests the bows of the trap that hold the net.[125] 1QH 11:26 is unusual in including fishing nets (מכמרת על פני מים) as well as traps more common from the Psalms (פחים and מצודות).

וַיְנַקְשׁוּ מְבַקְשֵׁי נַפְשִׁי וְדֹרְשֵׁי רָעָתִי דִּבְּרוּ הַוּוֹת וּמִרְמוֹת כָּל־הַיּוֹם יֶהְגּוּ:

Ps 38:12[13]: Those who seek my life lay their snares; those who seek to hurt me speak of ruin, and meditate treachery all day long.

ופח לפח יטמונו צמי רשעה

1QH 21:8: They have hidden trap upon trap, the snares of wickedness.

נָתְנוּ רְשָׁעִים פַּח לִי

Ps 119:110: The wicked have laid a snare for me.

פָּרַשׂ רֶשֶׁת לְרַגְלָי

Lam 1:13: He spread a net for my feet.

שָׁמְרֵנִי מִידֵי פַח יָקְשׁוּ לִי וּמֹקְשׁוֹת פֹּעֲלֵי אָוֶן: יִפְּלוּ בְמַכְמֹרָיו רְשָׁעִים יַחַד אָנֹכִי עַד־אֶעֱבוֹר:

Ps 141:9–10: Guard me from the jaws of the traps they have set for me and the snares of evildoers. May the wicked fall one and all into their own nets, while I myself escape.[126]

---

125. Keel, *Symbolism*, 91.
126. Allen, *Psalms 101–150*, 270.

Distress and the Constraint Schema

בהפתח כל פחי שחת ויפרשו כול מצודות רשעה ומכמרת
חלכאים על פני מים

> 1QH 11:26: When all the traps of the pit open, all the snares of wickedness are spread and the nets of scoundrels are upon the surface of the sea.

In these verses, the petitioners' experience of distress is the fear of an animal faced by snares, rather than being trapped already. However, this mapping still reflects the conceptualization that being caught in a trap would be a kind of distress, an even worse scenario than the current predicament. That is, the entailed result of this image, whether in a trap or in fear of falling into one, is that of being caught and held utterly at the mercy of one's enemies.

Turning to Job, he never positions himself as trapped or in danger of being snared, but his friends do, either explicitly or implicitly (as they discuss the fate of the wicked). In Job 22:10, Eliphaz describes Job's plight as one surrounded (סבב) by snares, a double use of the CONSTRAINT schema, both being surrounded by the snares collectively, and at danger of being held by any particular one. In Job 18:8–10, Bildad's summary of the plight of the wicked (and Job by inference) devotes six cola to understanding the disasters they face as being trapped by a net (רֶשֶׁת), a snare (פַּח), a noose (צַמִּים), a rope (חֶבֶל), and a trap (מַלְכֹּד), as well as the less easily identified שְׁבָכָה.

עַל־כֵּן סְבִיבוֹתֶיךָ פַחִים וִיבַהֶלְךָ פַּחַד פִּתְאֹם׃

> Job 22:10: Therefore snares are around you, and sudden terror overwhelms you.

כִּי־שֻׁלַּח בְּרֶשֶׁת בְּרַגְלָיו וְעַל־שְׂבָכָה יִתְהַלָּךְ׃ יֹאחֵז בְּעָקֵב פָּח
יַחֲזֵק עָלָיו צַמִּים׃ טָמוּן בָּאָרֶץ חַבְלוֹ וּמַלְכֻּדְתּוֹ עֲלֵי נָתִיב׃

> Job 18:8–10: For they are thrust into a net by their own feet, and they walk into a pitfall. A trap seizes them by the heel; a snare lays hold of them. A rope is hid for them in the ground, a trap for them in the path.

Surrounded by Bitterness

c) Entailments

Nets and traps frame the CONSTRAINT schema to draw explicit attention to the *agentive cause* of distress (in contrast to narrow places, water, or prison), mapping the hunter setting the trap onto the agent causing distress. The cause is very deliberate: nets and snares are not left accidentally, they are deliberately set to catch prey. By using this metaphor, petitioners attribute deliberate action against them by others, whether human adversaries (the wicked [Ps 119:110], "workers of iniquity" [Ps 141:9]), or God himself, to whom the petition is addressed (as in Lam 1:13). Ps 18:5[6] even grants personification to death as the one trying to snare the petitioner.

חֶבְלֵי שְׁאוֹל סְבָבוּנִי קִדְּמוּנִי מוֹקְשֵׁי מָוֶת׃

Ps 18:5[6]: The cords of Sheol entangled me; the snares of death confronted me.

Other entailments of the "trap" script are explicitly highlighted in the metaphors of the specific corpus. First, being caught is no fault of the animal. In the mapping, this conceptual metaphor highlights the innocence of the petitioner in contrast to his adversaries' cunning, so that the distress falling upon him is *unjustified*. This is explicit in Ps 35:7.

כִּי־חִנָּם טָמְנוּ־לִי שַׁחַת רִשְׁתָּם חִנָּם חָפְרוּ לְנַפְשִׁי׃

Ps 35:7: For without cause they hid their net[127] for me, without cause they dug a pit for my life.

Second, being caught is also *unsuspected*, with the hidden nature of nets and traps frequently made explicit. Just as the prey is unable to perceive a hidden trap, the petitioner is concerned about a source of distress that he is unable to discern until it is too late. The root טמן is used for this concealment in Ps 31:4[5]; 1QH 21:8 (both cited above); Pss 64:5[6]; 142:3[4]; and 1QH 21:4.

---

127. "Net" and "pit" are the other way around in Hebrew, but the sentence only makes sense this way, as in Craigie, *Psalms 1–50*, 285.

Distress and the Constraint Schema

יַחַזְּקוּ־לָמוֹ דָּבָר רָע יְסַפְּרוּ לִטְמוֹן מוֹקְשִׁים אָמְרוּ מִי יִרְאֶה־לָּמוֹ׃

Ps 64:5[6]: They hold fast to their evil purpose; they talk of laying snares secretly, thinking, "Who can see us?"

בְּאֹרַח־זוּ אֲהַלֵּךְ טָמְנוּ פַח לִי׃

Ps 142:3[4]: In the path where I walk they have hidden a trap for me.

[...] ופעמי על מט(מ)יני פחיה ומפרשי ר[שת]

1QH 21:4: [...] my steps over those who hide its traps and who stretch a n[et ...].

Several verses map release from the confines of a net or trap to relief from distress. Psalms 25:15 and 31:4[5] (cited above) use this entailment in individual lament, whereas Ps 124:7 gives an example from a communal lament. The former two examples also demonstrate the helplessness of the prey, the only way out of distress is by the action of an outsider. Psalm 124 is a rare example where the animal manages to escape on its own, through the trap "breaking."

עֵינַי תָּמִיד אֶל־יְהוָה כִּי הוּא־יוֹצִיא מֵרֶשֶׁת רַגְלָי׃

Ps 25:15: My eyes are ever toward the LORD, for he will pluck my feet out of the net.

נַפְשֵׁנוּ כְּצִפּוֹר נִמְלְטָה מִפַּח יוֹקְשִׁים הַפַּח נִשְׁבָּר וַאֲנַחְנוּ נִמְלָטְנוּ׃

Ps 124:7: We have escaped like a bird from the snare of the fowlers; the snare is broken, and we have escaped.

A final frequent entailment is the possibility of the hunters being trapped in their own devices. Within the source domain this is at least theoretically possible, but in the target domain this idea is variously elaborated to become a significant feature of this conceptual metaphor. In Ps 141:10 (cited above), the petitioner sees all the wicked falling into their own traps while he alone escapes. In Ps 57:6[7], the psalmist's enemies use a net and a pit, but they themselves fall in, and in Ps 35:8 the psalmist asks for his adversaries to be caught in the net they set for him in v. 7. Nets and traps both capture those who set them in 1QH 10:29. Finally, Ps 7:15[16] and Ps 9:15[16] both assert that those who dig holes and set nets end up trapped by their own activities.

רֶשֶׁת הֵכִינוּ לִפְעָמַי כָּפַף נַפְשִׁי כָּרוּ לְפָנַי שִׁיחָה נָפְלוּ בְתוֹכָהּ סֶלָה׃

Ps 57:6[7]: They set a net for my steps; my soul was bowed down. They dug a pit in my path, but they have fallen into it themselves.

תְּבוֹאֵהוּ שׁוֹאָה לֹא־יֵדָע וְרִשְׁתּוֹ אֲשֶׁר־טָמַן תִּלְכְּדוֹ בְּשׁוֹאָה יִפָּל־בָּהּ׃

Ps 35:8: Let ruin come on them unawares. And let the net that they hid ensnare them; let them fall in it—to their ruin.

והם רשת פרשו לי תלכוד רגלם ופחים טמנו לנפשי נפלו בם

1QH 10:29: But they, the net which they spread for me, entangled their own feet, in the traps they hid for my life, they have fallen.

בּוֹר כָּרָה וַיַּחְפְּרֵהוּ וַיִּפֹּל בְּשַׁחַת יִפְעָל׃

Ps 7:15[16]: They make a pit, digging it out, and fall into the hole that they have made.

טָבְעוּ גוֹיִם בְּשַׁחַת עָשׂוּ בְּרֶשֶׁת־זוּ טָמָנוּ נִלְכְּדָה רַגְלָם׃ נוֹדַע יְהוָה מִשְׁפָּט עָשָׂה בְּפֹעַל כַּפָּיו נוֹקֵשׁ רָשָׁע הִגָּיוֹן סֶלָה׃

Ps 9:15–16[16–17]: The nations have sunk in the pit that they made; in the net that they hid has their own foot been caught. The LORD has made himself known, he has executed judgment; the wicked are snared in the work of their own hands.

Finally, do any aspects of this image map onto the *intensity* of distress? One way is through the contrast between being surrounded by nets and actually being in the net itself. Being caught expresses a more severe situation than just being worried about the traps. Another way of expressing intensity is through highlighting the number of traps, either by reduplication, as in the reference to ופח לפח in 1QH 21:8, or through the multiplication of different kind of traps, as in the six different images of Job 18:8–10.

These mappings and entailments are summarized in the following table.

Domain	Agonist's Force Tendency	Antagonist's Force Tendency	Causation	Resultant Action
Source	Animal to move and act freely	Net / trap to hold the animal until hunters arrive to kill it	Deliberate action of hunters directed at prey	Animal is held and, ultimately, captured and killed by hunters
Target	Self to act freely	Distressing experiences to bring self under the control of adversaries	Deliberate action of adversaries directed at self	Person is completely under the control / at the mercy of the adversaries
Other Entailments: Prey is innocent (not responsible for getting caught) → Situation of distress is unjustified Prey does not suspect the trap → Situation of distress comes suddenly and unexpectedly Trap can snare the hunter → Situation of distress can fall on the adversary				

6.4.7. Experiencing Distress is Being Confined in a Pit

Closely related to these images are those of being trapped in a pit. These images were discussed in some detail in chapter five. However, as they conflate both being down and being constrained (by the walls of a pit) they need brief revisiting.

The two main types of pits mentioned are בּוֹר and שַׁחַת, the former prototypically referring to a pit dug for water or produce storage, whereas the latter is dug deliberately for trapping animals,[128] and thus fits closely with trap images. References to being in, or on the way to, a בּוֹר occur in Lam 3:53, 55; Pss 40:2[3]; 88:6[7]; and 143:7.

צָמְתוּ בַבּוֹר חַיָּי וַיַּדּוּ־אֶבֶן בִּי׃

Lam 3:53: They flung me alive into a pit and hurled stones on me.

---

128. See chapter 5.

Surrounded by Bitterness

קָרָאתִי שִׁמְךָ יְהוָה מִבּוֹר תַּחְתִּיּוֹת׃

Lam 3:55: I called on your name, O LORD, from the depths of the pit.

וַיַּעֲלֵנִי מִבּוֹר שָׁאוֹן מִטִּיט הַיָּוֵן וַיָּקֶם עַל־סֶלַע רַגְלַי כּוֹנֵן אֲשֻׁרָי׃

Ps 40:2[3]: He drew me up from the desolate pit, out of the miry bog, and set my feet upon a rock, making my steps secure.

שַׁתַּנִי בְּבוֹר תַּחְתִּיּוֹת בְּמַחֲשַׁכִּים בִּמְצֹלוֹת׃

Ps 88:6[7]: You have put me in the depths of the pit, in the regions dark and deep.

אַל־תַּסְתֵּר פָּנֶיךָ מִמֶּנִּי וְנִמְשַׁלְתִּי עִם־יֹרְדֵי בוֹר׃

Ps 143:7: Do not hide your face from me, or I shall be like those who go down to the pit.

Since a בּוֹר already exists, where the agent is mentioned (Ps 88:6[7], Lam 3:53) it is someone who has put the petitioner into the pit. Where שַׁחַת or related words are used, by contrast, the agent has more premeditated intentions, actually digging the pit out, as in Jer 18:20, 22; and Ps 119:85.

הַיְשֻׁלַּם תַּחַת־טוֹבָה רָעָה כִּי־כָרוּ שׁוּחָה לְנַפְשִׁי

Jer 18.20: Is evil a recompense for good? Yet they have dug a pit for my life.

כִּי־כָרוּ שׁוּחָה לְלָכְדֵנִי וּפַחִים טָמְנוּ לְרַגְלָי׃

Jer 18.22: For they have dug a pit to catch me, and laid snares for my feet.

כָּרוּ־לִי זֵדִים שִׁיחוֹת אֲשֶׁר לֹא כְתוֹרָתֶךָ׃

Ps 119:85: The arrogant have dug pitfalls for me; they flout your law.

The result of being in a pit is eventual death, whether it is a prison from which one cannot escape, or a pit dug for animals in which one awaits the returning hunter to come and claim his catch. This result is mapped onto the target domain. Someone in a pit is doomed and awaiting the inevitable end.

1QH 13:6 uses the entailment that it is impossible to escape from a pit oneself, but is possible with another's help. Along with Ps 40:2[3] (above), this also shows that release from distress is being brought out to space from the pit. The lack of a verb of vertical upward movement for this release suggests that the confining aspect of pits is just as important as the vertical aspect.

> ולא עזבתני בזמות יצרי ותעזור משחת חיי

> 1QH 13:6: Nor did you abandon me to my wicked nature, but you helped my life out of the pit.[129]

In these examples, the pit (either בּוֹר or שַׁחַת) is frequently a metaphor for the ultimate situation of distress, existence in Sheol. This is often shown by the subsequent parallel expressions, as in 1QH 11:19–20.

> אודכה אדוני כי פדיתה נפשי משחת ומשאול אבדון העליתני
> לרום עולם ואתהלכה במישור לאין חקר

> 1QH 11:19–20: I thank you, Lord, because you have saved my life from the pit, and from the Sheol of Abaddon have lifted me up to an everlasting height, so that I can walk on a boundless plain.

Conceptualizing the ultimate end of humanity as in a "pit" is further evidence of the significance of this constraint schema for understanding distress. If the worst possible outcome of distress (the end of life) is understood as a confining pit, it is not surprising that less severe examples of distress in everyday life are also understood as restriction. Sheol is the paradigmatic example of confinement, where the force tendency for movement is once and for all restrained and there is no chance of return.

These mappings and entailments are summarized below:

---

129. Kittel, *Hymns*, 84.

Surrounded by Bitterness

Domain	Agonist's Force Tendency	Antagonist's Force Tendency	Causation	Resultant Action
Source	Person or animal To move freely	Pit walls To prevent the person or animal escaping	Pit may be dug deliberately to trap, or person may be thrown in	Person or animal perishes from lack of food or is taken and killed
Target	Self To live and act freely	Distressing Experiences To hold back the self	May be a result of deliberate action	Self ultimately perishes

Other Entailments:
Release from the pit → Relief from distress
Inability to help oneself out → Inability to get out of distress alone

6.4.8. Experiencing Distress is Being Tied Up with Cords

a) Examples

In several verses, the Antagonist is identified as binding ropes or fetters, tying either a hunted animal or a person bound in prison. Often חֶבֶל is used. In Ps 119:61, the ropes of the wicked are restricting the author, but in Pss 18:4–5[5–6]; 116:3; and the apocalyptic 1QH 11:28, they are more sinister ropes of death. Thus, these metaphors map an agent, although the agency is minimized by using a construct state rather than a verb of "tying." The roots expressing the ropes' restriction include אפף and סבב, already noted as accessing the surrounding part of the CONSTRAINT schema, and עוד which is used in the piel for "surrounding."

חֶבְלֵי רְשָׁעִים עִוְּדֻנִי תּוֹרָתְךָ לֹא שָׁכָחְתִּי׃

Ps 119:61: The cords of wicked men are all around me—I do not forget your Torah.[130]

---

130. Based on Allen, *Psalms 101–150*, 129.

Distress and the Constraint Schema

אֲפָפוּנִי חֶבְלֵי־מָוֶת וּמְצָרֵי שְׁאוֹל מְצָאוּנִי צָרָה וְיָגוֹן אֶמְצָא:

Ps 116:3: Death's cords were all around me, Sheol's nooses had seized me, I encountered distress and anguish.[131]

אֲפָפוּנִי חֶבְלֵי־מָוֶת וְנַחֲלֵי בְלִיַּעַל יְבַעֲתוּנִי: חֶבְלֵי שְׁאוֹל סְבָבוּנִי קִדְּמוּנִי מוֹקְשֵׁי מָוֶת:

Ps 18:4–5[5–6]: Death's cords were all around me;[132] the torrents of perdition assailed me. The cords of Sheol have surrounded me; the snares of death have confronted me.[133]

וקץ חרון לכול בליעל וחבלי מות אפפו לאין פלט

1QH 11:28: And the period of anger against any Belial, and the ropes of death enclose with no escape.

In Job 36:8 (implicitly directed at Job) and Ps 107:10, Agonists are bound by the more abstract Antagonist of "affliction" (עֳנִי / עֱנִי).

וְאִם־אֲסוּרִים בַּזִּקִּים יִלָּכְדוּן בְּחַבְלֵי־עֹנִי:

Job 36:8: And if they are bound in fetters and caught in the cords of affliction...

יֹשְׁבֵי חֹשֶׁךְ וְצַלְמָוֶת אֲסִירֵי עֳנִי וּבַרְזֶל:

Ps 107:10: ... those who lived in darkness grim as death, fettered in affliction's iron chains.[134]

Sometimes the verb אסר makes the agency of the aggressor more explicit, as in Job 36:13 (implicitly applied to Job), although at other times a passive or niphal is used, hiding the agent, as in Job 36:8 (above) and 1QH 13:36–37. The passive form of רתק also minimizes the agent of distress in 1QH 16:35.

---

131. Allen, *Psalms 101–150*, 111.
132. As in Psalm 116.
133. Craigie, *Psalms 1–50*, 166.
134. Based on Allen, *Psalms 101–150*, 56.

Surrounded by Bitterness

וְחַנְפֵי־לֵב יָשִׂימוּ אָף לֹא יְשַׁוְּעוּ כִּי אֲסָרָם׃

Job 36:13: The godless in heart cherish anger; they do not cry for help when he binds them.

כי נאסר[תי] בעבותים 37 לאין נתק וזקים ללוא ישוברו וחומת עוז יסבני ובריחי ברזל ודלתי[ן] נחושת לאי[ן] 38 [פתוח]

1QH 13:36–38: For [I] am tied with ropes which can not be untied, with fetters which can not be broken; a str[ong] wall [surrounds me,] iron bars and [bronze] doors [which can not] [be opened].

זרועי רותקו בזקי מכשול...

1QH 16:35: My arms are bound by fetters which cause stumbling.

Restricting chains are also intended by the heavy "bronzes" in Lam 3:7.

הִכְבִּיד נְחָשְׁתִּי׃

Lam 3:7: He has put heavy chains on me;

b) Entailments

Turning to entailments, several verses describe relief as removal of the bonds restraining the petitioner. This is specified as "opening" (פתח, Ps 116:16) or "cutting" (קצץ, Ps 129:4) the bonds, and in Psalm 107 as "snapping" (נתק) and "cutting in half" (גדע).

אָנָּה יְהוָה כִּי־אֲנִי עַבְדֶּךָ אֲנִי־עַבְדְּךָ בֶּן־אֲמָתֶךָ פִּתַּחְתָּ לְמוֹסֵרָי׃

Ps 116:16: O LORD, I am your servant; I am your servant, the child of your serving girl. You have undone my bonds.

יְהוָה צַדִּיק קִצֵּץ עֲבוֹת רְשָׁעִים׃

Ps 129:4: The LORD is righteous; he has cut the cords of the wicked.

יוֹצִיאֵם מֵחֹשֶׁךְ וְצַלְמָוֶת וּמוֹסְרוֹתֵיהֶם יְנַתֵּק: יוֹדוּ לַיהוָה חַסְדּוֹ
וְנִפְלְאוֹתָיו לִבְנֵי אָדָם: כִּי־שִׁבַּר דַּלְתוֹת נְחֹשֶׁת וּבְרִיחֵי בַרְזֶל
גִּדֵּעַ:

> Ps 107:14–16: He brought them out of darkness and gloom, and broke their bonds asunder. Let them thank the LORD for his steadfast love, for his wonderful works to humankind. For he shatters the doors of bronze, and cuts in two the bars of iron.

Being bound with fetters has the implication of being in the control of someone else, thus becoming totally at their mercy. In Psalms 18 and 116, the psalmist felt himself in the control of death and thus in danger of being taken prisoner forever to Sheol. This mapping then entails the result that the one tied is in danger of worse disaster from the agent who has tied him up and has him in control.

Domain	Agonist's Force Tendency	Antagonist's Force Tendency	Causation	Resultant Action
Source	Person or animal To move freely	Bonds / ropes / fetters To restrain movement of the body	Not often mentioned	Person or animal is completely under the control of the enemy
Target	Self To live and act freely	Situation of distress Restrains the person from living as he chooses	-	Self no longer has control of itself.
Other Entailments: Cutting the ropes → Freedom from distressing situation			

6.4.9. Experiencing Distress is Being Imprisoned

Imprisonment is also closely related, where elements of the prison become the surrounding Antagonist. Psalm 142:7[8] requests release from a מַסְגֵּר, to be surrounded (כתר) instead by the righteous, showing another positive evaluation of being "surrounded." 1QH 13:38 uses

כלא for the prison, a root focusing on restricted movement and also occurring as a verb of imprisonment in Ps 88:8[9].[135]

הוֹצִיאָה מִמַּסְגֵּר נַפְשִׁי לְהוֹדוֹת אֶת־שְׁמֶךָ בִּי יַכְתִּרוּ צַדִּיקִים כִּי תִגְמֹל עָלָי׃

Ps 142:7[8]: Bring me out of prison, so that I may give thanks to your name. The righteous will surround me, for you will deal bountifully with me.

וחומת עו[ן] יסבני ובריחי 38 [פתוח כ]לאי עם תהום נחשב לאין ברזל ודלתין נחושת לאין]

1QH 13:37–38: A str[ong] rampart [surrounds me,] iron bars and [bronze] doors [which can not] [be opened]; my [ga]ol is comparable to the deep without there being . . .

כָּלֻא וְלֹא אֵצֵא׃

Ps 88:8[9]: I am shut in so that I cannot escape.

Frequently, chains and bars explicitly highlight the restriction of imprisonment. References to chained arms in Lam 3:7 and in 1QH 16:35 were given in section 6.4.8. Bars, בְּרִיחִים, are used in 1QH 13:37 (above) and Jon 2:6[7].

יָרַדְתִּי הָאָרֶץ בְּרִחֶיהָ בַעֲדִי לְעוֹלָם

Jon 2:6[7]: I went down to the land whose bars closed upon me forever.

Elsewhere other restrictive elements are used. In Job 13:27, Job's feet are restricted, imprisoned within stocks, whereas in Job 7:12 a prison guard is mapped onto someone checking that the petitioner as Agonist is not able to manifest his force tendency to go out.

וְתָשֵׂם בַּסַּד רַגְלַי וְתִשְׁמוֹר כָּל־אָרְחוֹתָי עַל־שָׁרְשֵׁי רַגְלַי תִּתְחַקֶּה׃

Job 13:27: You put my feet in the stocks, and watch all my paths; you set a bound to the soles of my feet.

---

135. Oswalt, "כָּלָא."

Distress and the Constraint Schema

הֲיָם־אָנִי אִם־תַּנִּין כִּי־תָשִׂים עָלַי מִשְׁמָר׃

Job 7:12: Am I the Sea, or the Dragon, that you set a guard over me?

As for the pits in section 6.4.7, Sheol is frequently viewed as a prison, with bars (Jon 2:6[7], Job 17:16) and guards (Isa 38:10, if שַׁעֲרֵי שְׁאוֹל are gatekeepers keeping Hezekiah from escaping).[136] Again this shows how distressing life experiences cohere with the ultimate form of distress as prison.

The *result* of imprisonment again places the Agonist completely under the control of someone else. Whether imprisonment ends in death or release depends on a higher authority.

Domain	Agonist's Force Tendency	Antagonist's Force Tendency	Causation	Resultant Action
Source	*Person* To move freely	*Prison* To hold the prisoner captive	Not often mentioned.	Under the control of another—possibly death
Target	*Self* To act freely as one chooses	*Situation of distress* To prevent the self from acting as he chooses	-	Self has no control over actions or life choices

6.4.10. Experiencing Distress is Being Gripped by the Contractions of Labor

Metaphors conceptualizing distress as the experience of a woman in labor are also linked to this CONSTRAINT schema, through the roots צרר and חבל, as explained in section 6.2.2. This conceptualization is more common at Qumran than in the biblical texts, although Jer 6:24 describes Jerusalem's inhabitants on the brink of invasion by paralleling the general term צָרָה with חִיל, evoking writhing in labor, and demonstrating that צָרָה did still provide a cognitive point of access to the domain of labor and birth.

---

136. Barré, *Lord*, 63.

Surrounded by Bitterness

צָרָה הֶחֱזִיקַתְנוּ חִיל כַּיּוֹלֵדָה׃

Jer 6:24: Anguish has taken hold of us, pain as of a woman in labor.

In the Hodayot, the fullest example is 1QH 11:7–12. In v. 7, the distress (conceptualized as צוקה) is compared to a woman giving birth, and vv. 8, 9, 11, and 12 all use חבל. After the initial comparison the remaining verses discuss the pain of birth, especially for a firstborn male, infused throughout with Qumranic dualism, with children born either as sons of the light or sons of darkness. The relevance here is the collection of distress motifs that are linked together in this understanding of birth. Not only are צוקה and חבל mentioned, but also משברי מות and חבלי שאול (as in Ps 18:5[6]).

8 אהיה בצוקה כמו אשת לדה מבכרית כיא נהפכו ציריה
וחבל נמרץ על משבריה להחיל בכור הריה כיא באו בנים עד
משברי מות 9 והרית גבר הצרה בהבליה כיא במשברי מות
תמליט זכר ובחבלי שאול יניח 10 מכור הריה פלא יועץ עם
גבורתו ויפלט גבר ממשברים בהריתו החישו כול 11 משברים
וחבלי (נ)מרץ מולדיהם ופלצות להורותם ובמולדיו יהפכו
כול צירים 12 בכור הריה והרית אפעה לחבל נמרץ ומשברי
שחת לכול מעשי פלצות

1QH 11:7–12: I was in distress like a woman giving birth the first time when her labor-pains come on her and a pang racks the mouth of her womb to begin the birth in the <<crucible>> of the pregnant woman. For children come through the breakers of death and the woman expectant with a boy is racked by her pangs, for through the breakers of death she gives birth to a male, and through the pangs of Sheol there emerges, from the <<crucible>> of the pregnant woman a wonderful counselor with his strength, and the boy is freed from the breakers. In the woman expectant with him rush all the contractions and the racking pain at their birth; terror (seizes) those expectant with them, and at his birth all the labor-pains come suddenly, in the <<crucible>> of the pregnant woman. And she who is pregnant with a serpent is with a racking pang; and the breakers of the pit result in all deeds of terror.

Distress and the Constraint Schema

A simpler example is found in 1QH 13:30–31, again using חבל. Another reference to חבל in 1QH 17:6 may also provide cognitive access to this same domain.

זלעופות אחזוני וחבלים כצירי 31 יולדה

1QH 13:30–31: Resentment has taken hold of me and "pangs" like the labors of a woman giving birth.

ואני משאה למשואה וממכאוב לנגע ומחבלים 7 למשברים תשוחח נפשי בנפלאותיכה

1QH 17:6–7: As for me, from ruin to annihilation, from sickness to disease, from pangs to labors, my soul reflects on your wonders.

These are insufficient examples to be definitive about parts of the mapping or entailments. However, this mapping does not include an agentive cause, nor is this metaphor used to express the possibility of distress bringing about something good, through the entailment that labor pains can lead to the joy of new birth. The focus is more on labor pain as symptomatic of the pain of distress. The result is not in focus, unless it is the possibility that labor can result in death, much more frequent when these texts were written than now.

Domain	Agonist's Force Tendency	Antagonist's Force Tendency	Causation	Resultant Action
Source	Woman in labor / To bear the child	Womb / To constrict / immobilize the woman's body	None given	If constrictions too great, woman may die in birth
Target	Self / Pain free achievement of life goals	Distressing experiences / To constrict / immobilize the self	-	Self may be at risk of death
Other Entailments: Pain of birth → Pain of situation of distress				

6.4.11. Experiencing Distress is Being Stuck in Mud

Finally, in a few verses, movement of the Agonist's feet is restricted by mud, introduced in section 5.4.1, but actually fitting more accurately here, since טבע is more about "embedding" than a downward trajectory. By being fixed in one position, the petitioner is at greater risk from other elements, whether enemies coming to attack (1QH 15:2–3) or flooding waters (Ps 69:2[3]). The result of this map would thus be greater disaster, if there is no help.

ותטבע >ב< בבץ רגלי

1QH 15:2–3: My feet sink in the mud.

טָבַעְתִּי בִּיוֵן מְצוּלָה וְאֵין מָעֳמָד בָּאתִי בְמַעֲמַקֵּי־מַיִם וְשִׁבֹּלֶת שְׁטָפָתְנִי׃

Ps 69:2[3]: I sink in deep mire, where there is no foothold; I have come into deep waters, and the flood sweeps over me.

6.5. Further Evidence

6.5.1. Generalizations over Polysemy

Generalizations over polysemy give the starting point for summarizing the significance of the CONSTRAINT schema and conceptual metaphors based on it, showing the unity of the schema, its degree of elaboration in metaphor, and how embedded the metaphor is in the Hebrew language.

First, a great variety of concrete metaphorical images used in distress are unified by a relatively small number of Hebrew roots. The roots צרר, סבב, אפף, נקף, חבל, and צוק link the concrete images of tight spaces, traps, nets and pits, siege, imprisonment, and labor. Each root is polysemous, accessing a spatial domain of surrounding constraint and also the domain of psychological or emotional distress. Indeed, the unity between these images means it is sometimes difficult to identify which concrete image (if any) was in the author's mind. This diversity of images and yet schematic unity is the main justification for the CONSTRAINT schema posited here.

Several roots complementing the schema (relating to spaciousness) are also polysemous. The most significant are רחב, describing both wide spaces and the "width" of someone relieved from distress, and פתח, describing physical openings (in tents or houses) and the relief of enclosing distressing elements.

Second, the variety of less common roots linguistically elaborating this metaphor shows how well entrenched it is in Hebrew. These roots include: אסר 'bind'; גדר 'build a wall'; סוך 'make a hedge'; עוד (piel) 'go round'; כלא 'imprison'; בלע 'swallow' and טבע 'be embedded in'. This variety of verbs shows the metaphor is conventionalized enough that new roots can be used and understood by coherence with more common conceptualizations.

Third, this polysemy permeates the linguistic system, surfacing in several different parts of speech. Thus, the polysemy includes verbs (for example, גָּדַר 'he built a wall', וַיָּסֶךְ 'and he has caused to be hedged around' or סַבּוּנִי 'they surround me'), nouns (for example, פַּח 'bird snare', מְצָרִים 'narrow places', חֶבֶל 'rope'), and adverbs (for example, סָבִיב 'all around'). This demonstrates how entrenched this schema is for conceptualizing distressing situations.

Relating to Barr's criticisms, all of this evidence comes from a systematic, structural approach to the Hebrew language to suggest that the basic physical meaning of צרר does influence thought about distress when its derivatives are used in those contexts.

6.5.2. Generalizations over Inference Patterns

Alongside these lexemes, the analysis revealed several common inferences from the spatial domain being used to reason about more general distress. Several of these overlap with the entailments of the CONTAINMENT schema cited in section 6.2.1.

First, the most common inference is that if being in distress is being constrained, *relief* from distress is removal of the constraint. Specifically, where distress is bodily constriction, relief is opening of the constriction; where distress is being in a narrow place, relief is being brought to a wide place; where distress is being surrounded by water, relief is being lifted out of the water; where distress is being caught in a trap, relief is being set free; where distress is being tied with ropes, relief is having the bonds loosed; and where distress is imprisonment, relief is being released.

Second, the *cause* of such distress is always external, whether a very deliberate agent (a commander besieging a city, a hunter laying traps, someone building a wall, or dogs surrounding a city), or a more general external cause from the natural environment (surrounding waters, narrow places, or pits). The petitioner never voluntarily puts himself in a container. In the more psychological target domain, these metaphors highlight external factors and hide personal responsibility for distressing situations.

Third, there is a generalized *result* that the situation is dangerous and will probably get worse, expressing the danger posed by fixity of location, making the petitioner vulnerable. With this mapping, increased time being constrained maps to increased time in distress, which will lead to more serious consequences for most images, whether starvation in a pit or behind the enemies' siege works, withering away in prison, succumbing to surrounding waters, having the dogs finally attack or the hunters returning to capture their prey from the net. Thus, while constrained, there is still time to call out for help, before the petitioner finally loses hope. This fits a corpus of prayers where petitioners are precisely crying out for help at such a time. Psychologically, then, these images all conceptualize distress as a place of threat of impending disaster.

Fourth, an inference is absent: aside from the length of time, distress conceptualized this way does not readily provide a scale of *intensity*. With צַר and סָבִיב a person is either contained or not. A few examples in the Hebrew Bible have צַר לִי מְאֹד (Judg 2:15 and 10:9; 2 Sam 24:14 / 1 Chr 21:13), but these are outside the specific corpus, and the general quantifier מְאֹד is unrelated to the schema.

Finally, several images allow the inference that restricting the petitioner's force hinders him from pursuing life purposes, especially images where the petitioner's path is blocked, but also those of siege, imprisonment, and being tied. This uses the event-structure conceptual mapping that maps purposes onto paths.

6.5.3. Novel Metaphor

The active use of the source domain is shown by both novel and conventional metaphors all instantiating the CONSTRAINT schema. Most obviously, the common conventional conceptualization of distress using צרר, or as something סָבִיב the petitioner, is elaborated in all the different concrete images given above. For example, Gen 32:7[8] conventionally frames Jacob's emotional response to Esau's approach as וַיֵּצֶר לוֹ, but this same schematic understanding of emotional distress as constriction is expressed more poetically and creatively in Ps 116:3, אֲפָפוּנִי חֶבְלֵי־מָוֶת ('death's cords were all around me') or Lam 3:5, בָּנָה עָלַי וַיַּקַּף רֹאשׁ וּתְלָאָה ('he builds a rampart against me and surrounds me with poison and hardship'). In each case, the experiencer's emotional distress is framed as a constricting Antagonist holding the Agonist in place, although using more novel images.

Elsewhere in narrative texts conventional idioms describe distress using this schema. For example, Exod 14:3 associates the wilderness 'closing in on' (סָגַר עַל) the Israelites with their state of confused distress there. Such examples demonstrate that the more novel examples in the specific corpus have conventional parallels in narrative texts.

וְאָמַר פַּרְעֹה לִבְנֵי יִשְׂרָאֵל נְבֻכִים הֵם בָּאָרֶץ סָגַר עֲלֵיהֶם הַמִּדְבָּר׃

> Exod 14:3: Pharaoh will say of the Israelites, "They are wandering aimlessly in the land; the wilderness has closed in on them."

סגר also describes sick people "shut up" apart from the rest of the community, as for Miriam in Num 12:15: וַתִּסָּגֵר מִרְיָם מִחוּץ לַמַּחֲנֶה שִׁבְעַת יָמִים, 'Miriam was shut outside the camp for seven days'. Framing the afflicted person's banishment as "shutting" with סגר gives extra background to metaphors of imprisonment and containment where psalms may come from sick petitioners.

Within the specific corpus too, the conventionality varies. For example, the image of a surrounding barrier might be accessed simply with the word סָבִיב in the psalms. By contrast, Job more innovatively uses the image of a surrounding thorn hedge in Job 3:23, וַיָּסֶךְ אֱלוֹהַּ

בַּעֲדוֹ, surrounding walls in Job 19:8 or surrounding archers in Job 16:13, יָסֹבּוּ עָלַי רַבָּיו.

6.5.4. Larger Scale Metaphorical Systems

At a wider level, conceptualizing distress as constraint coheres with conceptualizing salvation as spaciousness, as researched by John Sawyer, who argued that "an important feature of OT tradition is the remarkable applicability of ideas like the spaciousness of salvation to an infinite variety of human situations."[137] By studying רחב (a root tied to physical dimensions), Sawyer showed the importance of spaciousness in God's promise of land to Israel from an early time, through idioms such as וְהִרְחַבְתִּי אֶת־גְּבוּלֶךָ "I will enlarge your borders" in Exod 34:24. This language then developed metaphorical senses from ideas of territorial freedom to become "colorful, poignant expressions for liberation from all kinds of restricting danger and distress," rooted in the time of David and Solomon when such a metaphor would have been particularly productive.[138] Sawyer rejects the idea that this spatial salvation language is late, supporting the idea that spatial conceptualizations of both distress and relief from distress (salvation) are firmly entrenched in the Hebrew language of the scriptures from every age.

6.5.5. Non-verbal Realizations

Finally, non-verbal realizations can show the entrenchment of a conceptual metaphor, possibly shown here in examples from Leviticus of "shutting in" diseased people.

In Leviticus 13–14, rules are given for treating various "diseases" affecting people, clothing or houses. In some cases, after an initial check of symptoms, the priest is commanded to "shut up" (סגר) the person, article, or house for seven days, check the symptoms again and then possibly repeat the process for another seven days. At the end of this time a pronouncement can be made as to whether the person or item

---

137. Sawyer, "Spaciousness," 31.
138. Ibid., 26, 31.

is clean or not. This process, framed with סגר, may provide a cognitive cultural background for the use of confinement language in the laments of sick people, as in Ps 88:8[9]. This use of confinement language also fits the inferences given above for the CONSTRAINT schema. The constraint is externally imposed, and in terms of results, the time of confinement is principally a time of waiting for an impending decision.

6.6. Universality and Variation

As there is very little cross-cultural information on CONSTRAINT schemas in emotion language with which to compare this research, this section focuses more on explaining cultural prototypes and types of linguistic expression that may vary when compared to other languages, than on providing explicit contrasts.

6.6.1. Variation within Source and Target Domain

The first area of potential variation is the preference for different metaphors to conceptualize experience. 129 of the expressions in the specific corpus used the CONSTRAINT schema, in comparison to 81 for the VERTICALITY schema. Thus, there is a slight preference for the CONSTRAINT schema over the VERTICALITY schema for individuals making sense of their negative physical, social, and emotional experiences. Certainly, the CONSTRAINT schema is more significant for this corpus than it was for those talking in English about depression, where depression as captor was only a minor metaphor.

Second, the target domain here is broader than that conceptualized via the category of "depression" in English. Comparing with English emotional categories, metaphors using the CONSTRAINT schema are often more closely related to fear than sadness. Further, while the CONSTRAINT schema can be used for general personal psychological or emotional distress, it is also used more broadly for social distress (problems in interpersonal relationships, or when enemies threaten), seen in the role of other personal agents in the various metaphors, who lay traps, hide nets, build walls, or surround like animals.

Third, for the source domain, cultural prototypes and entailments may differ from the instantiations of the CONSTRAINT metaphor in distress discourse in other cultures. For example, the פַּח snare is an important cultural prototype for understanding distress situations. The use of bait, the trap's hidden nature, and the suddenness of its enclosing are all entailed when used to describe distress. These differ from the entailments for an English-speaking person who more generally feels *trapped*, although both use the CONSTRAINT schema for understanding negative life experience. Similarly, siege is a salient cultural prototype for this schema. Here, the situation's severity increases the longer it lasts, ending in final disaster, and thus, when used in metaphor, implies the increasing severity of distress the longer it continues. This cultural prototype therefore adds extra structure to the containment schema.

6.6.2. Variation in Linguistic Expression

Kövecses also noted that conceptual metaphors may vary in the linguistic expressions used, including the degree of elaboration of different parts of the metaphor, the conventionalization of the linguistic expressions, and the syntactic expressions used.

First, the most striking thing here is the variety of verbs used to describe the experience of being constrained by an Antagonist. The roots include צוּק, אפף, סבב, נקף, עוד, אסר, גדר, סוך, and כתר, a much more elaborated set than those found for "descent." This demonstrates again the significance of this schema compared to the VERTICALITY schema for conceptualizing distress. Fewer different verbs describe relief from distress, but these include פתח, יצא, and רחב. There are also a large number of nouns used for these situations of distress, normally referencing the Antagonist, including פַּח, רֶשֶׁת, צָרָה, כֶּלֶא, חֶבֶל, and בּוֹר.

Second, concerning conventionalization, this schema is much more conventionalized in distress discourse than the VERTICALITY schema. This is seen by the frequency of the expression צַר לִי, both in the specific corpus and in narrative texts, and in the use of סָבִיב with many different abstract Antagonists.

Third, regarding syntactic expression, this schema is realized in a considerable variety of different syntactic forms. This includes single words, such as צַר and סָבִיב, short multiword phrases such as גָּדַר בַּעֲדִי or וְתָשֵׂם בַּסַּד רַגְלִי, through to longer and more elaborate constructions based on the schema, such as יַחַד יָבֹאוּ גְדוּדָיו וַיָּסֹלּוּ עָלַי דַּרְכָּם וַיַּחֲנוּ סָבִיב לְאָהֳלִי (Job 19:12). Further, it is impossible to translate the verbal phrase צַר־לִי into English and maintain the verbal syntax. The best approximation is by using a noun in a prepositional phrase, like *in straits*. This shows a syntactic difference between English and Hebrew.

6.7. Summary

In summary, this chapter identified the CONSTRAINT schema as a particularly significant image schema for conceptualizing distress in the specific corpus. The clarification of this image schema is one of the most striking results of this research, a schema relating to an entity that desires to move being surrounded and held fast by another entity. This schema is more frequent in distress discourse, more conventionalized and more highly elaborated than the VERTICALITY schema. This suggests that inferences from this schema may have been more significant for understanding distressing life experiences for an ancient Israelite than inferences from the VERTICALITY schema. Such inferences include being in a situation of imminent disaster, which could come suddenly. Without a mapping of intensity, there is less emphasis on a situation worsening. Rather it is an ongoing state of distress (one cannot gradually change from being contained to not contained) at a relatively constant level, which will eventually wear down defenses.

The next chapter will continue to investigate forceful interactions used to understand distressing experience, focusing on cases where the force is directed straight at the sufferer, rather than merely hindering the sufferer's own desire to move.

7

Distress and the Force Schema

"Your arrows have sunk into me, and your hand has come down on me."—Ps 38:2[3]

7.1. Introduction

This chapter investigates a more general FORCE schema than the previous one. Here, the petitioner resists a change of state or location, and the focus is on the forceful Antagonist seeking to change the Agonist's state or location, whether military opponents or wild animals, crashing waves, fire, or more general forces that crush and break. Contemporary English and ancient Akkadian also conceptualize emotional or psychophysical experiences as force encounters, so comparisons will be made with both. First, however, the FORCE schema will be clarified.

7.2. Establishing the Schema

7.2.1. Physiological / Universal Factors

Human existence entails constant experience of forces, whether external forces such as gravity or wind resistance, or forces exerted by a person, moving muscles to pump blood around the body, open eyelids, or manipulate objects. Thus, "our bodies are clusters of forces and . . . *every event of which we are a part consists, minimally, of forces in interaction . . .* Our daily reality is one massive series of forceful sequences."[1] Many are not consciously reflected upon, unless they are exceptionally strong, or cease to be balanced, yet they are ever present.

Six features of forces give a gestalt structure to the FORCE schema, potentially constraining inferences in metaphors.[2] First, every experience of force involves *interaction*. Second, force interactions usually involve movement of something through space in some *direction*, or at least a force exerted in a particular direction. Third, such force vectors prototypically have a *single path of motion*, as when gravity pulls an object to the ground. Fourth, forces have *sources*, and can be directed by *agents* at *targets*. Fifth, forces have *degrees* of power. Sixth, there is always a sequence of *causality* for forceful interaction. Prototypically, forces are not conceptualized as just happening, but as being caused by something, whether inanimate object, event, or purposive being.

This gestalt structure suggests inferences when forces conceptualize emotional experience, such as varying intensity, potential causes, or changes in state or location resulting from experiencing the emotion.

7.2.2. Culture-specific Factors

How did Classical Hebrew authors perceive force interactions? The corpus has no abstract discussion of forces, but can answer the following questions: What entities were perceived as forcefully interacting? Which kinds of force interaction were particularly salient, potentially shaping understanding and thinking about forces?

---

1. Johnson, *Body*, 42.
2. Ibid., 43–44.

First, force-exerting entities included humans, animals, Yahweh himself, and "natural" forces including winds, seas, rivers, lightning, fire, earthquakes, and heat. Force is prototypically exerted by direct contact between a human or animal and another object, and the results are generally predictable. Many common roots describe human exertion of force, including עשׂה 'make,' נתן 'give / put,' לקח 'take,' נשׂא 'lift,' שׂים 'put,' and נכה 'strike.' Forceful effects achieved without direct contact, or where direct contact has an "unpredictable" result, are presented as anomalous, demonstrating divine forces, as in the collapse of the walls of Jericho or Elisha's ability to make an axe head float. Force interactions are also attributed to God making physical contact with the environment. For example, God's feet touch the mountains and they quake, or he "hurls" a wind at the sea to stop Jonah. Sometimes, signs of God's presence make physical entities respond as if forcefully struck, his voice breaking cedars (Ps 29:5) or making the earth melt (Ps 46:6[7]) or the ark of the covenant causing Dagon to fall before it (1 Sam 5:1–4). Yahweh's messenger (מַלְאָךְ) also exerts force: pulling Lot into the house (Gen 19:10) or touching Elijah to arouse him (1 Kgs 19:5). Other spiritual entities only exert direct forces in visions, like the seraph who touches Isaiah's lips (Isa 6:6). "Natural" forces also impact the environment, although sometimes natural and supernatural forces are conflated together,[3] so that, for example, Jonah's storm is portrayed both as Yahweh hurling a great wind at the sea, and as the sea itself exerting an increasingly stormy force. Elsewhere, natural forces act without any reference to God, as in the wind that "struck" Job's children's house (Job 1:19), and perhaps more figuratively, the earth that "swallowed" Korah, and fire that "ate" his followers (Num 16:31–35). Thus, several agents act forcefully, and may exert force upon the sufferer in distress.

Second, salient cultural force interactions occur in domains of technology, economy, politics, social life, environment, and religion.[4] Regarding technology and economy, the texts derive from agricultural cultures, so salient force interactions relate to animal husbandry (particularly shepherding), vine tending, and farming cereals. These give verbs related to "driving," "pruning," "cutting," "ploughing," and "harvesting."

3. Deist, *Culture*, 109–10.
4. These domains of culture come from Deist, *Culture*, 103.

The material culture included clay pots, wooden plates, animal skins, and woven materials (shown by the categories of artifacts in Leviticus 11), explaining the salience of verbs for "breaking," "shattering," and "tearing," which would be framed against such prototypical materials.

Politically, Canaan's fertile location between Egypt and Mesopotamia made it the scene of conflict between these powers or with others. International conflict recurs throughout the Hebrew Bible,[5] so forces of warfare would be more salient than in contemporary English, providing an embodied background for drawing bows or swords, and striking.

Socially, physical interpersonal conflict within the community also pervades the corpus. Beginning with Cain's murder of Abel, through Moses' witnessing of fighting contemporaries, Torah regulations for those fighting, and the establishment of cities of refuge, to Shimei stoning David and his troops (1 Sam 16:1) or Nehemiah striking and pulling the hair of his fellow Jews (Neh 13:25), community disputes were frequently settled physically. Such conflicts are normally hand-to-hand, so the language of "striking," "blows," "seizing," or "grasping" would have been easily accessible, and it is sometimes difficult to decide whether a psalm refers to metaphorical blows or real ones. However, even for originally physical blows, repetition by the community over subsequent generations would have allowed wider application.

Environmentally, wind and rain powerfully affected Canaan, and thus were likely to be cognitively salient for Hebrew authors, including the weeklong sirocco, a dry, hot East wind (קָדִים).[6] Rain was also significant. Although limited to around 45 days per year, it often fell in heavy showers, potentially creating raging masses of water able to sweep away fertile soil, houses, people, and animals, especially in a wadi (נַחַל), a dry gorge for most of the year, but potentially channeling a tremendous force of water following heavy rain.[7]

---

5. Thompson, *Handbook*, 283.
6. Negenman, "Palestine," 15.
7. Ibid., 16–17.

7.3. Comparative Data on Emotion Language and the FORCE Schema

7.3.1. Contemporary Cross-Linguistic Comparisons

English will be considered for contemporary comparisons, having at least three areas where force conceptualizes negative life experiences. First, conflict language conceptualizes disease; second, force is used in *stress* discourse; and third, forces conceptualize emotions.

First, conversational English often conceptualizes sickness as an attacker and the sufferer as defender. Someone may *lose the fight against cancer*, or *battle a nasty infection*, or communally we fight *the war against AIDS*. Some parts of this mapping are so deeply entrenched they are not perceived as metaphoric:[8] referring to the immune system as the body's *defences*, or to a virus *attacking* a body function, are conventional descriptions of biological mechanisms. This "invasion" metaphor dates from Pasteur and the beginnings of germ theory,[9] although conceptualizing sickness as being overwhelmed by an aggressive force has a much longer history. The primary agent here is always non-human, related to the sickness itself, whether germs, cancer, or AIDS.

Second, the conceptual model of "stress" deserves separate consideration because of its salience in contemporary English and the possibility for the agentive force to be another person causing stress. Stress research started with Hans Selye identifying a "syndrome produced by diverse nocuous agents,"[10] common symptoms resulting from various shocks to the body system. These became known as a *stress response*, including aches and pains in the joints, intestinal distress, loss of appetite, fever, enlarged spleen or liver, inflamed tonsils, and skin rash.[11] From a Cognitive Linguistic perspective, Selye discovered that using a general FORCE schema to frame what happened to the body in various situations (such as exposure to cold, injury, intoxication, or excessive exercise) enabled a better problematization, and suggested new solutions.[12]

8. Gwyn, "Captain," 208.
9. Ibid.
10. Selye, "Syndrome."
11. Selye, *Stress*, cited in Johnson, *Body*, 128.
12. Johnson discusses Selye's breakthrough more thoroughly in ibid., 127–37.

Selye specifically refers to physical forces, arguing that "in the biological sense stress is the interaction between damage and defense, just as in physics tension or pressure represent the interplay between a force and the resistance offered to it."[13] Problematizing stress as a balance between forces prompted solutions which emphasized "supplementing the natural defensive measures" when they are suboptimal,[14] as well as dealing with the "attacking" force directly, forcing a paradigm shift in medicine.

From this physiological paradigm, a pervasive, well-elaborated cultural model of stress has developed, still based on forces impacting the individual, but prioritizing psychological responses,[15] and including emotional and social factors.[16] Such models evoke "a diffuse and invisible "force," somehow mediating between individuals (and their mental and physical state), and the social environment in which they live and work,"[17] blending Selye's concept with older conceptualizations of divine punishment, witchcraft, or demon possession, linking "popular, medical, and religious explanations for suffering."[18] Common conceptualization through the FORCE schema makes this blend possible.

Helman analyzed conceptual metaphors used by American patients with psychosomatic disorders, and found stress conceptualized as a heavy weight (an invisible force pressing down on individuals), a wire (that becomes tense under the application of force), a force causing internal chaos, a force causing fragmentation ("going to pieces" or "falling apart"), a machine malfunctioning, a depletion of vital liquid, an inner explosion (an internal force), or an interpersonal force, with one person causing another to feel stressed.[19] The omnipresence of forceful interactions shows the FORCE schema's significance for the model of stress in popular culture.

Third, the FORCE schema conceptualizes emotion, as presented in Kövecses' *Metaphor and Emotion*. Kövecses sees EMOTION IS FORCE

13. Selye, "Adaptation," 1384.
14. Ibid.
15. Helman, *Culture*, 297.
16. Dressler, "Culture."
17. Helman, *Culture*, 314.
18. Ibid.
19. Ibid., 315–16.

as a single "master metaphor" giving coherence to many specific emotion metaphors.[20] The self is an Agonist with a force tendency towards inaction (opposite to chapter six), and the Antagonist is the emotion exerting a force. This is instantiated by metaphors of emotion as internal pressure inside a container, an opponent, a wild animal (that needs controlling), a social force, a natural force, a mental force, insanity, heat, a physiological force (such as hunger), physical agitation, or a burden.[21] This overlaps somewhat with Helman's research, but differs because of the different target domains, of stress as opposed to emotion. For example, for Helman, being *all shook up* conceptualizes stress as internal chaos,[22] whereas for Kövecses the same phrase exemplifies EMOTION IS PHYSICAL AGITATION.[23] Such overlap demonstrates the difficulty in precisely defining target domains (and hence for choosing the broad topic of "distress" for this thesis, rather than a more specific emotion), but also supports the reality of these source domains as cognitive resources for understanding negative life experiences. This convergence above all shows the importance of the FORCE schema for these conceptualizations.

A significant generalized inference is that controlling emotions is consistently understood as resisting forces: by "keeping a lid" on them (EMOTION IS INTERNAL PRESSURE); by "taming" them (EMOTION IS A WILD ANIMAL); by "conquering" them (EMOTION IS AN OPPONENT) or by "extinguishing" them (EMOTION IS HEAT). This inference occurring across almost every source domain shows how important controlling emotions is in Anglo culture. Emotions are consistently problematized as potentially harmful forces, so that solutions are framed as ways of resisting these forces.

This survey of illness, stress, and emotions has revealed various source domains to contrast with the Hebrew examples, and some structural features to compare. For example, who are the agents in the Hebrew texts, and is it possible for a person to exert a psychological or emotional force on another (as in English stress)? Are there explicit en-

---

20. Kövecses, *Emotion*, 61.
21. Ibid., 65–83.
22. Helman, *Culture*, 315.
23. Kövecses, *Emotion*, 80.

tailments relating to controlling forces, as for English emotions? These questions will be investigated below.

7.3.2. Ancient Near Eastern Comparisons

Ancient Near Eastern literature is also comparable with Hebrew. Only illustrative examples will be given, from Akkadian. Negative experience is conceptualized as being gripped by an opponent, experiencing heat, or being "broken" hearted. The Diagnostic Handbook is particular useful for the conceptualization of diseases in Mesopotamia, listing symptoms followed by a diagnosis of the problem.

Many symptoms result from physical contact with spiritual beings, framed as "seizing" (ṣabātu), "touching" (lapātu), "striking" (mahāṣu), and "reaching" (kašādu).[24] A picture of a god holding someone upside down by the legs graphically displays seizure by disease.[25] Physical contact is also entailed by the omnipresent diagnosis "the hand of x," where x embraces great gods (like Marduk, Shamash, and Ishtar), less important deities (like Ningirsu or Baba), all kinds of demons (like Lamaštu, Kubu, or Alû lemnu), but also the hand of a ghost, the stars, the Underworld or of human beings.[26] This phrase attributes the disease to a particular agent (with whom reconciliation must be sought) rather than naming a specific disease.[27] Similarly, the demon Lamaštu "is a paramount evil force whose actions can (and regularly do) lead to a loss of health and subsequent or immediate death."[28] Thus, with this language, "diseases were understood by analogy with injuries received in battle, fights or accidentally at the hands of a fellow human being, the blows being administered this time by supernatural agents."[29]

With this problematization, finding the agent responsible is important for a solution, in order to be reconciled, usually through the āšipu

---

24. Heessel, "Hands," 125.
25. Black and Green, *Gods*, 67.
26. Heessel, "Hands," 121.
27. Ibid., 128–29.
28. Farber, "Lamaštu," 144–45.
29. Van der Toorn, *Sin*, 68.

"'exorcist'-psychologist, magician-diviner."[30] Usually, the force-exerting agent is supernatural, but sorcery by another human is also possible, framed as the "hand of man."[31] For supernatural forces, "only the physical separation of perpetrator and victim could guarantee long-term healing,"[32] hence the importance of knowing who to address. Further, conceptualizing disease as a superior supernatural force made it seem especially terrifying, bringing about an "apprehensive state of mind" and its own set of fear-induced psychosomatic symptoms.[33]

The FORCE schema is also instantiated in descriptions of fever. Fevers are consistently conceptualized as heat, but also as external forces that can "seize," "hold," "attack," or "fall on" the sufferer, "eating" or "gnawing" the body. Intermittent fevers may seize and then "release" the sufferer, and treatment is framed as "tearing out" or "loosening" the aggressor.[34] The scalarity of heat is used, with the fever's intensity evoked by words indicating various degrees of heat, so that, for example, *ummu danna* (very hot) is used for a strong fever "seizing" someone.[35]

Finally, references to a (forcefully) "broken heart," *ḫīp libbi*, provide interesting comparisons with Hebrew. It is always caused by divine wrath, occurs in contexts of anxiety, and iterative verb forms suggests it happens "again and again."[36] Someone suffering heartbreak may have lost possessions, be being ignored, be losing sleep, have a diminished appetite or become forgetful.[37] The psychological state describes someone who may be "ill-tempered, suspicious, have a nervous breakdown, be full of apprehensions, be worried, or in a panic."[38] Classifying this as fragmentation of the heart uses the FORCE schema even without explicitly attributing distress to the direct influence of supernatural forces. A "shattered" heart (*kusup libbi*) also occurs in similar contexts.

30. Wiseman, "Medicine," 17.
31. Stol, "Suffering," 57.
32. Farber, "Lamaštu," 138.
33. Stol, "Suffering," 57.
34. Stol, "Fevers."
35. Ibid., 1, 6.
36. Stol, *Epilepsy*, 28–29.
37. Ibid., 29.
38. Ibid., 32.

Distress and the Force Schema

As well as this conventional medical terminology, more poetic prayers and incantations also evoke distress through the FORCE schema. For example, an incantation against headache frames the sufferer as experiencing a forceful onslaught, using similes of reeds, rope, boats, and basket. The variety of forceful verbs is suggested by Foster's translations: "wastes"; "contorts"; "twists"; "chokes"; "crushes"; "snaps off"; "destroys"; "slits open"; "staves in"; "gets a grip"; "flattens"; "slaughters"; "strikes"; and "punctures."

> It makes the [b]elly(?) tremble, it wastes the body,
> It makes [the stomach] rumble like a porous pot,
> It contorts the tendons, it twists the sinews,
> It twists the sinews like a heavy rope,
> It contorts [the mus]cles,
> It chokes the mouth and nostrils as with pitch,
> It crushes the armpit like malt,
> It snaps off the [ha]nd like a thread in a tempest,
> It destroys the shoulder like an embankment,
> It slits open the breast like a (flimsy) basket
> It staves in the ribs like an old boat
> It gets a grip on the colon as if it were intestines,
> It flattens the tall like a reed
> It slaughters the great one like an ox
> . . .
> It punctures everything like a throw stick.[39]

Thus, Akkadian literature conceptualizes sickness and other negative psychological states as forces acting on the sufferer. Occurring in conventional, technical, and cultic language, this conceptualization is sufficiently entrenched to pervade many domains of discourse, and is instantiated in single conventional verbs through to stretches of poetic metaphor. Primarily, the agents are spiritual beings, although they can also be humans. Turning to Hebrew: do the texts use the force schema in similar ways to conceptualize illness? Is it entrenched as thoroughly into the language? What agents exert forces on those suffering?

---

39. Foster, *Muses*, 974–75, Akkadian transliteration not accessible.

7.4. Presentation and Analysis of Hebrew Mappings

The Hebrew mappings are grouped below according to different specific source domains, facilitating comparison with the comparative material. These groups are not mutually exclusive, since metaphors of gripping and seizing, for example, also fit the "opponent" metaphors. The presentation moves from more general instantiations of the FORCE schema to more specific source domains.

7.4.1. BEING IN DISTRESS IS EXPERIENCING FORCE DAMAGING PART OF THE BODY

This presentation again begins with metonymic mappings, with distress conceptualized as experiencing a force in different body parts, potentially motivating some of the metaphors considered later.

The heart, kidneys, bones, spirit, flesh, and self (נֶפֶשׁ) all experience force. For the heart, most commonly, one's heart is "broken" as in Ps 69:20[21]. Elsewhere, the heart melts in response to a force and is poured out, as in 1QH 16:32, fitting a conceptualization where distress makes the insides tremble, turn to liquid, and perhaps come out through the eyes as tears,[40] showing vitality draining away.[41] In Ps 109:22, the heart is "pierced,"[42] giving another kind of force impacting the heart.

חֶרְפָּה שָׁבְרָה לִבִּי וָאָנוּשָׁה

Ps 69:20[21]: Reproach—it has broken my heart and I am sick (with misery).[43]

כי נשבת מעוזי מגויתי וינגר כמים לבי וימס 33 כדונג בשרי ומעוז מותני היה לבהלה

1QH 16:32-33: For my vitality has left my body, my heart pours out like water, my flesh melts like wax, the vitality of my loins turns into listlessness.

---

40. Collins, "Physiology."
41. Johnson, *Vitality*.
42 Although frequently emended to "writhes" (חִיל), Allen, *Psalms 101–150*, 75.
43. Tate, *Psalms*, 187.

Distress and the Force Schema

וְלִבִּי חָלַל בְּקִרְבִּי׃

Ps 109:22: . . . and my heart is pierced within me.

The kidneys (כִּלְיוֹתַי) are also "pierced" (אֶשְׁתּוֹנָן) in Ps 73:21, a root used for sharpening arrows in the qal, and perhaps describing envious emotions in distress.[44]

וְכִלְיוֹתַי אֶשְׁתּוֹנָן׃

Ps 73:21: . . . and as to my kidneys, I was pierced.[45]

Forces also impact the skeleton (עֶצֶם). Job 30:17 has a third root translated "pierce" in English (נקר), used elsewhere for boring out eyes or quarries,[46] for the night forcefully impacting Job's bones. Psalm 42:10 has a deadly force striking the bones. Finally, bones, arms, and the general foundation of the person are all subject to a variety of forces in 1QH 15:2, 4 and 16:33.

לַיְלָה עֲצָמַי נִקַּר מֵעָלָי וְעֹרְקַי לֹא יִשְׁכָּבוּן׃

Job 30:17: The night pierces my bones, and those who gnaw me take no rest.[47]

בְּרֶצַח בְּעַצְמוֹתַי חֵרְפוּנִי צוֹרְרָי

Ps 42:10[11]: As with a deadly wound in my bones, my adversaries taunt me.

זרו]ע נשברת מקניה [. . .

1QH 15:2: My [ar]m is broken at the elbow.

וירועו כול אושי מבניתי ועצמי יתפרדו

1QH 15:4: The foundations of my build have crumbled, my bones have been disjointed.

---

44. BDB 1044.
45. Tate, *Psalms*, 227, 230.
46. BDB 669.
47. Clines, *Job 21–37*, 931.

וַתִּשָּׁבֵר זְרוֹעִי מִקָּנֶיהָ [וְאֵי]ן לְהָנִיף יָד

1QH 16:33: My arm is broken at the elbow [with]out my being able to wave my hand.

Occasionally the spirit (רוּחַ) is also impacted by forces, being "crushed" (דכא) in Ps 34:18[19], or possibly "broken" in Job 17:1.

קָרוֹב יְהוָה לְנִשְׁבְּרֵי־לֵב וְאֶת־דַּכְּאֵי־רוּחַ יוֹשִׁיעַ׃

Ps 34:18 [19]: The LORD is near to the brokenhearted, and saves the crushed in spirit.

רוּחִי חֻבָּלָה

Job 17:1: My spirit is broken.

Finally, the נֶפֶשׁ sometimes experiences forces in distress, as in 11Q5 24:5, where the petitioner fears his נֶפֶשׁ will be "hurled" (מגר), or in 1QH 13:17 where it is "crushed."

בנה נפשי ואל תמגרה

11Q5 (Psalm 155) 24:5: Build up my soul and do not demolish it.

וכול היום ידכאו נפשי

1QH 13:17: The whole day they crush my soul.

Thus several physiological parts experience force during distress, including heart, spirit, bones, and other internal organs. Further, several verbs are used, with fragmentation (crushing, crumbling, breaking) and piercing being the most common forces. However, there is no especially salient physiological symptom conceived as a force that might metonymically motivate other metaphors.

7.4.2. Being in Distress is Experiencing Fragmentation

Several Hebrew verbs describe a forceful impact transforming a unity into several pieces. These conceptualize distress experiences as experiencing fragmentation, mapping the sufferer onto an entity that is crushed or broken.

The most common root is שׁבר, used with trees, bows, gates, dishes, yokes, rocks, and snares as well as physiological terms. The verb's agent is almost always personal, either God or humans.[48] In physical usage, whole objects are fragmented into several pieces, becoming no longer functional.

The substantive שֶׁבֶר also occurs, usually translated as "wound" or "injury." However, its semantic development likely "never parted company with that of the verb,"[49] so it could still evoke situations of forceful fragmentation.

Several places refer to a "broken heart." With the לֵב as the organ of cognition and control, fragmentation is serious, affecting thinking and decision making, not just feelings. Outside the specific corpus, שׁבר occurs in the niphal or in a passive participle (both having no explicit agent), as in Pss 34:18[19] and 147:3. Within the corpus, the substantive in 11Q5 24:16 also leaves the agent implicit, whereas in Ps 69:20[21] fragmentation is caused by "reproach" (חֶרְפָּה).

קָרוֹב יְהוָה לְנִשְׁבְּרֵי־לֵב וְאֶת־דַּכְּאֵי־רוּחַ יוֹשִׁיעַ׃

Ps 34:18[19]: The LORD is near to the brokenhearted and saves the crushed in spirit.

הָרֹפֵא לִשְׁבוּרֵי לֵב

Ps 147:3: He heals the brokenhearted.

קראתי יהוה ויענני [וירפא את] שבר לבי

11Q5 24:16: I called <YHWH> and he answered me, [and he healed] my broken heart.

חֶרְפָּה שָׁבְרָה לִבִּי

Ps 69:20[21]: Reproach—it has broken my heart.[50]

In Lam 3:48, paralleling Lam 2:11, שֶׁבֶר links "brokenness" with the desolate state of Jerusalem's inhabitants. Jeremiah describes himself

---

48. Knipping, "שָׁבַר."
49. Ibid., 379.
50. Tate, *Psalms*, 187.

similarly in Jer 8:21, feeling himself "broken" for the "brokenness" of his people. In Jer 10:19, his "broken" situation (שִׁבְרִי) is paralleled by מַכָּתִי evoking the impact of being "struck."

פַּלְגֵי־מַיִם תֵּרַד עֵינִי עַל־שֶׁבֶר בַּת־עַמִּי׃

Lam 3:48: My eyes flow with rivers of tears because of the brokenness of my people.[51]

נִשְׁפַּךְ לָאָרֶץ כְּבֵדִי עַל־שֶׁבֶר בַּת־עַמִּי

Lam 2:11: My bile is poured out on the ground because of the brokenness of my people.[52]

עַל־שֶׁבֶר בַּת־עַמִּי הָשְׁבָּרְתִּי

Jer 8:21: For the brokenness of my people I am broken.[53]

אוֹי לִי עַל־שִׁבְרִי נַחְלָה מַכָּתִי

Jer 10:19: Woe is me because of my brokenness! My wound is severe.

Elsewhere, "bones" are broken. Bones often metonymically stand for a person's core, so that their "broken" condition covers physical and psychological distress.[54] Thus, English reference to "broken bones" in Lam 3:4 should not be understood literally, but as evoking fragmentation at the author's very foundation. Similarly, the "broken" arm in 1QH 15:2 and 1QH 16:33 expresses fragmentation of the petitioner's power.

בִּלָּה בְשָׂרִי וְעוֹרִי שִׁבַּר עַצְמוֹתָי׃

Lam 3:4: He has made my flesh and my skin waste away, and broken my bones.

[. . .]זרו[ע נשברת מקניה

1QH 15:2: My [ar]m is broken at the elbow.

51. Author's translation.
52. Author's translation.
53. Author's translation.
54. Beyse, "עֶצֶם," 308; Van der Toorn, *Sin*, 63.

Distress and the Force Schema

ותשבר זרועי מקניה [ואי]ן להניף יד

1QH 16:33: My arm is broken at the elbow [with]out my being able to wave my hand.

In 1QH 15:4, רעע evokes breaking, and separation of the bones is emphasized (יתפרדו). Fragmentation and separation at the petitioner's core signify the extent of distress.

וירועו כול אושי מבניתי ועצמי יתפרדו

1QH 15:4: The foundations of my build have crumbled, my bones have been disjointed.[55]

In Job 17:11, the root נתק describes Job's plans, fragmented as they are torn apart.

זִמֹּתַי נִתְּקוּ מוֹרָשֵׁי לְבָבִי׃

Job 17:11: My plans are broken off, the desires of my heart.

דכא also implies fragmentation. Forms from דכא, דכה, or דוך almost exclusively occur in non-concrete situations, with only Num 11:8 in a physical domain, for "crushing" manna in a mortar. However, two other facts suggest these roots still provided cognitive access to crushing, grinding, or pulverizing. First, poetic parallels include שבר (to break), תחן (to grind), נכה (to smite), and נגע (to touch or strike), all accessing force domains. Second, דכא is possibly linked to דקק,[56] a verb for crushing or grinding into small pieces, as when preparing sacred incense (Exod 30:36) or Moses' destroying the golden calf (Exod 32:20). This use is similar to דוך in Num 11:8, plus דקק occurs precisely in the books where דכא and derivatives are absent.[57] דקק conceptualizes the nations as ground in a mortar in Ps 18:42[43] and Mic 4:13. Thus, being ground to fine powder is potentially evoked when distress is described with דכא, highlighting "the grinding effect of oppression that penetrates the whole person."[58]

---

55. Martínez and Barrera, *People*, 177.
56. Fuhs, "דָּכָא," 201.
57. Ibid., 199.
58 Tamez, *Bible*, 9, cited in Swart, "Vocabulary," 188.

Surrounded by Bitterness

Psalm 34:18[19] (cited above) parallels דַּכְּאֵי־רוּחַ with a "broken heart," with the adjective hiding the "crushing" agent, as does the niphal in Ps 38:8[9], where the modifier עַד־מְאֹד expresses intensity. In Ps 143:3 and 1QH 13:17 (following the conceptualization of oppression as במצוקותם, a constricting force), the enemy causes crushing and consequent fragmentation. In Job 19:2, Job's friends' words "crush" him. God himself is the agent in Pss 51:8[10] and 44:19[20].

נְפוּגוֹתִי וְנִדְכֵּיתִי עַד־מְאֹד

Ps 38:8[9]: I am utterly spent and crushed.

כִּי רָדַף אוֹיֵב נַפְשִׁי דִּכָּא לָאָרֶץ חַיָּתִי

Ps 143:3: For the enemy has pursued me, crushing my life to the ground.

וימהרו עלי רשעי עמים במצוקותם וכול היום ידכאו נפשי

1QH 13:17: The wicked of the nations hustle me with their trials, and the whole day they crush my soul.[59]

עַד־אָנָה תּוֹגְיוּן נַפְשִׁי וּתְדַכְּאוּנַנִי בְמִלִּים׃

Job 19:2: How long will you torment me, and crush me with your words?[60]

תָּגֵלְנָה עֲצָמוֹת דִּכִּיתָ׃

Ps 51:8[10]: Let the bones that you have crushed rejoice.

כִּי דִכִּיתָנוּ בִּמְקוֹם תַּנִּים

Ps 44:19[20]: Yet you crushed us in the place of jackals.[61]

Thus, experiencing a fragmenting force is a salient way of conceptualizing distress, using שבר and דכא, but also elaborated with roots like רעע and נתק. This conceptualization may highlight an aggressive

---

59. Martínez and Tigchelaar, *Scrolls*, 173.
60. Gordis, *Job*, 196.
61. Basson, *Divine*, 162.

Distress and the Force Schema

agent (as typically for דכא), or use a less active form to hide it. Two non-personal agents occur: "words" and "reproach."

The linguistic forms suggest that שבר profiles the resultant broken state of the sufferer, whereas דכא profiles the agent causing fragmentation. They also evoke different manners of fragmentation. דכא evokes very deliberate and thorough fragmentation, whereas שבר neither requires a deliberate agent nor evokes such complete fragmentation.

These mappings are summarized as follows:

Domain	Agonist's Force Tendency	Antagonist's Force Tendency	Causation	Resultant Action
Source	*Whole object* To remain intact	*Fragmenting force* To break or grind into pieces	May be deliberate action	Object is no longer able to function as desired
Target	*Self* To keep life, thoughts, feelings together	*Distress* To fragment the self	May be deliberate action of another entity	Self is no longer able to function as desired
Other Entailments: Greater extent of fragmentation → More intense distress				

7.4.3. BEING IN DISTRESS IS BEING FORCEFULLY GRIPPED

Next, several conventional roots frame distress with verbs of object manipulation, specifically being touched or held by someone (or something).

First, אחז is used, physically describing holding or grabbing objects, usually implying "a certain vivacity or forcefulness,"[62] and often describing violent or aggressive action. Different agents "hold" the petitioner: in Job 21:6, the agent is "shuddering" (פַּלָּצוּת) and Job's flesh (בְּשָׂרִי) is "seized"; in Job 30:16 the agent is "days of affliction" (יְמֵי־עֹנִי); in 1QH 13:30 it is "heat"[63] (זלעופות); and in 1QH 12:33,

---

62. Konkel, "אחז," 354.

63. Martinez and Tigchelaar translate as "resentment," but the basic meaning of זלעפה is 'heat,' as in BDB 278.

"dread and dismay" (ראד ורתת), showing some similarities to the English phrase being "gripped by emotion."[64] In Ps 77:4[5], God himself grips the petitioner, holding open his eyelids. The various abstract agents indicate the conventionalization of this FORCE schema for conceptualizing distress. However, the absence of intensity modifiers (such as מְאֹד) suggests limited scalarity here.

וְאָחַז בִּשָׂרִי פַלָּצוּת:

Job 21:6: ... and shuddering seizes my flesh.

יֹאחֲזוּנִי יְמֵי־עֹנִי:

Job 30:16: Days of affliction have taken hold of me.

זלעופות אחזוני וחבלים כצירי 31 יולדה

1QH 13:30–31: Resentment [heat] has taken hold of me and pangs like the labors of a woman giving birth.

ואני ראד ורתת אחזוני

1QH 12:33: And I, dread and dismay have gripped me.

אָחַזְתָּ שְׁמֻרוֹת עֵינָי

Ps 77:4[5]: You held open my eyelids.[65]

The hiphil of חזק evokes a similar image, of "seizing" or "grasping."[66] In Jer 8:21 the agent is dismay (שַׁמָּה) and in 6:24 it is distress (צָרָה).

שַׁמָּה הֶחֱזִיקָתְנִי:

Jer 8:21: Dismay has taken hold of me.

צָרָה הֶחֱזִיקַתְנוּ חִיל כַּיּוֹלֵדָה:

Jer 6:24: Anguish has taken hold of us, pain as of a woman in labor.

64. Konkel, "אחז," 355.
65. Alter, *Psalms*, 268.
66. BDB 305.

Finally, נגע is used, frequently translated as "touch." It denotes both touches so gentle that they are unnoticed (Lev 5:2)[67] and powerful forces like the wind destroying Job's house (Job 1:19). The noun נֶגַע describes skin diseases in Leviticus, and Seybold identifies this word in certain Psalms as clear indication that they come from a life-setting of physical illness.[68] Sussman thinks it specifically represents epidemic diseases spread through contact.[69] However, in 1 Kgs 8:37, נֶגַע summarizes several distressing circumstances, including famine, pests, mildew, locusts, human enemies, and disease,[70] showing many disasters attributable to divine touch. It is also used for the disasters befalling Pharaoh in Gen 12:17 and Exod 11:1.

Sometimes, God's touch specifically causes distress, as in Ps 39:10[11] or Job 19:21. Elsewhere, distress is conceptualized simply as a "touch." Psalm 73:14 uses a passive to minimize the agent, whereas Ps 38:11[12] and 1QH 12:36 use a nominal.

הָסֵר מֵעָלַי נִגְעֶךָ מִתִּגְרַת יָדְךָ אֲנִי כָלִיתִי׃

Ps 39:10[11]: Take away from me your touch, from the blow of your hand I perish.[71]

יַד־אֱלוֹהַּ נָגְעָה בִּי׃

Job 19:21: The hand of God has touched me!

וָאֱהִי נָגוּעַ כָּל־הַיּוֹם

Ps 73:14: For all day long I have been plagued.

אֹהֲבַי וְרֵעַי מִנֶּגֶד נִגְעִי יַעֲמֹדוּ

Ps 38:11[12]: My friends and companions stand aloof from my affliction.

---

67. Emphasized by Schwienhorst, "נֶגַע," 204–5.
68. Seybold, *Gebet*.
69. Sussman, "Sickness," 8.
70. Harrison and Swart, "נֶגַע," 25.
71. Based on Alter, *Psalms*, 139.

Surrounded by Bitterness

ורוחי החזיקה במעמד לפני נגע

1QH 12:36: My spirit kept firmly in place in the face of affliction.

נגע, אחז, and חזק all evoke physical contact, but in different manners. אחז may focus on "forcefulness," and the intention to not let go, whereas נגע evokes more general physical contact. חזק may emphasize strength, given its qal meaning.

Conceptualizing distress as being gripped or touched is thus deeply entrenched, shown especially by these different roots and the variety of abstract agents. Rather than specific diseases gripping someone (as in Akkadian), Hebrew texts have general agents (more commonly than God or human enemies), such as "trouble" or "dismay." Despite this conventionality, few texts use source domain inferences, either related to intensity or potential solutions.

The following table summarizes this mapping, focusing on אחז and חזק.

Domain	Agonist's Force Tendency	Antagonist's Force Tendency	Causation	Resultant Action
Source	Material entity To remain at rest	Forceful entity To hold on with strength, and bring under control	May be deliberate	The gripped entity is under control of the stronger entity
Target	Self To remain at ease and in control	Emotions / God / distress To hold strongly onto the self and control it	May be deliberate	Self is under control of someone or something else

7.4.4. Being in Distress is Encountering a Moving Force

A third category conceptualizes distress as an entity coming forcefully towards the petitioner, and potentially penetrating him or her. Here, the potential forceful impact affects the author's feelings.

Distress and the Force Schema

Psalm 55:5[6] prototypically has emotion responses (יִרְאָה וָרַעַד) "coming into" the petitioner. Again in Job 3:25–26, substantives related to fear (פַּחַד, אֲשֶׁר יָגֹרְתִּי, רֹגֶז) "come" to Job, using both בוא and the much rarer אתה for the movement towards the sufferer. In Job 30:26, "evil" and "darkness" come.

יִרְאָה וָרַעַד יָבֹא בִי

Ps 55:5[6]: Fear and trembling come upon me.

כִּי פַחַד פָּחַדְתִּי וַיֶּאֱתָיֵנִי וַאֲשֶׁר יָגֹרְתִּי יָבֹא לִי: לֹא שָׁלַוְתִּי וְלֹא שָׁקַטְתִּי וְלֹא־נָחְתִּי וַיָּבֹא רֹגֶז:

Job 3:25–26: I feared a fear and it came to me, all that I dreaded has come upon me. I have no repose, no quiet, no rest. Turmoil has come.[72]

כִּי טוֹב קִוִּיתִי וַיָּבֹא רָע וַאֲיַחֲלָה לְאוֹר וַיָּבֹא אֹפֶל:

Job 30:26: But when I looked for good, evil came; and when I waited for light, darkness came.

In Ps 119:143, trouble and anguish have come to meet the psalmist. The same verb in Ps 116:3 describes the pangs of Sheol (מְצָרֵי שְׁאוֹל) "meeting" (מְצָאוּנִי) the psalmist. Psalm 22:11[12] uses a "path" entailment, describing trouble as not just coming but "near" (קְרוֹבָה).

צַר־וּמָצוֹק מְצָאוּנִי

Ps 119:143: Trouble and anguish have come upon me.

וּמְצָרֵי שְׁאוֹל מְצָאוּנִי צָרָה וְיָגוֹן אֶמְצָא:

Ps 116:3: The pangs of Sheol laid hold on me; I suffered distress and anguish.

אַל־תִּרְחַק מִמֶּנִּי כִּי־צָרָה קְרוֹבָה כִּי־אֵין עוֹזֵר:

Ps 22:11[12]: Do not be far from me, for trouble is near and there is no one to help.

---

72. Clines, *Job 1–20*, 68, 75.

Job 30:27 uses the rarer קדם for days of affliction which "come to meet" Job. In 1QH 19:21, thoughts of man's sin and guilt have "penetrated" (ויגעו) the author, and cause him emotional distress.

קִדְּמֻנִי יְמֵי־עֹנִי׃

Job 30:27: Days of affliction come to meet me.

ויבואו בלבבי ויגעו בעצמי

1QH 19:21: These things have entered my heart, they have penetrated my bones.

All these expressions conceptualize distress as moving forcefully towards the sufferer, inferring that the closer the entity is, the more imminent distress is. The situation is most serious when it penetrates "into" a person. These mappings are shown below:

Domain	Agonist's Force Tendency	Antagonist's Force Tendency	Causation	Resultant Action
Source	Material entity To remain at rest	Forceful entity To move towards the other entity and even penetrate it	Deliberate, inescapable movement towards the other entity	Material is penetrated by the forceful entity
Target	Self To remain unaffected and in control	Emotions / distress To come to the self and even penetrate it	Deliberate, inescapable occurrence of distress is coming	Distress reaches and penetrates the self
Other Entailments: The closer the force is → The more serious the distress				

7.4.5. Being in Distress is Experiencing Enforced Movement

The previous mappings leave the Agonist in one place. Elsewhere, metaphors frame distress as enforced movement, where an irresistible

Distress and the Force Schema

Antagonist overcomes the Agonist's tendency to rest. Such "compulsion" frequently results in the Agonist involuntarily following an undesired path.[73] Within the English event-structure conceptual metaphor, self-propelled motion maps onto purposeful action, whereas other-propelled motion maps onto caused events.[74] The Hebrew mapping may similarly have important entailments regarding control and causation.

Different verbs evoke different manners of enforced movement. First, sometimes the sufferer is an inanimate object sent along a trajectory over which it has no control. Psalm 102:10[11] uses שׁלך, prototypically describing "thrown" inanimate objects, with God as the agent. In Ps 118:13, דחה evokes "violent pushing" by the psalmist's enemies. The infinitive absolute highlights this force's intensity. Psalm 109:23 pictures the psalmist as a locust shaken (נִנְעַרְתִּי) from a garment, using a niphal and hiding the agent, but still suggesting a deliberate action.

כִּי נְשָׂאתַנִי וַתַּשְׁלִיכֵנִי׃

Ps 102:10[11]: For you have lifted me up and thrown me aside.

דָּחֹה דְחִיתַנִי לִנְפֹּל וַיהוָה עֲזָרָנִי׃

Ps 118:13: You pushed me hard so that I was falling, but the LORD helped me.[75]

נִנְעַרְתִּי כָּאַרְבֶּה׃

Ps 109:23: I am shaken off like a locust.

Second, some verbs evoke more personal enforced movement. In the "anti-Psalm 23" of Lam 3:1–6,[76] a long-term, purposeful, directing force leads the sufferer like an animal (נהג)[77] into darkness, not green pastures and still waters. נהג also fits a shepherding context, used for

---

73. Johnson, *Body*, 45.

74. Kövecses, *Emotion*, 51–60.

75. NRSV, but following the Masoretic "you pushed me hard" rather than the LXX "I was pushed hard," taking this verse as addressing the hostile nations, as in Alter, *Psalms*, 416.

76. Van Hecke, "Lamentations."

77. Gross, "נָהַג."

driving sheep from their pasture (Jer 23:2),⁷⁸ or a bird from a nest, and in 1QH 12:8–9, for the author "driven" from his land. In Jon 2:4[5], נרש evokes "forcible or violent expulsion,"⁷⁹ with the niphal minimizing the agent. In Ps 36:11[12], the hiphil of נוד suggests causing someone to wander aimlessly,⁸⁰ describing the threat of the wicked. These verses thus show several verbs evoking someone forcing another to move.

אוֹתִי נָהַג וַיֹּלַךְ חֹשֶׁךְ וְלֹא־אוֹר׃

Lam 3:2: He has driven and brought me into darkness without any light.

כיא ידיחני מארצי 9 כצפור מקנה וכול רעי ומודעי נדחו ממני

1QH 12:8–9: For they drive me from my land like a bird from its nest; all my friends and my acquaintances have been driven away from me.

וַאֲנִי אָמַרְתִּי נִגְרַשְׁתִּי מִנֶּגֶד עֵינֶיךָ אַךְ אוֹסִיף לְהַבִּיט אֶל־הֵיכַל קָדְשֶׁךָ׃

Jon 2:4[5]: Then I said, "I am driven away from your sight; how shall I look again upon your holy temple?"

אַל־תְּבוֹאֵנִי רֶגֶל גַּאֲוָה וְיַד־רְשָׁעִים אַל־תְּנִדֵנִי׃

Ps 36:11[12]: Do not let the foot of the arrogant tread on me, or the hand of the wicked drive me away.

Third, the petitioner is occasionally lifted up, using the root נשא. In Ps 102:10[11] (cited above) the psalmist is lifted before being thrown, and in Job 30:22 he is then forced to even more violent movement, riding the wind. In both cases this image shows a harmful intent that the sufferer cannot do anything about.

תִּשָּׂאֵנִי אֶל־רוּחַ תַּרְכִּיבֵנִי

Job 30:22: You snatch me up and make me ride on the wind.⁸¹

78. Kronholm, "נָדַח," 239.
79. Stigers, "גָּרַשׁ."
80. BDB 627.
81. Clines, *Job 21–37*, 931.

Distress and the Force Schema

Job being moved by the wind is also implicit in Job 13:25.

הֶעָלֶה נִדָּף תַּעֲרוֹץ וְאֶת־קַשׁ יָבֵשׁ תִּרְדֹּף׃

Job 13:25: Will you frighten a windblown leaf and pursue dry chaff?

Fourth, some texts show the concept of enforced movement being particularly appropriate for the wicked, whose plight is being "moved away," presumably in death. In both Pss 28:3 and 26:9 the psalmist asks not to be moved as the wicked are, first with משׁך, being drawn away by a stronger force, and second with אסף, being gathered together with the wicked by a stronger force.

אַל־תִּמְשְׁכֵנִי עִם־רְשָׁעִים

Ps 28:3: Do not drag me away with the wicked.

אַל־תֶּאֱסֹף עִם־חַטָּאִים נַפְשִׁי

Ps 26:9: Do not gather up my soul with sinners.[82]

These metaphors all conceptualize distress as movement against the will of the sufferer, evoking different manners of movement. שׁלך and דחה evoke violent movement after an initial contact with the one causing movement, whereas the shepherding roots גרשׁ, נהג, and נדח evoke the force causing the movement accompanying the moved body. Further, several verses explicitly entail movement from a good place (a bird in its nest, or within God's sight) to a negatively conceptualized place (such as darkness, or with the wicked).

---

82. Craigie, *Psalms 1-50*, 233.

Domain	Agonist's Force Tendency	Antagonist's Force Tendency	Causation	Resultant Action
Source	Material entity To remain at rest, in control of own movement	Forceful agent To cause the entity to move	Usually deliberate and purposeful	Entity is forcibly moved
Target	Self To remain in control of own life events	Distress causing agent To control what happens to the self	Usually deliberate and purposeful	Self's life events are in the control of another
Other Entailments: Undesirable destination → Undesirable life situation				

7.4.6. Being in Distress is Being Attacked by Wild Animals

Considering more specific scripts, several examples conceptualize the petitioner as stalked or attacked by animals. The Palestinian lion was the prototypical predator,[83] being fairly common and living amongst dense vegetation.[84] Its cultural significance is seen by seven Hebrew denotations,[85] including אַרְיֵה / אֲרִי, כְּפִיר, לָבִיא, שַׁחַל, and אֲרִי. גּוּר is probably the basic-level term, used for a prototypical lion but also a male adult lion in distinction to the other words marking sex and maturity.[86]

Lions symbolized power across the ancient Near East, whether positively representing fertility, protection, or strength, or negatively

---

83. Dogs and bulls are also mentioned, but mainly as surrounding the petitioner and cited in the previous chapter. The closest to their exerting a direct force is the psalmist saved from the hand of the dog (מִיַּד־כֶּלֶב) and from the horns of the wild oxen (מִקַּרְנֵי רֵמִים) in Ps 22.20–21[21–22]. Psalm 74.19 also refers generally to wild animals (חַיַּת).

84. Negenman, "Palestine," 18, although very few bone remains have been found, Hesse, "Husbandry," 203.

85. Rechenmacher, "Kognitive," 51.

86. Ibid., 51–54.

representing chaos and destruction.[87] In the corpus, lions are unequivocally negative. Power (כח) is highlighted in 1QH 13:18–19.

ונפש אביון פלטתה כ . . .].[. . .]. טרף מכח 19 אריות

1QH 13:18–19: and have freed the soul of the poor like [. . .] prey from the power of lions.

Psalm 35:15–17 typically instantiates lion metaphors, framing the mockers as lions surrounding a stumbling prey, gnashing their teeth as they tear it apart.

וּבְצַלְעִי שָׂמְחוּ וְנֶאֱסָפוּ נֶאֶסְפוּ עָלַי נֵכִים וְלֹא יָדַעְתִּי קָרְעוּ וְלֹא־דָמּוּ: בְּחַנְפֵי לַעֲגֵי מָעוֹג חָרֹק עָלַי שִׁנֵּימוֹ: אֲדֹנָי כַּמָּה תִּרְאֶה הָשִׁיבָה נַפְשִׁי מִשֹּׁאֵיהֶם מִכְּפִירִים יְחִידָתִי:

Ps 35:15–17: But at my stumbling they gathered in glee, they gathered together against me; ruffians whom I did not know tore at me without ceasing; they impiously mocked more and more, gnashing at me with their teeth. How long, O LORD, will you look on? Rescue me from their ravages, my life from the lions!

Such verses, alongside descriptions of typical leonine behavior, suggest a prototypical "lion attack" script. First, the lion stalks its prey under cover, preparing an ambush, then as it breaks cover, it snarls, showing its teeth, and opening wide its mouth. The attack itself involves ripping flesh with its mouth, tearing the body apart, breaking and shattering bones. Finally, the lion may drag the victim away to finish the destruction.

This script maps onto distressing experiences as follows:

---

87. Cornelius, "Lion."

Person being attacked	→	Person in distress
Lion(s)	→	Agent(s) causing distress
Lion in hiding / hunting	→	Agent premeditating to cause distress
Lion snarling / showing teeth / opening mouth	→	Agent using words to initiate distress
Ripping and tearing flesh	→	Painful experience of distress
Being dragged off	→	Distressed person is completely under the agent's control

First, the agent, mapped to the lion, may be non-specific enemies (Ps 17:12), or God himself (Job 10:16). Psalm 17:12 also maps the agent's desire to a lion longing to eat, inferring motivation from this script. Job 10:16 specifically maps the lion's boldness onto God's character.

דִּמְיֹנוֹ כְּאַרְיֵה יִכְסוֹף לִטְרוֹף וְכִכְפִיר יֹשֵׁב בְּמִסְתָּרִים׃

Ps 17:12: His appearance is like a lion, longing to tear apart, like a young lion lurking in ambush.[88]

וְיִגְאֶה כַּשַּׁחַל תְּצוּדֵנִי

Job 10:16: Bold as a lion you hunt me.

Second, the deliberate, premeditated nature of attack maps to the enemies' deliberate undertakings. An attacking lion may stalk prey silently under cover, before charging at the prey, or male lions may scare prey towards lionesses waiting in ambush to finish the job.[89] The hunting lion of Job 10:16 (תְּצוּדֵנִי, above) suggests the first script. The lions lying in wait in Lam 3:10 and Ps 10:8–9 are more like the second. A hiding lion evokes deliberate action, but also unsuspected distress. Explicating the "blameless" (נָקִי) prey highlights that distress is unjustified, the psalmist is as innocent as the lion's prey.

דֹּב אֹרֵב הוּא לִי אֲרִי בְּמִסְתָּרִים׃

Lam 3:10: He is a bear lying in wait for me, a lion in hiding.

---

88. Basson, *Divine*, 88.
89. Hope, *Creatures*, 2.24.

Distress and the Force Schema

יֵשֵׁב בְּמַאְרַב חֲצֵרִים בַּמִּסְתָּרִים יַהֲרֹג נָקִי עֵינָיו לְחֵלְכָה יִצְפֹּנוּ:
יֶאֱרֹב בַּמִּסְתָּר כְּאַרְיֵה בְסֻכֹּה יֶאֱרֹב לַחֲטוֹף עָנִי

Ps 10:8–9: He waits in ambush in a sheltered place, from a covert he kills the blameless, for the wretched his eyes look out. He lies in wait in a covert like a lion in his lair, lies in wait to snatch up the poor.[90]

Third, the script includes the lion's threatening behavior as it closes in. Whilst the stalking is silent, snarling accompanies the final approach "produced with exposed teeth, the body in a low crouch, and ears laid back flat"[91] and also the ensuing fight. This may explain חרק, usually translated as "gnashing" or "grinding" of teeth and clearly a gesture of hostility. Psalm 35:16 equates this with "contemptuous mocking chatter,"[92] in Ps 37:12 it is part of the enemies' plot, indicating desire to harm, and in Ps 112:10 failure to do more than this shows the inability of the wicked to fulfil their desire to harm the righteous. In Job 16:9, it more closely parallels "tearing." In most cases, this action could specifically conceptualize the opponents' threatening words.

בְּחַנְפֵי לַעֲגֵי מָעוֹג חָרֹק עָלַי שִׁנֵּימוֹ:

Ps 35:16: With contemptuous mocking chatter they gnashed their teeth against me.

זֹמֵם רָשָׁע לַצַּדִּיק וְחֹרֵק עָלָיו שִׁנָּיו:

Ps 37:12: The wicked plot against the righteous, and gnash their teeth at them;

רָשָׁע יִרְאֶה וְכָעָס שִׁנָּיו יַחֲרֹק וְנָמָס תַּאֲוַת רְשָׁעִים תֹּאבֵד:

Ps 112:10: The wicked see it and are angry; they gnash their teeth and melt away; the desire of the wicked comes to nothing.

אַפּוֹ טָרַף וַיִּשְׂטְמֵנִי חָרַק עָלַי בְּשִׁנָּיו צָרִי יִלְטוֹשׁ עֵינָיו לִי:

---

90. Alter, *Psalms*, 30.
91. Hope, *Creatures*, 2:24.
92. Following Kimchi's interpretation of מָעוֹג as 'empty talk,' Alter, *Psalms*, 124.

> Job 16:9: He has torn me in his wrath, and hated me; he has gnashed his teeth at me; my adversary sharpens his eyes against me.

The fourth stage is the attack and devouring of the prey, including grabbing the prey at the neck with the mouth to suffocate the animal,[93] then tearing it apart as it is eaten. The most common root for the lion's action here is טרף, but roots evoking tearing (פרק, קרע) or breaking bones (שבר) also occur.

For טרף, Wagner observes "the basic meaning is 'tear (to pieces),' especially with large beasts of prey as subject."[94] However, this overlooks the mouth's importance. All verbal uses could describe tearing prey with the mouth, and the noun טֶרֶף describes food, both for large beasts and humans (Prov 31:15). Assyrian art shows the lion's claws primarily holding down the victim, while the lion uses teeth to tear the prey.[95] Further, 1QH 13:14 emphasizes God's closing the teeth of the lions as the way to stop them "tearing" (with טרף). Thus, the prototypical meaning is more likely "tear apart *with the mouth*."

פרק highlights the prey's fate more than the lion's action, evoking forceful separation, whether positive (in rescue) or negative.[96] Psalm 7:2[3] uses both verbs for the pursuers' actions. Since the lion is the strongest animal, rescue is impossible.

> פֶּן־יִטְרֹף כְּאַרְיֵה נַפְשִׁי פֹּרֵק וְאֵין מַצִּיל׃
>
> Ps 7:2[3]: Lest they should rip me like a lion, tearing me up, with no deliverer.[97]

The lion's mouth (פֶּה) is always feared (rather than claws), with the teeth (שֵׁן) and tongue (לָשׁוֹן) specifically highlighted, as in Ps 22:13[14] and 21[22]. In Ps 35:16, cited above, the teeth are associated with mocking. In Ps 57:4[5], the enemies are lions, then their teeth are arrows and tongues swords, perhaps in this context describing the accusers' words

---

93. Hope, *Creatures*, 2:24.
94. Wagner, "טָרַף," 351.
95. As shown in Cornelius, "Lion," 72–73.
96. Reiterer, "פָּרַק."
97. Craigie, *Psalms 1–50*, 96.

in a trial.⁹⁸ Thus, the enemies' "attacking" words may be specifically focused whenever this part of the script is invoked, as with "gnashing" teeth. Therefore, even the intensely physical language of a lion attack may describe psychological or social violence. As Firth notes for Psalm 7, "false accusation is in itself an intensely distressing thing."⁹⁹

נַפְשִׁי בְּתוֹךְ לְבָאִם אֶשְׁכְּבָה לֹהֲטִים בְּנֵי־אָדָם שִׁנֵּיהֶם חֲנִית וְחִצִּים וּלְשׁוֹנָם חֶרֶב חַדָּה:

Ps 57:4[5]: I lie down among lions that greedily devour human prey; their teeth are spears and arrows, their tongues sharp swords.

פָּצוּ עָלַי פִּיהֶם אַרְיֵה טֹרֵף וְשֹׁאֵג:

Ps 22:13[14]: They open wide their mouths at me, like a ravening and roaring lion.

הוֹשִׁיעֵנִי מִפִּי אַרְיֵה וּמִקַּרְנֵי רֵמִים עֲנִיתָנִי:

Ps 22:21[22]: Save me from the mouth of the lion! From the horns of the wild oxen you have rescued me.

בָּרוּךְ יְהוָה שֶׁלֹּא נְתָנָנוּ טֶרֶף לְשִׁנֵּיהֶם:

Ps 124:6: Blessed be the LORD, who has not given us as prey to their teeth.

ותסגור פי כפירים אשר 10 כחרב שניהם ומתלעותם כחנית חדה

1QH 13:9–10: You closed the mouth of the lion cubs, whose teeth are like a sword, whose fangs are like a sharpened spear.

ותצל נפש עני במעון אריות אשר שננו כחרב לשונם 14 ואתה אלי סגרתה בעד שניהם פן יטרפו נפש עני ורש ותוסף לשונם 15 כחרב אל תערה בלוא| כר|תה נפש עבדכה

---

98. Tate, *Psalms*, 78.
99. Firth, *Retribution*, 23.

Surrounded by Bitterness

1QH 13:13–15: And you rescued the life of the afflicted in the den of lions, whose tongue is like a sharpened sword. And you, O my God, you shut their teeth, lest they tear apart the life of the poor afflicted. And their tongue was drawn back like a sword to its sheath, lest it [dest]roy the life of your servant.[100]

Lamentations 3:11; Isa 38:13; and Job 16:9 most vividly describe someone who has actually been attacked by a lion. In Lamentations and Job the petitioner has been "torn" (טרף, פשח), whereas in Isaiah 38 all the sufferer's bones have been broken (שבר). None of these fit the contexts of accusation or trial common elsewhere, describing life threatening illness or the experience of Jerusalem's destruction. This stage of the script is the most serious. The possibility of lions breaking bones also occurs in 1QH 13:6–7.

דְּרָכַי סוֹרֵר וַיְפַשְּׁחֵנִי שָׂמַנִי שֹׁמֵם׃

Lam 3:11: He led me off my way and tore me to pieces; he has made me desolate.

אַפּוֹ טָרַף וַיִּשְׂטְמֵנִי

Job 16:9: He has torn me in his wrath, and hated me;

כַּאֲרִי כֵּן יְשַׁבֵּר כָּל־עַצְמוֹתָי מִיּוֹם עַד־לַיְלָה תַּשְׁלִימֵנִי׃

Isa 38:13: Like a lion he breaks all my bones; from day to night you bring me to an end.

ותתן . . . [. . .] . . . בתוך 7 לביאים מועדים לבני אשמה
אריות שוברי עצם אדירים ושותי ד[ם] גבורים

1QH 13:6–7: And you placed [me] in the midst of lions, those appointed for the sons of guilt, lions who shatter the bones of the noble, and who drink the blood of the mighty.[101]

Further, problematizing a situation as a lion attack entails particular solutions. Psalm 58:6[7] asks God to tear out the lions' fangs,

---

100. Kittel, *Hymns*, 85.
101. Ibid., 84.

a plea to nullify the words of the unjust judges addressed in v. 1[2].[102] Similarly, 1QH 13 thanks God for "closing" (סגר) the teeth of those he dwelt amongst (v. 14, cited above). The only solution for a helpless prey facing a powerful enemy is for a stronger power to vanquish the predator. Sufferers never ask for increased strength to fight back.

אֱלֹהִים הֲרָס־שִׁנֵּימוֹ בְּפִימוֹ מַלְתְּעוֹת כְּפִירִים נְתֹץ יְהוָה׃

> Ps 58:6[7]: O God, break the teeth in their mouths; tear out the fangs of the young lions, O LORD!

Finally, the petitioner's perceived position within the script also constrains inferences. If the lion is waiting in ambush, escape is still possible. The predicament is more serious when the lion breaks cover and is snarling in full view, but still a stronger power may intervene and rescue the prey. Where the petitioner has actually been torn to pieces, or had his bones shattered, hope is very limited, showing the greatest intensity of distress.

These metaphors show a well-structured source domain giving structure to distressing experiences perceived to be caused by deliberate aggressive agents. The structured script of leonine attack, and the various entailments regarding motives and character of predator and prey, enable petitioners to understand their distressing situation, predicting what will happen next and guiding their prayers for God to intervene.

The mappings are summarized as follows:

---

102. Tate, *Psalms*, 87.

Domain	Agonist's Force Tendency	Antagonist's Force Tendency	Causation	Resultant Action
Source	*Prey* To survive, escape	*Lion* To capture with the jaws and then eat the prey	Deliberate premeditated attack	Serious harm and finally death
Target	*Self* To live in safety and security	*Enemies* To harm the self with words, and possibly more seriously, for their own benefit	Deliberate premeditated action of enemies	Serious harm.

Other Entailments:
Temporal progress of the lion attack script → Temporal progress of the distressing predicament
Lion attacks from hiding → Distress comes unexpectedly
Desire of lion to eat → Desire of enemies to cause harm
Boldness of lion → Boldness of enemies
Innocence of the prey (attack is unjustified) → Innocence of the sufferer (distress is unjustified)
Supreme strength of the lion → Supreme strength of the opponent (no-one can rescue)
Gnashing and tearing with teeth → Opponents verbal attacks
Breaking the teeth / closing the mouth → Being saved from distress

7.4.7. BEING IN DISTRESS IS BEING ATTACKED BY A HUMAN OPPONENT

Forceful interpersonal human conflict also frequently conceptualizes distress. Sometimes, informal hand-to-hand fighting is evoked. Elsewhere, images evoke more formal, armed combat. Although more than one script is evoked, a general overarching script (similar to that of lion attack) maps to distressing situations, as shown below.

Distress and the Force Schema

Person being attacked	→	Person in distressing circumstances
Adversary / enemy	→	Agent causing distress
Enemy hunts / pursues his opponent	→	Premeditated action of adversaries towards the sufferer
Enemy waits to ambush	→	Distress comes unawares
Enemy prepares for attack (drawing bow or sword)	→	Further premeditated action by adversaries towards the sufferer
Enemy attacks (with sword, arrow, or hand)	→	The sufferer experiences distress

a) Various Adversaries

Considering these individually, first, the enemy (אֹיֵב), or adversary (צַר), maps onto the agent causing distress. Job consistently conceptualizes his situation (of loss and sickness) as conflict with God, a strong opponent, against whom he has no chance of prevailing (Job 13:24; 19:11; and 9:19). Jeremiah 20:7 also conceptualizes God as an overpowering strong opponent.

לָמָּה־פָנֶיךָ תַסְתִּיר וְתַחְשְׁבֵנִי לְאוֹיֵב לָךְ׃

Job 13:24: Why do you hide your face, and count me as your enemy?

וַיַּחְשְׁבֵנִי לוֹ כְצָרָיו׃

Job 19:11: He counts me as his adversary.

אִם־לְכֹחַ אַמִּיץ הִנֵּה

Job 9:19: If it is a contest of strength, he is the strong one!

חֲזַקְתַּנִי וַתּוּכָל

Jer 20:7: You have overpowered me, and you have prevailed.

Similarly, in Lamentations God has become the enemy. He has caused the disastrous circumstances, not the Babylonian army, as in Lam 2:5 and 3:1.

הָיָה אֲדֹנָי כְּאוֹיֵב

Lam 2:5: The Lord has become like an enemy.

אֲנִי הַגֶּבֶר רָאָה עֳנִי בְּשֵׁבֶט עֶבְרָתוֹ׃

Lam 3:1: I am the man who has seen affliction under the rod of his wrath.

In the Psalms, people are more frequently conceptualized as enemies or adversaries. Whilst some psalms may originate from the king during national conflict with very real enemies, many do not fit this context very well, especially when the psalmist is apparently suffering from disease, yet still mentions enemies. No identification of these enemies has yet gained wide scholarly acceptance.[103] The enemies are depersonalized, so that distinguishing physical and psychological scenarios is rarely possible.[104] Thus, this analysis will not presume that enemy references necessitate there being opponents bent on physical harm.

b) Deliberate Preparation

The earliest stages of the script conceive the enemies pursuing, plotting or hunting down their opponent. רדף sometimes occurs, evoking "active pursuit of one or more persons, with hostile intent."[105] In narrative, pursuit frequently follows a battle, to complete victory over a fleeing enemy.[106] The psalmists' use is depersonalized and generalized, but still suggests aggressors deliberately setting out to apprehend their opponents and "finish them off."

In Ps 71:10–11, the enemies deliberately plot together to pursue and seize (תפשׂ) the petitioner, exploiting his vulnerability, whereas in Lam 3:43 God has set out in pursuit. Both emphasize deliberate intent to harm.

---

103. Johnston, "Distress," 75.
104. Frevel, "רָדַף," 349.
105. Ibid., 343.
106. Ibid., 344.

כִּי־אָמְרוּ אוֹיְבַי לִי וְשֹׁמְרֵי נַפְשִׁי נוֹעֲצוּ יַחְדָּו׃ לֵאמֹר אֱלֹהִים עֲזָבוֹ
רִדְפוּ וְתִפְשׂוּהוּ כִּי־אֵין מַצִּיל׃

Ps 71:10–11: For my enemies speak concerning me, and those who watch for my life consult together. They say, "God has forsaken him; pursue and seize him, for there is no one to deliver."[107]

סַכֹּתָה בָאַף וַתִּרְדְּפֵנוּ הָרַגְתָּ לֹא חָמָלְתָּ׃

Lam 3:43: You have wrapped yourself with anger and pursued us, killing without pity.

Elsewhere, the enemies' perceived intentions map onto those of hunters, as in Lam 3:52 and 4:18 (using צוּד) and Ps 55:3[4] (using שׂטם). In Lam 3:52, the modifier חִנָּם emphasizes unjustified distress, typical of this motif.

צוֹד צָדוּנִי כַּצִּפּוֹר אֹיְבַי חִנָּם׃

Lam 3:52: Those who were my enemies without cause have hunted me like a bird.

צָדוּ צְעָדֵינוּ מִלֶּכֶת בִּרְחֹבֹתֵינוּ קָרַב קִצֵּינוּ מָלְאוּ יָמֵינוּ כִּי־בָא קִצֵּינוּ׃

Lam 4:18: They dogged our steps so that we could not walk in our streets; our end drew near; our days were numbered; for our end had come.

כִּי־יָמִיטוּ עָלַי אָוֶן וּבְאַף יִשְׂטְמוּנִי׃

Ps 55:3[4]: For they move evil over on me, and hunt me down in their wrath.[108]

In Ps 86:14, this intention is framed as enemies "seeking my life" (בִּקְשׁוּ נַפְשִׁי).

אֱלֹהִים זֵדִים קָמוּ־עָלַי וַעֲדַת עָרִיצִים בִּקְשׁוּ נַפְשִׁי וְלֹא שָׂמוּךָ לְנֶגְדָּם׃

---

107. Author's translation.
108. Tate, *Psalms*, 50, understanding שׂטם as "hunt" from the parallel in Job 16:9.

Ps 86:14: O God, the insolent rise up against me; a band of ruffians seeks my life, and they do not set you before them.

Deliberate actions are also mapped when enemies hide or lie in ambush. Whereas pursuing and hunting highlight harmful intent, hidden enemies (usually using ארב) evoke unexpected or unjustified distress, as in Ps 59:3[4].

כִּי הִנֵּה אָרְבוּ לְנַפְשִׁי יָגוּרוּ עָלַי עַזִים לֹא־פִשְׁעִי וְלֹא־חַטָּאתִי יְהוָה׃

Ps 59:3[4]: Even now they lie in wait for my life; the mighty stir up strife against me. For no transgression or sin of mine, O LORD.

Other verses reflect deliberate intentions with opponents surrounding the petitioner, setting traps or digging pits, but these were considered in chapter six.

Beyond these preparations, conceptualizations vary depending on whether hand-to-hand conflict is assumed, or with bow and arrow, with sword, or some more comprehensive military endeavor.

c) The Enemy's Hand

First, the opponent's hand is often upon the petitioner. Usually, it is God's hand, (Job 19:21; Ps 77:10[11]), but occasionally it is the hand of the wicked (Pss 71:4; 82:4), although not in the sickness contexts common in Akkadian texts. Whereas most references use יָד, Ps 77:10[11] specifically highlights the right hand (יָמִין), used for holding weapons, and symbolizing power and strength, while Ps 71:4 uses the palm (כַּף) in parallel to hand. This elaboration shows the entrenchment of this conceptual metaphor.

יַד־אֱלוֹהַּ נָגְעָה בִּי׃

Job 19:21: The hand of God has touched me!

וָאֹמַר חַלּוֹתִי הִיא שְׁנוֹת יְמִין עֶלְיוֹן׃

Ps 77:10[11]: And I say, "It is my grief that the right hand of the Most High has changed."

Distress and the Force Schema

אֱלֹהַי פַּלְּטֵנִי מִיַּד רָשָׁע מִכַּף מְעַוֵּל וְחוֹמֵץ׃

Ps 71:4: Rescue me, O my God, from the hand of the wicked, from the grasp of the unjust and cruel.

פַּלְּטוּ־דַל וְאֶבְיוֹן מִיַּד רְשָׁעִים הַצִּילוּ׃

Ps 82:4: Rescue the weak and the needy; deliver them from the hand of the wicked.

Sometimes, this image evokes the particular script of hand-to-hand combat, as in Ps 39:10[11], using נגע to demonstrate a consistent conceptualization of distress as divine touch. Job 19:21 (above) also links יָד and נגע.

הָסֵר מֵעָלַי נִגְעֶךָ מִתִּגְרַת יָדְךָ אֲנִי כָלִיתִי׃

Ps 39:10[11]: Take away from me your scourge, from the blow of your hand I perish.[109]

The Akkadian parallels have sickness or plague as normal results of being touched by a divine hand.[110] Similarly, in Hebrew, with God as agent, the expression most commonly designates "the 'disastrous manifestation of the supernatural power' especially in sickness or plague."[111]

Several texts elaborate this image to express intensity. In Job 30:21, the hand's might (עֹצֶם) is emphasized; in Lam 3:3, repeated attacks evoke intensity (כָּל־הַיּוֹם, יָשֻׁב); and in Ps 38:2[3], repeating נחת for both the penetrating arrows and the hand coming down increases the intensity of the description.

בְּעֹצֶם יָדְךָ תִשְׂטְמֵנִי׃

Job 30:21: With the might of your hand you persecute me.

אַךְ בִּי יָשֻׁב יַהֲפֹךְ יָדוֹ כָּל־הַיּוֹם׃

Lam 3:3: Against me alone he turns his hand, again and again, all day long.

---

109. Alter, *Psalms*, 139.
110. Roberts, "Hand," 96.
111. Ibid., 99.

Surrounded by Bitterness

כִּי־חִצֶּיךָ נִחֲתוּ בִי וַתִּנְחַת עָלַי יָדֶךָ׃

Ps 38:2[3]: For your arrows have sunk into me and your hand has come down on me.

1QH 10:34–35 again emphasizes the strength of the hand (חזק ממנו, אדירים), whereas in Ps 32:4 and Job 23:2 the hand's weight (כבד) expresses intensity. These various syntactic frameworks demonstrate how entrenched this conceptualization is, and how freely it can be elaborated to portray distress.

ואתה אלי עזרתה נפש עני ורש 35 מיד חזק ממנו וחפף נפשי מיד אדירים

1QH 10:34–35: But you my God have freed the soul of the poor and needy from the hand of someone stronger than him: from the hand of the powerful you have saved my soul.

כִּי יוֹמָם וָלַיְלָה תִּכְבַּד עָלַי יָדֶךָ

Ps 32:4: For day and night your hand was heavy upon me.

יָדִי כָּבְדָה עַל־אַנְחָתִי׃

Job 23:2: The heavy hand upon me is because of my groaning![112]

As in Mesopotamia, relief is achievable by removing God's hand and ending this forceful contact, as in Job 13:21, but by prayer rather than other rites.

כַּפְּךָ מֵעָלַי הַרְחַק וְאֵמָתְךָ אַל־תְּבַעֲתַנִּי׃

Job 13:21: Withdraw your hand far from me, and do not let dread of you terrify me.

d) Other Hand-to-Hand Combat

Other examples evoke unarmed combat without mentioning the hand. The sufferer is fighting God or another opponent. Job 30:18–19 is especially vivid, and must, despite difficult Hebrew, describe a physical

---

112. Wolfers, *Deep*, 346. The owner of the hand here is difficult to ascertain.

attack, with God grabbing Job by his clothes and throwing him into the mud. Job 16:14 pictures God more generally as a warrior, expressing intensity by the threefold repetition of the root פרץ. Jeremiah 14:17, 19 also has the people struck by forceful blows.

בְּרָב־כֹּחַ יִתְחַפֵּשׂ לְבוּשִׁי כְּפִי כֻתָּנְתִּי יַאַזְרֵנִי: הֹרָנִי לַחֹמֶר וָאֶתְמַ־
שֵׁל כֶּעָפָר וָאֵפֶר:

Job 30:18–19: With great power he grasps my garment, he holds me tight by the collar of my tunic. He has hurled me into the mire, and I have become dust and ashes.[113]

יִפְרְצֵנִי פֶרֶץ עַל־פְּנֵי־פָרֶץ יָרֻץ עָלַי כְּגִבּוֹר:

Job 16:14: He bursts upon me again and again; he rushes at me like a warrior.

כִּי שֶׁבֶר גָּדוֹל נִשְׁבְּרָה בְּתוּלַת בַּת־עַמִּי מַכָּה נַחְלָה מְאֹד:
מַדּוּעַ הִכִּיתָנוּ וְאֵין לָנוּ מַרְפֵּא

Jer 14:17, 19: For the virgin daughter—my people—is broken by a crushing blow, by a very grievous blow . . . Why have you struck us down so that there is no healing for us?[114]

Elsewhere, the opponent's blows and their effect are emphasized, particularly using נכה, prototypically evoking hitting an object with one non-fatal strike.[115] In 1QH 10:5 the "blows" probably refer to the comforters' words, given the next verbs are about them "announcing" and "proclaiming." Similarly, in Ps 42:9–10[10–11], the "murderous blows to my bones" (בְּרֶצַח בְּעַצְמוֹתַי) represent the enemies' words. Psalm 62:3[4] also uses רצח for the enemies' battering (alongside הות), again implying verbal attack by the subsequent switch to the issue of speech.

מחץ מכ[ת]י[ן] מנחמי. . .]

1QH 10:5: [. . .] smitten by bl[ows of the comforters . . .]

---

113. Gordis, *Job*, 326.
114. Author's translation.
115. Wilson, "נָכָה."

Surrounded by Bitterness

לָמָּה־קֹדֵר אֵלֵךְ בְּלַחַץ אוֹיֵב: בְּרֶצַח בְּעַצְמוֹתַי חֵרְפוּנִי צוֹרְרָי בְּאָמְרָם אֵלַי כָּל־הַיּוֹם אַיֵּה אֱלֹהֶיךָ:

Ps 42:9–10[10–11]: Why must I walk about mournfully because the enemy oppresses me? With a murderous blow to my bones, my adversaries taunt me, while they say to me continually, "Where is your God?"[116]

עַד־אָנָה תְּהוֹתְתוּ עַל אִישׁ תְּרָצְּחוּ כֻלְּכֶם

Ps 62:3[4]: How long will you assail a person, will you batter your victim, all of you.

In Jer 14:17–19 (above), enemy attack and famine are described as being "struck" by God (הִכִּיתָנוּ), and thus totally "broken" (שֶׁבֶר גָּדוֹל נִשְׁבְּרָה). נכה is also used (without referring to words) in Ps 69:26[27] (where the author is "struck" [הִכִּיתָ] by God), in Ps 102:4[5]; Jer 15:18; 1QH 17:27 (these three all hiding the agent by using a noun or passive); and Lam 3:30. The root in Lam 3:16 (גרס) also likely evokes a physical fight.

כִּי־אַתָּה אֲשֶׁר־הִכִּיתָ רָדָפוּ

Ps 69:26[27]: For you—whom you struck they pursued.[117]

לָמָּה הָיָה כְאֵבִי נֶצַח וּמַכָּתִי אֲנוּשָׁה מֵאֲנָה הֵרָפֵא

Jer 15:18: Why is my pain unceasing, my wound incurable, refusing to be healed?

הוּכָּה־כָעֵשֶׂב וַיִּבַשׁ לִבִּי כִּי־שָׁכַחְתִּי מֵאֲכֹל לַחְמִי:

Ps 102:4[5]: My heart is stricken and withers like grass, so I forget to eat my bread.[118]

[. . . מח]ץ מכתי ולמכשולי גבורת פלא

1QH 17:27:]. . . the wou]nd inflicted on me, my weakness to wonderful force.

116. Author's translation.
117. Alter, *Psalms*, 240.
118. Ibid., 353.

יִתֵּן לְמַכֵּהוּ לֶחִי יִשְׂבַּע בְּחֶרְפָּה׃

Lam 3:30: To give one's cheek to the smiter, and be filled with insults.

וַיַּגְרֵס בֶּחָצָץ שִׁנָּי הִכְפִּישַׁנִי בָּאֵפֶר׃

Lam 3:16: He has made my teeth grind on gravel, and made me cower in ashes;

Two inferences from this script are used. In Lam 1:13, a person struck by God sees himself consequently "stunned" (שֹׁמֵמָה) and "faint" (דָּוָה) all day long. Elsewhere, relief is conceptualized as the opponent looking away from the sufferer so that he is no longer the target for his blows (as in Job 7:19–20) or as the opponent ceasing the attack (as in Job 9:34).

הֱשִׁיבַנִי אָחוֹר נְתָנַנִי שֹׁמֵמָה כָּל־הַיּוֹם דָּוָה׃

Lam 1:13: He turned me back; he has left me stunned, faint all day long.

כַּמָּה לֹא־תִשְׁעֶה מִמֶּנִּי לֹא־תַרְפֵּנִי עַד־בִּלְעִי רֻקִּי׃ חָטָאתִי מָה אֶפְעַל לָךְ נֹצֵר הָאָדָם לָמָה שַׂמְתַּנִי לְמִפְגָּע לָךְ

Job 7:19–20: Will you not look away from me for a while, let me alone until I swallow my spittle? If I sin, what do I do to you, you watcher of humanity? Why have you made me your target?

יָסֵר מֵעָלַי שִׁבְטוֹ

Job 9:34: If he would take his rod away from me . . .

e) Bows and Arrows

Armed conflict most frequently involves bow and arrow, used in warfare or for hunting animals. Archers (particularly Assyrians with powerful composite bows) were the most important infantry in ancient Near Eastern armies, alongside spearmen and slingmen.[119] Bows and arrows were also salient in art, a salience possibly reflected in Hebrew

---

119. Yadin, *Warfare*, 293–97.

distress language. Specifically, bows symbolize kingship, emphasizing the "immediate and potential power fit for gods and kings."[120] Some reliefs explicitly link the bow with divine ordination of kingship, the god giving the king a bow, assuring his victory, or riding beside him in his chariot helping him to draw the bow.[121]

More practically, bows and arrows allow the separation of attacker and victim (impossible for sword or mace) thus it was possible "to surprise the enemy and attack him from beyond his range of retaliation, of hearing, and, on occasion, of vision."[122] The bow's range means hidden assailants can surprise their enemy without any danger of harm themselves.[123] This implication is used in Ps 64:2–4[3–5], conceiving the enemies' words as arrows.

תַּסְתִּירֵנִי מִסּוֹד מְרֵעִים מֵרִגְשַׁת פֹּעֲלֵי אָוֶן: אֲשֶׁר שָׁנְנוּ כַחֶרֶב לְשׁוֹנָם דָּרְכוּ חִצָּם דָּבָר מָר: לִירוֹת בַּמִּסְתָּרִים תָּם פִּתְאֹם יֹרֻהוּ וְלֹא יִירָאוּ:

Ps 64:2–4[3–5]: Hide me from the secret plots of the wicked, from the scheming of evildoers, who whet their tongues like swords, who aim bitter words like arrows, shooting from ambush at the blameless; they shoot suddenly and without fear.

Distress here is always caused by a deliberate agent, usually God (Lam 3:13) or human enemies (Ps 64:2–4[3–5], above), although in 1QH 11:17 the construct formation חצי שחת suggests a more abstract enemy.

הֵבִיא בְּכִלְיוֹתָי בְּנֵי אַשְׁפָּתוֹ:

Lam 3:13: He shot into my kidneys the arrows of his quiver.[124]

---

120. Wilkinson, "Representation," 83.

121. Cornelius, "Divine," 16–18. Egyptian reliefs also show a scimitar sword being given by the gods as a victory symbol, Keel, "Victory."

122. Yadin, *Warfare*, 8.

123. Ibid., 6.

124. Author's translation.

בהתעופף כול חצי שחת לאין השב ויודו לאין תקוה

1QH 11:17: When all the arrows of the pit fly forth without return then they rend beyond hope.[125]

Several verses highlight the agent's premeditated, secret preparation. Psalms 11:2[3]; 37:14; and Lam 2:4 and 3:12 describe the agent "bending the bow" (דרך), holding the bow with the foot to attach the cord and prime it for action.[126] Other preparations include fitting the arrow to the string (Ps 11:2[3]) or deliberately setting up the petitioner as a target (Job 16:12–13), showing significant elaboration of this part of the script.

חַרְבּוֹ יִלְטוֹשׁ קַשְׁתּוֹ דָרַךְ וַיְכוֹנְנֶהָ׃ וְלוֹ הֵכִין כְּלֵי־מָוֶת חִצָּיו לְדֹלְקִים יִפְעָל׃

Ps 7:12–13[13–14]: He[127] sharpens his sword; he has bent his bow and prepared it, and for it he has made ready instruments of death. He will make his arrows fiery shafts.[128]

כִּי הִנֵּה הָרְשָׁעִים יִדְרְכוּן קֶשֶׁת כּוֹנְנוּ חִצָּם עַל־יֶתֶר לִירוֹת בְּמוֹ־אֹפֶל לְיִשְׁרֵי־לֵב׃

Ps 11:2[3]: For look, the wicked bend the bow, they have fitted their arrow to the string, to shoot in the dark at the upright in heart.

חֶרֶב פָּתְחוּ רְשָׁעִים וְדָרְכוּ קַשְׁתָּם לְהַפִּיל עָנִי וְאֶבְיוֹן לִטְבוֹחַ יִשְׁרֵי־דָרֶךְ׃

Ps 37:14: The wicked draw the sword and bend their bows to bring down the poor and needy, to kill those who walk uprightly.

דָרַךְ קַשְׁתּוֹ כְּאוֹיֵב

Lam 2:4: He has bent his bow like an enemy.

125. Kittel, *Hymns*, 59.
126. Craigie, *Psalms 1–50*, 99.
127. It is unclear whether the antecedent of this pronoun is God, the righteous judge of v. 11[12], or the unrepentant wicked person of vv. 12a[13a] and 14[15].
128. Craigie, *Psalms 1–50*, 97.

דָּרַךְ קַשְׁתּוֹ וַיַּצִּיבֵנִי כַּמַּטָּרָא לַחֵץ:

Lam 3:12: He bent his bow and set me as a mark for his arrow.

וַיְקִימֵנִי לוֹ לְמַטָּרָה: יָסֹבּוּ עָלַי רַבָּיו

Job 16:12–13: He set me up as his target; his archers surround me.

Distressing situations are then described as arrows striking. Separation of archer and opponent may allow retreat once struck and before possible death (as in Ahab's demise in 1 Kgs 22:34–35), making being pierced by an arrow suitable for lingering, potentially terminal, illness. In Ps 38:2[3], arrows have "gone down" (נְחָתוּ) into the sufferer, whereas in Job 6:4 they are "with" him, both implying a serious attack, but recovery may yet be possible. Arrows penetrating the kidneys (כִּלְיוֹתָי) in Lam 3:13 (above) imply a more hopeless predicament. The modifying phrase "without cure" (לאין מרפא) in 1QH 10:26, also emphasizes severity, using arrows to conceptualize verbal attacks.

כִּי־חִצֶּיךָ נִחֲתוּ בִי

Ps 38:2[3]: For your arrows have sunk into me.

כִּי חִצֵּי שַׁדַּי עִמָּדִי אֲשֶׁר חֲמָתָם שֹׁתָה רוּחִי

Job 6:4: For the arrows of the Almighty are in me; my spirit drinks their poison.

ויפרו חצים לאין מרפא

1QH 10:26: They loose off arrows without any cure.

Thus, various methods map intensity to the distressing situation. Further, this source domain maps to a broad target domain including illness and verbal attack.

Finally, distress problematized as enemies firing arrows is solved by destroying the weapons of war, as in Ps 37:15.

חַרְבָּם תָּבוֹא בְלִבָּם וְקַשְּׁתוֹתָם תִּשָּׁבַרְנָה:

Ps 37:15: Their sword shall enter their own heart, and their bows shall be broken.

f) Swords

Elsewhere, swords appear in the attack part of the script, often paralleled with arrows (as in Pss 7:12[13] and 37:14). However, some distinctives of sword metaphors utilize the Hebrew cognitive and cultural background.

Two types of swords were used, one with a curved blade for slashing at the enemy, the other being a shorter double-edged sword for stabbing, but both referenced by חֶרֶב.[129] In most verses, swords conceptualize oppressors' words, fitting the use of swords when both assailant and victim are within arm's reach of each other. There is less surprise than for bow and arrow.

Again premeditation is emphasized. Psalm 7:12[13] pictures the enemy "sharpening" (יִלְטוֹשׁ) a sword in preparation for attack, whereas in Ps 64:2–3[3–4] and 1QH 13:13–15 a different verb describes the tongue being sharpened (שׁנן) like a sword.

חַרְבּוֹ יִלְטוֹשׁ קַשְׁתּוֹ דָרַךְ וַיְכוֹנְנֶהָ׃

Ps 7:12–13[13–14]: He sharpens his sword; he has bent his bow and prepared it.[130]

תַּסְתִּירֵנִי מִסּוֹד מְרֵעִים מֵרִגְשַׁת פֹּעֲלֵי אָוֶן׃ אֲשֶׁר שָׁנְנוּ כַחֶרֶב לְשׁוֹנָם דָּרְכוּ חִצָּם דָּבָר מָר׃

Ps 64:2–3[3–4]: Hide me from the secret plots of the wicked, from the scheming of evildoers, who whet their tongues like swords, who aim bitter words like arrows.

ותצל נפש עני במעון אריות אשר שננו כחרב לשונם 14 ואתה
אלי סגרתה בעד שניהם פן יטרפו נפש עני ורש ותוסף לשונם
15 כחרב אל תערה בלוא[כר]נתה נפש עבדכה

1QH 13:13–15: And you rescued the life of the afflicted in the den of lions, whose tongue is like a sharpened sword. And you, O my God, you shut their teeth, lest they tear apart the life of the

---

129. Kaiser, "חֶרֶב," 155.
130. Craigie, *Psalms 1–50*, 97.

poor afflicted. And their tongue was drawn back like a sword to its sheath, lest it [dest]roy the life of your servant.[131]

Elsewhere, distress itself is an encounter with the opponent's sword. In Ps 144:11[10–11] the attacking sword is explicitly "evil" (רָעָה), and in Ps 55:21[22] the hapax legomenon פְּתִחוֹת presumably refers to a drawn sword or knife.[132]

פְּצֵנִי וְהַצִּילֵנִי מִיַּד בְּנֵי־נֵכָר אֲשֶׁר פִּיהֶם דִּבֶּר־שָׁוְא וִימִינָם יְמִין שָׁקֶר מֵחֶרֶב רָעָה׃

Ps 144:11[10–11]: Rescue me from the cruel sword, and deliver me from the hand of aliens, whose mouths speak lies, and whose right hands are false.

רַכּוּ דְבָרָיו מִשֶּׁמֶן וְהֵמָּה פְתִחוֹת׃

Ps 55:21[22]: His words were softer than oil, but in fact were drawn swords.

Two verses resolve the sword attack problematization of distress. In 1QH 13:15 (cited above), the tongue is withdrawn like a sword into its sheath. In Ps 37:15 (cited above), the enemies' swords more dramatically pierce their own hearts.

g) Military Battle

Sometimes distress is being beset by a more comprehensive attack force than a single individual. Job, especially, conceptualizes the intensity and duration of his suffering as a whole army attacking. Elsewhere, this image conceptualizes several people causing distress (Pss 3:1[2]; 69:4[5]; and 27:2). The number and strength of these foes are highlighted.

יְהוָה מָה־רַבּוּ צָרָי רַבִּים קָמִים עָלָי׃

Ps 3:1[2]: O LORD, how many are my foes! Many are rising against me.

---

131. Kittel, *Hymns*, 85.
132. Tate, *Psalms*, 54.

רַבּוּ מִשַּׂעֲרוֹת רֹאשִׁי שֹׂנְאַי חִנָּם עָצְמוּ מַצְמִיתַי אֹיְבַי שֶׁקֶר

Ps 69:4[5]: More in number than the hairs of my head are those who hate me without cause; many are those who would destroy me, my enemies who accuse me falsely.

בִּקְרֹב עָלַי מְרֵעִים לֶאֱכֹל אֶת־בְּשָׂרִי צָרַי וְאֹיְבַי לִי הֵמָּה כָשְׁלוּ וְנָפָלוּ׃

Ps 27:2: When evildoers assail me to devour my flesh—my adversaries and foes—they shall stumble and fall.

The battle script's first stage has the army preparing by encamping around the petitioner (Job 19:12; 1QH 10:25–26; and Ps 27:3), with a whole army ready to attack evoking both premeditating agents and intense anticipated distress.

יַחַד יָבֹאוּ גְדוּדָיו וַיָּסֹלּוּ עָלַי דַּרְכָּם וַיַּחֲנוּ סָבִיב לְאָהֳלִי׃

Job 19:12: His troops come forth all together. They have paved their road against me and have encamped around my tent.[133]

ואני אמרת חנו עלי גבורים סבבים בכל 26 כלי מלחמותם

1QH 10:25–26: I thought: heroes have set up camp against me, surrounding with all their weapons of war.

אִם־תַּחֲנֶה עָלַי מַחֲנֶה לֹא־יִירָא לִבִּי אִם־תָּקוּם עָלַי מִלְחָמָה בְּזֹאת אֲנִי בוֹטֵחַ׃

Ps 27:3: Though an army encamp against me, my heart shall not fear; though war rise up against me, yet I will be confident.

When the army attacks, this conceptualization can highlight intensity (through the multiplicity of enemies), or the opponents' perceived co-ordination. In Job 16:10–13, God violently attacks Job, with the ungodly as an accompanying army. In Job 10:17 and 30:12–14 the multiplicity of foes conveys the intensity of suffering, inflicted by God through repeated changes of the troops (חֲלִיפוֹת וְצָבָא), or as a storm noisily "rolling on" (תַּחַת שֹׁאָה הִתְגַּלְגָּלוּ).

---

133. Gordis, *Job*, 196.

Surrounded by Bitterness

פָּעֲרוּ עָלַי בְּפִיהֶם בְּחֶרְפָּה הִכּוּ לְחָיָי יַחַד עָלַי יִתְמַלָּאוּן: יַסְגִּירֵנִי
אֵל אֶל עֲוִיל וְעַל־יְדֵי רְשָׁעִים יִרְטֵנִי: שָׁלֵו הָיִיתִי וַיְפַרְפְּרֵנִי וְאָחַז
בְּעָרְפִּי וַיְפַצְפְּצֵנִי וַיְקִימֵנִי לוֹ לְמַטָּרָה: יָסֹבּוּ עָלַי רַבָּיו יְפַלַּח
כִּלְיוֹתַי וְלֹא יַחְמוֹל יִשְׁפֹּךְ לָאָרֶץ מְרֵרָתִי:

Job 16:10–13: They have gaped at me with their mouths; they have struck me insolently on the cheek; they mass themselves together against me. God gives me up to the ungodly, and casts me into the hands of the wicked. I was at ease, and he broke me in two; he seized me by the neck and dashed me to pieces; he set me up as his target; his archers surround me. He slashes open my kidneys, and shows no mercy; he pours out my gall on the ground.

תְּחַדֵּשׁ עֵדֶיךָ נֶגְדִּי וְתֶרֶב כַּעַשְׂךָ עִמָּדִי חֲלִיפוֹת וְצָבָא עִמִּי:

Job 10:17: You constantly send new witnesses against me and increase your hostility toward me; wave after wave of foes assails me.[134]

עַל־יָמִין פִּרְחַח יָקוּמוּ רַגְלַי שִׁלֵּחוּ וַיָּסֹלּוּ עָלַי אָרְחוֹת אֵידָם:
נָתְסוּ נְתִיבָתִי לְהַוָּתִי יֹעִילוּ לֹא עֹזֵר לָמוֹ: כְּפֶרֶץ רָחָב יֶאֱתָיוּ תַּחַת
שֹׁאָה הִתְגַּלְגָּלוּ:

Job 30:12–14: On my right the young rabble rises, sending me sprawling and casting up against me their destructive ways. They hedge my path with thorns, they promote my calamity with no-one to restrain them. Like a wide torrent they rush in, like a storm they roll on.[135]

Ps 109:2–3 pictures the opponents together attacking (וַיִּלָּחֲמוּנִי) with words, with חִנָּם again emphasizing the unjustified nature. Lamentation 3:62 also highlights forceful words, as does Psalm 55 where the recurring theme of speech suggests that the "battle" (קְרָב) in v. 18[19] is a verbal war.

כִּי פִי רָשָׁע וּפִי־מִרְמָה עָלַי פָּתָחוּ דִּבְּרוּ אִתִּי לְשׁוֹן שָׁקֶר: וְדִבְרֵי
שִׂנְאָה סְבָבוּנִי וַיִּלָּחֲמוּנִי חִנָּם:

---

134. Ibid., 100.
135. Ibid., 326.

Distress and the Force Schema

Ps 109:2–3: For wicked mouths, deceitful mouths have they opened against me, they have spoken to me with lying tongues, and surrounded me with hateful talk and attacked me without reason.[136]

שִׂפְתֵי קָמַי וְהֶגְיוֹנָם עָלַי כָּל־הַיּוֹם׃

Lam 3:62: The whispers and murmurs of my assailants are against me all day long.

פָּדָה בְשָׁלוֹם נַפְשִׁי מִקְּרָב־לִי כִּי־בְרַבִּים הָיוּ עִמָּדִי׃

Ps 55:18[19]: He will redeem me unharmed from the battle that I wage, for many are arrayed against me.

h) Summary

These mappings from the domain of conflict are summarized in the following table.

Domain	Agonist's Force Tendency	Antagonist's Force Tendency	Causation	Resultant Action
Source	*Unarmed person* To go on living in peace	*Opponent* To attack, harm, and possibly kill, by hand, sword or arrow	Deliberate premeditated attack	Serious harm and potential death
Target	*Self* To continue living in safety and security	*Enemies* To harm the self with words, and possibly more seriously, for their own benefit	Deliberate premeditated action	Serious harm and potentially complete destruction

---

136. Allen, *Psalms 101–150*, 70.

> **Other Entailments:**
> Greater number of attackers → Greater intensity of distress
> Pursuit of attackers → Deliberate actions of those causing distress to harm the self
> Deliberate actions taken to prepare to fight (bending the bow, drawing the sword) → Actions taken to prepare to cause distress
> Unsuspected nature of attack (for example, from ambush) → Unsuspected nature of distress
> Unjustified nature of attack → Unjustified nature of distress
> Being struck by arrows, blows or swords → Being accused by the words of others
> Cessation of attack (through broken bow or attacker turning away) → Relief from distress

7.4.8. BEING IN DISTRESS IS EXPERIENCING THE FORCES OF NATURE

Next, distress is sometimes experiencing the powerful "natural" forces of water, sea and wind. The cause of distress may be either the natural forces themselves (1QH 10:12), or extend further to God who owns and controls the natural phenomena (Ps 42:7[8]) or puts the petitioner in their path (Job 30:22).

ועלי קהלת רשעים תתרגש ויהמו כנחשולי ימים בהרגש גליהם
רפש 13 וטיט יגרושו

1QH 10:12–13: And the assembly of the wicked is roused against me; they roar like the breakers of the seas: when their waves beat they spew out slime and mud.

תְּהוֹם־אֶל־תְּהוֹם קוֹרֵא לְקוֹל צִנּוֹרֶיךָ כָּל־מִשְׁבָּרֶיךָ וְגַלֶּיךָ עָלַי עָבָרוּ׃

Ps 42:7[8]: Deep calls to deep at the thunder of your cataracts; all your waves and your billows have gone over me.

תִּשָּׂאֵנִי אֶל־רוּחַ תַּרְכִּיבֵנִי וּתְמֹגְגֵנִי תֻּשִׁיָּה׃

Job 30:22: You snatch me up and make me ride on the wind; you dissolve me with a downpour.[137]

---

137. Clines, *Job 21–37*, 931, following most other translations in finding a word for noisy water that fits the Ketiv, rather than trying to use the Qere.

a) Torrents

Many references highlight the power of water, especially dry wadis (נַחַל) transforming into surging torrents following heavy rain. שׁטף describes these torrents surging and overflowing, sweeping everything away. It is normally used with water in a negative sense in the Bible.[138] In Job 14:18–19, this and other powerful natural forces that transform the environment picture how powerfully God wears away human hopes.

וְאוּלָם הַר־נוֹפֵל יִבּוֹל וְצוּר יֶעְתַּק מִמְּקֹמוֹ: אֲבָנִים שָׁחֲקוּ מַיִם
תִּשְׁטֹף־סְפִיחֶיהָ עֲפַר־אָרֶץ וְתִקְוַת אֱנוֹשׁ הֶאֱבַדְתָּ:

> Job 14:18–19: Yet as a mountain slips away and erodes, and a cliff is dislodged from its place, as water wears away stone and torrents scour the soil from the land—so you destroy man's hope.[139]

In Ps 124:4–5 the enemies' anger potentially drowns the petitioners in its flooding, syntactically emphasizing intensity by repeating that the waters would pass over the "neck" (נֶפֶשׁ), a life-threatening situation. "Raging torrents" in 1QH 16:14–15 are probably those who verbally opposed the author's teaching. In Psalm 69, the image may evoke someone stuck in a muddy wadi, vulnerable to the rising rushing torrent. In Ps 18:4[5] and the more apocalyptic sounding 1QH 11:29–30, the torrents of Belial exert a terrifying force.

אֲזַי הַמַּיִם שְׁטָפוּנוּ נַחְלָה עָבַר עַל־נַפְשֵׁנוּ: אֲזַי עָבַר עַל־נַפְשֵׁנוּ
הַמַּיִם הַזֵּידוֹנִים:

> Ps 124:4–5: Then the waters would have swept us up, the torrent come up past our necks. Then it would have come up past our necks—the raging waters.[140]

ואני הייתי ל[ב]זאי נהרות 15 שוטפים כי גרשו עלי רפשם

> 1QH 16:14–15: But I had become the mockery of the raging torrents for they threw their mire over me.

---

138. Hamilton, "שָׁטַף."
139. Clines, *Job 1–20*, 278.
140. Alter, *Psalms*, 444.

Surrounded by Bitterness

טָבַעְתִּי בִּיוֵן מְצוּלָה וְאֵין מָעֳמָד בָּאתִי בְמַעֲמַקֵּי־מַיִם וְשִׁבֹּלֶת שְׁטָפָתְנִי׃

Ps 69:2[3]: I am sinking in a deep swamp—and there is no foothold. I have reached the watery depths, and the current has swept me away.[141]

אַל־תִּשְׁטְפֵנִי שִׁבֹּלֶת מַיִם וְאַל־תִּבְלָעֵנִי מְצוּלָה

Ps 69:15[16]: Let the waters' current not sweep me away and let not the deep swallow me.[142]

וְנַחֲלֵי בְלִיַּעַל יְבַעֲתוּנִי׃

Ps 18:4[5]: The torrents of perdition assailed me.

וילכו נחלי בליעל על כול אגפי רום כאש אוכלת בכול שנא־ביהם להתם כול עץ לח 03 ויבש מפלניהם

1QH 11:29–30: And the torrents of Belial will overflow all the high banks like a devouring fire in all their watering channels, destroying every tree, green or dry, from their canals.

b) Waves

Elsewhere, מִשְׁבָּר 'breakers,' accesses the power of water, presumably prototypically the waves of the Mediterranean or Sea of Galilee. Explicit comparison with God's power in Ps 93:4 shows these typically evoke powerful force. In Jon 2:3[4], the literal waves passing over Jonah aptly symbolize his distress. The cause is clear as he emphasizes they are *God's* breakers. Psalm 42:7[8] (cited above) is identical, though the context is much less specific. The phrase highlights the intensity of the psalmist's distress. In Ps 88:7[8], the waves are powerfully "squashing" the petitioner (עִנִּיתָ).[143]

---

141. Based on Tate, *Psalms*, 186 and Alter, *Psalms*, 236.
142. Alter, *Psalms*, 238.
143. Taking the "press down" sense, following Tate, *Psalms*, 397.

וַתַּשְׁלִיכֵנִי מְצוּלָה בִּלְבַב יַמִּים וְנָהָר יְסֹבְבֵנִי כָּל־מִשְׁבָּרֶיךָ וְגַלֶּיךָ
עָלַי עָבָרוּ:

Jon 2:3[4]: You cast me into the deep, into the heart of the seas, and the flood surrounded me; all your waves and your billows passed over me.

וְכָל־מִשְׁבָּרֶיךָ עִנִּיתָ סֶּלָה:

Ps 88:7[8]: You have squashed (me) with all your waves.[144]

The Hodayot are even more vivid. In 1QH 14:22–24, waves (the enemies' opposition) are part of the extended conceptualization of the sufferer as in a storm-tossed boat. In 1QH 16:31, the author's ailments are waves "flying" against him, whereas in 1QH 17:3–4 the more serious waves of death surround the petitioner.

[והיי]תי כמלח באוניה בזעף 23 ימים גליהם וכול משבריהם
עלי המו רוח עוע[יים] לאין [דממה להשיב נפש ואין 24 נתיבת
לישר דרך על פני מים

1QH 14:22–24: I [have become] like a sailor in a ship in the raging seas: their waves and all their breakers roar over me, a whirlwind [without a] lull for taking breath, without a track to take a straight path over the surface of the water.

ויתעופפו עלי משברים

1QH 16:31: Breakers rush against me.

[. . .] אפפוני 4 משברי מות

1QH 17:3–4: The breakers of death [surround me].

The most prolific use of מִשְׁבָּרִים is in 1QH 11:7–18, uniting labor, sea travel, and death or Sheol. Again they symbolize powerful forces, in childbirth and the more eschatological forces restraining the "wonderful counsellor" and accompanying "deeds of terror." 1QH 10:12–13 (cited above) does not use מִשְׁבָּרִים, but still conceptualizes the opponents' words as waves spewing mud.

144. Ibid., 394.

Surrounded by Bitterness

אהיה בצוקה כמו אשת לדה מבכרית . . . 8 . . . כיא באו בנים
עד משברי מות 9 והרית גבר הצרה בחבליה כיא במשברי
מות תמליט זכר ובחבלי שאול יניח 10 מכור הריה פלא יועץ
עם גבורתו ויפלט גבר ממשברים בהריתו החישו כול 11
משברים וחבל (נ)מרץ מולדיהם ופלצות להורתם ובמולדיו
יהפכו כול צירים 12 בכור הריה והרית אפעה לחבל נמרץ
ומשברי שחת לכול מעשי פלצות וירועו 13 אושי קיר כאוניה
על פני מים ויהמו שחקים בקול המון ויושבי עפר 14 כיורדי
ימים נבעתים המון מים וחכמיהם למו כמלחים במצולות כי
תתבלע 15 כול חכמתם בהמות ימים ברתוח תהומות על נבוכי
מים ויתרגשו לרום גלים 16 ומשבתי מים בהמון

1QH 11:7–18: I was in distress like a woman giving birth the first time . . . For children come through the breakers of death and the woman expectant with a boy is racked by her pangs, for through the breakers of death she gives birth to a male, and through the pangs of Sheol there emerges, from the <<crucible>> of the pregnant woman a wonderful counselor with his strength, and the boy is freed from the breakers. In the woman expectant with him rush all the contractions and the racking pain at their birth; terror (seizes) those expectant with them, and at his birth all the labor-pains come suddenly, in the <<crucible>> of the pregnant woman. And she who is pregnant with a serpent is with a racking pang; and the breakers of the pit result in all deeds of terror. The foundations of the wall shake like a ship on the surface of the sea, and the clouds thunder with a roar. Those who live on the dust, as well as those who sail upon the sea are terrified by the din of the water. For them their wise men are like sailors on the deeps, for swallowed up is all their wisdom by the roar of the seas. When the deep boils over the springs of water, they rush forth to form huge waves, and breakers of water, with clamorous sound.

c) Storms

The force of storms (סַעַר), either at sea (as in Jonah) or as tempestuous winds on land (like the one that carried Elijah away), indicate "a danger deriving from something unstable, something from which people want to save themselves."[145] Job 9:17 conceptualizes Job as wounded by a stormy force, using שׂוּף and פצע for the physical impact, whereas in Ps 55:8[9] the enemies' speech is a stormy onslaught, intensified by the parallelism and the modifier סֹעָה highlighting the wind's speed.

אֲשֶׁר־בִּשְׂעָרָה יְשׁוּפֵנִי וְהִרְבָּה פְצָעַי חִנָּם:

Job 9:17: For he crushes me with a tempest, and multiplies my wounds without cause.

אָחִישָׁה מִפְלָט לִי מֵרוּחַ סֹעָה מִסָּעַר:

Ps 55:8[9]: I would hurry to find a shelter for myself from the raging wind and tempest.

In 1QH 21:6 the threat is a stormy wind, and 1QH 15:4–5 conceptualizes internal distress as experiencing strong stormy forces (בזעף חרישית and רוח עועיים). Job 30:14–15 is difficult to interpret, but again portrays Job's distress as being impacted by various stormy forces. Finally, in 1QH 10:27–28, a sea storm conceptualizes the author's opponents, with their words compared to a "hurricane storm" (נפץ זרם) and upward heaving waves.

איכה אעמוד לפני רוח סוע[רה ואני יכונני ב]

1QH 21:6: How can I stand firm before the hurric[ane? But me, he establishes me in . . .]

ותכמי עלו כאניה בזעף 5 חרישית ויהם לבי לכלה ורוח עועיים תבלעני מהוות פשעם

1QH 15:4–5: My entrails heave like a boat in the rage of the storm, my heart pulsates to destruction, a whirlwind swallows me, due to the destruction of their offence.

כְּפֶרֶץ רָחָב יֶאֱתָיוּ תַּחַת שֹׁאָה הִתְגַּלְגָּלוּ: הָהְפַּךְ עָלַי בַּלָּהוֹת תִּרְדֹּף כָּרוּחַ נְדִבָתִי וּכְעָב עָבְרָה יְשֻׁעָתִי:

Job 30:14–15: Like a wide torrent they rush in, like a storm they roll on, terrors are turned loose upon me, my lofty rank is driven off like a wind, my high position passing like a cloud.[146]

---

145. Fabry, "סָעַר," 294.
146. Gordis, *Job*, 326.

וכהמון מים רבים שאון קולם נפץ זרם להשחית רבים למזוררות
יבקעו 28 אפעה ושוא בהתרומם גליהם

> 1QH 10:27–28: Like the din of turbulent water is the roar of their voices, like a hurricane storm which destroys many. Right up to the stars burst emptiness and deceit when their waves heave upwards.

1QH 13:18 solves this problematization of distress as a storm by God restoring calm. Other ways of surviving such distress include finding shelter (Ps 55:8[9], above) or standing firm by God's help (1QH 21:6, above).

ואתה אלי תשיב סערה לדממה

> 1QH 13:18: But you, my God, have changed the storm to a calm.

d) Wind

Other images of strong winds include Job as a windblown leaf (Job 13:25) or where he complains God made him ride the wind in Job 30:22 (cited above).

הֶעָלֶה נִדָּף תַּעֲרוֹץ וְאֶת־קַשׁ יָבֵשׁ תִּרְדֹּף׃

> Job 13:25: Will you frighten a windblown leaf and pursue dry chaff?

These mappings can be summarized as follows:

Domain	Agonist's Force Tendency	Antagonist's Force Tendency	Causation	Resultant Action
Source	Entity in the natural environment To remain fixed in one place	Water / Wind / Storm To violently wash or blow away everything in its path	God is sometimes considered explicitly as the controller of wind and waves	Entity is damaged and swept away
Target	Self To remain firm and in control	Distressing experiences To move the self against his/her will	May be God or more general causation	Self is damaged and no longer in control of life events
Other Entailments: Easing of the storm → Relief from distress Shelter or help to stand upright → Protection during distress				

7.4.11. Being in Distress is Exposure to Heat / Fire

As well as Antagonist forces moving a restful Agonist, others try to cause a change of state for the Agonist. As in Mesopotamia, exposure to heat commonly conceptualizes distress. Considering only physical symptoms in the Psalms, Van der Toorn notes that "most of the descriptions group themselves around the theme of heat and aridity," linking them to "feverish conditions."[147] Within the wider category of distress language, heat is no longer the most common image, but still significant.

First, internal heat may typify distress. Psalm 39:3[4] frames the petitioner's distress as both heart-heat and burning fire. The context of pain (כְּאֵבִי) in v. 2[3] suggests the heart-heat here is not just building pressure to speak but emotional or physical distress.[148] In Ps 38:7[8] the sufferer's "loins" (כְסָלַי) experience heat (נִקְלָה), and in Job 30:30 it is his "bones" (perhaps his "core") that burn. 1QH 16:30–31 also apparently describes sickness, elaborating the burning fire within the bones

---

147. Van der Toorn, *Sin*, 63.

148. The same expression describes the emotional reaction on hearing of the death of a loved one (Deuteronomy 19.6).

by modifying the fire with בֹּעֵר to heighten the intensity, and utilizing the ability of fire to spread (וַיִּפְרַח) and consume (תּוֹאכַל) greater areas.

חַם־לִבִּי ׀ בְּקִרְבִּי בַּהֲגִיגִי תִבְעַר־אֵשׁ דִּבַּרְתִּי בִּלְשׁוֹנִי׃

Ps 39:3[4]: My heart became hot within me. While I mused, the fire burned; then I spoke with my tongue.

כִּי־כְסָלַי מָלְאוּ נִקְלֶה

Ps 38:7[8]: For my loins are filled with burning.

וְעַצְמִי־חָרָה מִנִּי־חֹרֶב׃

Job 30:30: My bones burn with heat.

ויפרח כאש בוער עצור בע[צמין] עד ימימה תואכל של(ה)בתה
31 להתם כוח לקצים ולכלות בשר עד מועדים

1QH 16:30–31: And it grows like a searing fire enclosed in [my] bo[nes] whose flame consumes for days without end, devouring my strength by periods, and destroying (my) flesh by seasons.

Lamentations 1:13 explicitly links internal heat to an external heating force.

מִמָּרוֹם שָׁלַח־אֵשׁ בְּעַצְמֹתַי וַיִּרְדֶּנָּה

Lam 1:13: From on high he sent fire; it went deep into my bones;

Conceptualizing distress as exposure to heat thus complements anger conceptualized as fire (Job 19:11; Ps 89:46[47]; and Lam 2:4).

וַיַּחַר עָלַי אַפּוֹ

Job 19:11: He has kindled his wrath against me.

לָנֶצַח תִּבְעַר כְּמוֹ־אֵשׁ חֲמָתֶךָ׃

Ps 89:46[47]: How long will your wrath burn like fire?

שָׁפַךְ כָּאֵשׁ חֲמָתוֹ׃

Lam 2:4: He has poured out his fury like fire.

Distress and the Force Schema

Elsewhere the fiery force is not linked to anger. In Ps 118:12 the surrounding enemies are a fire of thorns (a particularly intense, though short-lived fire),[149] whereas in Ps 66:12, fire is a general metaphor, linked to refining in v. 10.

סַבּוּנִי כִדְבוֹרִים דֹּעֲכוּ כְּאֵשׁ קוֹצִים

Ps 118:12: They surrounded me like bees, they were extinguished like a fire of thorns.[150]

בָּאנוּ־בָאֵשׁ וּבַמַּיִם וַתּוֹצִיאֵנוּ לָרְוָיָה׃

Ps 66:12: We went through fire and water, but you brought us out to abundance.[151]

The behavior of heated substances frequently maps to internal physiological behavior, especially in descriptions of "melting hearts," prototypically compared to wax. Thus, מסס is prototypically framed against a usually solid substance, changing it to an abnormal state. By contrast, English *melt* is prototypically framed against the ice-water transition, reverting to normality from an abnormal state. Thus, if someone's heart *melts* in English it is viewed positively, but in Hebrew this transition is negative. Psalm 22:14[15] exemplifies this conceptualization, describing both the self poured out like water, and the internal melted heart. 1QH 12:33 adds that the melting is like wax "in front of" (מִלִּפְנֵי) the fire, and in 1QH 22:14 it is prompted by the prevalence of sin.

כַּמַּיִם נִשְׁפַּכְתִּי וְהִתְפָּרְדוּ כָּל־עַצְמוֹתָי הָיָה לִבִּי כַּדּוֹנָג נָמֵס בְּתוֹךְ מֵעָי׃

Ps 22:14[15]: I have been poured out like water, and all my bones have become disjointed; my heart was like wax; it melted within my innards.[152]

וימס לבבי כדונג מפני אש

1QH 12:33: My heart has melted like wax in front of the fire.

---

149. Deist, *Culture*, 148.
150. Allen, *Psalms 101–150*, 119.
151. Tate, *Psalms*, 145.
152. Craigie, *Psalms 1–50*, 195.

Surrounded by Bitterness

ולבבי כדונג ימס על פשע וחטאה

1QH 22:14: And my heart melts like wax on account of offence and sin.

1QH 16:32–33 alternatively has the heart (לבי) poured out and the flesh (בשרי) melting like wax. In Ps 107:26, the life-breath (נֶפֶשׁ) melts on stormy seas. These similar images with various melting elements show this conceptualization is well entrenched, being elaborated differently in different contexts, rather than just being copied. Psalm 119:28 may also be related, with דלף suggesting the dripping of liquid, here applied to the melted נֶפֶשׁ.

כי נשבת מעוזי מגויתי וינגר כמים לבי וימס 33 כדונג בשרי ומעוז מותני היה לבהלה

1QH 16:32–33: For my vitality has left my body, my heart pours out like water, my flesh melts like wax, the vitality of my loins turns into listlessness.[153]

נַפְשָׁם בְּרָעָה תִתְמוֹגָג׃

Ps 107:26: Their life-breath melted away in their calamity.[154]

דָּלְפָה נַפְשִׁי

Ps 119:28: My being dissolves in anguish.

This idiom may reflect a particular cultural image. At least three activities involved wax "in front of the fire": separating wax from honey;[155] heating wax to cover writing tablets; and the "lost wax" process to create moulds for metallic objects,[156] known as early as the fourth millennium BCE in Palestine.[157] "Lost wax" casting involves making a wax model of a desired object, covering it with fine clay and placing it in the fire. The clay bakes into a hard mould, but the wax inside melts and pours out, leaving space for the molten metal. The solid wax melting within

---

153. Martínez and Tigchelaar, *Scrolls*, 183.
154. Based on NRSV and Alter, *Psalms*, 386.
155. Neufeld, "Apiculture," 238.
156. Petty, "Bees," 4.
157. Roaf, *Atlas*, 126.

another object exposed to heat, and then pouring out, coheres closely with these metaphors.

This becomes a conventional idiom for apprehension in battle, as in Josh 2:11; 5:1; 7:5; 2 Sam 17:10; Deut 1:28; and 20:8, or for response to a theophany, as in Ezek 21:7[12]; Isa 13:7; or Nah 2:10[11]. The War Scroll also refers to melting hearts several times (1QM 1:14; 8:10; and 14:5–6). מסס and מוג may thus have originated as semi-technical holy war vocabulary.[158] Nevertheless, they do help make sense of battle experiences, describing "the subjective side of things, the interior feeling of fear created by panic from outside."[159]

ו[רגלי הבנים יהיה להמס לבב וגבורת אל מאמצת ל[בב בני אור]

> 1QM 1:14: There will be infantry battalions to melt the heart, but God›s might will strengthen the hea[rt of the sons of light].

קול אחד תרועת מלחמה גדולה להמס לב אויב

> 1QM 8:10: a single blast, a deafening war alarm, to melt the heart of the enemy.

ולהרים במשפט 6 לב נמס

> 1QM 14:5–6: in order to raise up in justice the melting heart.

This mapping is summarized in the following table:

---

158. McCarthy, "Vocabulary."
159. Ibid., 230.

Domain	Agonist's Force Tendency	Antagonist's Force Tendency	Causation	Resultant Action
Source	Wax / combustible entity to remain solid or intact	Fire to burn, melt, and destroy anything it contacts	Sometimes deliberate, but usually not explicit	The entity's structure is dissolved or destroyed
Target	Self to remain firm and emotionally stable	Distressing experiences to gradually consume the person until he or she is destroyed	Can be caused by an agent	The self is eventually consumed or dissolved by the distressing experiences

Other Entailments:
Heat is a response to fire → Internal heat is a response to another's anger
The fire spreads and consumes more of the entity → The distressing experiences consume more of the person
The melted substance drains away, destroying the entity's integrity → The melted insides drain away removing the self's vitality

7.4.12. Being in Distress is Being Trampled

The Agonist also changes state as a result of forceful impact when trampled underfoot, either in battle or as grapes in a winepress. In Ps 7:5[6], רמס evokes the image of horses or people trampling someone into the ground. In Ps 57:3[4] and 56:1–2[2–3], שאף is traditionally rendered "trample" because of cognate roots,[160] but possibly just means "pant after."[161] In Ps 36:11[12], the foot (רֶגֶל) of the arrogant "coming" to the sufferer potentially evokes trampling. In all these cases the agent is human. Lamentations 1:15 more specifically has being trodden in a winepress (גַּת דָּרַךְ), with God as the agent.

יִרְדֹּף אוֹיֵב נַפְשִׁי וְיַשֵּׂג וְיִרְמֹס לָאָרֶץ חַיָּי וּכְבוֹדִי לֶעָפָר יַשְׁכֵּן

Ps 7:5[6]: May the enemy pursue and overtake me, trample to earth my life, and make my glory dwell in the dust.[162]

160. BDB 983.
161. Maiberger, "שָׁאַף," 269.
162. Alter, *Psalms*, 19.

Distress and the Force Schema

חֵרֵף שֹׁאֲפִי

Ps 57:3[4]: He will put to shame those who trample on me.

חָנֵּנִי אֱלֹהִים כִּי־שְׁאָפַנִי אֱנוֹשׁ כָּל־הַיּוֹם לֹחֵם יִלְחָצֵנִי: שָׁאֲפוּ
שׁוֹרְרַי כָּל־הַיּוֹם כִּי־רַבִּים לֹחֲמִים לִי

Ps 56:1–2[2–3]: Be gracious to me, O God, for people trample on me; all day long foes oppress me; my enemies trample on me all day long, for many fight against me.

אַל־תְּבוֹאֵנִי רֶגֶל גַּאֲוָה

Ps 36:11[12]: Do not let the foot of the arrogant tread on me.

גַּת דָּרַךְ אֲדֹנָי לִבְתוּלַת בַּת־יְהוּדָה:

Lam 1:15: The Lord has trodden as in a winepress the virgin daughter Judah.

Here, distress is a force which also evokes the VERTICALITY schema. The sufferer is both "down" and experiencing a violent force.

7.4.13. BEING IN DISTRESS IS CARRYING A WEIGHT

Finally, the opposing force may be something heavy, weighing down the petitioner. In Ps 38:4[5] and Lam 1:14 the petitioner's own sins (/ עֲוֺנֹתַי פְּשָׁעַי) are heavy, causing an emotional response, a rare occasion where something internal causes distress. Conversely, in Job 6:2–3 it is his "vexation" and "calamity" (כַּעְשִׂי וְהַוָּתִי), originating externally from God, that is weightier than he can bear.

כִּי עֲוֺנֹתַי עָבְרוּ רֹאשִׁי כְּמַשָּׂא כָבֵד יִכְבְּדוּ מִמֶּנִּי:

Ps 38:4[5]: For my iniquities have gone over my head; they weigh like a burden too heavy for me.

נִשְׂקַד עֹל פְּשָׁעַי בְּיָדוֹ יִשְׂתָּרְגוּ עָלוּ עַל־צַוָּארִי הִכְשִׁיל כֹּחִי

Lam 1:14: My transgressions were bound into a yoke; by his hand they were fastened together; they weigh on my neck, sapping my strength.

Surrounded by Bitterness

לוּ שָׁקוֹל יִשָּׁקֵל כַּעְשִׂי וְהַוָּתִי בְּמֹאזְנַיִם יִשְׂאוּ־יָחַד: כִּי־עַתָּה מֵחוֹל יַמִּים יִכְבָּד

Job 6:2–3: O that my vexation were weighed, and all my calamity laid in the balances! For then it would be heavier than the sand of the sea.

Lamentations 3:7 explicitly highlights the heaviness of the chains holding the petitioner. Similarly Ps 32:4 and Job 23:2 (cited in section 6.4.7.c) highlight the "heaviness" of God's hand in descriptions of distress.

הִכְבִּיד נְחָשְׁתִּי:

Lam 3:7: He has put heavy chains on me.

Less clearly, Ps 88:7[8] has God's wrath squashing the petitioner, and Ps 55:4[5] has "terrors of death" falling on the petitioner, suggesting an unexpected weight. Finally, Ps 66:11 also suggests something heavy weighing on the person through the use of מוּעָקָה, a hapax legomenon but presumably linked to עק 'press'.[163]

עָלַי סָמְכָה חֲמָתֶךָ וְכָל־מִשְׁבָּרֶיךָ עִנִּיתָ

Ps 88:7[8]: Your wrath has come down on me, you have squashed (me) with all your waves.[164]

וְאֵימוֹת מָוֶת נָפְלוּ עָלָי:

Ps 55:4[5]: The terrors of death have fallen upon me.

שַׂמְתָּ מוּעָקָה בְּמָתְנֵינוּ:

Ps 66:11: You put affliction on our backs.[165]

These examples show the common conceptualization of distress as experiencing weight, but several different abstract entities exert the weight (sin, calamity, wrath, affliction, or terrors), showing the degree

---

163. Tate, *Psalms*, 146.
164. Ibid., 394.
165. Ibid., 145.

Distress and the Force Schema

to which this conceptualization is entrenched and thus available to be elaborated.

7.5. Further Evidence

This FORCE schema is clearly a significant conceptual framework for understanding distress, uniting several metaphors including fragmenting forces, gripping forces, moving forces that may come towards or forcefully move the Agonist, the force of aggressive animals, the force of attack from enemy opponents, heating forces, the force of water or wind, the force of heavy weights, and the force of being trampled underfoot. The following sections use Lakoff and Johnson's criteria to quantify this significance.

7.5.1. Generalizations over Polysemy

The primary types of evidence for a structured conceptual metaphor are generalizations over polysemy. Here, the diverse roots evoking both forceful interaction and the experience of physical, social, psychological or emotional distress give good examples. These generalizations are sufficiently entrenched to highlight different perspectives on the distress experience, to cover several different parts of the scenario, and to be embedded throughout different parts of speech.

First, the schema's entrenchment is seen in the different *perspectives* afforded by polysemous forceful roots. Several focus on experiencing a violent physical force (נכה 'to strike,' סער 'to storm,' טרף 'to tear with teeth,' דחה 'to push violently,' or אחז 'to grip'). Another group emphasizes the petitioner's resultant state (שבר 'to break,' דכא 'to crush,' מסס 'to melt,' or פרק 'to tear apart'). Still others focus on the trajectory of the force (בוא 'to come,' שלך 'to throw,' נהג 'to lead,' נדה 'to drive,' נשא 'to lift'). These various perspectives enable sufferers to highlight different aspects of their distress, such as the perceived cause and strength of the distress, or on the feelings it has aroused. Further, these roots evoke different manners of forceful interaction, whether violent, sudden, prolonged, intense, destructive, personal, or impersonal, enabling sufferers to give nuanced perspectives on their own circumstances.

Second, various *parts* of the distress scenario are highlighted across many images. For example, preparation to cause distress is understood as preparation to exert a force, whether hunting, pursuing, sharpening a sword, drawing a bow, or gnashing teeth. That all these words fit both physical domains and the distress domain again shows a generalization over polysemy, and demonstrates the entrenchment of the metaphor. Another striking example is the number of ways that words are conceptualized as forceful entities, being things that can "crush" (Job 19:2) or "break" (Ps 69:20[21]), and pictured as physical blows (Ps 42:10[11]), the impact of an arrow (Ps 64:3[4]) or sharpened sword (1QH 13:13), the tearing teeth of a lion (Ps 35:16), a torrent of rushing water (1QH 16:14-15), or powerful breakers spewing mud (1QH 10:12-13).

Finally, entrenchment is demonstrated by generalizations over polysemy across different parts of speech. As well as across verb roots, many prototypical force-exerting agents map onto agents of distress, including אֲרִי 'lion,' נַחַל 'torrent,' סַעַר 'storm,' אֵשׁ 'fire,' and אוֹיֵב 'enemy.' Nouns for implements that prototypically exert a violent force are also common, including חֶרֶב 'sword,' חֵץ 'arrow,' שֵׁן 'tooth,' or רֶגֶל 'foot.'

These generalizations over polysemy pervading the linguistic system, and covering much of the target scenario, give good evidence that the FORCE schema is both important and well entrenched in Hebrew for conceptualizing distress.

7.5.2. Generalizations over Inference Patterns

Next, generalizations over inference patterns show that a conceptual metaphor maps inferential structure from physical domains to more abstract ones, demonstrating knowledge of forces being used to reason about distressing situations. Using Johnson's gestalt structure for the FORCE schema (section 7.2.1), some inference patterns can be highlighted.

First, every force experience involves interaction. Conceptualizing distress as force interaction, it is given external causation, usually by a personal agent, whether enemy, lion, crusher, breaker or, more indirectly, God controlling the natural elements. Thus, sufferers do not just "become sick." Rather, conceptualizing illness as being "touched" or

Distress and the Force Schema

"gripped" highlights life as something experienced in interaction with other entities, divine and human. Thus, distress conceptualized as a force constrains the inference that there must be something or someone interacting with the sufferer.

Second and third, forces involve movement or direction, making entities follow a path of motion. Section 7.4.4 showed distress "coming" towards someone, drawing "near" and then "meeting" or even "penetrating" the person, conceptualizing distress at varying distances away from the sufferer. The force quality constrains the inference that it will continue this trajectory until it reaches the sufferer. Similarly, when the Agonist is moved by a force, whether "driven," "led," "hurled," or "swept away," the motion trajectory of the distress-causing force impacts the sufferer, causing him or her to follow the same trajectory to new locations, an enforced movement evoking an externally caused scenario.

Fourth, forces have origins and can be directed by agents at targets. Usually, God or the petitioner's opponents deliberately direct a force at the sufferer as target. The sufferer is rarely impacted by "random" forces. Sometimes, agents use implements or direct other forces, as when the enemies' words are arrows shot at the sufferer, or God's breakers are the crushing element. The clearest examples of this inference are when the petitioner perceives himself as a "target" (as in Lam 3:12 or Job 16:12–13, both with God as agent), inferring that his distress results from a rational entity's deliberate choice to target him and cause harm.

As a corollary, agents may choose against directing forces at a target, or be restrained from doing so, as in descriptions of rescue or petitions for relief. Thus, God ended distress by shutting the lions' mouths (1QH 13:14), or turning the storm to a calm (1QH 13:18), a greater force restraining a lesser one. Elsewhere, Job pleads for God to look away (Job 7:19, 9:34), asking God to redirect his force and end his distress.

Fifth, forces have degrees of intensity. This scalar property conceptualizes distress through three different linguistic methods: modifying words or clauses; verb forms; and lexical variation. Sometimes intensity is expressed by a simple intensity modifier or modifying clause, as in Ps 38:8[9] (וְנִדְכֵּיתִי עַד־מְאֹד), or a clause giving the duration of the forceful interaction as in 1QH 13:17 (כול היום ידכאו נפשי). Other modifiers express intensity by highlighting the size or extent of the force (כָּל־מִשְׁבָּרֶיךָ וְגַלֶּיךָ עָלַי עָבָרוּ, Lam 2:14; or גָּדוֹל כַּיָּם שִׁבְרֵךְ, Ps 42:7[8]) or showing that the force was exerted to the limit, as in Ps 143:3 (דִּכָּא לָאָרֶץ חַיָּתִי). Second, the infinitive absolute verb form may show intensity, as in Ps 118:13 (דַּחֹה דְחִיתַנִי) or Lam 3:52 (צוֹד צָדוּנִי). Finally, some roots evoke more intense interaction than others. Thus, רצח prototypically evokes more intense contact than נגע, and דכא evokes more intense fragmentation than שבר. This lexical variation enables petitioners to choose roots that match the perceived intensity of their distress.

The sixth aspect is a possible sequence of causality. Inferences based on this can be seen, for example, in verses like Ps 42:7[8] where the psalmist refers to "*God's* waves" passing over him. The immediate understanding of the distressing situation is as caused by the pounding of waves, but this pounding is itself caused by God who directs the waves.

Thus, all six aspects of force gestalt structure constrain inferences about distressing situations conceptualized via the FORCE schema, showing the importance of this schema for thinking about distressing situations.

7.5.3. Novel Metaphor

The FORCE schema is instantiated both in conventional and novel distress expressions, again showing how entrenched the conceptual metaphor is. Indeed, forceful physical contact is the most common way to conceptualize God interacting with humans to cause harm throughout Classical Hebrew narrative. Thus, God struck (נכה) the inhabitants of Sodom (Gen 19:11) and Syrian invaders (2 Kgs 6:18) with blindness, and the Egyptians with his "plagues" (Exod 3:20 and elsewhere).

נֶגַע and שֶׁבֶר are both conventional nominal instances of the schema, used for illnesses and wounds in the corpus and other texts (as in Gen 12:17 and 1 Kgs 8:37 for נֶגַע and Prov 16:18 and Nah 3:19 for שֶׁבֶר). Both access the domain of physical contact ("touching" and "breaking"). Among the verbs, אחז takes several different abstract agents (such as "shuddering," "affliction," or "dread"), showing how conventional this word is for conceptualizing distress.

At the other end of the conventional-novel scale, Job conceptualizes himself as someone gripped by an aggressive agent and flung into the mud (Job 30:18–19), using highly poetic language, but accessing similar prototypical experiences of being gripped by a hostile entity. Here, the author creatively elaborates new expressions which can be understood because of the conventional mappings.

The forceful conceptualization of words also occurs across the conventionality spectrum. "Crushing" words (דכא, Job 19:2) are at the conventional end, using a relatively common root in a simple syntactic frame. Conversely, mocking words as lions tearing and gnashing their teeth in Ps 35:15–17 uses a vivid image, rare words and less standard syntax, demonstrating a more creative, novel use of the FORCE schema for a similar scenario.

7.5.4. Larger Scale Metaphorical Systems

Other evidence for conceptual metaphor comes from coherence with larger scale metaphorical systems. Here, at a larger scale, God's involvement with the world (whether for good or bad) is frequently understood as force interaction. God positively rescues distressed people by forcefully "lifting" them to a positively-valued high destination. Similarly, in narrative, Exod 19:4 describes the Exodus as being forcefully "carried" (נשא) on eagles' wings. In 1 Kgs 18:46, without a vertical sense, the hand of Yahweh is described as being forcefully on (אל) Elijah, positively giving him supernatural strength, rather than causing distress as above.

Thus, God's relationship with humans is frequently characterized as force interaction. The examples in this chapter are understood negatively because of the choices of roots (often those for violent actions), the aggressive agents exerting the forces, and the destinations to which enforced movement carries the subject.

7.5.5. Non-verbal Realizations

The fifth kind of evidence comes from non-verbal realizations. No clear examples of this have been found for the FORCE schema. Certainly there is no Israelite iconography showing sick humans in the hands of demons, as there is in Assyria. Neither are there rituals to remove God's hand as in the Akkadian texts.

7.6. Universality and Variation

7.6.1. Variation within Source and Target Domain

The most obvious observation here is the preference for the FORCE schema for conceptualizing distress in each of English (shown by Kövecses' study of emotional distress), Akkadian (seen in section 7.3.2), and Hebrew (presented above). As well as this universal preference, there is both overlap and variation in the target domains conceptualized and in the specific source domains instantiating the FORCE schema.

First, the target domains introduced in this chapter are English illness, stress, and emotion, Akkadian distress, and Hebrew distress. Some life scenarios could fit all these target domains (such as an anxious emotional state). However, the prototypes differ. For English stress, psychological and emotional distress is prototypical; for illness, distress is prototypically physical, as it is for the Akkadian data; for Hebrew, prototypical distress is physical or social; whereas for Kövecses' data it is specifically emotional distress. Thus, lists of source domains do not exactly compare like with like, although they do indicate commonalities in language and thought. For example, the social force of words is significant in Hebrew, being elaborated by several different linguistic expressions in different source domains. However, such powerful words are outside the target domains for Kövecses and Helman.

With this caveat, the Hebrew source domains can be compared to those for English *stress* and emotions,[166] as follows:

---

166. Kövecses himself does not distinguish metaphors for positive or negative emotions.

Distress and the Force Schema

Hebrew distress	English stress (Helman)	English negative emotions (Kövecses)
Fragmenting force	Fragmenting force	
Wild animal		Wild animal
Opponent	Interpersonal force	Opponent
Heat		Heat
Wind and water		Natural force
Crushing force		(Opponent)
Heavy weight	Heavy weight	Burden
Gripping force		(Opponent)
Moving force / enforced movement		
	Wire or line	
	Chaos causing force	
	Malfunctioning machine	
	Inner explosion	Internal pressure
		Social force
		Mental force
		Insanity

Thus, several similar source domains instantiating the FORCE schema describe psychophysical experiences in Hebrew and English. Specifically, heavy weights and opponents conceptualize all three targets, whereas fragmentation, heat, wild animals, and natural forces occur in Hebrew and one other list. Further, gripping and crushing forces are both subsumed under Kövecses' "opponent." The main source domain only found in Hebrew is distress as an approaching force, and indeed, these examples seem unusual to a native English speaker.

Helman noted that stress metaphors were based on artifacts and technology of everyday life: "machines, cars, batteries, electrical wires, strings, rubber bands, kettles, crockery, and pottery."[167] Although wires, machines, and kettles are (unsurprisingly) not used in Hebrew, the texts

---

167. Helman, *Culture*, 314.

283

do use corresponding "artifacts and technology of everyday life," such as grape presses, swords, arrows, and rods.

Even within overlapping source domains, this simple list hides differences. For example, both Hebrew and English conceptualize emotional distress using wild animals, with the self experiencing the force of a wild animal directed towards him or her. However, in English, the emotion itself is the wild animal, a force the subject can "rein in" or "unleash." In Hebrew, other people are wild animals, forcefully hunting and tearing the sufferer, reflecting the social emphasis in Hebrew, as opposed to the emotional and physiological focus of the English target domain. Similarly, in English, emotions themselves are opponents, natural forces or heat, whereas in Hebrew these forces map to external agents or situations.

The source domains also have different prototypes. Whereas Kövecses' heat domain is prototypically structured around boiling water in a container, the prototypical heat in Hebrew is a fire. Further, since wax is the prototypical melting solid (compared to ice in English), entailments differ. In English, heat can positively generate "warm" emotions and a heart "melting" towards you, like ice returning to normality. However, with wax being normally solid, a Hebrew heating force that causes melting is unequivocally negative.

Different entailments of a "broken heart" in English and Hebrew also reflect different prototypes. The English *heart* prototypically stands for feelings, so fragmentation affects these alone. In Hebrew, לֵב stands for feelings, thoughts, desires, and will, so fragmentation is more serious, forcefully affecting feeling, thinking, deciding, and controlling one's life. Similarly, a "melting heart" represents more comprehensive distress in Hebrew than English.

Comparing to Akkadian, domains again overlap. Source domains of fragmentation, gripping, heat, and opponents were all found. The key difference is the prototypical agent directing the forces. In Hebrew, only God or other humans direct forces, whereas in Akkadian many more personal deliberate agents (demons and deities) can direct such forces.

The prototypical agents also differ between English and Hebrew. Helman noted a few English stress conceptualizations where other humans direct a force at the subject,¹⁶⁸ however these are not prototypical, with either passives (*being churned up* or *under pressure*) or adjectives (*taut, tense, burnt out*) that minimize agency being much more common. For the Hebrew examples, the situation is reversed, with some passives (as in נִשְׁבְּרֵי־לֵב or נָגוּעַ) and others with non-rational agents (including "days of affliction," the "night," "trouble," "trembling," or "dismay"), but prototypically an agent exerts the force, as in the large cluster of metaphors involving wild animals and opponents.

Thus, all three languages conceptualize distress as experiencing forces, but most significantly, what (or who) exerts the force differs. In English, prototypically the emotion or illness exerts force, in Akkadian it is the demon or deity responsible for the disease, whereas in Hebrew it is other people or God himself.

7.6.2. Variation in Linguistic Expression

Conceptual metaphors may also vary across languages in the linguistic expressions used, including the degree of elaboration of different parts of the metaphor, the conventionalization of the linguistic expressions, and the syntactic expressions used.

First, the FORCE schema is elaborated more than the other schemas, having the largest number of different linguistic expressions. For example, the variety of roots evoking manner, resultant state or direction of the force is much greater than for the VERTICALITY schema or CONSTRAINT schema. The FORCE schema is also well elaborated for stress and emotions in English, as shown by Kövecses' and Helman's data.

Comparing with Akkadian, a similarly elaborate set of verbs for physical contact are used in distress discourse, including touching, seizing, striking, and gripping, and both languages fairly frequently use the expression "hand of . . ." In Akkadian these entail a personal agent inflicting the force, and impel sufferers to find out which one it is. This entailment is not elaborated at all in the Hebrew texts, it is always clear who the perpetrator is.

---

168. Ibid., 315–16.

The control of forces is also absent from Hebrew. Kövecses' study showed metaphors for controlling forces for almost every domain conceptualizing English emotion. By contrast, in Hebrew there are only occasional pleas to God to shut the mouths of the lions or remove the rod, since the Hebrew forces are external and outside the petitioner's control. The elaboration in English also reflects the importance of controlling emotions in Western thought, for which there is little evidence in Hebrew.

Second, regarding conventionalization, some of the most conventionalized Hebrew linguistic expressions use אחז (shown by the various forceful subjects it collocates with), נגע (used both as a verb and a noun) and שבר (again both as verb and noun). In English, *stress* is one of the "most pervasive—and multi-dimensional—folk illnesses of contemporary Western society,"[169] suggesting *stress* itself is a very conventional expression of this FORCE schema. This word also occurs as both verb and noun. Thus, both English and Hebrew have very conventional expressions of this schema. However, the Hebrew roots prototypically evoke a personal agent, whereas the word *stress* prototypically evokes mechanical systems and certainly does not need a personal agent. This suggests that while instantiations of the FORCE schema in English with personal agents are understandable, they are stylistically marked, and not as conventional as those with a hidden agent. For example, the English translation of Job 19:2 "you crush me with words" (with an explicit personal agent) is more stylistically marked than the more conventional phrase "I felt totally crushed by what you said," which uses a very similar conceptualization.

Third, the FORCE schema in Hebrew is cognitively accessed through various syntactic expressions, whether a single root like אחז or נגע in a sentence with no other links to the schema, or in longer multi-word phrases, using combinations of forceful verbs, prototypically powerful nouns and intensity modifiers, as in Ps 124:4, אֲזַי הַמַּיִם שְׁטָפוּנוּ נַחְלָה עָבַר עַל־נַפְשֵׁנוּ. Similarly, the single word *stress* accesses the force schema in English, as do longer phrases like *I felt like I had been run over by a truck*.

---

169. Ibid., 314.

Contrasts occur in the syntactic expression of intensity. In English, intensity is often expressed through an adverb giving the extent to which the force is exerted: "thoroughly crushed"; "totally shattered"; or "completely stressed-out." In Hebrew, this level of intensity is expressed through longer syntactic expressions, as in כָּל הַיּוֹם, עַד מְאֹד, or עַד נַפְשִׁי, or through other syntactic forms, like the infinitive absolute construction used in דָּחֹה דְחִיתַנִי.

Thus, although Hebrew, English, and Akkadian all conceptualize distress (whether physical, psychological, emotional, or social) with the FORCE schema, and share several individual source domains instantiating this schema, there are nevertheless several differences. Variations in the prototypical structure of source domains and target domains, in the different entailments, and in the different linguistic expressions, have confirmed Kövecses' parameters of variation. More importantly, they show how inferences from conceptual metaphors can differ even when similar source and target domains are mapped.

7.7. Summary

This chapter established the FORCE schema as the most significant schema for conceptualizing distress in the specific corpus. It is well entrenched, from simple verbs through to much more complex expressions, and is used to infer the cause of distressing situations, particularly their origin in a deliberate agent, and the intensity of distress. This conceptualization of distress shares many similarities with the discourse of stress or emotions in English, and Akkadian illness discourse, but also many differences. Although each language conceptualizes the subjective experience of various kinds of distress as experiencing force, the prototypical agents directing the force vary from language to language, and corpus to corpus. This understanding of the agency behind distressing situations, directing force at the experiencer, is one of the key variations between the languages considered, leading to different solutions for distress problematized linguistically in this way. In Akkadian, a multiplicity of personal agents coheres with the search for the true agent and a method to remove their touch. In English, internal or non-specific agents (such as our own emotions) lead to solutions in terms of self-control or self-help. Finally, in Hebrew, seeing God as the ultimate director of forces leads to solutions where he is asked to control his forces, or overpower other agents who are inflicting the sufferer.

In the next chapter, discussion turns from image schemas to primary metaphors, beginning with those based on sight, and especially darkness as a metaphor for distress.

8

Distress and DARKNESS

"I go about in sunless gloom"—Job 30:28

8.1. Introduction

The final two chapters concern primary metaphors rather than image schemas. A primary metaphor is "grounded in the everyday experience that links our sensory-motor experience to the domain of our subjective judgments,"[1] mapping different sense modalities to language. This chapter considers mappings from the sense of sight and begins by discussing the universal and cultural factors influencing vision, light and darkness, since even perception is influenced by language.[2]

---

1. Lakoff and Johnson, *Metaphors*, 255.
2. Recall section 2.2.3 and the following discussion.

8.2. Establishing the Source Domain

8.2.1. Physiological / Universal Factors

Lakoff and Johnson argue that "many primary metaphors are universal because everybody has basically the same kinds of bodies and brains and lives in basically the same kinds of environments."[3] At least three universal factors are important here: visual physiology; environmental experience of night and day; and a possible physiological connection between darkness and negative emotion. Conversely, universal correlations between darkness and distress in early infancy are unlikely.

First, human visual physiology has universal effects on language and cognition.[4] Vision differs from other senses in several ways, potentially affecting inferences when used in conceptual mappings. First, sight and hearing are "distant" senses, enabling perception without direct contact, or even proximity, to the perceived entity.[5] Second, vision can voluntarily focus on one stimulus within a multitude of input stimuli.[6] Third, since light does not bend (as sound does), the visual field is often limited, potentially mapping to "control" in a target domain, since entities within the limited visual field can often be controlled, whereas things outside are unknown and thus uncontrollable.[7]

Second, environmentally, both sunlight and lack of sunlight are universal experiences. Goddard suggests this diurnal experience is prototypical for understanding all experiences of light and dark. Thus, the darkness inside a cave is "like" situations where the sun is not shining.[8] Although such nighttime darkness may be prototypical for *dark* in English, it is not prototypical for the darkness used for English emotional distress (*gloomy* is more common), nor are words for prototypically "night-time" darkness used in distress metaphors in the other languages considered below.

---

3. Lakoff and Johnson, *Metaphors*, 257.
4. As in color-term research, summarized in Goddard, *Analysis*, 111–35.
5. Sweetser, *Etymology*, 39.
6. Ibid., 32.
7. Ibid., 33.
8. Goddard, *Analysis*, 128.

Even the daily experience of sunlight differs across the globe, affecting how this domain is structured. Day-length varies little in tropical regions, and daylight relatively quickly transitions to darkness. Conversely, polar regions experience winter days with no sunlight and summer days with no darkness. In between, long evenings have gradually decreasing light. This is reflected in language. Finnish *kaamos* refers specifically to the long midwinter darkness, and several words describe gradations of light. Further, words refer to the time of day without implying light levels. Thus *ilta* refers to roughly 6:00–9:00 p.m. without reference to darkness. Conversely, in Papua New Guinea, words for "night" as a time period are rarely distinguished from more abstract "darkness," so that in Gadsup (a non-Austronesian language of the Eastern Highlands) both are *ayafum*,[9] and there is also no clear intensity scale for darkness. Thus, night and day are not conceptualized identically across the globe, despite the universal experience of its rotation.

Third, lack of sunlight and emotional distress are potentially physiologically related. Seasonal Affective Disorder (SAD) describes a depressive condition found in higher-latitude regions during winter months. The human brain produces melatonin during dark periods, with the level depending on the darkness's duration,[10] perhaps contributing to negative emotional responses during dark periods. Certainly, light therapy works as effectively as drugs in treating this negative emotional condition,[11] so a universal physiological link between darkness and emotional experience is possible.

Fourth, primary metaphor research focuses on correlations of experience in early infancy as conceptual networks form in the brain and neurons "wire together" as they fire simultaneously. This suggests investigating universal correlations between darkness and distressing emotions in this timeframe. However, the very situations motivating the posited universal primary metaphor AFFECTION IS WARMTH (being in the womb or held close to parents) are also dark, suggesting that any universal correlations between darkness and distress come from later

---

9. Bokawa, personal communication.
10. Snyder et al., "Light."
11. Lam et al., "Can-SAD," 810.

cognitive development, from physiology or from cultural correlations passed on from generation to generation.

8.2.2. Culture-specific factors

Considering Hebrew specifics, this section focuses on "darkness," investigating its role in the ancient Near East, the places and entities prototypically associated with darkness in Hebrew, and then whether it is a scalar concept.

a) Darkness in the Ancient Near East

First, in Egypt, with the sun worshipped as the source of life, darkness opposes its power. Creation came from the darkness of the primeval ocean, and the daily cycle re-enacted the initial struggle of light against darkness, with light victorious at sunrise.[12] In the Hymn to Aten, when the sun is absent, "darkness is a shroud, and the earth is in stillness, for he who made them rests in his horizon."[13] The absence of the creator sun is like death, and his victory over death is celebrated in morning worship.[14] At death, consigning bodies to dark graves further consolidated the link between darkness and the underworld. Thus, darkness is negatively evaluated in Egypt, opposing the strongest divine power, and associated with death and the underworld.

In Mesopotamia, darkness is similarly threatening, and opposed to the sun god. It is always viewed negatively. Darkness is the natural habitat for demons, who even bring darkness during daytime. The netherworld is called the "house of darkness,"[15] so darkness is again negatively valued and associated with death and harmful spiritual forces.

In Hebrew too, darkness is "uniformly negative in its import."[16] Darkness is present from creation (Gen 1:2), but there is no sugges-

---

12. Ringgren et al., "חָשַׁךְ," 246.
13. Pritchard, *ANET*, 370.
14. Bleeker, "Remarks," 26.
15. Ringgren et al., "חָשַׁךְ," 247.
16. Ryken et al., *Dictionary*, 191.

tion of conflict with God,[17] nor that this darkness is an attribute of God himself.[18] Rather, God demonstrated control by ordering the darkness, naming it, and putting it under the moon's governance.[19] Throughout the Bible, darkness is always under God's control.[20]

Several scholars see Hebrew "darkness" (חֹשֶׁךְ) as a cosmic substance,[21] more than the absence of light.[22] Some verbs do conceptualize it as acting independently: "falling" (נפל) on people; "covering" (כסה) them; or "destroying / silencing" (צמת) them; and "created" by God in Isaiah 45:7 (בּוֹרֵא חֹשֶׁךְ). This conceptualization may affect inferences from the darkness domain, since a substance is not gradable in the same way as absence of light.

b) Prototypical Associations for Darkness

Several prototypical scenarios or locations are associated with Hebrew darkness (חֹשֶׁךְ), thus potentially evoked when darkness occurs in distress metaphors. First, darkness is associated with Sheol, using several different words, including חֹשֶׁךְ, אֹפֶל, and צַלְמָוֶת.[23] The netherworld association is thus common to Egypt, Mesopotamia, and Hebrew. Second, darkness is associated with theophany, including God's covenant ceremony with Abraham (Genesis 15), at Sinai, and in the poetry of Psalm 18. Often, עֲרָפֶל describes this kind of darkness. Third, darkness is the sphere of the wicked, who act at night. For example, Job 24:13–17, describes murderers and adulterers as "friends with the terrors of deep darkness" (יַכִּיר בַּלְהוֹת צַלְמָוֶת). Fourth, darkness is prototypically associated with captivity and imprisonment. Fifth, blindness is understood as darkness, as in Isa 29:18, וּמֵאֹפֶל וּמֵחֹשֶׁךְ עֵינֵי

---

17. Contra Piper, "Light," 130, Ryken et al., *Dictionary*, 191.
18. Contra Wyatt, "Darkness."
19. Ringgren et al., "חָשַׁךְ," 249.
20. Ryken et al., *Dictionary*, 193.
21. Aalen, "אוֹר," 156.
22. Piper, "Light," 130; Ringgren et al., "חָשַׁךְ," 248.
23. Even if צַלְמָוֶת does not derive from the folk etymology "shadow of death" (Niehr, "צַלְמָוֶת," 397).

עִוְרִים תִּרְאֶינָה "from gloom and from darkness, the eyes of the blind will see." Finally, Job 28:3 refers to a mine's darkness.

All of these prototypes fit חֹשֶׁךְ, but אֹפֶל has near identical associations, including the nighttime domain of the wicked, the netherworld, blindness, and the mine. The adjectives אֲפֵלָה and אָפֵל more specifically evoke darkness as judgment.[24] There is little evidence that אֹפֶל is associated with different situations, or with a greater intensity of darkness.

Three further metaphorical situations are understood as darkness: ignorance, evil, and affliction. Ecclesiastes 2:14, for example, describes the wise as having eyes, but the fool "walks in darkness" (בַּחֹשֶׁךְ הוֹלֵךְ). Evil and darkness contrast with good and light in Isa 5:20, and darkness as affliction is discussed below. These three metaphorical targets are not distinct, since a fool may experience the evil of affliction from the ignorant choices he makes, conceptualized as "walking in darkness." However, the three English domains show the breadth of this source domain in Hebrew.

c) Intensity of Darkness

Is darkness gradable in Hebrew? If so, it may conceptualize distress intensity. One approach is to investigate the words for degrees of darkness throughout the daily cycle. In Palestine "the light does not fade gradually after twilight . . . Within an hour, sunset has given way to the darkness of night,"[25] suggesting there may be few words for shades of darkness. However, as well as יוֹם 'day' and לַיְלָה 'night,' עֶרֶב describes the time as the sun prepares to set,[26] contrasting with בֹּקֶר for the start of daylight. The light quality at dusk and dawn is described by נֶשֶׁף.[27] עֲלָטָה gives another perspective, and, though glossed by BDB as "thick

---

24. Price, "אֹפֶל," 480.
25. Feinberg, "אפל."
26. Niehr, "עֶרֶב," 335.
27. Wakely, "נֶשֶׁף."

darkness,"[28] more accurately describes the "darkness that follows the setting of the sun."[29]

עֲרָפֶל is also glossed as "deep darkness," but is unconnected to the daily cycle. Since cognates describe "thick clouds"[30] it likely evokes the darkness of stormy clouds. Mulder argues it evokes intensity because it describes the temple's lightless interior (1 Kgs 8:20).[31] However, the point may rather be that God's dark cloudy dwelling is now in this thoroughly dark place. Price also claims it reflects "deep" darkness,[32] but all his examples could equally reflect "cloudy" or "obscuring" darkness, an explanation fitting a possible derivation from עָרַף, 'drop' or 'drip.'[33]

A possible intensity scale for darkness might also be entailed through modifiers, as for English *very dark*, or *thick, deep*, or *pitch* darkness. However, verbs from חשך never have a modifier like מְאֹד, nor do nouns have an intensifying modifier like רַב or גָּדוֹל. Only two verses potentially suggest more intense darkness through a modifier. First, in Prov 20:20, someone is destined for אִישׁוֹן חֹשֶׁךְ (Ketiv) or אֶשׁוּן חֹשֶׁךְ (Qere). The Ketiv could suggest the "middle" of the darkness,[34] or darkness as of the pupil, whereas the Qere may mean something like "blackest,"[35] or just the "approach of" night.[36] Thus, any potential evocation of intensity is far from certain.

Second, Exod 10:22 describes the ninth plague as חֹשֶׁךְ־אֲפֵלָה. The syntax is unusual compared to Joel 2:2 and Zeph 1:15, both describing the day of Yahweh as חֹשֶׁךְ וַאֲפֵלָה (with a conjunction). Further, no other examples of אֲפֵלָה, אֹפֶל, or אָפֵל clearly suggest increased intensity of darkness. אֲפֵלָה may rather evoke a quality of darkness (other than its intensity), such as the fear it induces, or the punitive cause. Nevertheless, the Exodus text is important, since in 10:21 the phrase

---

28. BDB 759.
29. Price, "עֲלָטָה."
30. Mulder, "עֲרָפֶל." 371.
31. Ibid., 373.
32. Price, "עֲרָפֶל."
33. Allen, "עָרַף."
34. BDB 36.
35. *NET*, 1074.
36. Wakely, "אֶשׁוּן," 549.

וַיְמֻשֶׁ֖שׁ חֹ֑שֶׁךְ 'and they feel darkness' is the clearest biblical evocation of intense darkness, with the root משׁשׁ also used for Isaac "touching" Jacob to identify him.

Thus, although several Hebrew words describe daily gradations of darkness, there are no clear examples using modifiers to evoke intensity. So, if this source domain expresses distress intensity, it is more likely to be by lexical variation than through modifiers.

8.3. Comparative data

8.3.1. Contemporary Cross-Linguistic Comparisons

The contemporary comparisons focus on English, Finnish, Japanese (originating from high latitudes) and Bamu (from Papua New Guinea). First, in English, intellection is the most significant target domain conceptualized through the domain of vision,[37] though not directly related to distress. Here, being *in the dark* conceptualizes lacking knowledge, solved by *shedding light* or a *bright* person *illuminating* the situation.[38] Thus, ideas are light sources and discourse is a light medium (which can be *opaque* or *clear*).[39]

Within distress language, several conventional expressions fit the conceptual metaphor DEPRESSION IS DARKNESS.[40] General expressions include feeling *dark* or *blue*, but others liken depression to rainy or cloudy weather, as when experiences are *black clouds*, a cloud sitting over someone, or a *rainy day*. McMullen and Conway saw here "not only the sense of decreased clarity of consciousness and pervasively negative attitude and affect that are two hallmarks of depression, but also the not uncommon way of talking about depression as if it autonomously descends upon a person, that is, occurs independently of one's will."[41] Thus, in English, darkness again implies an external cause for depression, even though the domain might not suggest that at first sight.

37. Sweetser, *Etymology*, 32–34.
38. Ibid., 40.
39. Lakoff and Johnson, *Metaphors*, 48.
40. McMullen and Conway, "Depression."
41. Ibid., 170.

Further, different "darkness" words describe different negative emotional experiences. When someone looks at another *blackly*, angry sentiment is implied, and if they looked *darkly* there may also be an intent to "get even." Conversely, if someone looks at another *gloomily*, they are sad or depressed, demonstrating that (fairly subtle) lexical variation in the source domain constrains different inferences in the target domain. *Gloomy* prototypically associates with dark, overcast clouds, dark forests or a night of particularly low visibility. The abnormality of gloominess (as for clouds darkening the sun's light) may make it appropriate for sadness rather than anger. Alternatively, *gloomy* may link to the sad feelings prototypically evoked by an overcast sky (for English people at least).

Second, in Finnish,[42] many words describe darkness, especially *musta* 'black' and *pimeä* 'dark'. *Pimeä* collocates with specific modifiers to express intensity: *sysipimeä* 'coal black'; *säkkipimeä* 'black like inside a sack'; and *pilkkopimeä* (meaning inaccessible). Several words describe shades of darkness, including *hämäryys* 'dusk, twilight,' *himmeä* 'dim,' *harmaa* 'grey,' *hämy* 'gloom,' *hämärä* 'dusky' and *hämyinen* 'shadowy, darkish'. *Kaamos* describes the long winter darkness, and *synkkä* evokes the darkness of a stormy autumn night (*synkkä yö*), a forest of tall trees (*synkkä metsä*), or very thick clouds (*synkkä taivas*). Both *kaamos* and *synkkä* describe emotional distress. *Kaamosmesennus*, 'kaamos depression' was described as SAD above. *Synkkä* is more general, so that someone with a *synkkä mieli* 'blue mood' is unhappy or hopeless, they may be having *synkät ajatukset* 'depressing thoughts', experiencing a *synkkä hetki* 'dark moment', and so may *kulkea synkän näköisenä* 'mope around'. More intense emotion is expressible with a standard modifier, as in *hyvin synkkä mieli*, a 'very' hopeless mood. Thus, as in English, a word prototypically linked to dark weather maps onto an emotion similar to "sadness." A mind that is *musta* 'black' may also be hopeless, but also suggests someone holding a grudge. Again this parallels English, with a more general dark word having overtones of resentment.

Third, Japanese *kurai* prototypically evokes nighttime darkness, that of a cloudy day, or in a cave.[43] *Yami* refers to more intense dark-

---

42. Finnish language information provided by Meinander, Sinnemäki, and Laihia and Laihia.

43. Japanese language information provided by Fukunaga.

ness, and the compound *kurayami* to the greatest intensity. Another quality is given by the Chinese character pronounced *in* in *inki* 'dark spirit', describing shadows, or sunless places, as in a cave or closed cupboard where something is kept hidden from sight. When applied to people, *kurai* 'dark' conventionally describes an emotional state similar to English "sad," "depressed," "anxious," or "worrying," so that '*kurai yo?*' is a normal way of asking someone if they are anxious. Describing someone as having *inki* 'shadowy spirit' means they have an anxious character, or are "sad" or "gloomy." The opposite is *youki*, someone with a bright or sunny character (*taiyou* refers to the sun). A longer idiomatic phrase cohering with these conventional linguistic descriptions is *an-un ga tachikomeru* 'it is crowded with dark clouds,' describing a depressing situation affecting an area, creating uncertainty and anxiety. Again, specifically words for dark weather phenomena describe emotions of "sadness."

Fourth, to provide a tropical contrast, in Bamu, the word *duwo* means "night," and more abstract darkness (as under the shade of a tree) is a reduplicated form *duwoduwo*. Unusually intense blackness, often associated with a supernatural cause is *sisibo*. There is no distinct word for twilight, just "morning" *duwoduwo* and "afternoon" *duwoduwo*. Intensity can be marked by the clitic *–ia,* so that *duwoduwoya* describes intense darkness. Dark objects are described as *gare'e* or *garegare*, as for the speakers' dark skin. Interestingly, these speakers do not use light and darkness for moral qualities at all, at odds with Bleeker's typology of light in world religions.[44] Where these words apply to people in any way, they can only refer to physical appearance.[45]

Though selective, these contemporary comparisons from four unrelated language families illustrate several features to compare with Hebrew. First, all three languages from high latitudes (Japanese, Finnish, and English) have a well-entrenched, conventional expression of sadness related to darkness, each using a word more prototypically evoking dark weather than night-time darkness. Does Hebrew have a similar expression? Second, these three languages map intensity of darkness to emotional discourse, using the scalarity of the darkness source domain

---

44. Bleeker, "Remarks," 27.
45. Bamu language information from Carr.

Distress and Darkness

to structure the emotional target domain. Is this possible in Hebrew? Finally, in English and Japanese at least, both conventional words and more syntactically complex idioms cohere with the same conceptual mapping from darkness to negative emotion. Do the Hebrew texts also show this variation?

8.3.2. Ancient Near Eastern Comparisons

Many ancient Near Eastern cultures also conceptualize distress through darkness, with examples in Egypt, Mesopotamia, and Greece, showing different entailments of the metaphorical mappings depending on other aspects of the culture.

In Egypt, darkness signified disaster,[46] as reflected in the three-day plague of darkness (Exod 10:21–23), a very serious omen for a country where the sun god demonstrated his supremacy over creation by bringing daylight every morning. Further, darkness "served as a metaphor for affliction and separation from the gods,"[47] with light and darkness signifying health or suffering, corresponding to the sun-god's bestowal, or otherwise, of light and life.

In Mesopotamia, darkness is associated with demons, whose grip caused most sickness, making it a natural source domain for sickness metaphors. Darkness surrounds a sick person, or afflicts his body. As an entailment, the sick person can ask a god to "pluck out his darkness," when asking for relief.[48] Further, greater risk (from demon attack, and thus sickness) is inferred during darkness. The moon kept demons at bay during the night, and Shamash banishes them during daytime. However, new moons and eclipses, when light is very limited, are very dangerous. Anyone might be vulnerable to the unimpeded arbitrary attack of demons, against which there is no magical incantation.[49]

Mesopotamian body idioms also associate distress and darkness. Gruber cites Akkadian expressions of the "sad person's gloomy

---

46. Ringgren et al., "חָשַׁךְ," 246.
47. Ibid., 247.
48. Ibid.
49. Ibid., 248.

countenance,"⁵⁰ including *pānū ukkulū* 'the face is darkened', *zīmī ukkuliššūwû* 'change the countenance to darkness', and *būnū uttû* 'darken the face'. However, these may not be best described as English "sadness." The first describes Enkidu's assailant in a dream,⁵¹ with no evidence this being is "sad." The second is the friend's description of the sufferer in the Babylonian theodicy,⁵² who has described his predicament as "anguish" and "trouble" rather than "sadness." The third comes from a boundary stone, in context reading, "May Sin, the lord of the crown, darken for him his shining face."⁵³ Thus, both the latter examples do conceptualize distress as a darkened face, if not specifically "sadness." Mitchell more accurately asserts that, in Mesopotamia, faces are said to darken in threatening situations.⁵⁴

Blackness in the internal organs is also a Mesopotamian concern, indicating fatal illness. However, in contrast to Greek humoral theories, this blackness is a result of an external (usually supernatural) cause, rather than the cause of the problem itself.⁵⁵

In ancient Greece, blackness conceptualizes illness in discussion of "melancholia." Humoral theory linked melancholia to excess black bile (as the etymology suggests), which threw a shadow over one's thoughts, impairing the ability to think. In terms of productivity, this metaphor "captured not only the sense of darkness-induced fear, gloom, or dejection experienced by sufferers of melancholia, but also the clouding of thought, consciousness, and judgment that was a dominant characteristic."⁵⁶

This well-entrenched conventional use of darkness was used to reason about melancholia. For example, the medicinal remedy of black hellebore was suitable because of the coloring.⁵⁷ However, black bile does not actually exist, with the origin maybe traceable to the idea that

50. Gruber, *Aspects*, 364.
51. Gilgamesh, VII iv, 17–18, in Dalley, *Myths*, 88.
52. Line 15, Arnold and Beyer, *Readings*, 180.
53. Gruber, *Aspects*, 364.
54. Ringgren et al., "חָשַׁךְ," 247.
55. Geller, "Phlegm," 192.
56. McMullen and Conway, "Depression," 168.
57. Stol, *Epilepsy*, 27.

"'black' or 'dark' intestines conveyed a feeling of depression," found in Homer and other ancient Greek texts.[58] This example shows how a simple conceptual mapping can have a profound impact on thought and practice for a long time, even when not based in reality.

Thus, there are two important ancient motivations for a conceptual metaphor linking darkness and physical, mental, or emotional distress. One is the cultural association of darkness with spiritual powers opposed to those of light and life. The other is an embodied motivation associating darkness in body parts with emotional or physical distress. These motivations may also be evident in the Hebrew texts.

8.4. Presentation and Analysis of Hebrew Mappings

8.4.1. Being in Distress is Darkness in Part of the Body

Metonymic mappings are considered first, where a physiological aspect of distress (such as a "dark face") stands for the distress scenario itself. These may motivate more metaphorical expressions, such as "sitting in darkness."

Most frequently, eyes are darkened in distress. Sometimes, the darkness is evoked by impaired vision, without a word for darkness. Several different roots and syntactic constructions express this aspect, showing its entrenchment within the language. Although outside the specific corpus, Ps 69:23[24] associates darkened eyes (using חשך) with distress desired for the enemies.

תֶּחְשַׁכְנָה עֵינֵיהֶם מֵרְאוֹת

Ps 69:23[24]: Let their eyes be darkened so that they cannot see.

Ps 38:10[11] evokes darkness through losing the "light of my eyes" (אוֹר־עֵינַי) in an illness context. Such loss is also implicit in Ps 13:3[4], where light must be returned to the eyes to avoid death. 1QH 15:2–3 claims impairment to both vision and hearing from experiencing distressing evil, with שעע evoking something "smeared over" or "closed

---

58. Ibid., 31.

up."[59] There is no suggestion in any of these verses that this visual impairment results from tears.

לִבִּי סְחַרְחַר עֲזָבַנִי כֹחִי וְאוֹר־עֵינַי גַּם־הֵם אֵין אִתִּי׃

Ps 38:10[11]: My heart throbs, my strength fails me; as for the light of my eyes—it also has gone from me.

הָאִירָה עֵינַי פֶּן־אִישַׁן הַמָּוֶת׃

Ps 13:3[4]: Give light to my eyes, or I will sleep the sleep of death.

שעו עיני מראות 3 רע אוזני משמוע דמים

1QH 15:2–3: My eyes are blind from having seen evil, my ears, through hearing the shedding of blood.

English translations of Ps 88:9[10] and Job 17:7 suggest darkened or "dim" eyes. כהה in Job 17:7 describes the dimly burning flame of Isa 42:3 and the condition of Isaac's eyes in Gen 27:1, as well as the cursed eyes of the worthless shepherd in Zech 11:17. It certainly suggests weakened vision. In Ps 88:9[10], דאב may be more accurately "fainting" or "wearying,"[60] describing eyes that have been watching too long for God's salvation and seeing no response.[61] However, it again suggests difficulty in vision during distress. 1QH 13:34 and Ps 6:7[8] both use עשש for the eyes' condition as a result of grief (כַּעַס). Although translated as "blinded" or "wasted away," the collocation with עֲצָמַי in Ps 31:10 shows it is more general than just blindness. These four verses all show impairment to vision resulting from emotional distress, and all explicitly attribute the eyes' problems to sorrow or affliction using מִן. These verses possibly conceptualize tears draining away the body's life force and thus weakening the eyes,[62] but only Ps 6:7[8] mentions tears in the context. It is equally likely that these verses should be processed along with those above as references to the eyes' diminishing power or light in distress.

59. BDB 1044.
60. Ibid., 178.
61. Goldingay, *Psalms* 2:651.
62. Collins, "Physiology."

וַתֵּכַהּ מִכַּעַשׂ עֵינִי וִיצֻרַי כַּצֵּל כֻּלָּם׃

Job 17:7: My eye has grown dim from grief, and all my members are like a shadow.

עֵינִי דָאֲבָה מִנִּי עֹנִי

Ps 88:9[10]: My eye grows dim through sorrow.

כי עששו מכעס עיני ונפשי במרורי יום

1QH 13:34: For my eyes are blinded by the grief and my soul by the bitterness of the day.

עָשְׁשָׁה מִכַּעַס עֵינִי עָתְקָה בְּכָל־צוֹרְרָי׃

Ps 6:7[8]: My eyes waste away because of grief; they grow weak because of all my foes.

In 1QH 13:32, the face (פני) rather than the eyes is darkened, using the verb חשך and nouns אפלה and משחור to comprehensively describe the darkness. This supports also reading darkness of the eyes in line 34 (above).

ויחשך מאור פני לאפלה והודי נהפך למשחור

1QH 13:32: The light of my face has become gloomy with deep darkness, my countenance has changed to gloom.[63]

Other verses use קדר. According to Schmoldt, "the main meaning is 'be dark, gloomy, dirty,'"[64] prototypically describing the sky or the stars, as in the sky darkened by clouds and wind in 1 Kgs 18:45. When predicated of people, it is usually translated "mourn" in English, although used for more situations than English mourning (prototypically linked to grief following someone's death). This extension to "mourning" may be motivated by the blackening by ashes used in penitential rites,[65] or a mourner's black (or dirty) clothes,[66] but equally could be

---

63. Martínez and Tigchelaar, *Scrolls*, 173.
64. Schmoldt, "קָדַר," 518.
65. Kraus, *Psalms 1–59*, 394.
66. BDB 871.

based on a "gloomy" facial expression,[67] or the "darkened eyes" metonymy described above. The physiological association of dark weather with negative emotion could also be a motivation. Clines claims that gloominess "cannot be substantiated," preferring to see a literal description of black clothes,[68] but his reasoning uses the verses listed below which can equally be understood as an emotional disposition. Further, the cross-cultural comparisons suggest a word like this for negative emotions may exist.

Frequently, the root occurs as a participle with הלך, describing the petitioner's condition as he "walks" (Pss 38:6[7]; 42:9[10]; and 43:2). Job 30:28 has identical syntax to Ps 38:6[7], but the additional modifier that there is no "sun" (חַמָּה) leads the NRSV to translate as walking in "sunless gloom" rather than "mournfully." Each verse could describe walking around with a countenance or emotional state like a dark sky, with Job 30:28 reaffirming this state by denying the opposite. His emotional frame is like a darkened sky, not a sunny one.

כָּל־הַיּוֹם קֹדֵר הִלָּכְתִּי׃

Ps 38:6[7]: All day long I go around gloomily.[69]

לָמָּה־קֹדֵר אֵלֵךְ בְּלַחַץ אוֹיֵב׃

Ps 42:9[10]: Why must I walk about gloomily because the enemy oppresses me?

לָמָּה־קֹדֵר אֶתְהַלֵּךְ בְּלַחַץ אוֹיֵב׃

Ps 43:2: Why must I walk about gloomily because of the oppression of the enemy?

קֹדֵר הִלַּכְתִּי בְּלֹא חַמָּה

Job 30:28: I go about in sunless gloom.

In 1QH 13:31, the phrase קדרות לבשתי 'I am clothed in darkness / dressed in black' apparently more clearly refers to donning dark

---

67. Schmoldt, "קָדַר," 519.
68. Clines, *Job 21–37*, 959.
69. *Mournfully* is changed to *gloomily* in each verse.

mourning clothes. However, the immediately preceding physiological context of a heart in turmoil and subsequent physiological reference to the tongue sticking to the palate, suggests even this is not literal. לבשׁ actually describes several emotional experiences: being clothed in desolation (יִלְבַּשׁ שְׁמָמָה, Ezek 7:27); shame (יִלְבְּשׁוּ־בֹשֶׁת, Job 8:22; Ps 35:26); trembling fear (חֲרָדוֹת יִלְבָּשׁוּ, Ezek 26:16); or humiliation (יִלְבְּשׁוּ כְלִמָּה, Ps 109:29), all using qal forms of the verb and the emotion noun without any preposition. The Qumran verse has nearly identical syntax, so could easily express the author's emotional state (something like "clothed with gloominess") rather than his apparel. Jeremiah 8:21 again uses a qal perfect of קדר in a context suggesting a distressed emotional state.

ויהם עלי לבי קדרות לבשתי ולשוני לחך תדבק וסבבוני בהוות לבם

> 1QH 13:31: My heart is in turmoil within me. I am clothed in gloominess and my tongue sticks to (my) palate, because they surrounded me with the calamity of their heart.[70]

עַל־שֶׁבֶר בַּת־עַמִּי הָשְׁבָּרְתִּי קָדַרְתִּי שַׁמָּה הֶחֱזִקָתְנִי׃

> Jer 8:21: For the hurt of my people I am hurt, I am gloomy, and dismay has taken hold of me.

This section has demonstrated three possible embodied motivations for darkness distress metaphors, showing responses to distress described as a darkened face, impaired (or darkened) vision, or darkness of the person himself or herself.

8.4.2. Being in Distress is Prototypically Suffering in the Dark

Other texts make nighttime or evening suffering particularly salient. Again this is a metonymic conceptual mapping, where distress suffered in the dark stands for the more general experience of distress.

In Ps 59:6[7], enemies attack at evening, and in Ps 11:2[3] the wicked shoot in the dark (אֹפֶל). It is also the "evening" (עֶרֶב) that

---

70. Author's translation.

continues until dawn twilight (נֶשֶׁף) that gives the "nights of misery" (לֵילוֹת עָמָל) Job complains of in Job 7:3–4. A similar sleepless night is highlighted in Ps 77:6[7], during which the author is troubled (v. 4[5]) and meditates on how God has spurned him (v. 7[8]). In Job 30:17, the night is a more active aggressor, piercing Job's bones (עֲצָמַי נִקַּר).

יָשׁוּבוּ לָעֶרֶב יֶהֱמוּ כַכָּלֶב וִיסוֹבְבוּ עִיר׃

Ps 59:6[7]: Each evening they come back, howling like dogs and prowling about the city.

כִּי הִנֵּה הָרְשָׁעִים יִדְרְכוּן קֶשֶׁת כּוֹנְנוּ חִצָּם עַל־יֶתֶר לִירוֹת בְּמוֹ־אֹפֶל לְיִשְׁרֵי־לֵב׃

Ps 11:2[3]: For look, the wicked bend the bow, they have fitted their arrow to the string, to shoot in the dark at the upright in heart.

כֵּן הָנְחַלְתִּי לִי יַרְחֵי־שָׁוְא וְלֵילוֹת עָמָל מִנּוּ־לִי׃ אִם־שָׁכַבְתִּי וְאָמַרְתִּי מָתַי אָקוּם וּמִדַּד־עָרֶב וְשָׂבַעְתִּי נְדֻדִים עֲדֵי־נָשֶׁף׃

Job 7:3–4: So I am allotted months of emptiness, and nights of misery are apportioned to me. When I lie down I say, "When shall I rise?" But the night is long, and I am full of tossing until dawn.

אֶזְכְּרָה נְגִינָתִי בַּלָּיְלָה עִם־לְבָבִי אָשִׂיחָה וַיְחַפֵּשׂ רוּחִי׃

Ps 77:6[7]: At night I remember my songs, I ponder in my heart, and my spirit seeks an answer.[71]

לַיְלָה עֲצָמַי נִקַּר מֵעָלָי וְעֹרְקַי לֹא יִשְׁכָּבוּן׃

Job 30:17: The night pierces my bones, and those who gnaw me take no rest.[72]

Night-time suffering is mentioned elsewhere, but explicit parallels with daytime suffering suggest these evoke continual suffering rather

---

71. Tate, *Psalms*, 268.
72. Clines, *Job 21–37*, 931.

Distress and Darkness

than giving particular salience to the night. Examples are in Isa 38:12 and Ps 77:2[3].

מִיּוֹם עַד־לַיְלָה תַּשְׁלִימֵנִי׃

Isa 38:12: From day to night you bring me to an end;

בְּיוֹם צָרָתִי אֲדֹנָי דָּרָשְׁתִּי יָדִי לַיְלָה נִגְּרָה וְלֹא תָפוּג מֵאֲנָה הִנָּחֵם נַפְשִׁי׃

Ps 77:2[3]: In the day of my trouble I seek the Lord; in the night my hand is stretched out without wearying; my soul refuses to be comforted.

Darkness is also mentioned when the sufferer considers death, suggesting again the cognitive salience of darkness during distress. In Job 10:21–22, descriptions of netherworld darkness are piled up, culminating with even the light there being darkness. Job 17:13 is a simpler parallelism of Sheol with darkness.

בְּטֶרֶם אֵלֵךְ וְלֹא אָשׁוּב אֶל־אֶרֶץ חֹשֶׁךְ וְצַלְמָוֶת׃ אֶרֶץ עֵיפָתָה כְּמוֹ אֹפֶל צַלְמָוֶת וְלֹא סְדָרִים וַתֹּפַע כְּמוֹ־אֹפֶל׃

Job 10:21-22: Before I go—I shall not return!—to the land of darkness and deep shadow, the land of gloom like blackness, of deep shadow without order, where the light is as darkness.[73]

אִם־אֲקַוֶּה שְׁאוֹל בֵּיתִי בַּחֹשֶׁךְ רִפַּדְתִּי יְצוּעָי׃

Job 17:13: If I look for Sheol as my house, if I spread my couch in darkness.

All these verses show a metonymic mapping in which suffering in darkness is a salient part of the author's distressing experience.

8.4.3. Being in Distress is Being in a Dark Place

Moving to conceptual metaphors, the main metaphor is that being in distress is being located in a dark place. First, Psalm 107 depicts those

---

73. Clines, *Job 1–20*, 216.

dwelling in darkness (צַלְמָוֶת, חֹשֶׁךְ) as one of four prototypes of distress elaborated in the psalm.

יֹשְׁבֵי חֹשֶׁךְ וְצַלְמָוֶת אֲסִירֵי עֳנִי וּבַרְזֶל׃

Ps 107:10: Some sat in darkness and in gloom, prisoners in misery and in irons,

יוֹצִיאֵם מֵחֹשֶׁךְ וְצַלְמָוֶת וּמוֹסְרוֹתֵיהֶם יְנַתֵּק

Ps 107:14: He brought them out of darkness and gloom, and broke their bonds asunder.

A dark location is also often ascribed to the wicked or desired for the authors' enemies. Job's friends frequently locate the wicked in darkness, implicitly suggesting that "darkness" appropriately conceptualizes Job's current condition. In Job 15:20–35, Eliphaz uses darkness (verses 22, 23 and 30) for the destination of the wicked in this life (given the context of living in reduced circumstances) and at death. The "day of darkness" (יוֹם־חֹשֶׁךְ) in v. 23 may connote death, causing present anxiety,[74] but if taken with v. 24, the terrifying effect of the day of darkness parallels being overwhelmed by distress (צַר) and anguish (מְצוּקָה),[75] suggesting a day of darkness before death.

לֹא־יַאֲמִין שׁוּב מִנִּי־חֹשֶׁךְ וְצָפוּי הוּא אֱלֵי־חָרֶב׃

Job 15:22: He cannot hope to escape the darkness; he is marked down for the sword.[76]

נֹדֵד הוּא לַלֶּחֶם אַיֵּה יָדַע כִּי־נָכוֹן בְּיָדוֹ יוֹם־חֹשֶׁךְ׃

Job 15:23: They wander abroad for bread, saying, "Where is it?" They know that a day of darkness is ready at hand.

לֹא־יָסוּר מִנִּי־חֹשֶׁךְ יֹנַקְתּוֹ תְּיַבֵּשׁ שַׁלְהָבֶת וְיָסוּר בְּרוּחַ פִּיו׃

Job 15:30: They will not escape from darkness; the flame will dry up their shoots and their blossom will be swept away by the wind.

74. Gordis, *Job*, 164.
75. Clines, *Job 1–20*, 341.
76. Ibid.

Distress and Darkness

In Job 18:5–6 and 18, Bildad's references to darkness more clearly evoke death, especially the end of the family line, with verse 19 suggesting that the darkness of verse 18 is partly about having no descendants to go on giving light in the world. In Job 12:24, Job says God strips leaders of understanding, so that in v. 25 their "groping in the darkness" (יְמַשְׁשׁוּ־חֹשֶׁךְ) expresses both their inability to plan wisely and the consequent distress that befalls them. In each verse darkness is evoked by the most general term, חֹשֶׁךְ.

גַּם אוֹר רְשָׁעִים יִדְעָךְ וְלֹא־יִגַּהּ שְׁבִיב אִשּׁוֹ: אוֹר חָשַׁךְ בְּאָהֳלוֹ וְנֵרוֹ עָלָיו יִדְעָךְ:

> Job 18:5–6: Surely the light of the wicked is put out, and the flame of their fire does not shine. The light is dark in their tent, and the lamp above them is put out.

יֶהְדְּפֻהוּ מֵאוֹר אֶל־חֹשֶׁךְ וּמִתֵּבֵל יְנִדֻּהוּ:

> Job 18:18: They are thrust from light into darkness, and driven out of the world.

יְמַשְׁשׁוּ־חֹשֶׁךְ וְלֹא־אוֹר וַיַּתְעֵם כַּשִּׁכּוֹר:

> Job 12:25: They grope in the dark without light; he makes them stagger like a drunkard.

Within the specific corpus, darkness is sometimes conceived as an independent agent of distress, sometimes as an entity used by other agents. First, sometimes darkness exists without referring to external agents or causes, as in 1QH 17:26–28, paralleling a dark situation (חושך) with a constricted soul and inflicted wound. Similarly, Eliphaz describes Job as overwhelmed by darkness (חֹשֶׁךְ) in Job 22:11. Psalm 88:18[19] concludes the psalm with the word מַחְשָׁךְ, summarizing the whole plight as "darkness." In Job 30:26, the darkness (אֹפֶל) is even given some agency of its own, "coming" (בֹּא) towards Job. This verse gives context for verse 28 (cited above) in which Job is walking "darkly" (קֹדֵר) without sun, demonstrating further that the meaning is not about being dressed in black.

Surrounded by Bitterness

כי מאור מחושך 27 האירותה ל[י . . . מח]ץ מכתי ולמכשולי גבורת פלא ורחוב 28 עולם בצרת נפש[י

> 1QH 17:26–28: For from darkness you make a light shine for [me, . . . the wou]nd inflicted on me, my weakness to wonderful force, the constriction of [my] soul to everlasting expanse.

אוֹ־חֹשֶׁךְ לֹא־תִרְאֶה

> Job 22:11: (Sudden terror overwhelms you) or darkness so that you cannot see.

הִרְחַקְתָּ מִמֶּנִּי אֹהֵב וָרֵעַ מְיֻדָּעַי מַחְשָׁךְ׃

> Ps 88:18[19]: You have caused lover and companion to stay away from me; my close friends—darkness![77]

כִּי טוֹב קִוִּיתִי וַיָּבֹא רָע וַאֲיַחֲלָה לְאוֹר וַיָּבֹא אֹפֶל׃

> Job 30:26: But when I looked for good, evil came; and when I waited for light, darkness came.

Job 23:17 also has darkness as an independent entity, using both חֹשֶׁךְ and אֹפֶל. The Hebrew text is difficult, because of the apparent contradiction between being both not destroyed by the darkness and having darkness covering Job's face. However, the first colon may mean Job has been destroyed by darkness, whether by giving an emphatic meaning for לֹא,[78] or omitting it altogether.[79] Although neither is totally satisfactory, it makes more sense if the darkness annihilating (נִצְמַתִּי) Job conceptualizes his distress, further described as gloom (אֹפֶל) in front of his face. This verse thus gives the greatest agency to darkness.

כִּי־לֹא נִצְמַתִּי מִפְּנֵי־חֹשֶׁךְ וּמִפָּנַי כִּסָּה־אֹפֶל׃

> Job 23:17: For I am annihilated by darkness and thick darkness covers my face.[80]

---

77. Tate, *Psalms*, 394.
78. Gordis, *Job*, 263.
79. Clines, *Job 21–37*, 581.
80. Ibid., 573.

Distress and Darkness

More frequently, the sufferer's dark location results from a premeditating agent. Thus, in Ps 44:19[20], God covered the community in "deathly darkness" (צַלְמָוֶת), whereas in 1QH 13:33 it is the author's enemies wrapping him in the same darkness (וישוכו בעדי בצלמות). In both, darkness has been brought to the petitioner's location.

כִּי דִכִּיתָנוּ בִּמְקוֹם תַּנִּים וַתְּכַס עָלֵינוּ בְצַלְמָוֶת:

Ps 44:19[20]: Yet you crushed us in the place of jackals and covered us with deathly darkness.[81]

ויוספוה לצוקה וישוכו בעדי בצלמות

1QH 13:33: But they have increased the narrowness and have wrapped me in darkness.

In Lam 3:2, the lamenter has been more aggressively forced against his will by God and driven (נהג) into darkness (חֹשֶׁךְ), taken to a new "dark" location. Similarly, in Ps 88:6[7], God has put the petitioner in a different, dark place. The plural form מַחֲשַׁכִּים is sometimes taken as an "intensive plural" translated as "great" or "utter" darkness,[82] but the combination with plural מְצֹלוֹת, consistently translated as "deep places" (rather than great depths) makes the identification as "dark places" more likely. The same word in Ps 143:3 and Lam 3:6 has the enemy or God making the petitioner sit in a dark place. Finally, Job 19:8 has God again as agent, bringing darkness (חֹשֶׁךְ) to Job's paths, obstructing his life journey. Thus, being in a dark place is frequently considered to be the result of an external agent (whether God or enemy), either bringing darkness to the sufferer or taking him to a dark place.

אוֹתִי נָהַג וַיֹּלַךְ חֹשֶׁךְ וְלֹא־אוֹר:

Lam 3:2: He has driven and brought me into darkness without any light.

שַׁתַּנִי בְּבוֹר תַּחְתִּיּוֹת בְּמַחֲשַׁכִּים בִּמְצֹלוֹת:

Ps 88:6[7]: You have put me in the depths of the Pit, in the regions dark and deep.

81. Basson, *Divine*, 162.
82. Tate, *Psalms*, 398; Goldingay, *Psalms* 2:649–50; Keel, *Symbolism*, 65.

Surrounded by Bitterness

כִּי רָדַף אוֹיֵב נַפְשִׁי דִּכָּא לָאָרֶץ חַיָּתִי הוֹשִׁיבַנִי בְמַחֲשַׁכִּים כְּמֵתֵי עוֹלָם:

Ps 143:3: For the enemy has pursued me, crushing my life to the ground, making me sit in darkness like those long dead.

בְּמַחֲשַׁכִּים הוֹשִׁיבַנִי כְּמֵתֵי עוֹלָם:

Lam 3:6: He has made me sit in darkness like the dead of long ago.

אָרְחִי גָדַר וְלֹא אֶעֱבוֹר וְעַל נְתִיבוֹתַי חֹשֶׁךְ יָשִׂים:

Job 19:8: He has walled up my way so that I cannot pass, and he has set darkness upon my paths.

The two words used most commonly are חֹשֶׁךְ and צַלְמָוֶת, and there is no clear evidence of the intensity of darkness being used to evoke the situation's seriousness.

However, various other entailments are highlighted. First, distress conceptualized as darkness coheres tightly with relief conceived as receiving light, as in Ps 18:28[29]. Psalm 43:3 also frames the plea for relief as a request for God to send his light and show the way out from the dark situation of distress and Ps 56:13[14] describes rescue from distress as returning to a state of walking in the light. In Job 11:17, Zophar conceptualizes Job's current distress as darkness, which on his restoration will appear only as morning light, compared to the "midday" light of his renewed life. 1QH 17:26–28 (cited above) also shows relief as light.

כִּי־אַתָּה תָּאִיר נֵרִי יְהוָה אֱלֹהַי יַגִּיהַּ חָשְׁכִּי:

Ps 18:28[29]: It is you who light my lamp; the LORD, my God, lights up my darkness.

שְׁלַח־אוֹרְךָ וַאֲמִתְּךָ הֵמָּה יַנְחוּנִי יְבִיאוּנִי אֶל־הַר־קָדְשְׁךָ וְאֶל־מִשְׁכְּנוֹתֶיךָ:

Ps 43:3: O send out your light and your truth; let them lead me; let them bring me to your holy hill and to your dwelling.

Distress and Darkness

וּמִצָּהֳרַיִם יָקוּם חָלֶד תָּעֻפָה כַּבֹּקֶר תִּהְיֶה׃

Job 11:17: Then your life will be brighter than the noonday; its darkness will be as morning.[83]

כִּי הִצַּלְתָּ נַפְשִׁי מִמָּוֶת הֲלֹא רַגְלַי מִדֶּחִי לְהִתְהַלֵּךְ לִפְנֵי אֱלֹהִים בְּאוֹר הַחַיִּים׃

Ps 56:13[14]: For you have delivered my soul from death, and my feet from falling, so that I may walk before God in the light of life.

Another entailment is the inability to see in the darkness. In Job 22:11 (cited above) the darkness specifically stops Job from seeing (לֹא תִרְאֶה). In Ps 40:12[13], again the psalmist cannot see, as a result of "evils" and "iniquities" (עֲוֹנֹתַי).

כִּי אָפְפוּ־עָלַי רָעוֹת עַד־אֵין מִסְפָּר הִשִּׂיגוּנִי עֲוֹנֹתַי וְלֹא־יָכֹלְתִּי לִרְאוֹת

Ps 40:12[13]: For evils have encompassed me without number; my iniquities have overtaken me, until I cannot see.

Such inability to "see" could evoke lack of understanding, as in English. However, a better interpretation comes through the general event-structure metaphor introduced in section 7.4.5, where voluntary movement maps onto purposeful action. The inability to see hinders voluntary movement, and thus prevents purposeful action. This interpretation is supported by Job 19:8 where darkness covers Job's "paths," hindering movement, and Ps 43:3 where the light shows the path out of distress. Further, darkness "wrapping" (וישוכו בעדי, 1QH 13:33) or "covering" (וַתְּכַס עָלֵינוּ, Ps 44:19[20]) the petitioner also evoke restricted movement as well as sight. Darkness is also part of a restriction to purposeful movement where the petitioner is forced to "sit" (ישב) in darkness (Pss 143:3; 107:10) or contained in a dark pit (Ps 88:6[7]). Thus, darkness metaphors cohere closely with metaphors of constraint and restriction (chapter six), suggesting the inability to see is closely linked to the inability to move, and explaining the salience of imprison-

---

83. Clines, *Job 1–20*, 253, revocalizing תָּעֻפָה to the noun תְּעָפָה.

ment as a prototypical place of darkness, where both these experiences occur together.

These mappings can be summarized as follows:

Person in dark place	→	Person in distressing situation
Agent causing the darkness (either making the place dark, or putting the person in a dark place)	→	Agent causing distress
Inability to see	→	Inability to act purposefully
Provision of light	→	Relief from distress, ability to see and act freely again

8.5. Further Evidence

8.5.1. Generalizations over Polysemy

The primary evidence that this conceptual metaphor is significant for understanding distress comes from generalizations over polysemy. First, several words describe both darkness and distressing experiences. For nouns, חֹשֶׁךְ and צַלְמָוֶת are most common, but אֹפֶל, מַשְׁחוֹר, and קַדְרוּת also occur. For verbs, קדר occurs frequently, but the widest variety is words for impaired vision, including כהה, עשש, חשך, שעע, and דאב, and longer phrases evoking a similar idea: לֹא־תִרְאֶה and וְאוֹר־עֵינַי גַּם־הֵם אֵין אִתִּי. These various nouns, verbs, and phrases all related to impaired vision or darkness demonstrate that this conceptual metaphor is well entrenched in the linguistic system.

8.5.2. Generalizations over Inference Patterns

Second, evidence of structure being mapped to the target domain may come from generalizations over inference patterns. Although this source domain is less structured than the preceding image schemas, it still constrains inferences in the target domain.

First, a "dark" situation is inferred to be negative. Prototypical associations with death, evil, ignorance, imprisonment, and the wicked make it clear that darkness is unequivocally "bad" for the sufferer. No text suggests a possible redeeming value of darkness.

Second, this source domain gives external causation to distress. Often an external agent is responsible for the darkness, but even the darkness itself is outside the person, and thus outside of his or her control. There is no suggestion that the sufferer can do anything about it. This coheres with the prototypical association of darkness with imprisonment by an external agent.

Third, relief from distress is inferred to be light, whether light given to darkened eyes (Ps 13:3[4]), or shining in the darkness surrounding the author (Ps 43:3). This coheres with the associations of darkness with death and the underworld, and light with life. Just as the darkness is externally imposed, the light must come from outside (from God) to transform the situation.

Fourth, impaired vision hinders someone from seeing the way ahead, and thus from progressing along a desired path. When desired for the enemy in Ps 69:23[24], the inability to see means they are unable to follow their plans to harm the petitioner. For the petitioner, however, inability to see and act is a salient feature of distress. The restoration of light would then enable them to see the way ahead.

Fifth, are there reasons why impaired sight is a more salient metaphor for distress than impaired hearing or other senses? References to deaf ears, numbness or inability to taste are rare. First, considering Sweetser's characteristics of sight (section 8.2.1), the ability to perceive at a distance may be significant. Sometimes the petitioner looks for help, but is unable to perceive it (most explicitly in Job 30:26). Even something on the horizon would bring hope, but with weakened eyes or darkness obscuring the view, potential relief cannot be seen. Second, the general ability to control what is within the visual field may be significant, with things outside that field uncontrollable and unknown (for other senses, we may be able to hear, smell, or taste something and still not know what it is). With darkness blocking most of the field of vision there is very little the petitioner can see, and thus very little that he or she can control.

8.5.3. Novel Metaphor

The examples presented covered both conventional and creative expressions, showing that this conceptual metaphor is being actively used by authors.[84] For example, the combination of קדר with הלךְ recurs in different contexts, demonstrating the conventionality of this idiom for "gloomy" emotions. This expression is developed more creatively in Job 30:28, where בְּלֹא חַמָּה intensifies the emotion. Even more innovatively, וּמִפָּנַי כִּסָּה־אֹפֶל (Job 23:17) expresses a similar idea, with more marked syntax and a rarer word for darkness.

8.5.4. Larger Scale Metaphorical Systems

The most obvious larger scale metaphorical system here is the common ancient Near Eastern mapping from light to life and from darkness to death. The mapping is explicit in references to the "light of life" (בְּאוֹר הַחַיִּים) in Ps 56:13[14] and Job 33:30. Conversely, Eccl 6:4–5 equates going to darkness with death (וּבַחֹשֶׁךְ יֵלֵךְ).

However, though darkness metaphors for distress cohere with this larger metaphorical system, it does not mean the biblical authors perceived their experiences of distress as real experiences of death when they position themselves in darkness,[85] since Job 15:20–35 uses darkness for distress that is something other than death itself. Rather, inferences about death and inferences about distress are both constrained by embodied experiences of darkness.

Further, light specifically in the eyes signifies renewed energy, as when Jonathan's eyes brighten (רְאוּ־נָא כִּי־אֹרוּ עֵינַי, 1 Sam 14:29), or accompanies joy, as in Prov 15:30 (מְאוֹר־עֵינַיִם יְשַׂמַּח־לֵב 'the light of the eyes rejoices the heart'). In the thanksgiving of Ezra 9:8, making the eyes light (לְהָאִיר עֵינֵינוּ) again expresses renewed positive emotion. These verses give a larger metaphorical framework for the dimmed eyes of sorrow and negative emotion.

---

84. However, there are no conventional expressions in narrative texts.
85. As argued by Pedersen, *Israel*, 464–67.

8.5.5. Non-verbal Realizations

Non-verbal realizations of a conceptual metaphor give further evidence of its entrenchment. Here, the actions of the distressed provide non-verbal realizations, with dark or dirty clothing or dust and ashes darkening the body also linking darkness to the experience of distress. For example, the king of Nineveh responds to impending disaster (Jonah 3:6) by covering (כָּסָה) himself in sackcloth (שַׂק) and sitting in ashes (אֵפֶר). Sackcloth was typically dark,[86] being used as a simile for the darkened sun in Revelation 6:12. It is worn on hearing distressing news, often in mourning (Gen 37:34), or in remorse and petition (1 Kgs 21:27), but also in more general distress (as when Hezekiah hears Sennacherib's threat in 2 Kgs 19:1, or Mordecai hears of Haman's plots in Esth 4:1). Thus, beyond mourning and penitence, it represents "the pain, grief, sorrow, or lack of or loss of hope, or the coming of tragedy."[87] Disfiguring oneself with ashes is also more than a mourning rite, being a reaction to more general tragedy, as when Tamar puts ashes on her head after being abused by Amnon (2 Sam 13:19). Ezekiel 27:30 has even more comprehensive covering with dark materials, with dust (עָפָר) being put on the head and then "rolling" (יִתְפַּלָּשׁוּ) in ashes to lament over Tyre. All of these actions darken the sufferer, removing the color that could be associated with glory, joy or honor.[88] Although these expressions do not necessarily directly motivate the metaphorical language of distress, they certainly cohere with it, again linking darkness to grief or distress.

8.6. Universality and Variation

8.6.1. Variation within Source and Target Domain

There are several comparisons between the Hebrew use of the darkness source domain and the examples listed earlier. First, a word prototypically describing "bad weather" consistently conceptualizes the

---

86. Cohen, "שַׂק."
87. Carpenter and Grisanti, "שַׂק."
88. Ibid.

physiological and emotional aspects of distress, as in English *gloomy*, Finnish *synkkä*, Japanese *kurai*, and Hebrew קדר. This conceptualization occurs in both climates where the weather is frequently overcast and from a Palestinian climate where an overcast sky is far rarer, and may bring much needed rain. A possible explanation comes from the negative physiological response to daytime darkness, mentioned earlier. However, this mapping is not as elaborated in Hebrew as in English or Japanese. The petitioner never sits under dark clouds; nor are there other references to meteorological conditions.

Second, regarding prototypes and entailments, whereas in English the prototypical dark place of depression is under a dark or cloudy sky, the prototypical dark location in Hebrew is imprisonment. In English, the darkness of black clouds, even though beyond individual control, does not result from a premeditating agent. The best solution is waiting for sunny skies to return, mapped onto an attitude in depression of waiting for situations to change. In Hebrew, being in a dark prison is also beyond individual control, but is the result of a premeditating agent, and waiting will not bring improvement. Sufferers are thus more urgent to find a way out of the darkness. Using צַלְמָוֶת for darkness also increases the salience of the prototypical association with death, further increasing the seriousness of a predicament conceptualized this way.

Third, another difference relates to intensity. In the contemporary examples, darkness is understood as graded amounts of light, so an intensity scale maps to experiences of distress. Life can be "very gloomy" or, in Finnish, *hyvin synkkä*. In Hebrew, possibly because darkness is understood as an entity, distinct to light, it does not have a natural scalar quality, and cannot easily express intensity of distress.

Fourth, the prototypical target domains differ between English and Hebrew. McMullen and Conway considered how darkness structured English depression. The target domain in Hebrew certainly overlaps with English depression, so that walking around gloomily (קדר with הלך) could be considered a metaphor of depression. However, scenarios also include verbal attack (Psalms 42–43) and sickness (Psalm 38), atypical for English depression. Certainly, this target domain reflects a negative emotional state, but it is more general, and often more active, than the long term despondency of English *depression*.

Distress and Darkness

Fifth, Hebrew and Mesopotamian examples have different entailments, despite superficial similarities. For example, both corpora describe being "wrapped" or "covered" in darkness. However, in the Akkadian texts, prototypical associations of darkness with demons means someone wrapped in darkness is particularly vulnerable to their attacks, and thus to sickness. There is no evidence of this association in Hebrew, with darkness firmly in God's control. This difference also affects the solutions looked for. In the Hebrew corpus, God's total control directs authors to complain to him for bringing darkness or to ask him to bring light into it, knowing that he is able to do this. In the Akkadian polytheistic context, where darkness is seen as the locus of forces in opposition to the gods associated with light, there is a need to resort to magic and other methods of resolving the problems of darkness.

8.6.2. Variation in Linguistic Expression

Alongside variation in the cognitive structure of a conceptual metaphor, linguistic expression may differ. As in previous chapters, different highlighted parts of the metaphor, different degrees of conventionalization and differences in syntactic expression will all be considered.

First, the most highlighted part of the Hebrew metaphor is darkened eyes, potentially representing the inability to see a way out of a situation. Although this is well elaborated in Hebrew, it is not used at all in English mappings from darkness to distress. From the opposite perspective, an important part of the English mapping is scalarity in the source domain. Situations of emotional distress can be understood as clouds getting "blacker," or "thicker," or a mental state becoming "increasingly gloomy," but this conceptualization of worsening distress is absent from Hebrew.

Second, conceptual metaphors differ cross-linguistically in the conventionalization of the linguistic expressions based on them. Comparing the English expression of *feeling gloomy* with the Hebrew example of קדר with הלך, both are relatively conventional and motivate more creative phrases like "sitting under a black cloud" (English) or having "darkness cover your face" (Hebrew). However, whereas in English "feeling gloomy" could be used in various registers of discourse,

קדר is restricted to poetic texts. In fact, no examples of the darkness source domain have been found conceptualizing distress in Hebrew narrative texts.[89] Thus, this source domain is more conventional for structuring distress in English than Hebrew. This result also contrasts with the constraint and force metaphors considered in previous chapters and the taste metaphors in the next chapter, all of which have conventional realizations in narrative and poetic texts.

Third, regarding syntactic expression, English evokes darkness using adjectives and adverbs ("gloomy," "gloomily") and more complex phrases with nouns prototypical of dark places ("sitting under a dark cloud"). Intensity can be marked by quantifiers like "very." Few examples use verbs. In Hebrew, קדר can be used as a participle or in the qal indicative (Jeremiah 8:21) to evoke the darkness source domain in a description of distress, so that verbal expression of this source domain is more common than in English. Where nouns are used they are usually general nouns for darkness (אֹפֶל, חֹשֶׁךְ) rather than words for dark places, although several verses do use צַלְמָוֶת, a darkness prototypically associated with death.

8.7. Summary

In summary, this chapter demonstrates a widespread tendency to map embodied experiences of darkness to situations of emotional, psychological, or physical distress, resulting in conceptual metaphors in Akkadian, Egyptian, English, Finnish, Japanese, and Hebrew. The counterexample of Bamu shows that this is not an absolute universal. In Hebrew, conceptual metaphors of being in a darkened location cohere with conceptual metonymies in which the lively "light of the eyes" is darkened.

Although this metaphorical conceptualization is not as well entrenched as those considered in other chapters (since there is no conventional expression used in narrative texts), there are nevertheless a significant number of both conventional and creative uses of this

---

89. The closest examples are where the "brightness" of the face changes (וְזִיוֹהִי שָׁנַיִן) in the Aramaic sections of Daniel (5.6, 9, 10b and 7.28) (Gruber, *Aspects*, 360–61).

primary metaphor within the specific corpus. The metaphor is likely grounded in the culturally embodied experiences of bad things happening at night, of the darkness of physical graves, and in the physiology of the eyes during times of grief. It leads to inferences for the situation of distress regarding the deathly seriousness of the situation, the inability to control the situation, and the blockage for the experiencer in fulfilling his purposes.

9

Distress and the BAD TASTE Primary Metaphor

"He has filled me with bitter herbs, he has sated me with wormwood"—Lam 3:15

9.1. Introduction

This final chapter investigates the primary metaphor associating distress with "bad" tastes, but also the wider domain of ingesting harmful food. Within Cognitive Linguistics, taste has received less attention than other senses, perhaps because (along with smell) the perceived objects disappear, making these senses "incapable of giving knowledge in Western metaphysics."[1] Nevertheless, taste provides a productive source domain for understanding distress.

---

1. Borthwick, "Olfaction," 127. Chinese, however, does use taste to understand cognition, Ye, "Taste."

9.2. Establishing the Source Domain

9.2.1. Physiological / Universal Factors

First, three aspects of taste can be explored from a universal perspective: human physiology; differences from other senses; and the typology of language describing tastes.

a) Physiology

First, "taste" physiology includes a complex interaction of perceptions. One aspect is the ability of taste cells to detect different chemicals, including the qualities called *salt* (sodium chloride), *sweet* (primarily glucose), *bitter* (many toxic substances, including quinine), and *sour* (acid). A fifth distinct "taste" is also detectable,[2] characteristic of seaweed broth[3] and named *umami* (the best English term is *savory*). The absence from conventional English shows that one cannot assume correlations between physiology and language, with even sense perception being culturally and linguistically channeled.

The variety of compounds with specific tastes differs. *Salt* sensation depends specifically on sodium chloride, and *umami* on monosodium glutamate or aspartate. However, many different stimuli evoke a uniform *bitter* taste,[4] warning the body of potentially harmful toxins and including structurally unrelated chemicals in citrus fruit, tea, red wine, coffee, dark chocolate, broccoli, cabbage, Brussels sprouts, cucumbers, almonds, and apricots.[5] Further, the concentrations required to perceive different tastes vary. Bitter compounds are detectable at concentrations a fraction that of detectable sucrose solutions, and their taste persists longer.[6]

Olfaction also contributes significantly to "taste," as do non-chemical perceptions analogous to the sensory perception elsewhere on the

---

2. Chandrashekar et al., "Receptors," 288.

3. Ikeda, "Seasonings," 847.

4. Although the mechanism is debated: Mueller et al., "Logic," 225; Caicedo and Roper, "Taste."

5. Drewnowski and Gomez-Carneros, "Phytonutrients."

6. Ibid., 1425.

skin of heat, cold, and pain, made salient in English words like *hot* and *spicy*. All these sensations are relevant when considering any linguistic domain of taste vocabulary.

b) Difference from Other Senses

Backhouse lists four areas where taste perception differs from other senses,[7] which may influence reasoning about distress. First, as noted above, the receptor systems are very *complex*, offering many different parameters that language could make salient.

Second, taste perception is *proximate*. Items need to contact the subject to be perceived. Further, this contact alters the object. An object cannot be tasted unless it dissolves and becomes part of the body.[8] Thus, it cannot be tasted again, whereas one can look repeatedly at an object without changing it at all. Anthropologically, integrating the outside world into the body may be why emotional responses are integral to taste.[9] Linguistically, "the agent in eating and drinking serves as a strong image of 'internalization.'"[10]

Third, "taste" is more *cultural* than vision. Things that should be tasted, and whether they are "good" or "bad," reflect cultural norms. Cultural norms can be transmitted through "disgust" faces, signaling to infants cultural aversion to specific foods.[11]

Fourth, taste inherently involves *evaluation*. Sweet and umami tastes are universally pleasant, alerting the body to nutritious foods; bitter taste is universally unpleasant, alerting the body to harmful substances.[12] This association is present from birth, depending on neural connections within the lower brain stem.[13] Further, the positive tastes

---

7. Backhouse, *Taste*, 12–14.
8. Borthwick, "Olfaction," 130.
9. Rozin et al., "Disgust," 68.
10. Newman, "Overview," 8.
11. Schiefenhövel, "Taste," 62.
12. Salty and sour tastes are more ambiguous. Small amounts are usually pleasant, but become unpleasant as concentration increases. However, some populations actually find sour tastes increasingly pleasant as concentration increases (Moskowitz et al., "Differences").
13. Smith and Margolskee, "Sense."

(sweet and umami), share a common receptor repertoire, whereas the receptors for bitter taste are different.[14] Thus even physiological differences distinguish unequivocally positive and negative tastes.

These characteristics of taste may constrain inferences in other domains. For example, the negative value of bitter taste is preserved in the English adverb *bitterly*. It functions as an intensifier, but only with verbs describing a negatively valued action, such as *attacked, criticized, jealous, resented,* or *divided*.[15]

c) Linguistic Typology

Given these universal physiological features, how universally are they reflected in language? For example, umami perception is not yet conventionalized in English. In general, taste words reflect prototypical substances and cultural uses, rather than just chemical composition,[16] although the physiology explains some universal features.

First, research suggests "all languages possess at least two basic terms within the domain of tongue-taste, one having a denotational range which includes sweetness, the other taking in disagreeable taste qualities."[17] The division of tastes between these and other words varies cross-culturally. Several languages categorize the "good" taste of sweet and salt together, and may have only one word for sour or bitter tastes, suggesting that the distinction between sour and bitter tastes is less salient than their unpalatability in these cultures.[18] Conversely, some languages have three words for bitter and sour tastes. In Spanish, *amargo* prototypically describes black coffee, quinine, and beer, *ácido* citric acid, limes, vinegar, and unripe fruits, whereas *agrio* is linked with orange peel.[19]

---

14. Chandrashekar et al., "Receptors," 289–90.
15. Popova, "Synaesthesia," 413.
16. As in the functional (rather than chemical) definitions of "salt" and "sugar" in Goddard and Wierzbicka, "Analyses," 771.
17. Backhouse, *Taste*, 166.
18. Ibid., 6–7.
19. Ibid., 12.

Second, the relationship of words describing taste "quality" ("sourness," "sweetness," or "bitterness") to those "evaluating" taste (such as "good," "bad," or "tasteless") differs typologically. Backhouse suggests three systems: first, a generalized system, in which the same words describe good and sweet tastes versus words for bad and bitter tastes; second, a differentiated system, in which evaluative words (good, bad) are thoroughly distinct from descriptive words (bitter, sweet); and finally an intermediate system where good and sweet tastes may have the same word, but bad tastes and bitter tastes have different expressions.[20] Whereas English officially has the second system, Section 9.2.2 shows Hebrew is more like the first system.

However, the English situation is different in conventional usage, often confusing the qualities "sour" and "bitter,"[21] with citric acids commonly termed "bitter" rather than "sour." This suggests that even in English *bitter* commonly describes any unpleasant taste, as people do not experience enough of the specific scientific "bitter" taste to recognize it.[22]

For Hebrew, this study shows typological comparisons for one, two, or three terms for tastes in the "bitter" and "sour" area, and also alerts to the possibility of words meaning just "unpleasant" taste, rather than a specific chemical taste description.

9.2.2. Culture-specific Factors

Next, which different tastes are recognized in Classical Hebrew, what are their prototypes and how are they valued? Many foodstuffs were available. Specifically, sweet dates, figs, and honey were all known. Mesopotamian shade gardens were used to grow cucumbers (which easily become bitter-tasting), turnips, peas, beans, chickpeas, garlic, leeks, lettuces, and melons, as well as more powerful herbs such as cumin, coriander, mustard, fennel, watercress, mint, rosemary, and fenugreek.[23] Walnuts and almonds were also cultivated, also having potentially bitter

20. Ibid., 168.
21. Robinson, "Misuse"; O'Mahony et al., "Confusion."
22. Backhouse, *Taste*, 11.
23. Renfrew, "Vegetables," 192–93.

tastes.[24] Bread was fermented overnight to create sourdough leaven, and beer and wine were produced.[25] Sheep were kept for milk, which could be soured to make dairy products.[26] Salt was also a well-known commodity. Relevant roots for the tastes of these substances include מתק, מרר, מלח, and חמץ.

מתק may imitate lips smacking in pleasure,[27] and is prototypically associated with דְּבַשׁ, which may be a date jam,[28] but parallels suggest honey is more likely. Honey was the only available sweetener,[29] hence its importance. Alongside clearly sweet substances, מתק describes generally pleasant, or palatable, tastes. Thus, the water at Marah changes from being "bitter" (מָרִים) to "potable" (וַיִּמְתְּקוּ). Similarly, in Prov 9:17, stolen waters are described with יִמְתָּקוּ, more likely evoking a "good" taste than a scientifically "sweet" one. These suggest Hebrew has a general linguistic system, using the same word for a "good" evaluation as well as the taste description "sweet."

"Salt" is מֶלַח, with cognates across all the Semitic languages showing its significance in these cultures.[30] Job 6:6 shows it adding flavor to "tasteless" food (הֲיֵאָכֵל תָּפֵל מִבְּלִי־מֶלַח, 'is tasteless food eaten without salt?'). Salt has negative associations (making land barren, Jer 17:6–8) and positive associations (rubbed on a newborn child, Ezekiel 16:4), and is also mentioned in connection with sacrifice. However, aside from Job 6:6, salt is nowhere connected with food.

חמץ is similar to English "sour," primarily describing leavened bread (made from sourdough).[31] The noun חֹמֶץ further describes vinegar, made by fermenting wine or beer. This "vinegar" made a tasty dip (Ruth 2:14), but the unpleasant effect on the teeth was also recognized (Prov 10:26). The prototypical association with sourdough and vinegar suggests fermentation is more salient here than for English "sour."

24. Ibid., 192.
25. Ibid., 195–97.
26. Hesse, "Husbandry," 212.
27. Kedar-Kopfstein, "מָתַק," 103.
28. Gruber, "Life," 639.
29. Fritz, *City*, 184.
30. Eising, "מֶלַח," 331.
31. Kellermann, "חמץ," 489.

Finally, the sensation evoked by מרר is most significant, usually glossed as "bitter."[32] The Akkadian cognate describes unpalatable breast milk, water, wine, seeds of some plants, dates, and gall.[33] The noun *marratu* describes the sea, a body of undrinkable water, suggesting no distinction between "salt" and "bitter" taste. In Ugaritic, *mrr* describes the bitter taste of almonds,[34] and *šmrr* snake venom, the form suggesting "causing bitterness."[35] In Hebrew, מרר is opposite to מָתוֹק in Isa 5:20, and in Prov 27:7 everything "bitter" is sweet to the hungry (כָּל־מַר מָתוֹק). Deuteronomy 32:32 ascribes this taste to grape clusters produced by a rebellious Israel. At the Passover, the Israelites ate unleavened bread and מְרֹרִים and in Isa 24:9, strong drink becomes bitter to those tasting it (יֵמַר שֵׁכָר לְשֹׁתָיו). Thus, מרר covers prototypical substances overlapping with those having the scientific English taste "bitter," including bad grapes, leafy vegetables, and fermented drink. These verses also show the changeability of taste judgments, with strong drink becoming bitter in Isaiah, and bitter things becoming sweet in Proverbs.

However, the adjective מָרִים describing Marah's undrinkable waters suggests a more general taste evaluation as "bad." This also helps interpret Numbers 5, where a wife drinks "bitter" waters that bring a curse (מֵי הַמָּרִים הַמְאָרֲרִים), which when they enter her may be "bitter" for her (וּבָאוּ בָהּ הַמַּיִם הַמְאָרֲרִים לְמָרִים). This is more understandable if it means "harmful" rather than merely "bitter" tasting. These examples again suggest that Hebrew has a general system merging taste and evaluation together, so the word for something tasting "bitter" also describes substances that are "bad" or "harmful."

The Ugaritic verb *mr* (parallel to *brk* 'bless') has confused analysis of Hebrew מרר, suggesting it means "strong" in places.[36] However, Pardee's comprehensive analysis shows the primary meaning of bad, "bitter" taste throughout the Bible. When used with נֶפֶשׁ, no examples evoke "strength" as a permanent state of enabling power, but only as a transitory, provoked state, where the "strength" results from the frus-

32. Ringgren and Fabry, "מרר," 16.
33. Pardee, "mrr," 252–53.
34. Ibid., 256.
35. Pardee, "Venom," 408.
36. For example, Kutler, "Case," Hamilton, "מָרַר."

tration or "bitterness" that מַר is signaling.³⁷ Similarly, when describing weapons or words, this root more likely evokes the bad, harmful associations of "bitter" taste, rather than being a separate homonym equivalent to English "strong."

A final semantic link is to gall and venom, specifically through the nouns מְרֵרָה and מְרוֹרָה (Job 16:13, 20:14, and 15). In Akkadian, these relate to the conceptualization that vipers "spit gall" (*martu*).³⁸ Pardee concludes that gall, a corrosive and poisonous substance used to tip arrows, was identified with snakes' poison, and so words for "gall" became used for poison more generally.³⁹ This association of venom and bitter taste through מרר motivates the inclusion of snakebite and poison below.

9.3. Comparative Data on Emotion Language and the BAD TASTE Metaphor

9.3.1. Contemporary Cross-Linguistic Comparisons

Contemporary comparisons come from English, Finnish, Hausa, and Guhu-Samane, a non-Austronesian language from Papua New Guinea.

First, in English, tastes can describe people as *sweet*, *sour*, or *bitter*. A sweet person prototypically displays admirable qualities, such as kindness or thoughtfulness, whereas sour and bitter people are viewed negatively. A sour person is unpleasant to encounter, but usually describes a short-lived disposition. Being bitter is more commonly a long-term character trait, often attributed to perceived harm from others, so that *I'm not bitter* means one is not allowing a grievance to have a lasting effect. A *bitter* person experiences a longer emotion that penetrates deeper into the character than someone *upset* or *angry*.

Several embodied experiences guide inferences here. First, nutritious foods can become unpleasant or toxic over time. Milk turns sour, cucumbers become bitter. Thus, somebody can *turn sour* or *become bitter*, but "becoming sweet" is less conventional. Second, something

---

37. Pardee, "mrr," 259.
38. Ibid., 254.
39. Pardee, "Venom," 415–16.

turned sour may still be palatable (like yoghurt), whereas something that has become bitter is usually inedible. Thus a sour person may yet be redeemable, whereas a bitter person's whole character has potentially irreversibly changed to something toxic. Other substances are naturally bitter, explaining why bitterness seems more intrinsic to someone's character than sourness, which often results from a process (like wine to vinegar or milk to yoghurt). Thus, the main meaning foci of English bitter taste are its negative connotations, its harmfulness, its persistence and its association with intrinsic properties.

Second, Finnish has several words for negative tastes.[40] *Hapan* describes acidic substances including sour milk, lemons, wine, tart apples, and bread made from sourdough. *Karvas* describes gooseberries, bitter almonds, dark chocolate, and Epsom salt. *Kirpeä* describes lemons, orange peel, and other citrus fruit, but also things sensed as "sharp" by smell, touch, or hearing, including spicy food. *Kitkerä* and *katkera* evoke especially negative tastes, the former more for tastes of substances, prototypically linked to bitter liquor, but also quinine or very bitter (undrinkable) coffee, the latter for emotions and situations.

These words conceptualize emotions, dispositions and distressing situations. A *karvas* experience might include losing everything, a disappointment, or a grievous event. Such experiences may cause someone to become *katkera*. A *katkera* condition is also often caused by others perceived to have treated the subject badly. As with English *bitterness*, this is prototypically a long-term character disposition. *Hapan*, conversely, more often describes someone's facial expression. Thus, a generally happy person may sometimes have a *hapan* expression, whereas a generally *katkera* person would show greater outbursts of their bitterness. *Hapan* and *katkera* differ in intensity in the taste domain, so that something tasting *hapan* may still be edible whereas something *kitkerä* is really unpleasant. This intensity difference maps onto character, so that someone *hapan* is in a less serious condition than a *katkera* person.

Third, Hausa provides interesting comparisons for verbs of eating (*ci*) and drinking (*shaa*).[41] Whereas eating conceptualizes agentive roles of overcoming or controlling something (like winning a war), drinking

---

40. This Finnish language information comes from SIL colleagues Pekka and Maiju Laihia, Tomas Kolkka, Kaius Sinnemäki, and Katri Linnasalo.

41. Jaggar and Buba, "Extensions."

expresses affected roles, undergoing experiences. Thus it is natural to say "they are drinking trouble," *sunàa shân wàhalàa*,⁴² with this use further evoking frequency and regularity. These entailments of drinking as opposed to eating reflect the unbounded nature of substances like water, and the relatively unobstructed ingestion associated with drinking.⁴³ Thus, drinking maps particularly onto the experience of negative emotional states over which the experiencer has little control, since there is "minimal physical manipulation" in the physical act of drinking.⁴⁴

Finally, in Guhu Samane, two words evoke potentially negative tastes. *Qaa* describes the taste of citrus fruit and ginger, something like "powerful" tastes in English. *Togo* describes the more specifically bitter taste of quinine or pawpaw seeds. Eating something *togo* may stimulate vomiting, whereas something *qaa* would not. Both of these words collocate with *qupa*, "heart." *Qupa qaa* may describe someone going through difficulties, or someone with just a sore throat. By contrast, *qupa togo* only describes someone going through difficult life experiences, such as a spouse's death. These also contrast with the more generic phrase, *qupa qanga*, a "bad" heart, normally associated with an anger scenario.

These examples offer several features to compare with Hebrew. Are taste descriptions applied to body parts, as in Guhu Samane? Are words for distinct taste experiences used to describe different emotional or psychological states, as in English and Finnish, indicating the intensity, seriousness or harmfulness of the situation? Do verbs of eating and drinking suggest different perspectives on life experiences, as in Hausa?

9.3.2. Ancient Near Eastern Comparisons

Turning to ancient Near Eastern comparisons, similar expressions in both Egypt and Mesopotamia link negative experiences to tasting bitter substances.

In Egypt, the Shipwrecked Sailor states "how joyful is one who relates what he has tasted (*dp*) after the bitter things (*ḥwt mrw*) have

---

42. Ibid., 232.
43. Newman, *Eating*, xi.
44. Jaggar and Buba, "Extensions," 241.

passed,"[45] with the "bitter" things referring to his negative experiences. Similarly, a Coffin Text reads, "I do not taste a bitter (that is, unpleasant) thing."[46] Both use the expression *dp ḫt mr* in the idiomatic sense of "experience an unpleasant affair."[47] Significantly here, a verb for "taste" (*dp*) is used for experiencing life events.

In Akkadian, the root *marāru*, cognate with Hebrew מרר, describes distressing experiences. In the vassal treaty of Esarhaddon, one line reads, "Just as (this) gallbladder is bitter (*martu marratuun*), so may you, your wives, your sons, (and) your daughters be bitter (*marrakunu*) towards each other."[48] This links the gall bladder and "bitter" taste, and explicitly links both with negative family relationships in some kind of ritual. Another religious text states that "they (the demons) seized my mouth and made my tongue bitter (*úmariru*)"[49] using bitterness to conceptualize sickness, and showing the potential agency of demons. Further, "illnesses like jaundice could also be caused by other external factors like *imtu* and *martu*, the poisonous saliva dripping from the mouths of angry gods and demons."[50] Finally, the statement, "You made mouths very bitter (*tumarriram*) toward / against me"[51] shows people can be bitter towards others.

Again, these texts suggest comparisons with Hebrew. What agents can cause bitterness? Do verbs for eating conceptualize experiencing events, as in Egyptian? Is gall the prototypical bitter substance, or something else?

---

45. 'The Shipwrecked Sailor,' 124, cited in Ward, "MR," 358.
46. Cited in Ward, "MR," 358.
47. Ibid.
48. Cited in Pardee, "mrr," 253.
49. Cited in Pardee, "mrr," 253.
50. Van der Toorn, *Sin*, 68–69.
51. Pardee, "mrr," 253.

9.4. Presentation and Analysis of Hebrew Mappings

9.4.1. Experiencing Distress is Experiencing Bitterness in the Body

This section investigates texts where tastes are localized within the person. Most commonly, מרר and נֶפֶשׁ are associated, with various syntactic expressions showing it is more than just a fixed idiom.[52] In Job 7:11 and 10:1, Job insists he will still speak "in the bitterness of his soul" (בְּמַר נַפְשִׁי). In Job 3:20, he includes himself among those with bitter souls (מָרֵי נָפֶשׁ). The parallels include having a "constrained spirit" (בְּצַר רוּחִי) or being in "misery" (עָמֵל), suggesting Job is goaded more by psychic torment than physical pain.[53] Job 21:25 has reversed syntax, for those dying with a bitter soul (בְּנֶפֶשׁ מָרָה), never having "eaten good things" (וְלֹא־אָכַל בַּטּוֹבָה). In Job 27:2, the hiphil attributes Job's bitterness to God. Outside Job, 1QH 13:12 also attributes bitterness to the soul, with yet another syntactic variant (מרורי נפשי). Finally, Hezekiah describes his bitter soul (מַר נַפְשִׁי) in Isa 38:15, describing the "negative physical and psychological state . . . occasioned by the threat of imminent death and by his afflictions."[54]

אֲדַבְּרָה בְּצַר רוּחִי אָשִׂיחָה בְּמַר נַפְשִׁי׃

Job 7:11: I will speak in the anguish of my spirit; I will complain in the bitterness of my soul.

נָקְטָה נַפְשִׁי בְּחַיָּי אֶעֶזְבָה עָלַי שִׂיחִי אֲדַבְּרָה בְּמַר נַפְשִׁי׃

Job 10:1: I loathe my life; I will give free utterance to my complaint; I will speak in the bitterness of my soul.

לָמָּה יִתֵּן לְעָמֵל אוֹר וְחַיִּים לְמָרֵי נָפֶשׁ׃

Job 3:20: Why is light given to one in misery, and life to the bitter in soul?

---

52. Contra Westermann, "נֶפֶשׁ," 752.
53. Clines, *Job 1-20*, 188.
54. Barré, *Lord*, 152.

זֶה יָמוּת בְּעֶצֶם תֻּמּוֹ כֻּלּוֹ שַׁלְאֲנַן וְשָׁלֵיו: עֲטִינָיו מָלְאוּ חָלָב וּמֹחַ
עַצְמוֹתָיו יְשֻׁקֶּה: וְזֶה יָמוּת בְּנֶפֶשׁ מָרָה וְלֹא־אָכַל בַּטּוֹבָה:

Job 21:23–25: One dies in full prosperity, being wholly at ease and secure, his loins full of milk and the marrow of his bones moist. Another dies in bitterness of soul, never having tasted of good.

וְשַׁדַּי הֵמַר נַפְשִׁי:

Job 27:2: . . . and the Almighty, who has made my soul bitter.

כי בצרת נפשי לא עזבתני ושועתי שמעתה במרורי נפשי

1QH 13:12: For in the distress of my soul you did not desert me, you heard my call in the bitterness of my soul.

אֶדַּדֶּה כָל־שְׁנוֹתַי עַל־מַר נַפְשִׁי:

Isa 38:15: Must I wander about all my years because of the bitterness of my soul?[55]

מרר and נֶפֶשׁ are also collocated in narrative, providing concrete instantiations. Hannah's barrenness and Peninnah's provocation made her soul bitter (הִיא מָרַת נָפֶשׁ), driving her to cry to God (1 Sam 1:10). After the Shunammite's son dies, Elisha recognizes her soul is bitter "to her" (נַפְשָׁהּ מָרָה־לָהּ, 2 Kgs 4:27). The men gathering around David in 1 Sam 22:2 are "under pressure" (כָּל־אִישׁ מָצוֹק), those in debt, and those with a bitter soul (כָּל־אִישׁ מַר־נֶפֶשׁ), with the parallels suggesting these men have experienced some external difficulty (similar to pressure or debt), rather than being "strong" warriors.[56] In 1 Sam 30:6, מָרָה נֶפֶשׁ describes those wanting to stone David after the Amalekites raided Ziklag and took their wives and children. Here a specific external distressing situation provokes a dangerous emotional and psychological state. Again, in 2 Sam 17:8, David's men are מָרֵי נֶפֶשׁ after fleeing from Absalom. The previous word, גִּבֹּרִים ("heroes") could suggest this phrase refers to strong warriors.[57] However, the following phrase, כְּדֹב

---

55. Barré, *Lord*, 151–52.
56. Kutler claims this "can only refer to warriors" (Kutler, "Case," 113).
57. Ibid., 112–13.

שַׁכּוּל בַּשָּׂדֶה 'like a bear robbed of her cubs in the field', is more important, qualifying the description. Such a bear is not "stronger" than others, but has been provoked (by stolen cubs), producing a dangerous, emotional state. David's men were similarly provoked by Absalom's rebellion, separation from family and taunting on the road.

Proverbs 31:6 recommends wine for bitter souls (מָרֵי נָפֶשׁ), paralleled with those who are "poor" (רָשׁ) and need to forget their "misery" (עֲמָלוֹ). Finally, Judg 18:25 describes the Danites who might attack Micah as אֲנָשִׁים מָרֵי נֶפֶשׁ. There is little contextual evidence to clarify this description, possibly evoking strong "warriors" as Kutler argues,[58] but equally that they are in a dangerous emotional state, provoked either by their hardship of having no territory allotted to them (18:1), or more immediately by Micah and his neighbors (18:22). The comparisons above suggest the phrase describes their emotional and psychological state, not their innate strength.

These scenarios outline a script for the condition designated by מרר with נֶפֶשׁ. In each scenario, emotional, physical, or psychological distress results from experiencing negatively viewed life events, usually at the hands of others (being mocked or hard pressed, living in poverty, having family taken away, the death of a loved one). Thus, it typically "depicts a provoked state of distress, frustration, and anger,"[59] expressing "the emotional response to a destructive, heart-crushing situation."[60] However, "anger" is not always involved (neither Hannah nor Hezekiah are prototypically "angry") and the destructive situation is almost always caused by others.

Almost always, this state leads to action, either physical or verbal. Hannah calls to God, Job speaks in bitterness, such people come to David, and the likelihood of violent action makes such men dangerous for Micah. Thus מַר־נֶפֶשׁ is not typical despondency or depression,[61] both characterized by inaction. This tendency to action may be inferred from the desire to eject bitter tasting substances from the mouth, or to eat something else to mask the taste. Giving alcohol to solve the prob-

58. Ibid., 113.
59. Pardee, "mrr," 259.
60. Hamilton, "מָרַר."
61. Argued by Barré, *Lord*, 152.

lems of a "bitter soul" in Prov 31:6 hints at masking the bitter taste, a non-verbal realization of this inference.

As נֶפֶשׁ can refer to the throat, embodied motivation may come from bitter gastric acid rising into the throat, or possibly from the bitter taste of tears.[62] Further, the נֶפֶשׁ is associated with hunger and thirst, giving another relation to food.[63] However, in Ps 106:33, bitter taste is attributed to Moses' spirit (רוּחַ), showing this is not restricted to the throat. The hiphil shows people as the agents causing bitterness, again describing a provoked emotional state causing Moses to speak strongly.

כִּי־הִמְרוּ אֶת־רוּחוֹ וַיְבַטֵּא בִּשְׂפָתָיו׃

> Ps 106:33: They had made him so bitter that he spoke with temerity.[64]

Esau's wives also provoke a "bitter spirit" (וַתִּהְיֶיןָ מֹרַת רוּחַ, Gen 26:35), presumably causing distress to his parents, as for מַר נֶפֶשׁ above, rather than making them harbor resentment, as for an English "bitter spirit."

The "heart" (לֵב) is a further locus of bad taste sensations. In Ps 73:21, the heart is fermenting like vinegar (יִתְחַמֵּץ). As this use of חמץ is so rare, one cannot claim more than that this shows another word for bad taste applied to the interior during distress.

כִּי יִתְחַמֵּץ לְבָבִי

> Ps 73:21: When my heart was as sour as vinegar . . .[65]

Elsewhere, references to toxic substances in a distressed person do not specify particular body parts. Most common is מרר with the preposition לְ, to give מַר לִי, for example. This occurs in Isa 38:17 and in Lamentations 1:4, attributed to Jerusalem, expressing that bad things have happened to the subject.

הִנֵּה לְשָׁלוֹם מַר־לִי מָר

> Isa 38:17: Surely it was for my welfare that I had great bitterness.

---

62. Pardee, "mrr," 259.
63. Seebass, "נֶפֶשׁ," 505–6.
64. Allen, *Psalms 101–150*, 46.
65. Tate, *Psalms*, 227.

Distress and the Bad Taste Primary Metaphor

וְהִיא מַר־לָהּ׃

Lam 1:4: . . . and her lot is bitter.

Lam 3:19 has an internal thought process generating an experience conceptualized as toxic substances (לַעֲנָה וָרֹאשׁ). Finally, in 1QH 16:27–28 it is a disease or "stroke" (נגעי) that has "sprouted" (פרח) into something bitter (לַמְּרוֹרִים), with the verb and the use of the preposition לְ here suggesting that the "bitterness" results from the disease.

זְכָר־עָנְיִי וּמְרוּדִי לַעֲנָה וָרֹאשׁ׃

Lam 3:19: The thought of my affliction and my homelessness is wormwood and gall!

כי פרח נגעי 28 למרורים וכאיב אנוש לאין עצור

1QH 16:27–28: For my disease has sprouted into bitterness and an incurable pain which does not stop.

Thus, bad tastes are attributed to the נֶפֶשׁ (most commonly), רוּחַ and לֵב, as well as to the distressed person in general. The various syntactic forms show this is a well-entrenched conceptualization.

9.4.2. Experiencing Distress Produces Bitterness

The corpus also uses taste language for sufferers expressing their distress. Job 23:2 possibly has Job giving a "bitter" complaint (מְרִי שִׂחִי).[66] 1QH 19 refers first to a "source" (מקור) of "bitter" mourning (לאבל מרורים, in v. 19), and then in v. 22 to "bitter" wailing (מספד מרורים). מקור describes springs or fountains, evoking a spring of "bad" water opened up to pour out the mourning and wailing of distress. Perhaps internal bitterness results in bitterness "flowing" from the person, as a spring which has bitterness at its source can only produce bitter water.

גַּם־הַיּוֹם מְרִי שִׂחִי

Job 23:2: Today also my complaint is bitter.

---

66. Although a "rebellious" complaint (from מרה) is perhaps better, Clines, *Job 21–37*, 572; Gordis, *Job*, 254.

ואני נפתח לי מקור לאבל מרורים

1QH 19:19: As for me, a spring of bitter mourning has opened for me.

ואנחה בכנור קינה לכול אבל יגו[ן] ומספד מרורים

1QH 19:22: I have sighed on the harp of lament for every sorrow of anguish, with bitter wailing.

מרר also occurs with verbs of expressing distress outside the corpus in Ezek 27:30 (וְיִזְעֲקוּ מָרָה 'and they will cry bitterly'), Gen 27:34 (וַיִּצְעַק צְעָקָה גְּדֹלָה וּמָרָה 'and he cried a loud and bitter cry'), and in Esth 4:1 (וַיִּזְעַק זְעָקָה גְדֹלָה וּמָרָה 'and he cried a loud and bitter cry').[67] Zechariah 12:10 also links the expression of distress with bitterness, וְסָפְדוּ עָלָיו כְּמִסְפֵּד עַל־הַיָּחִיד וְהָמֵר עָלָיו כְּהָמֵר עַל־הַבְּכוֹר, 'they will mourn over him as the mourning for an only child, and show bitterness over him as showing bitterness over a firstborn'.

Whereas in English, the adverb "bitterly" intensifies verbs already construed negatively,[68] in Hebrew it more narrowly collocates with verbal expressions of distress. Thus, it is more likely these expressions evoke the experience of a sufferer, so that "bitter" cries are sounds typical of those with a "bitter" soul, describing more the character of the person crying than the cry itself.

9.4.3. Experiencing Distress is Ingesting an Unpleasant Substance

The mappings considered so far have been metonymic, highlighting parts of the distress experience using the "taste" source domain. A complementary metaphorical mapping describes distress experiences as ingesting unpleasant or potentially harmful substances. Although some examples are outside the specific corpus, they give a helpful interpretive background. For example, in Ps 75:8[9] Yahweh will force the wicked to drink a cup of wine, conceptualizing the distress that will come upon them. Similarly, Ps 11:6 describes a cup containing a scorching wind,

---

67. Showing צעק and זעק are "mere variants," Wood, "זְעַק."
68. Popova, "Synaesthesia," 413.

Distress and the Bad Taste Primary Metaphor

conceptualizing distress for the wicked. In Job 20:23, Zophar conceptualizes God giving the wicked his anger as food (לֶחֶם). Job's reply repeats the image of "consuming" God's anger in 21:20, but returns to drinking (יִשְׁתֶּה) harmful liquids.

כִּי כוֹס בְּיַד־יְהוָה וְיַיִן חָמַר מָלֵא מֶסֶךְ וַיַּגֵּר מִזֶּה אַךְ־שְׁמָרֶיהָ יִמְצוּ יִשְׁתּוּ כֹּל רִשְׁעֵי־אָרֶץ:

Ps 75:8[9]: For in the hand of the LORD there is a cup with foaming wine, well mixed; he will pour a draught from it, and all the wicked of the earth shall drain it down to the dregs.

וְרוּחַ זִלְעָפוֹת מְנָת כּוֹסָם:

Ps 11:6: A scorching wind shall be the portion of their cup.

יְהִי לְמַלֵּא בִטְנוֹ יְשַׁלַּח־בּוֹ חֲרוֹן אַפּוֹ וְיַמְטֵר עָלֵימוֹ בִּלְחוּמוֹ:

Job 20:23: To fill their belly to the full God will send his fierce anger into them, and rain it upon them as their food.

וּמֵחֲמַת שַׁדַּי יִשְׁתֶּה:

Job 21:20: Let them drink of the wrath of the Almighty.

Similarly, the specific corpus describes distress through eating and drinking. In Job 9:18, God has "filled" (יַשְׂבִּעַנִי) Job with "bitter things" (מַמְרֹרִים). שׂבע prototypically means "to be satisfied with nourishment,"[69] an image reversed here, with Job fully satisfied not with good food but bad, bitter food. Lamentations 3:15 is similar, subsequently asserting that God has "satiated" (or filled with liquid, הִרְוַנִי) the author with לַעֲנָה. Although often translated "wormwood," the referent is unclear. At least, it is a dangerous or poisonous herbal substance that can be eaten or taken in liquid form.[70] Proverbs 5:3–4 ("bitter like לַעֲנָה," מָרָה כַלַּעֲנָה), shows it is a prototypical "bitter" substance that can be masked by sweet tasting honey.

---

69. Waltke, "שָׂבֵעַ."
70. Seybold, "לַעֲנָה," 15.

Surrounded by Bitterness

כִּי יַשְׂבִּעַנִי מַמְּרֹרִים׃

Job 9:18: He fills me with bitterness.

הִשְׂבִּיעַנִי בַמְּרוֹרִים הִרְוַנִי לַעֲנָה׃

Lam 3:15: He has filled me with bitter herbs, he has sated me with wormwood.[71]

References to being given "poison" (רֹאשׁ) for food and vinegar (חֹמֶץ) for drink in Ps 69:21[22] are also likely metaphorical, expressing how the enemies harmful words have caused distress. רֹאשׁ is another prototypically "bitter" plant-derived poison (paralleled with מרר in Deut 32:32) of uncertain identification,[72] but also describes snake venom. Job's spirit also drinks poison (חֲמָתָם שֹׁתָה רוּחִי) in Job 6:4. The source here is God's arrows, rather than oral consumption, yet שׁתה still evokes drinking. Finally, 1QH 12:11 also describes people given vinegar (חומץ) to drink, to make them act like fools and enable enemies to "catch them in their nets," emphasizing the negative consequences of this drink.

וַיִּתְּנוּ בְּבָרוּתִי רֹאשׁ וְלִצְמָאִי יַשְׁקוּנִי חֹמֶץ׃

Ps 69:21[22]: They gave me poison for food, and for my thirst they gave me vinegar to drink.

כִּי חִצֵּי שַׁדַּי עִמָּדִי אֲשֶׁר חֲמָתָם שֹׁתָה רוּחִי

Job 6:4: For the arrows of the Almighty are in me; my spirit drinks their poison.

יעצורו משקה דעת מצמאים ולצמאם ישקום חומץ למע(ן)
הבט אל 12 תעותם
מתודוצמב שפתהל מ (superscript) הידעומב ללוהתהל

1QH 12:11–12: They have denied the drink of knowledge to the thirsty, but for their thirst they have given them vinegar to drink, to consider their mistake, so they may act like fools in their feasts so they will be caught in their nets.

---

71. Author's translation.
72. Fleischer, "רֹאשׁ," 262.

Distress and the Bad Taste Primary Metaphor

Sometimes it is inferred that the object sensed is incorporated into the body, passing the food's quality to the person ingesting it. In Job 21:23–25 (cited in section 9.4.1), the bitter soul is explicitly someone who "never tasted anything good" (וְלֹא־אָכַל בַּטּוֹבָה). Here, bad-tasting experiences produce a bitter soul, whereas good life experiences, conceptualized as good-tasting milk, result in a person wholly at ease. In 1QH 13:35, bread (לחמי) has turned into quarrel and drink (שקוי) into argument, but more significantly, they have entered into the bones and affected the whole person.

ויהפך לי לחמי לריב ושקוי לבעל מדנים ויבוא[ו] בעצמ[י] 36
[לה]כשיל רוח ולכלות כוח

> 1QH 13:35–36: My bread has turned into quarrel and my drink into argument. They have entered in [my] bones to make my spirit stagger and make an end of strength.

Other verses use the consequences of eating to highlight the effects of distressing life events. Thus, Ps 60:3[5] conceptualizes the suffering following enemy attacks as reeling after drinking the wine God has given them, as in references to the cup of wrath above. The parallelism explicitly links drinking wine with suffering "hard things" (קָשָׁה).

הִרְאִיתָה עַמְּךָ קָשָׁה הִשְׁקִיתָנוּ יַיִן תַּרְעֵלָה׃

> Ps 60:3[5]: You have made your people suffer hard things; you have given us wine to drink that made us reel.

A further set of verses describes experiences of distress as consuming tears, sighing, or weeping, again non-nutritious food. Psalm 42:3[4] makes tears (דִמְעָתִי) the psalmist's daily food (לֶחֶם). In Ps 102:9[10] weeping (בְּכִי) is consumed as drink (שִׁקּוּי), and ashes are food (לֶחֶם). In 1QH 13:33–34, "sighing" (אנחה) is food, and tears (דמעות) are drink. Psalm 80:5[6] has tears (דִמְעָה) as both food and drink. In each verse, the events the sufferer is experiencing (crying, weeping, sighing, shedding tears) are conceptualized as food consumed. Where these are abstract nouns based on a fairly common verb (בְּכִי, אנחה) rather than concrete nouns (like דִמְעָה), these cohere with the mappings in which bad life experiences are conceptualized as bad food that is eaten (as in

Job 9:18). The difference here is that the foods eaten are events where the self is an agent, rather than an undergoer.

הָיְתָה־לִּי דִמְעָתִי לֶחֶם יוֹמָם וָלָיְלָה

Ps 42:3[4]: My tears have been my food day and night.

כִּי־אֵפֶר כַּלֶּחֶם אָכָלְתִּי וְשִׁקֻּוַי בִּבְכִי מָסָכְתִּי׃

Ps 102:9[10]: Ashes I eat for my food, with my drink I mix my weeping.[73]

ואוכלה בלחם אנחה 34 ושקוי בדמעות אין כלה

1QH 13:33–34: I am eating the food of sighing; my drink is tears without end.

הֶאֱכַלְתָּם לֶחֶם דִּמְעָה וַתַּשְׁקֵמוֹ בִּדְמָעוֹת שָׁלִישׁ׃

Ps 80:5[6]: You have fed them [your people] with the food of tears, and given them tears to drink in full measure.

Outside the corpus, Isa 30:20–21 has וְנָתַן לָכֶם אֲדֹנָי לֶחֶם צָר וּמַיִם לָחַץ "and though the Lord gives you the food of distress and the water of adversity." Here, food and drink are again bad life experiences. Similarly, Jer 9:15[14] has God giving his people wormwood to eat and poison to drink (מַאֲכִילָם אֶת־הָעָם הַזֶּה לַעֲנָה וְהִשְׁקִיתִים מֵי־רֹאשׁ). Carroll sees God here as "a *chef of death*, that is . . . one who serves food and drink to his creatures in order to punish and to destroy them."[74]

This metaphor maps significant structure onto the experience of distress. First, *agency* is frequently highlighted, mapping the person offering "bad" food or drink onto the agent responsible for distress. Sometimes, this is very deliberate (Ps 75:8[9]), with God mixing and pouring a toxic drink. Elsewhere (Ps 60:3[5]; Lam 3:15; and Job 9:18), God is perceived more generally as responsible for what is consumed. In Ps 80:5[6] even the food of tears is given by God. Rarely, other humans are agents, as in Ps 69:21[22].

---

73. Author's translation.
74. Carroll, "Grapes," 114.

Second, this mapping can evoke *intensity*, sometimes by how much of a toxic substance has been ingested. Lamentations 3:15 and Job 9:18 highlight the severity of distress by claiming the authors are completely "filled" (שׂבע) with bitterness. Similarly, Ps 80:5[6] likely refers to a "full," or "triple," measure[75] (שָׁלִישׁ) of tears given as drink. Intensity can also be evoked by the frequency of consuming "bad" food. In Ps 42:3[4], the repeated consumption of tears "day and night" shows ongoing distress. In 1QH 13:34, the drinking tears "without end" (אין כלה), evokes both the amount of tears being ingested and the ongoing nature of the distress.

Third, *consequences* of consuming bad food map onto consequences of distress. Just as wine causes staggering, distress hinders purposeful movement, and thus the ability to carry out purposeful action. Another consequence of eating bad food is the lasting bad taste, seen explicitly in Job 21:23–25, but also implicitly in all the examples of מרר with נֶפֶשׁ listed earlier. Ongoing bitterness in the person is a result of eating the bitter food of experience.

These mappings can be summarized as follows:

Person ingesting bad food	→	Person experiencing distress
Agent offering bad food	→	Agent responsible for distress (God or human enemies)
Premeditated preparation of noxious food	→	Premeditated action to cause distress
Amount of bad food ingested	→	Intensity of distress experienced
Frequency of consumption of bad food	→	Frequency of experiencing distress
Negative results of eating bad food (reeling, staggering)	→	Negative symptoms of distress

9.4.4. Experiencing Distress is Being Exposed to Poison

The use of מרר for bile and thus for snake's venom (through the common ancient Near Eastern conceptualization that snakes' venom consists of their bile), links venom (and general examples of being exposed

---

75. Alter, *Psalms*, 285.

to poison) conceptually to the other examples in this chapter.[76] A toxic substance is still being incorporated into the person, though not necessarily administered orally.

1QH 13:26–29 offers a fairly full script. The petitioner's opponents have "vipers' venom' (כחמת תנינים) on their tongues, subsequently described as "serpents' poison' (מבלגות פתנים). The poison's spreading nature is highlighted, so that it infuses the person, going on to make the sufferer stagger, lose strength, and unable to stand in his place.

> וא[נ]שי ב[ל]יעל פתחו 27 לשון שקר כחמת תנינים פורחת לק-
> צים וכזוחלי עפר יורו לחתונ[ף מבלגות] פתנים 28 לאין חבר
> ותהי לכאיב אנוש ונגע נמאר בתכמי עבדכה להכשיל [רוח]
> ולהתם 29 כוח לבלתי החזק מעמד

> 1QH 13:26–29: M[en of Be]lial have opened a lying tongue, like vipers' venom that spreads to the extremities, like crawlers in the dust they shoot to gra[b], serpents' [poison], against which there is no incantation. It has become an incurable pain, a wasting disease in the innards of your servant, which makes [the spirit] stagger and makes an end of strength, so that he is unable to remain firm in his place.

The poison specifically describes the opponents' words both here and in Ps 140:3[4], where the poison is under the enemies' lips (תַּחַת שְׂפָתֵימוֹ).

> שָׁנֲנוּ לְשׁוֹנָם כְּמוֹ־נָחָשׁ חֲמַת עַכְשׁוּב תַּחַת שְׂפָתֵימוֹ

> Ps 140:3[4]: They make their tongue sharp as a snake's, and under their lips is the venom of vipers.

Elsewhere, poison is attributed to the thoughts and plans of the enemies. 1QH 12:14–15 locates poisonous taste in the enemies' thoughts, as a root that "produces" (פורה) poisonous substances, evoking a plant growing in the enemies' minds which will cause harm to others later. 1QH 13:10 locates the venom in the enemies' schemes (מזמותם).

> שורש פורה רוש ולענה במחשבותם

> 1QH 12:14: A root which produces poison and bitterness is on their thoughts.

76. Pardee, "Venom."

Distress and the Bad Taste Primary Metaphor

חמת תנינים כול מזמותם לחתף

1QH 13:10: Vipers' venom is all their scheming to snatch away.

This mapping develops extra inferences related to the general conceptual mapping from toxic substances to distress. Toxic substances here are not just given by the enemy, but may have their very source in the enemy, as a snake produces its own poison. Further, there are extra inferences when the toxic substance reaches the petitioner. Just as a poison enters a person and then spreads within the body, so distress caused by an enemy (particularly through their words) can increase in severity and take over more of the person.

9.4.5. Experiencing Distress is Other Exposure to Something Bitter/Noxious

Finally, sometimes the petitioner is exposed to something bitter or noxious in a more general way than ingesting it or being bitten by a snake.

First, some texts conceptualize something toxic outside the person. Lamentations 3:5 positions the petitioner as enveloped by poison (וַיַּקַּף רֹאשׁ), conflating the CONSTRAINT schema of chapter six with the danger of poison. Similarly, 1QH 13:31–32 uses both the surrounding schema and "bitterness." The enemies intend to create bitterness for the author, intending to act to harm him. In Ps 64:3[4], the psalmist is exposed to "bitter words" (דָּבָר מָר). As when the enemies' words were viper's venom, this highlights their power to harm when they make contact and are absorbed by the target. In Job 13:26, God's written words are "bitter" (תִכְתֹּב עָלַי מְרֹרוֹת), rather than spoken words, causing harm to Job, just as a noxious substance would do. Finally, Ps 71:4 uses the word חוֹמֵץ to describe the unjust ones persecuting the psalmist. Usually this is translated as "robbers," based on the parallel with חמס, covering robbery in rabbinic Hebrew,[77] but it could also provide cognitive access to the domain of taste. These men who are "sour" could have an unpleasant effect on others just as vinegar does to the teeth.

---

77. Gruber, *Rashi*, 469.

Surrounded by Bitterness

בָּנָה עָלַי וַיַּקַּף רֹאשׁ וּתְלָאָה:

Lam 3:5: He has besieged and enveloped me with bitterness and tribulation.

וסבבוני בהוות לבם ויצרם 32 הופיע לי למרורום

1QH 13:31–32: They surrounded me with the calamity of their heart; and their intention appeared to me for bitterness.

אֲשֶׁר שָׁנְנוּ כַחֶרֶב לְשׁוֹנָם דָּרְכוּ חִצָּם דָּבָר מָר

Ps 64:3[4]: [Evildoers,] who whet their tongues like swords, who aim bitter words like arrows.

כִּי־תִכְתֹּב עָלַי מְרֹרוֹת וְתוֹרִישֵׁנִי עֲוֹנוֹת נְעוּרָי:

Job 13:26: For you write bitter things against me, and make me reap the iniquities of my youth.

אֱלֹהַי פַּלְּטֵנִי מִיַּד רָשָׁע מִכַּף מְעַוֵּל וְחוֹמֵץ:

Ps 71:4: Rescue me, O my God, from the hand of the wicked, from the grasp of the unjust and cruel (sour).

In these examples the main inference is the harmfulness of "bitter" substances, the potential to cause damage being mapped to the words, thoughts or other aspects of the sufferer's enemies to which he is exposed.

9.5. Further Evidence

9.5.1. Generalizations over Polysemy

Generalizations over polysemy can be seen both in the various roots used for ingesting substances and the various unpleasant or harmful substances that are ingested.

Roots used for ingesting substances (and also for experiencing distress) include general words like אכל 'eat', שתה 'drink', שקה 'cause to drink' (in the hiphil), but also words indicating specific parts of the experience such as שבע 'fill with food', רוה 'fill with drink', and מלא

'fill'. Words for the substances taken into the body also include general words like לֶחֶם 'food', כּוֹס 'cup', and מַשְׁקֶה / שִׁקּוּי 'drink', but also several specific unpleasant or toxic substances, such as חוֹמֶץ 'vinegar', לַעֲנָה 'wormwood(?)', רֹאשׁ 'poison / gall', חֵמָה 'venom', מְרוֹרִים 'bitter herbs / foods'. Finally, roots describing tastes themselves (מרר, חמץ) occur both in the physical domain and to describe emotional or psychological states. The various words here, potentially allowing significant lexical variation, show how elaborated this mapping is.

9.5.2. Generalizations over Inference Patterns

Generalizations over inference patterns include both inferences from the domain of taste (enumerated in section 9.2.1.b) and those from eating and drinking more generally.

First, of the complex taste receptors available, predominantly the chemical sense of potentially harmful, "bitter" taste (מרר) is used, although חמץ 'sour' also occurs twice. Different concentrations of toxicity are not used, with no modifiers evoking intensity of a "bitter" soul or spirit. Bitter tastes lingering beyond other tastes are used in Prov 5:4 and 2 Sam 2:26, where something that seems good ends in bitterness, although less explicit in the specific corpus.

Second, taste's *proximate* nature allows several inferences. Food disappears when it is ingested, and similarly, when life events are conceptualized as ingested substances, they are experienced, their taste is perceived, but the events themselves cannot be experienced again. The taste of food lingers in the mouth, while it itself is internalized by the subject. Correspondingly, the bitterness of life events may be internalized by the subject, resulting in a מַר נֶפֶשׁ. Job 21:25 most clearly shows this inference, explicit linking what has been consumed and the condition of the נֶפֶשׁ. Further, one may get rid of a persistent bitter taste by eating something else or by actively ejecting the substance from the body. This motivation to action is mapped to those with a "bitter soul."

Third, the *evaluative* aspect of taste is significant. מרר evokes "bad" tastes, not just chemically "bitter" ones, suiting it for negatively evaluating life experiences. Just as eating "bad" tasting substances is unpleasant and harmful to the body, experiences conceived as ingesting or being exposed to bitterness are unpleasant and harmful.

Other inferences come from the broader domain of consumption. First, some inferences relate to *consequences*. Ingested food has an ongoing effect on the body. Wine tastes good, but as it is absorbed by the body causes staggering. Similarly, some life experiences or choices may seem good at the time, but result in distress, as in Ps 60:3[5]. Consuming poison also has inferred harmful, or even fatal, consequences. Elsewhere, consequences are understood as a noxious substance spreading within the body (1QH 13:27). The active tendency of those with a "bitter" soul fits again here. They acknowledge the ongoing consequences of tasting something harmful and seek to do things to get rid of it.

Second, embodied experiences of eating and drinking conceptualize *intensity* more than taste perception. The regularity of eating and the amount consumed map onto the intensity of suffering.

Finally, conceptualizing distress as an ingested foodstuff again emphasizes its external origin. It is something from the outside that enters a person, rather than a characteristic of people themselves. Even the "bitter" soul is always a result of something negative and external affecting the person.

These various inferences show that this metaphor maps significant structure from the domain of taste to the domain of physical distress.

9.5.3. Novel Metaphor

Next, instantiations found in both very conventional idioms and in more poetic phrases show the entrenchment of this mapping. First, associating מרר with נֶפֶשׁ is very conventional, found within and outside the corpus. By contrast, God filling Job with bitterness (Job 9:18) is more poetic, with increased impact through extra entailments about who is causing the bitterness, and the implicit contrast with God's expected filling of the person with good food.

Second, the conceptualization of life experiences as "drinking a cup" is likely conventional (from the references considered here, the extended symbolism of Jer 25:15–19, and even Jesus' reference to his suffering as a cup in Gethsemane in Matt 25:39, 42). Psalm 75:8[9] then elaborates this conventional mapping, describing the type of wine and how God mixes and pours it. Understanding this novel expression relies on awareness of the common conventional mapping that understands life events as drinking a cup.

Thus, this conceptual mapping appears in conventional idioms in narrative and within the corpus, and also in highly creative instances, showing ongoing active use of this source domain to understand distress situations.

9.5.4. Larger Scale Metaphorical Systems

The mapping from negative life experiences to eating bitter food coheres with a larger scale metaphorical mapping in which various life events or actions are classified as food or drink.

Thus, the wife in Prov 31:27 does not "eat the food of idleness" (וְלֶחֶם עַצְלוּת לֹא תֹאכֵל). She does not act in a lazy way, but this is conceptualized through the domain of eating. In Prov 4:17, the wicked eat "the food of wickedness" and drink "the wine of violence" (כִּי לָחֲמוּ לֶחֶם רֶשַׁע וְיֵין חֲמָסִים יִשְׁתּוּ), where the wickedness and violence consumed describe the actions of the wicked. In Job 15:16, man drinks "evil like water" (אִישׁ־שֹׁתֶה כַמַּיִם עַוְלָה), where what is ingested is the evil committed. Similarly, in Job 34:7, Job's complaints are "drinking scoffing like water" (יִשְׁתֶּה־לַּעַג כַּמָּיִם). In each case, a person's attitude and actions are understood as the food or drink they consume.[78] This most closely coheres with the agentive examples of drinking or eating "weeping" or "sighing" given above. However, since elsewhere food conceptualizes life experiences more generally (like the food of affliction and drink of adversity in Isa 30:20–21), this larger metaphorical system also coheres with metaphors of distress as drinking a cup of wrath or being filled with bitterness. Both eating and drinking can conceptualize either more agentive activities or more passive experiences that are "undergone."

The proverb quoted in Jer 31:29 and Ezek 18:2 also makes sense in this context, "the fathers have eaten sour grapes and the children's teeth are set on edge" (אָבוֹת אָכְלוּ בֹסֶר וְשִׁנֵּי בָנִים תִּקְהֶינָה). The fathers' sinful actions are conceptualized as eating bad-tasting food. The prov-

---

78. As in Hausa, the drinking examples may evoke repeated acts more than the eating examples.

erb then expands on the inferred consequences. Eating bad food affects the body, similarly bad actions result in negative consequences.

Job 20:12–15 also uses this larger metaphorical system, first describing how wicked actions are "sweet" in the mouth of the wicked (אִם־תַּמְתִּיק בְּפִיו רָעָה). The way they savor these actions is elaborated: hiding them under their tongues; not letting go; holding them in their mouths. Yet, in v. 14 this food turns within their stomachs (לַחְמוֹ בְּמֵעָיו נֶהְפָּךְ) to the poisonous bitterness of snakes (מְרוֹרַת פְּתָנִים בְּקִרְבּוֹ), linking מרר with snake venom. Here again, something tasting sweet at first may become toxic inside the person. Further, the eating metaphor again highlights the consequences of actions.

Thus, life events are understood as food being consumed throughout several Hebrew texts. Positive events or experiences are good food, whereas events that have harmful consequences are characterized as unpleasant or toxic food. The specific mapping from distressing events to eating toxic food fits coherently within this larger structure.

9.5.5. Non-verbal Realizations

Non-verbal realizations are found in the bitter herbs of the Passover celebration and the ordeal of Numbers 5.

The Passover regulations in Exod 12:8 require eating "bitter herbs" (עַל־מְרֹרִים יֹאכְלֻהוּ). Within Exodus this is verbally linked to the distress in Egypt, since Exodus 1:14 describes the Egyptian taskmasters making the Hebrews' lives "bitter" with hard service (וַיְמָרְרוּ אֶת־חַיֵּיהֶם בַּעֲבֹדָה קָשָׁה). By the time the Haggadah was compiled (between 200 and 500 CE), the bitter herbs eaten at Passover were explicitly connected with the distress of Egyptian slavery through the words recited as these symbolic elements are eaten, "a reminder of the bitter treatment to which the Jews were subjected in Egypt."[79]

The "bitter water" ordeal of Num 5:11–31 gives another non-verbal consolidation of the mapping from bitter-tasting substances to distress. A wife suspected of adultery must drink "bitter water" (מֵי הַמָּרִים), and if she is guilty, the water will cause internal distress and pain, whereas if she is innocent it has no effect. This non-verbal symbolism consolidates

---

79. Hamilton, "מָרַר."

a link between eating and drinking and distress that comes as some kind of punishment.

Both situations link situations of distress with the consumption of bad-tasting food, though the Passover Seder would be most significant neurologically, cross-modally linking words and taste experiences, and repeated year after year.

9.6. Universality and Variation

9.6.1. Variation within Source and Target Domain

Comparing with other languages, the closest similarities are with the other ancient Near Eastern languages and Guhu Samane. English and Finnish have commonalities in the use of the same sensory source domain to conceptualize emotional, psychological and physical distress, but there are also significant variances. As in previous chapters, these differences can be described as differences in the target domain, in the prototypical structure of the source domain and in the entailments drawn from it.

First, this source domain conceptualizes wider experiences in Hebrew than in European languages like English and Finnish. In Hebrew, the source domain conceptualizes emotional and psychological dispositions common with English words like *bitter* or *sour*. However, the Hebrew target domain also encompasses physical distress, such as Hezekiah's illness.

Within emotional discourse there is a further difference. The English emotion of *bitterness* is a long-lasting state similar to *anger* or *resentment*. Similarly, a *katkera* Finnish person would likely display angry behavior. Hebrew scenarios and actions are closer to English *grief* than *anger* (for example, Hannah's childlessness or Naomi's and Job's loss of family members). Guhu-Samane is more similar, linking a "bitter" heart to grief rather than anger (which is referred to as *qupa qanga*, "bad" heart).

Second, the source domain's prototypical structure differs. For example, in English, *bitter* taste is prototypically associated with orange peel, certain vegetables, and (for some) quinine. In Hebrew, מרר is

351

prototypically associated with undrinkable water, certain leaves, bad grapes, bile, and snake venom, as well as רֹאשׁ and לַעֲנָה. Such substances are more harmful than prototypical English *bitter* tasting substances, thus entailing a more dangerous situation described with מרר than one conceptualized through *bitterness*, and a greater need to act to remedy the situation.

Third, entailments from the domain of experiencing bad tastes differ between Hebrew and English. In Hebrew, applying the root מרר to someone entails something bad has happened to them, conceptualized as eating something bad, an entailment not significantly utilized with English *bitterness*. An English *bitter* person is prototypically compared to a bitter substance, with the bitterness belonging to the nature of the substance. This internal origin means a bitter person would be held (at least partially) responsible for their bitterness, so that solutions should be found internally, by the person finding a way to get over it or change their character. This individual control is seen in phrases like, *I'm not bitter*. By contrast, in Hebrew, the entailment that "bitterness" is caused by an external toxic substance entering the body means that the person is not prototypically responsible for the bitterness, nor able to control it. Attempts to solve such a situation thus revolve around changing external circumstances, for example by pleading for God to change the situation.

Fourth, compared with Hausa, there are few obviously different entailments between eating and drinking as ways of consuming bad food in distress. Whereas in Hausa eating suggested agentive control over a situation and drinking an undergoer type of passivity, in Hebrew both express either agency or passivity. As well as mappings similar to Hausa where drinking is passive (as in the cup of God's wrath) and eating active (as in the bread of tears), drinking sometimes emphasizes agency (as in drinking "scoffing") and eating sometimes emphasizes passivity (as in eating the food of affliction). The context defines whether the source domain maps to an agentive or passive experience, rather than specific features of the embodied experiences.

Finally, comparing with the Akkadian examples, the target domains and prototypical substances are fairly similar. However, the agents feeding with harmful food differ. In Hebrew, the only agents are God or occasionally other people. In the Akkadian texts there are many more spiritual beings, particularly demons, who could be feeding poison to the sufferer. Thus a very similar embodied conceptualization occurs in a polytheistic context, multiplying the possible agents who could offer food or drink.

9.6.2. Variation in Linguistic Expression

The linguistic expression of this conceptual metaphor also varies. Differences can be seen in the parts of the experience of taste or eating that are highlighted across different cultures, in the degree of conventionalization of the mapping across cultures and in the syntactic expressions used.

First, Hebrew and English differ in the elaboration of the "eating" part of the mapping. Eating "tears," "scorn," or "the food of affliction" sound unusual in English, yet the variety of similar Hebrew expressions suggests this is fairly conventional. Thus, Hebrew highlights the part of an "ingestion" script where food is actually eaten (as a way of conceptualizing activities carried out in life). When people are described as becoming "sour" or "bitter" in English, this part of the script is not used. The Hebrew highlighting of this aspect highlights both the relationship between action and consequence, and the external cause of emotional and psychological symptoms of distress.

Second, degrees of conventionalization across languages may vary. Since expressions using מרר to conceptualize distress occur relatively frequently throughout narrative and poetic genres in the limited Classical Hebrew corpus, it is likely a fairly conventional expression. Descriptions of "bitter" people or experiences are also fairly conventional in English. Noticeably, these metaphors of distress are more conventionalized in Hebrew than either the VERTICALITY schema or the DARKNESS primary metaphor (as these are very rarely used in narrative texts, if at all) even though there are fewer tokens in the specific corpus.

Finally, syntactic expression differs. For example, it is more common in English to talk of someone being bitter or sour than to use these as an adjective combined with a body part. In Guhu Samane, "bitter" emotions are commonly referred to with the adjective-noun combination *qupa togo*. In the Classical Hebrew texts, the most common syntax is also an adjective-noun combination, associating מרר with the נֶפֶשׁ. In English, the most common use of the source domain of "bitterness" is in the description of verbs through the adverb "bitterly." Hebrew does not have this kind of adverbial construction, with the source domain being used much more frequently to describe nouns than verbs.

9.7. Summary

The universal physiology of taste receptors that tell us when a "bad" substance is being ingested provides a useful source domain in several languages for conceptualizing negatively valued situations. Whereas in English negative character disposition or verbal ideas are expressed with this source domain, in Classical Hebrew, it is particularly negatively valued life events that are conceptualized this way, so that the users of the language "expressed tragic, unpleasant experiences in terms of the sense of taste, the bitter."[80] This chapter has shown the significant parts of this structured mapping, in which negative, harmful experiences are conceptualized as toxic substances being ingested, and the resulting emotional and psychological state as the persisting toxicity or bitterness in the body. The high degree of entrenchment has also been demonstrated through the conventional and poetic uses of the same conceptual mappings.

---

80. Hamilton, "מָרַר."

10

Conclusion

10.1. Introduction

This conclusion summarizes the results of this work, offers some implications for linguistics, Biblical Studies, and translation, and finally suggests some directions for future research.

10.2. Summary of Results

This book investigated the five most significant source domains and image schemas used to conceptualize situations of physical, emotional, and psychological distress in the first person statements of distress found in a corpus of Classical Hebrew texts, concentrated in lament psalms, Job, Lamentations, and the Hodayot from Qumran. It was shown that these embodied experiences consisted of the VERTICALITY schema, the CONSTRAINT schema, the FORCE schema, and the source domains of DARKNESS and BAD TASTE.

It was possible to identify which domains were preferred most for conceptualizing distress. The most frequently occurring is the FORCE schema, then the CONSTRAINT schema, then VERTICALITY, DARKNESS, and BAD TASTE. The overwhelming significance of the FORCE schema is revealed in the frequency of instantiations and the variety of images and mixture of conventional and novel linguistic expressions that illustrate it. The CONSTRAINT schema is also surprisingly significant, especially when compared to conceptualizations of distress in English, instantiated by many different images, and again being reflected in both very conventional and more creative expressions.

As claimed in chapter three, these metaphors together conceptualize a gestalt experience of distress, including a prototypical scenario with participants, parts, stages, causes, and results. This prototypical scenario, with its different elements structured by these different conceptual metaphors, is summarized in the following table and then discussed below.[1] As the scenario is prototypical, not all experiences of distress follow every aspect, but these elements are most frequently highlighted in the metaphorical conceptualizations.[2]

---

1. For comparable summaries, see Lakoff and Johnson, *Metaphors*, 80–81, Lakoff, *Women*, 397–409.

2. The prototypical scenario may also differ in other corpora.

Conclusion

	Distress Scenario	Source Domain Scenarios
Participants	Person suffering distress (S)	Hunted animal, person under attack, eating bad food or in darkness
	Agent(s) causing distress (A)	Hunter, enemy opponent, lion, snake, military commander, "chef" or archer
	Other hostile persons in the community	Enemies, animals
Causation	Deliberate, premeditated	A baits traps, hunts prey, plots, sets ambushes, mixes wine, prepares food, guides to bad place
	Unjustified	S is innocent prey or innocent victim
	Unsuspected	A uses traps or ambushes
Stage 1: Distress approaches	S becomes aware that A intends to cause distress and cries for help	S detects ambush, senses traps, sees surrounding animals
Stage 2: Distress	S experiences distress as a forceful impact	S is struck, crushed, broken, gripped, seized, moved, pushed, pierced, or torn
	S experiences physiological symptoms	S experiences constrained, melted, or broken heart, bowed soul, crushed spirit, broken "bones," weakened eyes, or bitter throat/soul
	S is harmed by words of others	S impacted by tearing teeth of animals, ocean waves, arrows and swords, or poison
Stage 3: Distress continues	Distress continues, constraining S and preventing from fulfilling life purposes	S is tied, held in a net, besieged, imprisoned, walled in, gripped, surrounded, blocked by darkness, feels toxic substances spreading within

	Distress Scenario	Source Domain Scenarios
	S is unable to do anything physical to alleviate the situation	S is imprisoned in a cistern, a helpless prey in a net, besieged by an enemy, ingested substances are no longer controllable
	Increased duration of distress intensifies the experience	Gravity pulls S closer to Sheol, the siege progresses, toxins spread in S's body
Stage 4: Relief	External agent causes relief from distress	S is lifted up, set free from a net or trap, the wild animals' power is defeated

Alongside this prototypical scenario, there are other atypical situations, varying at one or more points from this scenario. For example:

Unrelieved distress: Stage 4 does not happen, and the metaphors are carried to their inferred conclusions, as in Psalm 88 where the author is now situated in the deepest possible location, and darkness has overcome everything.

Non-specific agent of distress: Prototypically, the agents causing distress are deliberate and personal, but occasional metaphors conceptualize a more generic, though still external, cause. Such causes might be conceptualized as gravity bringing the person to a low place, or the buffeting of water and the waves that are not explicitly in anyone's control.

Interrupted preparations: Sometimes the scenario is evoked through a script that has an inferred sequence of increasingly desperate situations (such as bird trapping or lion attack). However, God's actions at an early stage prevent the script continuing and the actual distress occurring. Thus, hunters may be caught in their own traps or the lions' teeth are broken.

For the prototypical scenario, the agent causing distress may be either God or human enemies. Noticeably, the same metaphors conceptualize either God or enemies acting in the same way towards the distressed petitioner, such as a hunting lion. This gives further validity to framing the prototypical distress scenario from the perspective of the sufferer. The first person experience is similarly conceived whether the agent causing the suffering is human or divine. This is also comparable to English and Mesopotamian examples that have similar verbs of forceful interaction to conceptualize sufferers' experiences, but different agents causing them, such as demons or objectified emotions.

This highlighting of external agents in all the metaphorical conceptualizations is very significant. Causes of distress are almost always external to the sufferer, predominantly problematizing the situation as being in the control of some other rational entity. This problematization within each image schema or primary metaphor constrains the petitioner's inferences so that only external solutions are sought. The only potential relief can come from an external source, so all the sufferer can do to affect change is utter a petition to God, pleading for help. This helplessness is especially emphasized in the significant CONSTRAINT schema conceptualizations, highlighting the powerlessness of the petitioner to act as he or she desires. Significantly, this metaphorical problematization prompts different courses of action to conceptualizations of similar target domains in English and other languages, even when similar source domains are used. As has been shown, English metaphors of distress place much more emphasis on the distressed individual acting to resolve the situation: to climb out of the pit, to keep a leash on emotions or hold it together when under stress.

This culture-specific, structured, prototypical conceptualization of distress and the atypical variants show the importance of metaphorical thinking for understanding, problematizing and acting to resolve situations of distress. The differences from English show that language, and in particular metaphorical conceptualization, prototypes and conventional inferences, is important for constraining how people think about situations, and thus how they choose to act upon them. Thus, this research confirms linguistic relativity, as described in chapter two. Different groups of people can be guided to think and act differently by the linguistic conceptualizations their community gives to life experiences.

These results, and the broader methodological considerations of this work, have a number of implications for the fields of biblical studies, cognitive linguistics, and translation.

10.3. Implications

10.3.1. Implications for Biblical Studies

Within the field of Biblical Studies the most significant contributions relate to the controversial area of claims about Hebrew thought based on linguistic texts. This work has endeavored to navigate a way past James Barr's minimalist conclusions that a language can tell us very little about the mental processes of its users. Rather, words can provide points of access to structures of encyclopedic knowledge including experiential gestalts, scripts, and cognitive scenarios, which might constrain inferences about causation, purposes, or results in non-trivial ways.

The contribution of this book has been the presentation of new strands of evidence that can be used to argue that words might provide access to these structures, especially where words have been metaphorically transferred to a more abstract domain of use. The methodology has introduced at least four analytical concepts that can argue for the influence of a root meaning on Hebrew thought, beyond mere assertion.

First, *elaboration* describes the extent to which a source domain or image schema is used in many different linguistic examples, being revealed in generalizations over polysemy. As Sawyer noted, several words used in each of two domains provide greater evidence that there is a mapping cognitively linking these domains for at least some users of the language than if there is only an isolated example. For example, the variety of individual words and longer expressions using the domain of surrounding or constraining to conceptualize distress suggests that צרר still provides cognitive access to this domain when it too is used in descriptions of distress.

Second, *entrenchment* describes the variety of linguistic expressions based on a possible conceptual metaphor. When these linguistic expressions include both highly conventional idioms and creative novel language usage, it shows speakers actively accessing the source domain

Conclusion

to creatively elaborate set forms of language. Conversely, it suggests novel utterances are processed and understood through the internalization of more conventional expressions. Thus, the existence of both the conventional expression מַר נֶפֶשׁ 'bitter soul', found throughout the Classical Hebrew texts, and the more creative יַשְׂבִּעַנִי מַמְּרֹרִים 'he fills me with bitter things', Job 9:18, suggests that the domain of bad taste is still evoked by the conventional description, and that the more novel use is processed and understood because of the familiarity of the mapping established in part by the conventional idiom. Entrenchment can also be seen when a conceptual metaphor is not just realized linguistically but also in non-verbal expressions.

Third, texts may show *inferential structure* from an embodied source domain constraining inferences in a more abstract target domain (such as distressing circumstances). Thus, when the author of Psalm 88 describes his plight as being in the deepest pit (using a modifier specifically from the domain of vertical position), the more basic domain of vertical position is being used to understand the intensity of a situation that is more abstract (his experience of feeling close to death). Further, this embodied prototypical situation constrains the inference that he is not able to help himself. Elsewhere, metaphors of distressing situations as consuming bitter substances constrain inferences regarding the external cause of distress.

Fourth, *coherence* describes the way in which a particular proposed metaphorical mapping coheres with other larger scale conceptual metaphors in the language. Where a proposed metaphorical extension fits in with larger scale metaphorical systems, it is more likely that people may think in line with the metaphor.

All of these kinds of evidence together give powerful support to a claim that an embodied source domain affects the way people thought about and acted upon more abstract situations. Conversely, where some or all of these strands are absent, it is hard to claim that an embodied domain still affected thinking.

Finally, alongside these methodological implications, the actual results of this work have implications for Hebrew semantics for those who are studying emotions or conceptual metaphors in Hebrew. In particular, the data collected here questions the assertion that "being down" is the major metaphor for depression in the Hebrew Scriptures. By seeking to take a comprehensive approach, both to the possible emotional, physical, and psychological states in the target domain and to the possible source domains that could be being accessed, this work has shown that "depression" as conceived in English is rarely (if ever) evidenced in the Hebrew texts, and that FORCE and CONSTRAINT schemas are more significant for conceptualization of the most similar conditions to depression than the VERTICALITY schema.

10.3.2. Implications for Cognitive Linguistics

Within Cognitive Linguistics, this research gives further data for those investigating emotion language, by applying the theory to Hebrew in new ways. Specifically, Lakoff's methodology for demonstrating evidence of conceptual metaphor has been tested, as have Kövecses's criteria for cross-cultural variation in conceptual metaphor. As such, it gives useful data for discussion of universals and cultural variation in the conceptualization of emotions across languages.

A specific focus of this book has been to develop a methodology that recognizes both the importance of conceptual metaphors and the universal domains they may use (in the tradition of Lakoff and Kövecses) and the importance of culture-specific conceptualizations (in the tradition of Wierzbicka). Kimmel's concept of compound image schema was significant here[3] in directing attention not just to the canonical universal image schema but also to the way they have been specifically consolidated in the Hebrew language (seen especially for the CONSTRAINT schema). Similarly, the decision to focus on general distress language (defined by form criticism) rather than any specific emotion defined by Anglo ethnopsychology has attempted to avoid imposing Anglo categories onto other cultural data.[4] The methodology used here thus provides guidelines for future Cognitive Linguistics research seeking to avoid the dangers of ethnopsychology. However, it also highlights the difficulties of doing such research for an ancient language where native intuition is inaccessible.

3. See section 4.5.1.
4. See section 3.3.1.

10.3.3. Implications for Translation

Finally, there are implications here for translation, although this has not been a focus in the research. Since words, and in particular metaphors, are not understood in isolation but in the context of wider cognitive structures based on conceptual mappings, gestalt experiences, and cultural prototypes, literal translations can lead to unexpected and misleading inferences.

For example, when Job says he will continue to speak in the bitterness of his soul in an English translation of בְּמַר נַפְשִׁי, the most relevant interpretation by English speakers (and thus the one arrived at first) is that Job is talking about his long-standing resentment against God, as this is what the source domain of bitterness maps onto in English. Within the wider Hebrew conceptual system, however, this bitterness is prototypically the result of suffering bad experiences (conceptualized as eating bad food), which is harming Job's very insides. Thus, his drive to go on speaking comes from what he has suffered and the desire to do something about it, rather than his frustration and resentment towards God. A literal translation would have more similar entailments in a language such as Guhu Samane in Papua New Guinea, for example. In each culture, translators need to be aware of the prototypical ways such basic embodied experiences as tasting bad food are structured in order to meaningfully translate conventional metaphors.

To avoid incorrect inferences, translations can remove active links to the embodied source domains, for example, translating the Job passage as "in the desperation of my soul" or the NET Bible translation of the "bowed soul" in Psalm 42:5[6] as "*Why are you depressed?*" However, this impoverishes the potential conceptual links to other passages making use of the same domain such as those of eating and drinking tears in distress, or of having an otherwise low posture. Alternatively, maintaining source domain terminology keeps these links but allows possible false inferences where the embodied domain is construed differently. In this case, the context of surrounding passages, footnotes, and church teaching may be needed to help avoid miscommunication. These choices need to be made for individual translation projects, but the significance of this research is the way metaphorical expressions cohere with one another in a structure that pervades many texts, so that such decisions cannot be made on a text-by-text basis without the danger of removing or confusing wider conceptual links.

10.4. Future Directions

Finally, this research could be taken in various directions by subsequent studies. First, the cross-cultural comparisons within each chapter have only been illustrative, suggestive of what may be found in the Hebrew texts. Any of the source domains covered in this book could be examined further from a typological perspective. Thus, for example, it would be helpful to devote a full study to taste terminology across languages (following Backhouse's initial work)[5] and to the way this domain is mapped onto the domain of positive and negative life experience. This would give a much stronger set of data with which to compare the Hebrew examples and investigate in more detail linguistic universals and areas of variation.

Second, it would be possible to compare the findings of this work with the results produced by an analysis of further ancient Near Eastern texts. This would bring the common heritage into clearer focus, and enable a better perspective on how the different theological worldviews interact with the common embodied domains to give the similarity and variety in the inferences that have been shown in this book.

Third, the methodology established in this book would be applicable to any area of metaphor research within Biblical Studies. The most natural direction to pursue would be to look at the conceptualizations of positively valued experiences (whether emotional, psychological, or physical).

Fourth, this book kept a deliberately broad target domain, covering all the experiences of distress occasioning the use of lament or complaint style genres. A further study could endeavor to narrow down the target domain and see if any of the conceptual metaphors are particularly related to one category of emotion. This was avoided within the book because of the inherent difficulties, particularly the use of an ethnopsychology alien to the world of the text, but it may be possible

---

5. Backhouse, *Taste*.

to find a way around this, especially as research progresses in the cross-cultural study of emotion.

Nevertheless, this book has taken the first step in showing how the writers and users of the Classical Hebrew texts organized, problematized and reasoned about the "kaleidoscope flux of impressions" they encountered as they perceived themselves in situations of distress. As they perceived themselves in the depths, hemmed in, struck down, wrapped in darkness, and surrounded by poison, they looked outside themselves to the God who alone could bring them relief. And it is precisely this cultural solution to the problems they perceived that has left us the rich treasury of texts on which this book is based.

Appendix

The following table lists all the verses considered within the specific corpus for this study and how they were categorized according to canonical image-schemas and primary metaphors, as detailed in section 4.4. Blank lines show verses that were considered in the specific corpus and did evoke some image schema or primary source domain, but not one of the main ones listed in this table.

Reference	Force	Containment	Verticality	Darkness	Bad Taste	Source / Path / Goal	Near / Far
Job 3:20					x	x	
Job 3:21							
Job 3:22			x				
Job 3:23		x				x	
Job 3:24							
Job 3:25	x						
Job 3:26	x						
Job 6:2–3	x						
Job 6:4	x					x	
Job 6:9							
Job 6:10	x						
Job 6:11–12						x	
Job 6:13	x						
Job 6:15–17							
Job 6:30					x		
Job 7:3				x			

Appendix

Reference	Force	Containment	Verticality	Darkness	Bad Taste	Source / Path / Goal	Near / Far
Job 7:4				x			
Job 7:5							
Job 7:6						x	
Job 7:8–10			x				
Job 7:11		x			x		
Job 7:12		x					
Job 7:13–14							
Job 7:15							
Job 7:16							
Job 7:19–20	x	x					
Job 9:11–12	x						
Job 9:17	x						
Job 9:18					x		
Job 9:19	x						
Job 9:21							
Job 9:25–26							
Job 9:30–31							
Job 9:34	x						
Job 10:1					x		
Job 10:8	x	x					
Job 10:15							
Job 10:16	x						
Job 10:20	x						
Job 10:21–22				x		x	
Job 12:5						x	
Job 12:14	x	x					
Job 12:19							
Job 12:22			x	x			
Job 12:24						x	
Job 12:25				x	x		
Job 13:21	x						x
Job 13:24	x						
Job 13:25	x						

Appendix

Reference	Force	Containment	Verticality	Darkness	Bad Taste	Source / Path / Goal	Near / Far
Job 13:26					x		
Job 13:27		x				x	
Job 13:28							
Job 14:1–2		x		x			
Job 14:3							
Job 14:5							
Job 14:6							
Job 14:10							
Job 14:11–12			x				
Job 14:13			x				
Job 14:16							
Job 14:18–19	x						
Job 14:20	x						
Job 14:21							
Job 14:22							
Job 16:6	x						
Job 16:7							
Job 16:8	x						
Job 16:9	x						
Job 16:10–11	x						
Job 16:12–13	x	x					
Job 16:14	x						
Job 16:15			x				
Job 16:16							
Job 16:20							
Job 17:1	x	x	x				
Job 17:2		x					
Job 17:7				x			
Job 17:11	x						
Job 17:12				x			
Job 17:13–14			x	x			
Job 17:15–16		x	x				
Job 19:2	x						

369

Appendix

Reference	Force	Containment	Verticality	Darkness	Bad Taste	Source / Path / Goal	Near / Far
Job 19:6	x	x					
Job 19:8		x		x		x	
Job 19:9	x						
Job 19:10	x	x					
Job 19:11	x						
Job 19:12	x	x					
Job 19:20							
Job 19:21	x						
Job 19:27							
Job 21:6	x						
Job 21:17	x	x		x			
Job 21:18	x						
Job 21:20					x		
Job 21:21							
Job 21:23–25					x		
Job 21:26			x				
Job 23:2	x				x		
Job 23:8–10						x	x
Job 23:15–16							
Job 23:17	x			x			
Job 26:2							
Job 27:2					x		
Job 30:11							
Job 30:13	x					x	
Job 30:14	x						
Job 30:15	x						
Job 30:16	x						
Job 30:17	x			x			
Job 30:18	x						
Job 30:19	x		x				
Job 30:20							
Job 30:21	x						
Job 30:22	x						

Appendix

Reference	Force	Containment	Verticality	Darkness	Bad Taste	Source / Path / Goal	Near / Far
Job 30:26				x			
Job 30:27	x						
Job 30:29				x		x	
Job 30:30	x			x			
Job 30:31							
Ps 3:1[2]	x		x				
Ps 3:6[7]		x					
Ps 4:1[2]		x					
Ps 4:4[5]							
Ps 6:2[3]							
Ps 6:3[4]							
Ps 6:6[7]							
Ps 6:7[8]							
Ps 7:1–2[2–3]	x					x	
Ps 7:5[6]	x		x				
Ps 9:13[14]			x				
Ps 11:2[3]	x			x			
Ps 12:8[9]		x					
Ps 13:1[2]							
Ps 13:2[3]							
Ps 13:3[4]				x			
Ps 13:4[5]							
Ps 17:9	x	x					
Ps 17:11	x	x	x				
Ps 17:12	x						
Ps 18:4[5]	x	x					
Ps 18:5[6]		x	x				
Ps 18:6[7]		x					
Ps 18:16[17]		x	x				
Ps 18:17[18]	x						
Ps 18:19[20]		x					
Ps 18:28[29]				x			
Ps 18:29[30]		x					

Appendix

Reference	Force	Containment	Verticality	Darkness	Bad Taste	Source / Path / Goal	Near / Far
Ps 18:36[37]		x					
Ps 22:1–2[2–3]							x
Ps 22:6[7]							
Ps 22:11[12]	x	x					x
Ps 22:12–13[13–14]	x	x					
Ps 22:14[15]	x						
Ps 22:15[16]	x		x				
Ps 22:16–17[17–18]		x					
Ps 22:19–21[20–22]	x						x
Ps 25:15		x					
Ps 25:16	x						
Ps 25:17		x					
Ps 25:18							
Ps 25:22							
Ps 27:2	x				x	x	
Ps 27:3	x						
Ps 28:1		x	x				
Ps 28:3	x						
Ps 30:1[2]			x				
Ps 30:2[3]							
Ps 30:3[4]			x				
Ps 30:7[8]							
Ps 30:9[10]			x				
Ps 30:10[11]							
Ps 31:4[5]		x					
Ps 31:7–8[8–9]		x					
Ps 31:9[10]		x					
Ps 31:11[12]							
Ps 31:12[13]							
Ps 31:13[14]		x					

Appendix

Reference	Force	Containment	Verticality	Darkness	Bad Taste	Source / Path / Goal	Near / Far
Ps 31:21[22]		x					
Ps 32:3–4	x						
Ps 32:10							
Ps 34:6[7]		x					
Ps 35:7–8		x	x				
Ps 35:17	x						
Ps 38:3[4]							
Ps 38:4[5]	x						
Ps 38:5[6]	x	x					
Ps 38:6[7]			x	x			
Ps 38:7[8]	x						
Ps 38:8[9]	x						
Ps 38:9[10]							
Ps 38:10[11]				x			
Ps 38:11[12]	x						
Ps 38:12[13]		x					
Ps 38:13–14[14–15]							
Ps 38:16–17[17–18]			x			x	
Ps 39:2–3[3–4]	x						
Ps 39:4–5[5–6]							
Ps 39:6[7]							
Ps 39:9[10]							
Ps 39:10[11]	x						
Ps 39:11[12]	x						
Ps 39:13[14]						x	
Ps 40:2[3]		x	x			x	
Ps 40:12[13]	x	x		x			
Ps 40:17[18]							
Ps 41:4[5]							
Ps 41:8[9]	x		x				
Ps 41:9[10]							

Appendix

Reference	Force	Containment	Verticality	Darkness	Bad Taste	Source / Path / Goal	Near / Far
Ps 42:3[4]					x		
Ps 42:4[5]							
Ps 42:5[6]			x				
Ps 42:6[7]			x				
Ps 42:7[8]	x		x				
Ps 42:9[10]	x			x			
Ps 42:10[11]	x						
Ps 43:2	x			x			
Ps 44:9[10]							
Ps 44:19[20]	x			x			
Ps 44:25[26]			x				
Ps 49:5[6]		x					
Ps 51:8[10]	x						
Ps 54:3[4]							
Ps 55:2–3[3–4]	x						
Ps 55:4[5]	x						
Ps 55:5[6]	x	x					
Ps 55:8[9]	x						
Ps 55:10[11]		x					
Ps 55:17–18[18–19]	x						
Ps 55:21[22]	x						
Ps 56:1–2[2–3]	x						
Ps 56:5–7[6–8]						x	
Ps 56:8[9]							
Ps 56:13[14]			x	x			
Ps 57:1[2]	x						
Ps 57:3[4]	x						
Ps 57:4[5]	x						
Ps 57:6[7]	x	x	x				
Ps 59:1–3[2–4]	x						
Ps 59:6–7[7–8]		x		x			
Ps 61:2[3]							x

Appendix

Reference	Force	Containment	Verticality	Darkness	Bad Taste	Source / Path / Goal	Near / Far
Ps 62:3[4]	x						
Ps 62:4[5]			x				
Ps 63:1[2]					x		
Ps 64:2-4[3-5]	x				x		
Ps 64:5[6]		x					
Ps 66:10	x						
Ps 66:11	x	x					
Ps 69:1-2[2-3]	x	x	x				
Ps 69:3[4]	x	x					
Ps 69:4[5]	x						
Ps 69:7-8[8-9]							
Ps 69:14-15[15-16]	x	x	x				
Ps 69:17[18]		x					
Ps 69:18[19]							
Ps 69:20[21]	x						
Ps 69:21[22]					x		
Ps 69:26[27]	x						
Ps 69:29[30]	x						
Ps 69:33[34]		x					
Ps 71:4	x				x		
Ps 71:9							x
Ps 71:10-11	x						
Ps 71:12							x
Ps 71:20		x	x				
Ps 73:2						x	
Ps 73:14	x						
Ps 73:21	x				x		
Ps 73:22							
Ps 73:26							
Ps 77:2[3]		x		x			
Ps 77:3[4]							
Ps 77:4[5]	x						

Appendix

Reference	Force	Containment	Verticality	Darkness	Bad Taste	Source / Path / Goal	Near / Far
Ps 77:6[7]				x			
Ps 77:10[11]	x						
Ps 86:1							
Ps 86:7		x					
Ps 86:13			x				
Ps 86:14	x						
Ps 86:16							x
Ps 88:3[4]			x			x	x
Ps 88:4[5]			x				
Ps 88:5[6]	x		x				
Ps 88:6[7]		x	x	x			
Ps 88:7[8]	x						
Ps 88:8[9]		x					x
Ps 88:9[10]				x			
Ps 88:14[15]	x						x
Ps 88:15[16]	x						
Ps 88:16[17]	x						
Ps 88:17[18]		x					
Ps 88:18[19]				x			x
Ps 94:17							
Ps 94:18						x	
Ps 94:19							
Ps 102:0[1]							
Ps 102:2[3]		x					
Ps 102:3[4]							
Ps 102:4[5]	x				x		
Ps 102:5[6]							
Ps 102:6[7]							
Ps 102:7[8]							
Ps 102:8[9]							
Ps 102:9[10]					x		
Ps 102:10[11]	x						
Ps 102:11[12]				x			

Appendix

Reference	Force	Containment	Verticality	Darkness	Bad Taste	Source / Path / Goal	Near / Far
Ps 102:23-24[24-25]							
Ps 109:2-3	x	x					
Ps 109:22	x						
Ps 109:23	x			x			
Ps 109:24							
Ps 116:3	x	x	x				
Ps 116:6			x				
Ps 116:8						x	
Ps 116:9	x						
Ps 116:16		x					
Ps 118:5		x					
Ps 118:10-12	x	x					
Ps 118:13	x					x	
Ps 118:18	x						
Ps 119:25			x				
Ps 119:28	x		x				
Ps 119:50							
Ps 119:61	x	x					
Ps 119:78							
Ps 119:81							
Ps 119:82							
Ps 119:83	x			x			
Ps 119:85	x	x	x				
Ps 119:92							
Ps 119:107							
Ps 119:109							
Ps 119:110	x	x					
Ps 119:120							
Ps 119:123							
Ps 119:134	x						
Ps 119:136							
Ps 119:141							

Appendix

Reference	Force	Containment	Verticality	Darkness	Bad Taste	Source / Path / Goal	Near / Far
Ps 119:143	x	x					
Ps 119:150	x						
Ps 119:153							
Ps 123:4							
Ps 129:3	x						
Ps 129:4	x	x					
Ps 130:1			x				
Ps 140:1–3[2–4]	x				x		
Ps 140:5[6]							
Ps 140:9–11[10–12]	x	x	x				
Ps 141:8–10[8–10]		x					
Ps 142:2–3[3–4]		x				x	
Ps 142:4[5]							
Ps 142:6[7]			x				
Ps 142:7[8]		x					
Ps 143:3	x		x	x			
Ps 143:4	x						
Ps 143:6					x		
Ps 143:7		x	x				
Ps 143:11		x					
Ps 144:7	x	x	x				
Ps 144:11	x						
Isa 38:10		x	x			x	
Isa 38:11				x			
Isa 38:12	x			x			
Isa 38:13	x						
Isa 38:14			x				
Isa 38:15	x						
Isa 38:16							
Isa 38:17–18	x		x		x		

Appendix

Reference	Force	Containment	Verticality	Darkness	Bad Taste	Source / Path / Goal	Near / Far
Jer 8:21	x				x		
Jer 9:1[8:23]							
Jer 10:19	x						
Jer 10:20	x						
Jer 10:24							
Jer 15:18	x						
Jer 18:20		x	x				
Jer 18:22		x	x				
Jer 20:7	x						
Jer 20:9		x					
Jer 20:18						x	
Lam 1:13	x	x	x				
Lam 3:1	x						
Lam 3:2	x			x			
Lam 3:3	x						
Lam 3:4	x						
Lam 3:5		x			x		
Lam 3:6				x			
Lam 3:7	x	x					
Lam 3:8		x					
Lam 3:9		x				x	
Lam 3:10	x						
Lam 3:11	x	x				x	
Lam 3:12	x						
Lam 3:13	x						
Lam 3:14							
Lam 3:15					x		
Lam 3:16	x		x				
Lam 3:17							
Lam 3:18							
Lam 3:19	x				x		
Lam 3:20			x				
Lam 3:27	x						

Appendix

Reference	Force	Containment	Verticality	Darkness	Bad Taste	Source / Path / Goal	Near / Far
Lam 3:28			x				
Lam 3:29			x				
Lam 3:30	x						
Lam 3:48	x						
Lam 3:49							
Lam 3:51							
Lam 3:53	x	x					
Lam 3:54		x					
Lam 3:55		x	x				
Lam 3:57							x
Lam 3:58							
Lam 3:62	x						
Jonah 2:2[3]		x	x				
Jonah 2:3[4]	x	x	x				
Jonah 2:4[5]	x						x
Jonah 2:5[6]		x	x				
Jonah 2:6[7]		x	x				
Jonah 2:7[8]							
1QH 10:5	x						
1QH 10:5–6							
1QH 10:6							
1QH 10:7–8		x				x	
1QH 10:12–13	x						
1QH 10:16–17	x						
1QH 10:17							
1QH 10:20–21		x	x				
1QH 10:23–24	x						
1QH 10:25–26	x	x					
1QH 10:27–28	x		x				
1QH 10:28							
1QH 10:32–33	x						
1QH 10:34–35	x						
1QH 11:6		x	x				

Appendix

Reference	Force	Containment	Verticality	Darkness	Bad Taste	Source / Path / Goal	Near / Far
1QH 11:7		x					
1QH 11:7-18	x	x	x				
1QH 11:19-20		x	x				
1QH 11:23-25		x					
1QH 11:25						x	
1QH 11:38							
1QH 12:8-9	x						
1QH 12:33-34	x						
1QH 12:35-36	x						
1QH 13:6		x					
1QH 13:9-10	x				x		
1QH 13:12		x			x		
1QH 13:13-15	x						
1QH 13:17	x						
1QH 13:18	x						
1QH 13:18-19	x						
1QH 13:26-29	x				x	x	
1QH 13:29-30	x	x					
1QH 13:30-31	x	x					
1QH 13:31-32		x		x	x		
1QH 13:32				x			
1QH 13:32-33		x		x			
1QH 13:33-34				x	x		
1QH 13:34-36		x			x		
1QH 13:36-39		x	x				
1QH 14:22-24	x	x	x			x	
1QH 14:24-25		x					
1QH 15:1							
1QH 15:2-3	x	x	x	x			
1QH 15:4-5	x						
1QH 16:14-15	x						
1QH 16:26-28					x		
1QH 16:28-29			x				

Appendix

Reference	Force	Containment	Verticality	Darkness	Bad Taste	Source / Path / Goal	Near / Far
1QH 16:30–31	x						
1QH 16:31–32	x						
1QH 16:32–33	x						
1QH 16:33–34	x	x				x	
1QH 16:35		x				x	
1QH 17:3–4	x	x	x				
1QH 17:5–6							x
1QH 17:8–9	x		x				
1QH 17:24–28	x	x		x			
1QH 18:33–34		x	x				
1QH 19:19–20		x			x		
1QH 19:21–22	x				x		
1QH 19:31–32	x	x					
1QH 21:4		x				x	
1QH 21:6	x						
1QH 21:8		x					
1QH 22:14	x						
4Q381 Frag 31:2		x					
11Q6 (Plea for Deliverance) 19:9–11			x				

Bibliography

Aalen, Sverre. "אוֹר." In *TDOT* 1:147–67.
Allen, Leslie C. *Psalms 101–150.* WBC 21. Waco: Word, 1983.
Allen, Ronald B. "עָרךְ." In *TWOT.* Electronic database. NavPress Software, 1999. In *The Translator's Workplace 5.0* DVD, by SIL International, 2009.
Allwood, Jens. "Meaning Potential and Context: Some Consequences for the Analysis of Variation in Meaning." In *Cognitive Approaches to Lexical Semantics,* edited by Hubert Cuyckens et al., 29–65. Cognitive Linguistics Research 23. Berlin: Mouton de Gruyter, 2003.
Alter, Robert. *The Art of Biblical Poetry.* New York: Basic Books, 1985.
———. *The Book of Psalms.* New York: Norton, 2007.
Anderson, Bernhard W. *Creation versus Chaos: The Reinterpretation of Mythical Symbolism in the Bible.* New York: Association, 1967.
Armstrong, Karen. *Jerusalem: One City, Three Faiths.* London: HarperCollins, 1996.
Arnold, Bill T., and Bryan E. Beyer. *Readings from the Ancient Near East.* Encountering Biblical Studies. Grand Rapids: Baker Academic, 2002.
Athanasiadou, Angeliki and Elżbieta Tabakowska. "Introduction." In *Speaking of Emotions: Conceptualisation and Expression,* edited by Angeliki Athanasiadou and Elżbieta Tabakowska, xi–xxii. Cognitive Linguistics Research 10. Berlin: Mouton de Gruyter, 1998.
———. *Speaking of Emotions: Conceptualisation and Expression.* Cognitive Linguistics Research 10. Berlin: Mouton de Gruyter, 1998.
Backhouse, A. E. *The Lexical Field of Taste: A Semantic Study of Japanese Taste Terms.* Cambridge Studies in Linguistics. Cambridge: Cambridge University Press, 1994.
Barcelona, Antonio. *Metaphor and Metonymy at the Crossroads: A Cognitive Perspective.* Topics in English Linguistics 30. Berlin: Mouton de Gruyter, 2000.
———. "On the Plausibility of Claiming a Metonymic Motivation for Conceptual Metaphor." In *Metaphor and Metonymy at the Crossroads: A Cognitive Perspective,* edited by Antonio Barcelona, 31–58. Topics in English Linguistics 30. Berlin: Mouton de Gruyter, 2000.
Barr, James. *The Semantics of Biblical Language.* London: Oxford University Press, 1961.
———. "Etymology and the Old Testament." In *Language and Meaning: Studies in Hebrew Language and Biblical Exegesis,* edited by James Barr et al., 1–28. OtSt 19. Leiden: Brill, 1974.

Bibliography

———. "The Limitations of Etymology as a Lexicographical Instrument in Biblical Hebrew." *Transactions of the Philological Society* (1983) 41–65.

———. "Hebrew Lexicography: Informal Thoughts." In *Linguistics and Biblical Hebrew*, edited by Walter R. Bodine, 137–51. Winona Lake, IN: Eisenbrauns, 1992.

———. "Scope and Problems in the Semantics of Classical Hebrew." *ZAH* 6 (1993) 3-14.

———. "Three Interrelated Factors in the Semantic Study of Ancient Hebrew." *ZAH* 7 (1994) 33–44.

———. "The Synchronic, the Diachronic and the Historical: A Triangular Relationship." In *Synchronic or Diachronic? A Debate on Method in Old Testament Exegesis*, edited by Johannes C. de Moor, 1–14. OtSt 34. Leiden: Brill, 1995.

Barré, Michael L. *The Lord Has Saved Me: A Study of the Psalm of Hezekiah (Isaiah 38:9-20)*. CBQMS 39. Washington, DC: Catholic Biblical Association of America, 2005.

Barsalou, L. W. "The Instability of Graded Structure: Implications for the Nature of Concepts." In *Concepts and Conceptual Development: Ecological and Intellectual Factors in Categorization*, edited by Ulric Neisser, 101–40. Emory Symposia in Cognition 1. Cambridge: Cambridge University Press, 1987.

Barth, Christoph. *Die Errettung vom Tode in den Individuellen Klage-un Dankliedern des Altes Testaments*. Zollikon: Theologischer, 1947.

Basson, Alec. *Divine Metaphors in Selected Biblical Hebrew Psalms of Lamentation*. FAT 2/15. Tübingen: Mohr/Siebeck, 2006.

———. "'People are Plants'—A Conceptual Metaphor in the Hebrew Bible." *OTE* 19 (2006) 573–83.

Baumann, G. "Er hat mir den Weg mit Quadersteinen Vermauert (Thr, 3,9) Ein Vorschlag zur Auslegung einer ungewöhnlichen Metapher." In *Metaphor in the Hebrew Bible*, edited by Pierre van Hecke, 139–46. BETL 187. Leuven: Peeters, 2005.

Baumgartner, Walter. *Jeremiah's Poems of Lament*. Historic Texts and Interpreters in Biblical Scholarship 7. Sheffield, UK: Almond, 1988.

Becker, J. *Das Heil Gottes: Heils- und Sündenbegriffe in den Qumrantextenund in Neuen Testament*. SUNT 3. Göttingen: Vandenhoeck & Ruprecht, 1964.

Berman, Ruth A. "Children's Lexical Innovations: Developmental Perspectives on Hebrew Verb Structure." In *Language Processing and Acquisition in Languages of Semitic, Root-Based Morphology*, edited by Joseph Shimron, 243–88. Language Acquisition & Language Disorders 28. Amsterdam: Benjamins, 2003.

Beuken, W. "שָׁכַב." In *TDOT* 14:659–71.

Beyse, K.-M. "עֶצֶם." In *TDOT* 11:304–9.

———. "עָמַק." In *TDOT* 11: 202–8.

Black, Jeremy, and Anthony Green. *Gods, Demons and Symbols of Mesopotamia: An Illustrated Dictionary*. London: British Museum Press, 1992.

Black, Max. "More about Metaphor." In *Metaphor and Thought*, edited by Andrew Ortony, 19–41. 2nd ed. Cambridge: Cambridge University Press, 1993.

Bleeker, C. J. "Some Remarks on the Religious Significance of Light." *JANESCU* 5 (1973) 23–34.

Boas, Franz. *Introduction to the Handbook of American Indian Languages*. Washington: Government Printing Office, 1911.

Boers, Frank. "When a Bodily Source Domain Becomes Prominent: The Joy of Counting Metaphors in the Socio-economic Domain." In *Metaphor in Cognitive*

Bibliography

Linguistics, edited by Raymond W. Gibbs Jr. and Gerard J. Steen, 47–56. Current Issues in Linguistic Theory 175. Amsterdam: Benjamins, 1999.
Bokawa, Nancy. Personal communication, 2009.
Boman, Thorlief. "Review: 'The Semantics of Biblical Language' and 'Biblical Words for Time.'" *SJT* (1962) 319–24.
Borthwick, Fiona. "Olfaction and Taste: Invasive Odours and Disappearing Objects." *The Australian Journal of Anthropology* 11 (2000) 127-140.
Briggs, Charles Augustus, and Emilie Grace Briggs. *A Critical and Exegetical Commentary on the Book of Psalms.* Edinburgh: T. & T. Clark, 1906.
Bright, John. *Jeremiah.* AB 21. Garden City, NY: Doubleday, 1965.
Brown, William P. *Seeing the Psalms: A Theology of Metaphor.* Louisville: Westminster John Knox, 2002.
Brueggemann, Walter. "The Formfulness of Grief." In *The Psalms and the Life of Faith,* edited by Patrick D. Miller, 84–97. Minneapolis: Fortress, 1995.
———. "Psalms and the Life of Faith: A Suggested Typology of Function." In *The Psalms and the Life of Faith,* edited by Patrick D. Miller, 3–32. Minneapolis: Fortress, 1995.
Brugman, Claudia, and George Lakoff. "Cognitive Topology and Lexical Networks." In *Cognitive Linguistics: Basic Readings,* edited by Dirk Geeraerts, 109–39. Berlin: Cognitive Linguistics Research 34. Berlin: Mouton de Gruyter, 2006.
Bullock, C. Hassell. *An Introduction to the Poetic Books of the Old Testament.* Chicago: Moody, 1979.
Caicedo, Alejandro, and Stephen D. Roper. "Taste Receptor Cells that Discriminate between Bitter Stimuli." *Science* 291 (2001) 1557–60.
Cameron, Lynne. "Identifying and Describing Metaphor in Spoken Discourse Data." In *Researching and Applying Metaphor,* edited by Lynne Cameron and Graham Low, 105–32. Cambridge Applied Linguistics Series. Cambridge: Cambridge University Press, 1999.
———. "Operationalising 'metaphor' for applied linguistic research." In *Researching and Applying Metaphor,* edited by Lynne Cameron and Graham Low, 3–28. Cambridge: Cambridge University Press, 1999.
Cameron, Lynne, and Graham Low, editors. *Researching and Applying Metaphor.* Cambridge Applied Linguistics Series. Cambridge: Cambridge University Press, 1999.
Carpenter, Eugene, and Michael A. Grisanti. "שׁקן." In *NIDOTTE* 3:1270.
Carr, Phil. Personal communication with the author, 2009.
Carroll, Robert P. "YHWH's Sour Grapes: Images of Food and Drink in the Prophetic Discourses of the Hebrew Bible." *Semeia* 86 (1999) 113–31.
Chandrashekar, Jayaram et al. "The Receptors and Cells for Mammalian Taste." *Nature* 444 (2006) 288–94.
Childs, Brevard S. *Introduction to the Old Testament as Scripture.* London: SCM, 1979.
Cienki, Alan. "Straight: An Image Schema and Its Metaphorical Extensions." *Cognitive Linguistics* 9 (1998) 107–49.
———. "Image Schemas and Gesture." In *From Perception to Meaning: Image Schemas in Cognitive Linguistics,* edited by Beate Hampe, 395–420. Cognitive Linguistics Research 29. Berlin: Mouton de Gruyter, 2005.
Clines, David J. A. *Job 1–20.* WBC 17. Waco, TX: Word, 1989.
———. *Job 21–37.* WBC 18A. Nashville: Nelson, 2006.

Bibliography

Clines, David J. A., and John Elwolde, editors. *The Dictionary of Classical Hebrew*. 7 vols. Sheffield, UK: Sheffield Academic, 1993.

Cohen, Gary G. "שָׁקַד." In *TWOT*. Electronic database. NavPress Software, 1999. In *The Translator's Workplace 5.0* DVD, by SIL International, 2009.

Collins, Terence. "The Physiology of Tears in the Old Testament, Part I." *CBQ* 33 (1971) 18-38.

Cooley, Robert E., and Gary D. Pratico. "Gathered to His People: An Archaeological Illustration from Tell Dothan's Western Cemetery." In *Scripture and Other Artifacts: Essays on the Bible and Archaeology in Honor of Philip J. King*, edited by Michael D Coogan et al., 70-92. Louisville: Westminster John Knox, 1994.

Cornelius, Izak. "The Lion in the Art of the Ancient Near East: A Study of Selected Motifs." *JNSL* 15 (1989) 53-85.

———. "The Visual Representation of the World in the Ancient Near East and the Hebrew Bible." *JNSL* 20 (1994) 193-218.

———. "The Iconography of Divine War in the Pre-Islamic Near East: A Survey." *JNSL* 21 (1995) 15-36.

Cortazzi, Martin, and Lixian Jin. "Bridges to Learning: Metaphors of Teaching, Learning and Language." In *Researching and Applying Metaphor*, edited by Lynne Cameron and Graham Low, 149-76. Cambridge Applied Linguistics Series. Cambridge: Cambridge University Press, 1999.

Cotterell, Peter, and Max Turner. *Linguistics and Biblical Interpretation*. Downers Grove, IL: InterVarsity, 1989.

Craigie, Peter C. *Psalms 1-50*. WBC 19. Waco, TX: Word, 1983.

Craigie, Peter C. et al. *Jeremiah 1-25*. WBC 26. Dallas: Word, 1991.

Cruse, D. Alan. "Aspects of the Micro-Structure of Word Meanings." In *Polysemy: Theoretical and Computational Approaches*, edited by Yael Ravin and Claudia Leacock, 30-51. Oxford Linguistics. Oxford: Oxford University Press, 2000.

Dahood, Mitchell. *Psalms 1-50*. AB 16. Garden City, NY: Doubleday, 1965.

Dalley, Stephanie. *Myths from Mesopotamia: Creation, the Flood, Gilgamesh and Others*. 2nd revised ed. Oxford World's Classics. Oxford: Oxford University Press, 2000.

Davies, Philip R. "The Society of Biblical Israel." In *Second Temple Studies*. Vol. 2, *Temple Community in the Persian Period*, edited by T. C. Eskenazi and K. H. Richards, 22-33. JOSTSup 175. Sheffield, UK: Sheffield Academic, 1994.

———. *In Search of 'Ancient Israel.'* 2nd ed. JSOTSup 148. Sheffield, UK: Sheffield Academic, 1995.

Day, John. *Psalms*. OTG. Sheffield, UK: Sheffield Academic, 1990.

De Blois, Renier. "Towards a New Dictionary of Biblical Hebrew Based on Semantic Domains." Presented at Society of Biblical Literature Annual Meeting, Nashville, TN, 2000.

———. "Lexicography and Cognitive Linguistics: Hebrew Metaphors from a Cognitive Perspective." Presented at Society of Biblical Literature Annual Meeting, Toronto, ON, 2002.

Deignan, Alice. "Corpus-Based Research into Metaphor." In *Researching and Applying Metaphor*, edited by Lynne Cameron and Graham Low, 177-99. Cambridge Applied Linguistics Series. Cambridge: Cambridge University Press, 1999.

Deist, Ferdinand E. *The Material Culture of the Bible: An Introduction*. Biblical Seminar 70. Sheffield, UK: Sheffield Academic, 2000.

Delitzsch, F. *Job*. Grand Rapids: Eerdmans, 1949.

Bibliography

Dever, William G. *What Did the Biblical Writers Know and When Did They Know it? What Archaeology Can Tell Us about the Reality of Ancient Israel.* Grand Rapids: Eerdmans, 2001.

Dimant, Devorah. "The Composite Character of the Qumran Sectarian Literature as an Indication of its Date and Provenance." *RevQ* 88 (2006) 615–30.

Dirven, René. "Emotions as Cause and the Cause of Emotions." In *The Language of Emotions: Conceptualization, Expression and Theoretical Foundation,* edited by Susanne Niemeier and René Dirven, 55–83. Amsterdam: Benjamins, 1997.

Dobbs-Allsopp, F. W. *Lamentations.* Interpretation: A Bible Commentary for Teaching and Preaching. Louisville: John Knox, 2002.

Douglas, Michael C. "The Teacher Hymn Hypothesis Revisited: New Data for an Old Crux." *Dead Sea Discoveries* 6 (1999) 239–66.

Dressler, William W. "Culture, Stress and Disease." In *Medical Anthropology: Contemporary Theory and Method,* edited by Carolyn Sargent and Thomas Johnson, 248–67. New York: Greenwood, 1990.

Drewnowski, Adam, and Carmen Gomez-Carneros. "Bitter Taste, Phytonutrients and the Consumer: A Review." *American Journal of Clinical Nutrition* 72 (2000) 1424–35.

Eidevall, Göran. "Images of God, Self and the Enemy in the Psalms: On the Role of Metaphor in Identity Construction." In *Metaphor in the Hebrew Bible,* edited by Pierre van Hecke, 55–66. BETL 187. Leuven: Peeters, 2005.

———. "Spatial Metaphors in Lamentations 3,1–9." In *Metaphor in the Hebrew Bible,* edited by Pierre van Hecke, 133–37. BETL 187. Leuven: Peeters, 2005.

Eising, H. "כרע." In *TDOT* 7:336–39.

———. "מֶלַח." In *TDOT* 8:331–33.

European Association of Biblical Studies. "Metaphor in the Hebrew Bible." No pages. Online: http://www.eurassbibstudies.group.shef.ac.uk/mhb.htm

Fabry, Heinz-Josef. "דַּל." In *TDOT* 3:208–30.

———. "חבל I." In *TDOT* 4:172–79.

———. "חבל IV." In *TDOT* 4:188–92.

———. "מְצוּלָה." In *TDOT* 8:514–19.

———. "סָעַר." In *TDOT* 10:291–96.

———. "צַר I." In *TDOT* 12:455–64.

Fabry, Heinz-Josef and R. E. Clements. "מַיִם." In *TDOT* 8:265–88.

Farber, Walter. "Lamaštu—Agent of a Specific Disease or a Generic Destroyer of Health?" In *Disease in Babylonia,* edited by I. L. Finkel and M. J. Geller, 137–45. Cuneiform Monographs 36. Leiden: Brill, 2007.

Fauconnier, Gilles. *Mappings in Thought and Language.* Cambridge: Cambridge University Press, 1997.

Fauconnier, Gilles, and Mark Turner. "Conceptual Integration Networks." In *Cognitive Linguistics: Basic Readings,* edited by Dirk Geeraerts, 303–71. Berlin: Mouton de Gruyter, 2006.

———. *The Way We Think: Conceptual Blending and the Mind's Hidden Complexities.* New York: Basic Books, 2003.

Feinberg, Charles L. "אפל." In *TWOT.* Electronic database. NavPress Software, 1999. In *The Translator's Workplace 5.0* DVD, by SIL International, 2009.

Bibliography

Fillmore, Charles. "Frames and the Semantics of Understanding." *Quaderni di Semantica* 6 (1985) 222–53.

———. "Frame Semantics." In *Cognitive Linguistics: Basic Readings*, edited by Dirk Geeraerts, 373–400. Berlin: Mouton de Gruyter, 2006.

Fillmore, Charles, and Beryl T. Sue Atkins. "Describing Polysemy: The Case of 'Crawl.'" In *Polysemy: Theoretical and Computational Approaches*, edited by Yael Ravin and Claudia Leacock, 91–110. Oxford Linguistics. Oxford: Oxford University Press, 2000.

Firmage, E. et al. "רום." In *TDOT* 13:403–12.

Firth, David G. *Surrendering Retribution in the Psalms: Responses to Violence in the Individual Complaints*. Eugene, OR: Wipf & Stock, 2007.

Fleischer, G. "ראש." In *TDOT* 13:262–64.

Foley, William A. *Anthropological Linguistics: An Introduction*. Language in Society 24. Malden, MA: Blackwell, 1997.

Foster, Benjamin R. *Before the Muses: An Anthology of Akkadian Literature*. 3rd ed. Bethesda, MD: CDL, 2005.

Foster, Stuart J. "A Prototypical Definition of ברית, 'Covenant' in Biblical Hebrew." *OTE* 19 (2006) 35–46.

Frevel, C. "רדף." In *TDOT* 13:340–51.

Fritz, Volkmar. *The City in Ancient Israel*. The Biblical Seminar 29. Sheffield, UK: Sheffield Academic, 1995.

Frymer-Kemsky, Tikva. "Biblical Cosmology." In *Backgrounds for the Bible*, edited by Michael Patrick O'Connor and David Noel Freedman, 231–40. Winona Lake: Eerdmans, 1987.

Fuhs, H. F. "דָּכָא." In *TDOT* 3:195–208.

———. "עָלָה." In *TDOT* 11:76–95.

Fukunaga, Kie. Personal communication, 2009.

Gamberoni, J. "חָבַל III." In *TDOT* 4:185–88.

———. "קוּם." In *TDOT* 12:589–612.

Garcia-López, F. "סבב." In *TDOT* 10:126–39.

Geeraerts, Dirk, editor. *Cognitive Linguistics: Basic Readings*. Cognitive Linguistics Research 34. Berlin: Mouton de Gruyter, 2006.

———. "Introduction: A Rough Guide to Cognitive Linguistics." In *Cognitive Linguistics: Basic Readings*, edited by Dirk Geeraerts, 1–28. Cognitive Linguistics Research 34. Berlin: Mouton de Gruyter, 2006.

Geller, M. J. "Phlegm and Breath—Babylonian Contributions to Hippocratic Medicine." In *Disease in Babylonia*, edited by I. L. Finkel and M. J. Geller, 187–99. Cuneiform Monographs 36. Leiden: Brill, 2007.

Gerstenberger, Erhard S. "Life Situations and Theological Concepts of Old Testament Psalms." *OTE* 18 (2005) 82–92.

———. *Psalms: Part 1 with an Introduction to Cultic Poetry*. The Forms of the Old Testament Literature 15. Grand Rapids: Eerdmans, 1988.

Gibbs, Raymond W., Jr. *The Poetics of Mind: Figurative Thought, Language, and Understanding*. Cambridge: Cambridge University Press, 1994.

———. "Researching Metaphor." In *Researching and Applying Metaphor*, edited by Lynne Cameron and Graham Low, 29–47. Cambridge Applied Linguistics Series. Cambridge: Cambridge University Press, 1999.

———. "Taking Metaphor Out of Our Heads and Putting It into Our Cultural World." In *Metaphor in Cognitive Linguistics*, edited by Raymond W. Gibbs Jr. and Gerard J. Steen, 145–66. Current Issues in Linguistic Theory 175. Amsterdam: Benjamins, 1999.

———. "The Psychological Status of Image Schemas." In *From Perception to Meaning: Image Schemas in Cognitive Linguistics*, edited by Beate Hampe, 113–36. Cognitive Linguistics Research 29. Berlin: Mouton de Gruyter, 2005.

Gibbs, Raymond W., Jr. et al. "Metaphor in Idiom Comprehension." *Journal of Memory and Language* 37 (1997) 141–54.

Gibbs, Raymond W. Jr., and Herbert L. Colston. "The Cognitive Psychological Reality of Image Schemas and their Transformations." In *Cognitive Linguistics: Basic Readings*, edited by Dirk Geeraerts, 239–68. Cognitive Linguistics Research 34. Berlin: Mouton de Gruyter, 2006.

Goddard, Cliff. *Semantic Analysis: A Practical Introduction*. Oxford Textbooks in Linguistics. Oxford: Oxford University Press, 1998.

Goddard, Cliff, and Anna Wierzbicka. "NSM Analyses of the Semantics of Physical Qualities: Sweet, Hot, Hard, Heavy, Rough, Sharp in Cross-Linguistic Perspective." *Studies in Language* 31 (2007) 765–800.

Goldingay, John. "Psalm 4: Ambiguity and Resolution." *TynBul* 57 (2006) 161–72.

———. *Psalms*. Vol. 1, *Psalms 1–41*. Baker Commentary on the Old Testament Wisdom and Psalms. Grand Rapids: Baker Academic, 2006.

———. *Psalms:* Vol. 2, *Psalms 42–89*. Baker Commentary on the Old Testament Wisdom and Psalms. Grand Rapids: Baker Academic, 2007.

Gordis, Robert. *The Song of Songs and Lamentations: A Study, Modern Translation and Commentary*. 3rd ed. New York: KTAV, 1974.

———. *The Book of Job: Commentary, New Translation and Special Studies*. New York: Jewish Theological Seminary of America, 1978.

Gottwald, Norman K. *Studies in the Book of Lamentations*. London: SCM, 1954.

Grady, Joseph E. "Image Schemas and Perception: Refining a Definition." In *From Perception to Meaning: Image Schemas in Cognitive Linguistics*, edited by Beate Hampe, 35–56. Cognitive Linguistics Research 29. Berlin: Mouton de Gruyter, 2005.

Groom, Sue. *Linguistic Analysis of Biblical Hebrew*. Carlisle, UK: Paternoster, 2003.

Gross, W. "גָּעָה." In *TDOT* 9:255–59.

Gruber, Mayer I. *Aspects of Non-Verbal Communication in the Ancient Near East*. 2 vols. Rome: Biblical Institute Press, 1980.

———. "Was Cain Angry or Depressed? Background of a Biblical Murder." *BAR* 6 (1980) 35–36.

———. "Private Life in Canaan and Ancient Israel." In *Civilizations of the Ancient Near East*, edited by Jack M. Sasson, 1:633–48. 2 vols. Peabody, MA: Hendrickson, 1995.

———. *Rashi's Commentary on the Psalms*. Philadelphia: The Jewish Publication Society, 2007.

Gunkel, Hermann. *The Psalms: A Form-Critical Introduction*. Facet Books. Biblical Series 19. Philadelphia: Fortress, 1967.

———. *Einleitung in die Psalmen*. 3rd ed. Göttingen: Vandenhoeck & Ruprecht, 1975.

Gwyn, Richard. "'Captain of my Own Ship': Metaphor and the Discourse of Chronic Illness." In *Researching and Applying Metaphor*, edited by Lynne Cameron and

Bibliography

Graham Low, 203–20. Cambirdge Applied Linguistics Series. Cambridge: Cambridge University Press, 1999.

Hallo, William W., and K. Lawson Younger Jr. *The Context of Scripture*. Vol. 1, *Canonical Compositions from the Biblical World*. Leiden: Brill, 1997.

Hamilton, Victor P. "מָרַד." In *TWOT*. Electronic database. NavPress Software, 1999. In *The Translator's Workplace 5.0* DVD, by SIL International, 2009.

———. "שָׁטַף." In *TWOT*. Electronic database. NavPress Software, 1999. In *The Translator's Workplace 5.0* DVD, by SIL International, 2009.

Hampe, Beate. *From Perception to Meaning: Image Schemas in Cognitive Linguistics*. Cognitive Linguistics Research 29. Berlin: Mouton de Gruyter, 2005.

———. "Image Schemas in Cognitive Linguistics: Introduction." In *From Perception to Meaning: Image Schemas in Cognitive Linguistics*, edited by Beate Hampe, 1-12. Cognitive Linguistics Research 29. Berlin: Mouton de Gruyter, 2005.

———. "When *Down* is Not Bad, and *Up* Not Good Enough: A Usage-Based Assessment of the Plus-Minus Parameter in Image-Schema Theory." *Cognitive Linguistics* 16 (2005) 81–112.

Harrison, R. K. and I. Swart. "נָגַע." In *NIDOTTE* 3:24–25.

Hausmann, J. "כָּלָא." In *TDOT* 7:143–45.

Hecke, P. van. "Lamentations 3,1–6: An Anti-Psalm 23." *SJOT* 16 (2002) 264–82.

Heessel, Nils P. "The Hands of the Gods: Disease Names, and Divine Anger." In *Disease in Babylonia*, edited by I. L. Finkel and M. J. Geller, 120–30. Cuneiform Monographs 36. Leiden: Brill, 2007.

Helman, Cecil G. *Culture, Health and Illness: An Introduction for Health Professionals*. 3rd ed. Oxford: Butterworth Heinemann, 1994.

Hesse, Brian. "Animal Husbandry and Human Diet in the Ancient Near East." In *Civilizations of the Ancient Near East, Volumes I and II*, edited by Jack M. Sasson, 1:203–22. 2 vols. Peabody, MA: Hendrickson, 1995.

Hillers, Delbert R. *Lamentations*. Rev. ed. AB 7A. New York: Doubleday, 1972.

———. "Dust: Some Aspects of Old Testament Imagery." In *Love & Death in the Ancient Near East: Essays in Honor of Marvin H. Pope*, edited by John H. Marks and Robert M. Good, 105–9. Guilford, CT: Four Quarters, 1987.

Hoftijzer, Jacob. "The History of the Database Project." In *Studies in Ancient Hebrew Semantics*, edited by Takamitzu Muraoka, 65–85. Abr-Nahrain Supplement Series 4. Leuven: Peeters, 1995.

Holm-Nielsen, Svend. *Hodayot: Psalms from Qumran*. Acta theologica Danica 2. Aarhus: Universitetsforlaget, 1960.

Hope, Edward Reginald. *All Creatures Great and Small: Living Things in the Bible*. New York: United Bible Societies, 2003. Electronic database. NavPress Software, 1999. In *The Translator's Workplace 5.0* DVD, by SIL International, 2009.

Humboldt, Carl Wilhem von. *On Language: The Diversity of Human Language-Structure and Its Influence on the Mental Development of Mankind*. Texts in German Philosophy. Cambridge: Cambridge University Press, 1988.

Ibarretxe-Antuñano, Iraide. "Metaphorical Mappings in the Sense of Smell." In *Metaphor in Cognitive Linguistics*, edited by Raymond W. Gibbs Jr. and Gerard J. Steen, 29–45. Current Issues in Linguistic Theory 175. Amsterdam: Benjamins, 1999.

Ikeda, Kikunae. "New Seasonings." *Chemical Senses* 27 (2002 [1909, Japanese]) 847–49.

Bibliography

Jacob, Edmond. *Theology of the Old Testament*. Translated by Arthur W. Heathcoate. London: Hodder & Stoughton, 1958.

Jaggar, Philip J. and Malami Buba. "Metaphorical Extensions of 'Eat' → [OVERCOME] and 'Drink' → [UNDERGO] in Hausa." In *The Linguistics of Eating and Drinking*, edited by John Newman, 229–52. Typological Studies in Language 84. Amsterdam: Benjamins, 2009.

Jäkel, Olaf "Hypotheses Revisited: The Cognitive Theory of Metaphor Applied to Religious Texts." *Metaphorik.de* 2 (2002) 20–42.

Janzen, J. Gerald. *Job*. Interpretation: A Bible Commentary for Teaching and Preaching. Atlanta: John Knox, 1985.

Jassen, Alex. "Intertextual Readings of the Psalms and the Dead Sea Scrolls: *4Q160 (Samuel Apocryphon)* and *Psalm 40*." *RevQ* 87 (2006) 403–30.

Jeremias, G. *Der Lehrer der Gerechtigkeit*. Franz-Delitzsch-Vorlesung 5. Göttingen: Vandenhoeck & Ruprecht, 1963.

Johnson, Aubrey R. *The Vitality of the Individual in the Thought of Ancient Israel*. 2nd ed. Cardiff: University of Wales Press, 1964.

Johnson, Mark. *The Body in the Mind: The Bodily Basis of Meaning, Imagination, and Reason*. Chicago: University of Chicago Press, 1987.

Johnston, Philip S. *Shades of Sheol: Death and Afterlife in the Old Testament*. Leicester: Apollos, 2002.

———. "The Psalms and Distress." In *Interpreting the Psalms: Issues and Approaches*, edited by Philip S. Johnston and David G. Firth, 63–84. Leicester: Apollos, 2005.

Joyce, Paul. "Lamentations and the Grief Process: A Psychological Reading." *BibInt* 1 (1993) 304–20.

Kaiser, O. "חֶרֶב." In *TDOT* 5:155–65.

Kaiser, Walter C., Jr. *A Biblical Approach to Personal Suffering*. Chicago: Moody, 1982.

Kedar-Kopfstein, B. "מֶתֶק." In *TDOT* 9:103–7.

Keel, Othmar. *The Symbolism of the Biblical World: Ancient Near Eastern Iconography and the Book of Psalms*. Winona Lake: Eisenbrauns, 1997.

———. "Powerful Symbols of Victory: The Parts Stay the Same, the Actors Change." *JNSL* 25 (1999) 205–40.

Kellermann, D. "חמץ." In *TDOT* 4:487–93.

———. "פֶּה." In *TDOT* 11:513–16.

Kimmel, Michael. "Culture Regained: Situated and Compound Image Schemas." In *From Perception to Meaning: Image Schemas in Cognitive Linguistics*, edited by Beate Hampe, 285–312. Cognitive Linguistics Research 29. Berlin: Mouton de Gruyter, 2005.

Kittel, Bonnie. *The Hymns of Qumran: Translation and Commentary*. SBLDS. Chico: Scholars, 1981.

Knibb, Michael A. "Life and Death in the Old Testament." In *The World of Ancient Israel: Sociological, Anthropological and Political Perspectives*, edited by R. E. Clements, 395–415. Cambridge: Cambridge University Press, 1989.

Knipping, B. "שָׁבַר." In *TDOT* 14:367–81.

Koch, K. "קָבַר." In *TDOT* 12:492–98.

Koerner, E. F. K. "Towards a 'Full Pedigree' of the 'Sapir-Whorf Hypothesis': From Locke to Lucy." In *Explorations in Linguistic Relativity*, edited by Martin Pütz and Marjolijn H. Verspoor, 1–23. Amsterdam Studies in the Theory and History

Bibliography

of Linguistic Science. Current Issues in Linguistic Theory i 199. Amsterdam: Benjamins, 2000.

Konkel, A. H. "אזח." In *NIDOTTE* 1:354–58.

Koptak, Paul E. "Intertextuality." In *Dictionary for Theological Interpretation of the Bible*, edited by Kevin J. Vanhoozer et al., 332–34. Grand Rapids: Baker Academic, 2005.

Kotzé, Zacharias. "A Cognitive Linguistic Approach to the Emotion of Anger in the Old Testament." *HvTSt* 60 (2004) 843–63.

———. "The Conceptualisation of Anger in the Hebrew Bible." PhD diss., Stellenbosch University, 2004.

———. "Women, Fire and Dangerous Things in the Hebrew Bible: Insights from the Cognitive Theory of Metaphor." *OTE* 17 (2004) 242–51.

———. "A Cognitive Linguistic Methodology for the Study of Metaphor in the Hebrew Bible." *JNSL* 31 (2005) 107–17.

Kövecses, Zoltán. *Metaphors of Anger, Pride, and Love: A Lexical Approach to the Structure of Concepts*. Pragmatics & Beyond: VII:8. Amsterdam: Benjamins, 1986.

———. *Emotion Concepts*. New York: Springer, 1990.

———. "Anger: Its Language, Conceptualization, and Physiology in the Light of Cross-Cultural Evidence." In *Language and the Cognitive Construal of the World*, edited by J. R. Taylor and R. MacLaury, 181–96. Trends in Linguistics. Studies and Monographs 82. Berlin: Mouton de Gruyter, 1995.

———. "Metaphor: Does It Constitute or Reflect Cultural Models?" In *Metaphor in Cognitive Linguistics*, edited by Raymond W. Gibbs Jr. and Gerard J. Steen, 167–88. Current Issues in Linguistic Theory 175. Amsterdam: Benjamins, 1999.

———. *Metaphor and Emotion: Language, Culture, and Body in Human Feeling*. Studies in Emotion and Social Interaction. 2nd Series. Cambridge: Cambridge University Press, 2000.

———. "The Scope of Metaphor." In *Metaphor and Metonymy at the Crossroads. A Cognitive Perspective*, edited by Antonio Barcelona, 79–92. Topics in English Linguistics 30. Berlin: Mouton de Gruyter, 2000.

———. "Emotion Concepts: Social Constructionism and Cognitive Linguistics." In *The Verbal Communication of Emotions: Interdisciplinary Perspectives*, edited by Susan R. Fussell, 109–24. Mahwah, NJ: Erlbaum, 2002.

———. *Metaphor: A Practical Introduction*. Oxford: Oxford University Press, 2002.

———. *Metaphor in Culture: Universality and Variation*. Cambridge: Cambridge University Press, 2005.

———. *Language, Mind and Culture: A Practical Introduction*. Oxford: Oxford University Press, 2006.

Kraus, Hans-Joachim. *Psalms 1–59: A Commentary*. Minneapolis: Augsburg, 1988.

———. *Psalms 60–150: A Commentary*. Minneapolis: Augsburg, 1989.

Krause, I. B. "Sinking Heart: A Punjabi Communication of Distress." *Social Science and Medicine* 29 (1989) 563–75.

Kronholm, T. "נדה." In *TDOT* 9:235–41.

Kruger, Paul A. "A Cognitive Interpretation of the Emotion of Anger in the Hebrew Bible." *JNSL* 26 (2000) 181–93.

———. "A Cognitive Interpretation of the Emotion of Fear in the Hebrew Bible." *JNSL* (2002) 77–89.

———. "On Emotions and the Expression of Emotions in the Old Testament: A Few Introductory Remarks." *BZ* 48 (2004) 213–28.

———. "Depression in the Hebrew Bible: An Update." *JNES* 64 (2005) 187–92.
———. "The Face and Emotions in the Hebrew Bible." *JNSL* 18 (2005) 651–63.
Kryk-Kastovsky, Barbara. "Surprise, Surprise: The Iconicity-Conventionality Scale of Emotions." In *The Language of Emotions: Conceptualization, Expression and Theoretical Foundation*, edited by Susanne Niemeier and René Dirven, 155–69. Amsterdam: Benjamins, 1997.
Krzeszowski, Tomasz. "The Axiological Parameter in Preconceptual Image Schemata." In *Conceptualizations and Mental Processing in Language*, edited by Richard Geiger and Brygida Rudzka-Ostyn, 307–29. Cognitive Linguistics Research 3. Berlin: Mouton de Gruyter, 1993.
Kübler-Ross, Elisabeth. *On Death and Dying*. New York: Macmillan, 1969.
Kutler, Laurence. "A 'Strong' Case for Hebrew *Mar*." *UF* 16 (1984) 111–18.
Kutscher, Eduard Y. *A History of the Hebrew Language*. Edited by Raphael Kutscher Leiden: Brill, 1982.
———. *The Language and Linguistic Background of the Isaiah Scroll (1QIsaa)*. STDJ 6. Leiden: Brill, 1974.
Labahn, Antje. "Bitterkeit und Asche als Speiser—das Leiden Jeremias am Schicksall Jerusalem, Metaphern und Metaphervariationen in Thr. 3, 1–21 LXX." In *Metaphor in the Hebrew Bible*, edited by Pierre van Hecke, 147–83. BETL 187. Leuven: Peeters, 2005.
———. "Wild Animals and Chasing Shadows: Animal Metaphors in Lamentations as Indicators of Individual Threat." In *Metaphor in the Hebrew Bible*, edited by Pierre van Hecke, 67–97 BETL 187. Leuven: Peeters, 2005.
———. "Fire from Above: Metaphors and Images of God's Actions in Lamentations 2.1–9." *JSOT* 31 (2006) 239–56.
Laihia, Pekka, and Marjut Laihia. Personal communication, 2009.
Lakoff, George. *Women, Fire, and Dangerous Things: What Categories Reveal about the Mind*. Chicago: University of Chicago Press, 1987.
———. "The Contemporary Theory of Metaphor." In *Cognitive Linguistics: Basic Readings*, edited by Dirk Geeraerts, 185–238. Cognitive Linguistics Research 34. Berlin: Mouton de Gruyter, 2006.
Lakoff, George and Mark Johnson. *Metaphors We Live By*, with a new afterword. 2nd ed. Chicago: University of Chicago Press, 2003 [1980].
———. *Philosophy in the Flesh: The Embodied Mind and Its Challenge to Western Thought*. New York: Basic Books, 1999.
Lakoff, George and Zoltán Kövecses. "The Cognitive Model of Anger Inherent in American English." In *Cultural Models in Language and Thought*, edited by Dorothy Holland and Naomi Quinn, 195–221. Cambridge: Cambridge University Press, 1987.
Lakoff, George, and Mark Turner. *More Than Cool Reason: A Field Guide to Poetic Metaphor*. Chicago: University of Chicago Press, 1989.
Lam, Raymond W. et al. "The Can-SAD Study: A Randomized Controlled Trial of the Effectiveness of Light Therapy and Fluoxetine in Patients with Winter Seasonal Affective Disorder." *American Journal of Psychiatry* 163 (2006) 805–12.
Lamb, Sydney M. "Neuro-Cognitive Structure in the Interplay of Language and Thought." In *Explorations in Linguistic Relativity*, edited by Martin Pütz and Marjolijn H. Verspoor, 173–96. Current Issues in Linguistic Theory. Amsterdam: Benjamins, 2000.

Bibliography

Lambert, William G. *Babylonian Wisdom Literature*. Oxford: Clarendon, 1960.

———. "The Cosmology of Sumer and Babylon." In *Ancient Cosmologies*, edited by Carmen Blacker and Michael Loewe, 42–65. London: Allen & Unwin, 1975.

Lamberty-Zielinski, Hedwig. "צוק." In *TDOT* 12:301–6.

Langacker, Ronald. *Foundations of Cognitive Grammar*. Vol. 1, *Theoretical Prerequisites*. Stanford: Stanford University Press, 1987.

Lauha, R. *Psychophysicher Sprachgebrauch im Alten Testament: Eine Struktursemantische Analyse von ruaḥ, nepeš, lēb*. Helsinki: Suomalainen Tiedeakatemia, 1983.

Licht, Jacob. *The Thanksgiving Scroll*. Jerusalem: Bialik Institute, 1957.

Loader, James Alfred. "Qumran, Text and Intertext: On the Significance of the Dead Sea Scrolls for Theologians Reading the Old Testament." *OTE* 19 (2006) 892–911.

Long, Gary Alan. "שׁחח." In *NIDOTTE* 4:76–77.

Low, Graham. "Validating Metaphor Research Projects." In *Researching and Applying Metaphor*, edited by Lynne Cameron and Graham Low, 48–65. Cambridge Applied Linguistics Series. Cambridge: Cambridge University Press, 1999.

Lucas, Ernest. *Exploring the Old Testament*. Vol. 3, *The Psalms and Wisdom Literature*. London: SPCK, 2003.

Lucy, John A. "The Scope of Linguistic Relativity: An Analysis and Review of Empirical Research." In *Rethinking Linguistic Relativity*, edited by John G. Gumperz and Stephen C. Levinson, 37–69. Studies in the Social and Cultural Foundations of Language 17. Cambridge: Cambridge University Press, 1996.

Lutz, Catherine. "Ethnopsychology Compared to What? Explaining Behaviour and Consciousness among the Ifaluk." In *Person, Self and Experience: Exploring Pacific Ethnopsychologies*, edited by Geoffrey M. White and John Kirkpatrick, 35–79. Berkeley: University of California Press, 1985.

———. "Goals, Events, and Understanding in Ifaluk Emotion Theory." In *Cultural Models in Language and Thought*, edited by Dorothy Holland and Naomi Quinn, 290–312. Cambridge: Cambridge University Press, 1987.

Mahon, James Edwin. "Getting Your Sources Right: What Aristotle Didn't Say." In *Researching and Applying Metaphor*, edited by Lynne Cameron and Graham Low, 69–80. Cambridge Applied Linguistics Series. Cambridge: Cambridge University Press, 1999.

Maiberger, P. "שׂאף." In *TDOT* 14:268–70.

Martin-Achard, Robert, and S. Paul Re'emi. *God's People in Crisis*. ITC. Edinburgh: Handsel, 1984.

Martínez, Florentino García. *The Dead Sea Scrolls Translated: The Qumran Texts in English*. Grand Rapids: Eerdmans, 1996.

Martínez, Florentino García, and Julio Trebolle Barrera. *The People of the Dead Sea Scrolls: Their Writings, Beliefs and Practices*. Leiden: Brill, 1995.

Martínez, Florentino García and Eibert J. C. Tigchelaar. *The Dead Sea Scrolls: Study Edition*. Eerdmans: Grand Rapids, 1997.

Mayer, G. "ירד." In *TDOT* 6:315–22.

Mazar, Amihai. *Archaeology of the Land of the Bible, 10,000–586 B.C.E.* ABRL. New York: Doubleday, 1992.

McCarthy, Dennis J. "Some Holy War Vocabulary in Joshua 2." *CBQ* 33 (1971) 228–30.

McConville, J. Gordon. *Exploring the Old Testament*. Vol. 4, *A Guide to the Prophets*. Downers Grove, IL: InterVarsity, 2002.

Bibliography

McElhanon, Kenneth. "From Word to Scenario: The Influence of Linguistic Theories upon Models of Translation." *SIL Journal of Translation* 1 (2005) 29–67.

———. "From Simple Metaphors to Conceptual Blending: The Mapping of Analogical Concepts and the Praxis of Translation." *SIL Journal of Translation* 2 (2006) 31–81.

McKane, William. *A Critical and Exegetical Commentary on Jeremiah*. ICC. Edinburgh: T. & T. Clark, 1986.

McMullen, Linda B., and John B. Conway. "Conventional Metaphors for Depression." In *The Verbal Communication of Emotions: Interdisciplinary Perspectives*, edited by Susan R. Fussell, 167–82. Mahwah, NJ: Erlbaum, 2002.

Meinander, Seija. Personal Communication, 2009.

Middlemas, Jill. "Did Second Isaiah Write Lamentations III?" *VT* 56 (2006) 505–25.

Mikołajczuk, Agnieszka. "The Metonymic and Metaphorical Conceptualisation of Anger in Polish." In *Speaking of Emotions: Conceptualisation and Expression*, edited by Angeliki Athanasiadou and Elżbieta Tabakowska, 153–90. Cognitive Linguistics Research 10. Berlin: Mouton de Gruyter, 1998.

Mommer, P. "רֶשֶׁת." In *TDOT* 14:16–19.

Mondry, Henrietta, and John R. Taylor. "The Cultural Dynamics of 'National Character': The Case of the New Russians." In *Speaking of Emotions: Conceptualisation and Expression*, edited by Angeliki Athanasiadou and Elżbieta Tabakowska, 29–48. Cognitive Linguistics Research 10. Berlin: Mouton de Gruyter, 1998.

Moore, Michael S. "Human Suffering in Lamentations." *RB* 90 (1983) 534–55.

Morag, Shelomo. "Qumran Hebrew: Some Typological Observations." *VT* 38 (1988) 148–64.

Moskowitz, Howard W. et al. "Cross-cultural Differences in Simple Taste Preferences." *Science* 190 (1975) 1217–18.

Mostovaja, Anna D. "On Emotions that One can 'Immerse Into,' 'Fall Into' and 'Come To': The Semantics of a Few Russian Prepositional Constructions." In *Speaking of Emotions: Conceptualisation and Expression*, edited by Angeliki Athanasiadou and Elżbieta Tabakowska, 295–330. Cognitive Linguistics Research 10. Berlin: Mouton de Gruyter, 1998.

Mowinckel, Sigmund. *The Psalms in Israel's Worship*. 2 vols. Oxford: Blackwell, 1962.

Mueller, Ken L. et al. "The Receptors and Coding Logic for Bitter Taste." *Nature* 434 (2005) 225–29.

Mulder, H.-P. "עֲרָפֶל." In *TDOT* 11:371–75.

Mullen, E. Theodore, Jr. *The Assembly of the Gods: The Divine Council in Canaanite and Early Hebrew Literature*. HSM 24. Chico: Scholars, 1980.

Muraoka, Takamitzu. "A New Dictionary of Classical Hebrew." In *Studies in Ancient Hebrew Semantics*, edited by Takamitzu Muraoka, 87–101. Abr-Nahrain Supplement Series 4. Leuven: Peeters, 1995.

Naudé, Jacobus. "A Perspective on the Chronological Framework of Biblical Hebrew." *JNSL* 30 (2004) 87–102.

Negenman, J. H. "Geography of Palestine." In *The World of the Bible*, edited by Adam S. van der Woude et al., 2–20. Bible Handbook 1. Grand Rapids: Eerdmans, 1986.

Nel, Philip J. "The Symbolism and Function of Epic Space in Jonah." *JNSL* 25 (1999) 215–24.

NET Bible 2nd Beta ed. Dallas: Biblical Studies Press, 1996–2003.

Neufeld, Edward. "Apiculture in Ancient Palestine (Early and Middle Iron Age) Within the Framework of the Ancient Near East." *UF* 10 (1978) 219–47.

Bibliography

Neusner, Jacob. *The Mishnah: Introduction and Reader*. Philadelphia: Trinity, 1992.

Newman, John. "A Cross-linguistic Overview of 'Eat' and 'Drink.'" In *The Linguistics of Eating and Drinking*, edited by John Newman, 1–26. Amsterdam: Benjamins, 2009.

———. *The Linguistics of Eating and Drinking*. Amsterdam: Benjamins, 2009.

Newsom, Carol A. "Kenneth Burke Meets the Teacher of Righteousness: Rhetorical Strategies in the Hodayot and the Serek ha-Yahad." In *Of Scribes and Scrolls: Studies in the Hebrew Bible, Intertestamental Judaism and Christian Origins*, edited by Harold W. Attridge et al., 121–31. College Theology Society Resources in Religion 5. Lanham, MD: University Press of America, 1990.

Niehr, H. "עֶרֶב." In *TDOT* 11:335–41.

———. "צַלְמָוֶת." In *TDOT* 12:396–99.

Niemeier, Susanne, and René Dirven, editors. *The Language of Emotions: Conceptualization, Expression and Theoretical Foundation*. Amsterdam: Benjamins, 1997.

Nørager, Troels. "'Heart' as Metaphor in Religious Discourse." In *Metaphor and God-Talk*, edited by Lieven Boeve and Kurt Feyaerts, 215–32. Religions and Discourse 2. Bern: Lang, 1999.

North, Robert. "Brain and Nerve in Biblical Outlook." *Biblica* 74 (1993) 577–97.

O'Mahony, M. et al. "Confusion in the Use of the Taste Adjectives 'Sour' and 'Bitter.'" *Chemical Senses* 4 (1979) 301–18.

Oakley, Todd. "Force-dynamic Dimensions of Rhetorical Effect." In *From Perception to Meaning: Image Schemas in Cognitive Linguistics*, edited by Beate Hampe, 443–474. Cognitive Linguistics Research 29. Berlin: Mouton de Gruyter, 2005.

Oeming, M. "צוד." In *TDOT* 12:270–75.

Oppenheim, A. Leo. *The Assyrian Dictionary of the Oriental Institute of the University of Chicago*. Vol. 1/2, *AM–AZ*. Chicago: The Oriental Institute, 1968.

Oswalt, John N. "כָּלָא." In *TWOT*. Electronic database. NavPress Software, 1999. In *The Translator's Workplace 5.0* DVD, by SIL International, 2009.

Panther, Klaus-Uwe, and Günter Radden, editors. *Metonymy in Language and Thought*. Human Cognitive Processing 4. Amsterdam: Benjamins, 1999.

Pardee, Dennis. "The Semitic Root mrr and the Etymology of Ugaritic mr(r) | brk." *UF* 10 (1978) 249–83.

———. "merôrăt-petanîm ›Venom‹ in Job 20.14." *ZAW* 91 (1979) 401–16.

Patterson, R. D. "סוּף." In *TWOT*. Electronic database. NavPress Software, 1999. In *The Translator's Workplace 5.0* DVD, by SIL International, 2009.

Pearsall, Judy, editor. *The New Oxford Dictionary of English*. Oxford: Clarendon, 1998.

Pedersen, Johannes. *Israel: Its Life and Culture*. 2 vols. London: Oxford University Press, 1926.

Petty, Alice. "So Work the Honey Bees: The Introduction of Apiculture as an Assertion of Royal Legitimacy." Paper presented at the American Schools of Oreintal Research (ASOR) Annual Meeting (held in Boulder, Colorado, in 2001).

Piper, O. A. "Light, Light and Darkness." In *IDB* 3:130–32.

Pohlig, James N. "Cognition and Biblical Documents: Towards Overcoming Theoretical and Methodological Obstacles to Recovering Cultural Worldviews." *JNSL* 29 (2003) 21–35.

Pope, Marvin H. *Job*. AB 15. Garden City, NY: Doubleday, 1965.

Popova, Yanna. "Image Schemas and Verbal Synaesthesia." In *From Perception to Meaning: Image Schemas in Cognitive Linguistics*, edited by Beate Hampe, 395–420. Berlin: Mouton de Gruyter, 2005.

Porteous, Norman W. "The Present State of Old Testament Theology." *ET* 75 (1963) 70–74.
Preuss, H. "חוה." In *TDOT* 4:248–56.
Price, James D. "אֹפֶל." In *NIDOTTE* 1:479–81.
———. "עָלָטָה." In *NIDOTTE* 3:421.
———. "עֲרָפֶל." In *NIDOTTE* 3:421.
Pritchard, James B. *Ancient Near Eastern Texts Relating to the Old Testament (ANET)*. 3rd ed. Princeton: Princeton University Press, 1969.
Rabin, Chaim. "Lexicostatistics and the Internal Divisions of Semitic." In *Hamito-Semitica*, edited by James and Theodora Bynon, 85–102. Janua linguarum Series Practica 200. The Hague: Mouton, 1975.
Rad, Gerhard von. *Old Testament Theology*. Vol. 1, *The Theology of Israel's Historical Traditions*. Edinburgh: Oliver & Boyd, 1962.
Radden, Günter. "The Conceptualisation of Emotional Causality by Means of Prepositional Phrases." In *Speaking of Emotions: Conceptualization and Expression*, edited by Angeliki Athanasiadou and Elżbieta Tabakowska, 273–94. Cognitive Linguistics Research 10. Berlin: Mouton de Gruyter, 1998.
———. "How Metonymic are Metaphors?" In *Metaphor and Metonymy at the Crossroads. A Cognitive Perspective*, edited by Antonio Barcelona, 93–108. Topics in English Linguistics 30. Berlin: Mouton de Gruyter, 2000.
Radden, Günter, and Zoltán Kövecses. "Towards a Theory of Metonymy." In *Metonymy in Language and Thought*, edited by Klaus-Uwe Panther and Günter Radden, 17–59. Human Cognitive Processing 4. Amsterdam: Benjamins, 1999.
Rechenmacher, H. "Kognitive Linguistik und Althebräische Lexicographie." *JNSL* 30 (2004) 43–59.
Reddy, Michael J. "The Conduit Metaphor: A Case of Frame Conflict in our Language about Language." In *Metaphor and Thought*, edited by Andrew Ortony, 164–201. 2nd ed. Cambridge: Cambridge University Press, 1993.
Reiner, Erica, editor. *The Assyrian Dictionary of the Oriental Institute at the University of Chicago Š/1*. Chicago: The Oriental Institute, 1989.
Reiterer, F. "נָקַף." In *TDOT* 10:10–14.
———. "פָּרַק." In *TDOT* 12:111–14.
Renfrew, Jane M. "Vegetables in the Ancient Near Eastern Diet." In *Civilizations of the Ancient Near East*, edited by Jack M. Sasson et al., 1:191–202. 4 vols. Peabody, MA: Hendrickson, 1995.
Renkema, Johan. *Lamentations*. Historical Commentary on the Old Testament. Leuven: Peeters, 1998.
Riede, Peter. "Der Sprache der Bilder. Zur bedeutung und funktion der Metaphorik in den Feindpsalmen des Alten Testaments am Beispiel der Psalmen 57 und 59." In *Metaphor in the Hebrew Bible*, edited by Pierre van Hecke, 19–40. BETL 187. Leuven: Peeters, 2005.
Ringgren, Helmer. "יָקַשׁ." In *TDOT* 6:288–90.
———. "סָגַר." In *TDOT* 10:148–52.
———. "צָר II." In *TDOT* 12:464–68.
Ringgren, Helmer et al. "חָשַׁךְ." In *TDOT* 5:245–59.
Ringgren, Helmer, and Heinz-Josef Fabry. "מרר." In *TDOT* 9:15–19.
Roaf, Michael. *Cultural Atlas of Mesopotamia and the Ancient Near East*. New York: Facts on File, 1990.

Bibliography

Roberts, J. J. M. "The Hand of Yahweh." In *The Bible and the Ancient Near East: Collected Essays*, edited by J. J. M. Roberts, 95–101. Winona Lake: Eisenbrauns, 2002.

Robinson, J. O. "The Misuse of Taste Names by Untrained Observers." *British Journal of Psychology* 61 (1970) 375–78.

Rochberg, Francesca. "Mesopotamian Cosmology." In *A Companion to the Ancient Near East*, edited by Daniel C. Snell, 316–29. Blackwell Companions to the Ancient World. Ancient History. Oxford: Blackwell, 2005.

Rogerson, John William. *Chronicles of the Bible Lands*. London: Angus, 2003.

Rosaldo, Michelle Z. "Toward an Anthropology of Self and Feeling." In *Culture Theory: Essays on Mind, Self, and Emotion*, edited by Richard A. Shweder and Robert A. LeVine, 137–57. Cambridge: Cambridge University Press, 1984.

Rosaldo, Renato. "Grief and a Headhunter's Rage." In *Death, Mourning, and Burial: A Cross-Cultural Reader*, edited by Antonius C. G. M. Robben, 167–78. Oxford: Blackwell, 2004.

Rosch, Eleanor. "Natural Categories." *Cognitive Psychology* 4 (1973) 328–50.

———. "Principles of Categorization." In *Cognition and Categorization*, edited by Eleanor Rosch and B. B. Lloyd, 27–48. Hillsdale, NJ: Erlbaum, 1978.

Rosch, Eleanor et al. "Basic Objects in Natural Categories." *Cognitive Psychology* 8 (1976) 382–439.

Roth, Martha T., editor. *Chicago Assyrian Dictionary (P)*. Chicago: The Oriental Institute, 2005.

Rozin, Paul et al. "Disgust: Preadaptation and the Cultural Evolution of a Food-Based Emotion." In *Food Preferences and Taste: Continuity and Change*, edited by Helen Macbeth, 65–82. Anthropology of Food and Nutrition 2. Oxford: Bergahn, 1997.

Rudman, Dominic. "The Use of Water Imagery in Descriptions of Sheol." *ZAW* 113 (2001) 240–44.

Rumelhart, David E. "Some Problems with the Notion of Literal Meaning." In *Metaphor and Thought*, edited by Andrew Ortony, 71–82. 2nd ed. Cambridge: Cambridge University Press, 1993.

Ruppert, L. "שחח." In *TDOT* 14:558–62.

Ryken, Leland et al., editors. *Dictionary of Biblical Imagery*. Downers Grove: InterVarsity, 1998.

Sáenz-Badillos, Angel. *A History of the Hebrew Language*. Translated by John Elwolde. Cambridge: Cambridge University Press, 1993.

Salters, R. B. *Jonah & Lamentations*. OTG. Sheffield, UK: JSOT Press, 1994.

Sapir, Edward. *Culture, Language and Personality: Selected Essays*. Berkeley: University of California Press, 1966.

Sawyer, John F. A. "Root-Meanings in Hebrew." *JSS* (1967) 37–50.

———. "Spaciousness (An Important Feature of Language about Salvation in the Old Testament)." *ASTI* 6 (1968) 20–34.

———. *Semantics in Biblical Research: New Methods of Defining Hebrew Words for Salvation*. SBT, 2nd ser., 24. London: SCM, 1972.

Schank, Roger, and Robert C. Abelson. *Scripts, Plans, Goals, and Understanding: An Inquiry into Human Knowledge Structures*. The Artificial Intelligence Series. Hillsdale, NJ: Erlbaum, 1977.

Schiefenhövel, Wulf. "Good Taste and Bad Taste: Preferences and Aversions as Biological Principles." In *Food Preferences and Taste: Continuity and Change*, edited by Helen Macbeth, 55–64. Anthropology of Food and Nutrition 2. Oxford: Bergahn, 1997.

Bibliography

Schmidt, Hans. *Das Gebet der Angeklagten im Alten Testament*. BZAW 49. Giessen: Töppelmann, 1928.

Schmoldt, H. "קדר." In *TDOT* 12:518–20.

Schuller, Eileen M. "Thanksgiving Hymns (1QH)." In *Dictionary of New Testament Background*, edited by Craig A. Evans and Stanley R. Porter, 1214–18. Leicester: InterVarsity, 2000.

———. "Some Contributions of the Cave Four Manuscripts (4Q427–32) to the Study of the Hodayot." *Dead Sea Discoveries* 8 (2001) 278–87.

Schultz, Carl. "עוד." In *TWOT*. Electronic database. NavPress Software, 1999. In *The Translatior's Workplace 5.0* DVD, by SIL International, 2009.

Schüpphaus, J. "בלע." In *TDOT*. Revised ed. 2:136–39.

Schwienhorst, L. "נגע." In *TDOT* 9:203–9.

Seebass, H. "נפש." In *TDOT* 9:497–519.

Segal, M. H. *A Grammar of Mishnaic Hebrew*. Oxford: Clarendon, 1927.

Selye, Hans "Stress and the General Adaptation Syndrome." *British Medical Journal* 1 (1950) 1383–92.

———. *The Stress of Life*. New York: McGraw-Hill, 1956.

———. "A Syndrome Produced by Diverse Nocuous Agents." *Nature* 138 (1936) 32.

Seybold, Klaus. *Das Gebet des Kranken im Alten Testament*. BWANT 5/1. Stuttgart: Kohlhammer, 1973.

———. "לענה." In *TDOT* 8:14–16.

Shea, William H. "The *qinah* Structure of the Book of Lamentations." *Biblica* 60 (1979) 103–7.

Shimron, Joseph. *Language Processing and Acquisition in Languages of Semitic, Root-Based, Morphology*. Language Acquisition and Language Disorders 28. Amsterdam: Benjamins, 2003.

———. "Semitic Languages: Are They Really Root-based?" In *Language Processing and Acquisition in Languages of Semitic, Root-Based, Morphology*, edited by Joseph Shimron, 1–28. Language Acquisition and Language Disorders 28. Amsterdam: Benjamins, 2003.

Silva, Moisés. *Biblical Words and Their Meanings: An Introduction to Lexical Semantics*. 2nd ed. Grand Rapids: Zondervan, 1994.

Sinnemäki, Kaius. Personal Communication, 2009.

Smith, David V., and Robert F. Margolskee. "Making Sense of Taste." *Scientific American* 16:3 (2006) 84–92.

Smith, Morton. "On the Differences Between the Culture of Israel and the Major Cultures of the Ancient Near East." *JANESCU* (1973) 389–95.

Snaith, Norman H. "The Language of the Old Testament." In *The Interpreter's Bible*, edited by George A. Buttrick et al., 1:220–32. 12 vols. New York: Abingdon-Cokesbury, 1952.

Snyder, Solomon H. et al. "Discovering Light Effects on the Brain." *American Journal of Psychiatry* 163 (2006) 771.

Spiegel, Yorick. *The Grief Process*. Nashville: Abingdon, 1977.

Steen, Gerard. "Metaphor and Discourse: Towards a Linguistic Checklist for Metaphor Analysis." In *Researching and Applying Metaphor*, edited by Lynne Cameron and Graham Low, 81–104. Cambridge Applied Linguistics Series. Cambridge: Cambridge University Press, 1999.

Bibliography

Steen, Gerard J. "From Linguistic to Conceptual Metaphor in Five Steps." In *Metaphor in Cognitive Linguistics,* edited by Raymond W. Gibbs Jr. and Gerard J. Steen, 57–77. Current Issues in Linguistic Theory 175. Amsterdam: Benjamins, 1999.

Stigers, Harold G. "גֵּרֵשׁ." In *TWOT*. Electronic database. NavPress Software, 1999. In *The Translator's Workplace 5.0* DVD, by SIL International, 2009.

Still, Judith, and Michael Worton. "Introduction." In *Intertextuality: Theories and Practice,* edited by Michael Worton and Judith Still, 1–44. Manchester, UK: Manchester University Press, 1990.

Stol, Marten. *Epilepsy in Babylonia.* Cuneiform Monographs 2. Groningen: STYX, 1993.

Stol, Marten. "Psychosomatic Suffering in Ancient Mesopotamia." In *Mesopotamian Magic: Textual, Historical and Interpretive Perspectives, Vol. 1999,* edited by I. Tzvi Abusch and Karel van der Toorn, 57–68. Groningen: Brill, 1999.

———. "Fevers in Babylonia." In *Disease in Babylonia,* edited by I. L. Finkel and M. J. Geller, 1-39. Leiden: Brill, 2007.

Stuart, Douglas. *Hosea-Jonah.* WBC. Waco: Word, 1987.

Summer Institute of Linguistics (SIL). "Key Terms in Biblical Hebrew: A Guide for Researchers." Online: http://www.ktbh-team.org/Project%20Information/Abridged%20Guide.doc

———. *The Translator's Workplace 5.0* DVD, 2009.

Sussman, Max. "Sickness and Disease." In *ABD* 6:6–15. New York: Doubleday, 1992.

Swart, I. "The Hebrew Vocabulary of Oppression: The State of Semantic Description." *JNSL* 16 (1990) 179–97.

Swart, Ignatius and Robin Wakely. "צרר." In *NIDOTTE* 3:853-858.

Sweetser, Eve. *From Etymology to Pragmatics: Metaphorical and Cultural Aspects of Semantic Structure.* Cambridge Studies in Linguistics 54. Cambridge: Cambridge University Press, 1990.

Talmon, Shemaryahu. "Har and Midbār: An Antithetical Pair of Biblical Motifs." In *Figurative Language in the Ancient Near East,* edited by M. Mindlin et al., 117–42. London: School of Oriental and African Studies, 1987.

Talmy, Leonard. "Force Dynamics in Language and Cognition." *Cognitive Science* 12 (1988) 49–100.

———. *Toward a Cognitive Semantics.* Vol. 1, *Concept Structuring Systems.* Language, Speech, and Communication. Cambridge: MIT Press, 2000.

Tamez, Elsa. *Bible of the Oppressed.* Maryknoll, NY: Orbis, 1982.

Tångberg, K. Arvid. "Linguistics and Theology: An Attempt to Analyze and Evaluate James Barr's Argumentation in The Semantics of Biblical Language and Biblical Words for Time." *BT* 24 (1973) 301–10.

Tate, Marvin E. *Psalms 51–100.* WBC 20. Waco: Word, 1990.

Taylor, John R. *Cognitive Grammar.* Oxford Textbooks in Linguistics. Oxford: Oxford University Press, 2002.

———. *Linguistic Categorization: Prototypes in Linguistic Theory.* 3rd ed. Oxford: Oxford University Press, 2003.

Taylor, John R., and Thandi G. Mbense. "Red Dogs and Rotten Mealies: How Zulus Talk about Anger." In *Speaking of Emotions: Conceptualisation and Expression,* edited by Angeliki Athanasiadou and Elżbieta Tabakowska, 191–226. Cognitive Linguistics Research 10. Berlin: Mouton de Gruyter, 1998.

Thompson, John A. *Handbook of Life in Bible Times.* Leicester: InterVarsity, 1986.

Toorn, Karel, van der. *Sin and Sanction in Israel and Mesopotamia: A Comparative Study*. SSN 22. Assen: Van Gorcum, 1985.
Tromp, Nicholas J. *Primitive Conceptions of Death and the Nether World in the Old Testament*. Rome: Pontifical Biblical Institute, 1969.
Tuggy, David. "The Nawatl Verb *kīsa*: A Case Study in Polysemy." In *Cognitive Approaches to Lexical Semantics*, edited by Hubert Cuyckens et al., 323–62. Cognitive Linguistics Research 23. Berlin: Mouton de Gruyter, 2003.
Turner, Mark. *The Literary Mind*. New York: Oxford University Press, 1996.
Turner, Mark, and Gilles Fauconnier. "Metaphor, Metonymy and Binding." In *Metaphor and Metonymy at the Crossroads: A Cognitive Perspective*, edited by Antonio Barcelona, 133–45. Topics in English Linguistics 30. Berlin: Mouton de Gruyter, 2000.
Ullendorf, Edward. "Is Biblical Hebrew a Language?" *BSOAS* 34 (1971) 241–55.
Unger, Merrill F. *Archaeology and the Old Testament*. Grand Rapids: Zondervan, 1954.
Ussishkin, David. "Gate 1567 at Megiddo and the Seal of Shema, Servant of Jeroboam." In *Scripture and Other Artifacts: Essays on the Bible and Archaeology in Honor of Philip J. King*, edited by Michael D. Coogan et al., 410–28. Louisville: Westminster John Knox, 1994.
Van der Merwe, Christo H. J. "Lexical Meaning in Biblical Hebrew and Cognitive Semantics: A Case Study." *Biblica* 87 (2006) 85–95.
———. "Towards a Principled Model of Biblical Hebrew Lexicology." *JNSL* 30 (2004) 119–37.
Van der Merwe, Christo H. J., and Lisa Hendriks. "Translating Metaphors in a Source Language Oriented Translation of the Bible in Afrikaans." Paper presented at Context and Translation: Bible Translation Conference (held in Horsleys Green, UK, 2006).
Wächter, L. "שְׁאוֹל." In *TDOT* 14:239–48.
———. "שַׁחַת." In *TDOT* 14:595–99.
Wagner, S. "טָרַף." In *TDOT* 5:350–57.
Wakely, Robin. "אָשׁוּן." In *NIDOTTE* 1:549–50.
———. "נֶשֶׁף." In *NIDOTTE* 3:191–96.
Waldman, Nahum M. "The Imagery of Clothing, Covering and Overpowering." *JANESCU* 19 (1989) 162–70.
———. *The Recent Study of Hebrew: A Survey of the Literature with Selected Bibliography*. Bibliographica Judaica 10. Cincinatti: Hebrew Union College Press, 1989.
Waltke, Bruce K. "עֶצֶב." In *TWOT*. Electronic database. NavPress Software, 1999. In *The Translator's Workplace 5.0* DVD, by SIL International, 2009.
Walton, John H. *Ancient Near Eastern Thought and the Old Testament: Introducing the Conceptual World of the Hebrew Bible*. Grand Rapids: Baker Academic, 2006.
Ward, W. A. "Egypto-Semitic MR, 'Be Bitter, Strong.'" *UF* 12 (1980) 356–60.
Warren-Rothlin, Andy L. "Body Idioms and the Psalms." In *Interpreting the Psalms: Issues and Approaches*, edited by Philip S. Johnston and David G. Firth, 195–212. Leicester: Apollos, 2005.
Werth, Paul. *Text Worlds: Representing Conceptual Space in Discourse*. Textual Explorations. Harlow, UK: Longman, 1999.
Westermann, Claus. *Lamentations: Issues and Interpretation*. Edinburgh: T. & T. Clark, 1994.

Bibliography

———. "נֶפֶשׁ." In *Theological Lexicon of the Old Testament*, edited by Ernst Jenni and Claus Westermann, 2:743–59. 3 vols. Peabody, MA: Hendrickson, 1997.

Whorf, Benjamin Lee. "A Linguistic Consideration of Thinking in Primitive Communities." In *Language, Thought, and Reality: Selected Writings of Benjamin Lee Whorf*, edited by John B. Carroll, 65–85. Cambridge: MIT Press, 1956.

———. "The Relation of Habitual Thought and Behavior to Language." In *Language, Thought and Reality: Selected Writings of Benjamin Lee Whorf*, edited by John B. Carroll, 134–59. Cambridge: MIT Press, 1956.

———. "Science and Linguistics." In *Language, Thought and Reality: Selected Writings of Benjamin Lee Whorf*, edited by John B. Carroll, 207–19. Cambridge: MIT Press, 1956.

Wierzbicka, Anna. *Emotions across Languages and Cultures: Diversity and Universals*. Studies in Emotion and Social Interaction, 2nd ser. Cambridge: Cambridge University Press, 1999.

———. "'Metaphors Linguists Live By: Lakoff and Johnson contra Aristotle' Review of Lakoff and Johnson 1980." *Papers in Linguistics* (1986) 287–313.

———. "Russian 'National Character' and Russian Language: A Rejoinder to H. Mondry and J. Taylor." In *Speaking of Emotions: Conceptualisation and Expression*, edited by Angeliki Athanasiadou and Elżbieta Tabakowska, 49–54. Cognitive Linguistics Research 10. Berlin: Mouton de Gruyter, 1998.

———. "'Sadness' and 'Anger' in Russian: The Non-universality of the So-called 'Basic Human Emotions.'" In *Speaking of Emotions: Conceptualisation and Expression*, edited by Angeliki Athanasiadou and Elżbieta Tabakowska, 3–28. Cognitive Linguistics Research 10. Berlin: Mouton de Gruyter, 1998.

———. *Semantics, Culture, and Cognition: Universal Human Concepts in Culture-Specific Configurations*. New York: Oxford University Press, 1992.

———. "The Semantics of Metaphor and Parable: Looking for Meaning in the Gospels." *Theoria et Historia Scientiarum* 4 (2002) 85–106.

———. *Understanding Cultures through Their Key Words: English, Russian, Polish, German, and Japanese*. Oxford Studies in Anthropological Linguistis 8. New York: Oxford University Press, 1997.

———. *What Did Jesus Mean? Explaining the Sermon on the Mount and the Parables in Simple and Universal Human Concepts*. Oxford: Oxford University Press, 2001.

Wilkinson, Richard H. "The Representation of the Bow in the Art of Egypt and the Ancient Near East." *JNES* 20 (1991) 83–99.

Willey, Patricia Tull. *Remember the Former Things: The Recollection of Previous Texts in Second Isaiah*. SBLDS 161. Atlanta: Scholars, 1997.

Williamson, H. G. M. "Reading the Lament Psalms Backwards." In *A God so Near: Essays in Old Testament Theology in Honor of Patrick D. Miller*, edited by Brent A. Strawn and Nancy R. Bowen, 3–15. Winona Lake: Eisenbrauns, 2003.

Wilson, Marvin R. "נָכָה." In *TWOT*. Electronic database. NavPress Software, 1999. In *The Translator's Workplace 5.0* DVD, by SIL International, 2009.

Wiseman, Donald J. "Medicine in the Old Testament World." In *Medicine and the Bible*, edited by Bernard Palmer, 13–42. Exeter, UK: Paternoster, 1986.

Wittgenstein, Ludwig. *Philosophical Investigations*. New York: Macmillan, 1953.

Wolf, Herbert M., and Robert Holmstedt. "שִׂיחַ." In *NIDOTTE* 4:98.

Wolfers, David. *Deep Things out of Darkness: The Book of Job, Essays and a New English Translation*. Kampen: Kok Pharos, 1995.

Wood, Leon J. "זָעַק." In *TWOT*. Electronic database. NavPress Software, 1999. In *The Translator's Workplace 5.0 DVD*, by SIL International, 2009.

Wyatt, Nick. "The Darkness of Genesis 1.2." In *The Mythic Mind: Essays on Cosmology and Religion in Ugaritic and Old Testament Literature*, edited by Nick Wyatt, 92–101. London: Equinox, 2005.

Wyatt, Nicolas. *Space and Time in the Religious Life of the Near East*. The Biblical Seminar 85. Sheffield, UK: Sheffield Academic, 2001.

Yadin, Yigael. *The Art of Warfare in Biblical Lands in the Light of Archaeological Discovery*. London: Weidenfeld & Nicolson, 1963.

Ye, Zhengdao. "Taste as a Gateway to Chinese Cognition." In *Mental States*. Vol. 2, *Language and Cognitive Structure*, edited by Andrea Schalley and Drew Khlentzos, 109–32. 2 vols. Studies in Language Companion Series 92–93. Amsterdam: Benjamins, 2007.

Scripture Index

OLD TESTAMENT

Genesis

1	174
1:2	292
4:5	134
12:17	229, 280
15	293
19:5	167
19:10	212
19:11	280
22:5	109
26:35	336
27:1	302
27:34	338
32:7[8]	145, 147, 205
32:11	117
37:34	317

Exodus

1:14	350
3:20	280
10:21–22	295, 299
11:1	229
12:8	350
12:34	144, 146
14:3	205
15:4–5	115
19:4	281
20:3	105
30:36	225
32:20	225
34:24	206

Leviticus

5:2	229
11	213
13–14	206–7

Numbers

5	328, 350–51
11:8	225
12:15	205
16:31–35	212

Deuteronomy

1:28	273
19:6	269
20:8	273
20:20	181
28:43	108
28:52	147
32:32	328, 340

Joshua

2:11	134, 273
5:1	273
7:5	273
9:4	146

Scripture Index

Judges

2:15	147, 204
7:18	167
10:9	147, 204
11:7	147
14:17	150
16	151
16:2	167
18	335
19:22	167
20:5	167
20:16	24

Ruth

2:14	327

1 Samuel

1:10	334
5:1–4	212
13:6	147
14:29	316
16:1	213
22:2	334
25:29	146
26:5	151
28:15	147
30:6	147, 334

2 Samuel

1:26	147
2:26	347
12:16	109
13:2	147
13:19	317
13:31	109
17:8	334
17:10	273
20:3	147
23:15	103
23:20	104
24:14	147, 204

1 Kings

5:3[17]	151
7:24	151
8:20	295
8:30–31	80
8:37	148, 229, 280
18:42	135
18:45	303
18:46	281
19:5	212
21:27	317
22:34–35	256

2 Kings

3:1	151
4:27	334
6:1	147
6:14	151
6:18	280
7:10	151
11:8	151
17:7	135
19:1	317

1 Chronicles

11:17	103
21:13	204

2 Chronicles

6:28	148

Ezra

9:8	316

Nehemiah

7:6	135
9:18	135
13:25	213

Esther

3:2	110
4:1	317, 338

Scripture Index

Job

Reference	Page(s)
1:5	151
1:10	154, 162
1:19	212, 229
3:20	333
3:23	154, 162, 205–6
3:25–26	231
6:2–3	275–276
6:4	89, 256, 340
6:6	327
7:3–4	306
7:11	160, 333
7:12	198–99
7:19–20	253, 279
8:22	305
9:17	267
9:18	339, 342–43, 348, 361
9:19	245
9:34	253, 279
10:1	333
10:8	170
10:16	238
10:17	259–60
10:21–22	307
11:17	312–13
12:14	163
12:24–25	309
13:21	250
13:24	245
13:25	235, 268
13:26	345–46
13:27	198
14:18–19	263
15:16	349
15:20–35	308, 316
16:9	239–40, 242
16:10–13	259–60
16:12–13	255–56, 279
16:13	169–70, 206, 329
16:14	251
17:1	152, 160, 222
17:7	302
17:11	225
17:13	307
17:16	199
18:5–6	309
18:7	147
18:8–10	187, 191
18:11	171
18:18	309
19:2	226, 278, 281, 286
19:6	180–81
19:8	161–63, 164, 206, 311–13
19:10	169–70
19:11	245, 270
19:12	180–81, 209, 259
19:21	229, 248–49
20:12–15	350
20:14–15	329
20:22	147
20:23	339
21:6	227–28
21:20	339
21:23–25	333–34, 341, 343, 347
22:10	187
22:11	176–77, 309–10, 313
23:2	250, 276, 337
23:17	310, 316
24:13–17	293
26:8	146
27:2	333–34
28:3	294
30:12–14	259–60
30:14–15	267
30:16	227–28
30:17	221, 306
30:18–19	250–51, 281
30:19	130, 134
30:21	249
30:22	234, 262, 268
30:26	231, 309–10, 315
30:28	3, 304, 316
30:30	269–70
33:30	316
34:7	349
36:8	152, 195

Scripture Index

Job (*cont.*)
36:13	195–96
36:16	163–64
38:8–11	174
38:40	110

Psalms
1	19
3:1[2]	258
3:6[7]	168
4:1[2]	90, 149, 165–66
6	80
6:7[8]	302–3
7	241
7:2[3]	240
7:5[6]	130, 274
7:12–13[13–14]	255, 257
7:15[16]	190
9:13[14]	122–23, 132
9:15[16]	190
10:8–9	238–39
11:2[3]	89, 255, 305–6
11:6	338–39
12:8[9]	168
13	80
13:3[4]	301–2, 315
17:9	168
17:11	130, 168, 173
17:12	238
18	293
18:4–5[5–6]	91, 194–95
18:4[5]	263–64
18:5[6]	118, 188, 200
18:6[7]	165
18:16[17]	117, 122, 132
18:19[20]	165
18:28[29]	312
18:29[30]	162–63
18:36[37]	165
18:42[43]	225
20:8[9]	131
22:11[12]	164, 231
22:12[13]	169
22:13[14]	240–41
22:14[15]	271
22:15[16]	130
22:16[17]	88, 169
22:20[21]	88
22:21[22]	240–41
24:2	105
25:15	189
25:17	149, 157
26:9	235
27:2	258–59
27:3	259
28.1	121, 123
28:3	235
29:5	212
30:1[2]	122–23, 132
30:3[4]	117, 121, 122
31	80
31:4[5]	185, 188–89
31:7[8]	149, 158, 165
31:8[9]	165–66
31:9[10]	147, 164
31:13[14]	171, 173
31:21[22]	180, 182
32:4	250, 276
32:6–7	154, 176–77
34:6[7]	164
34:18[19]	222–23, 226
35	80
35:7–8	119, 188–90
35:15–17	237, 281
35:16	239, 240, 278
35:26	305
36:11[12]	234, 274–75
37:12	239
37:14	255, 257
37:15	256, 258
37:24	129
38	79, 318
38:2[3]	249–50, 256
38:4[5]	275
38:6[7]	127, 129, 304
38:7[8]	269–70

Scripture Index

Psalms (*cont.*)

38:8[9]	226, 279
38:10[11]	301–2
38:11[12]	229
38:12[13]	186
38:16–17[17–18]	129
39:3[4]	269–70
39:10[11]	229, 249
40:2[3]	116, 122, 132, 134, 191–93
40:12[13]	172, 313
42–43	318
42	128
42:3[4]	341–43
42:5–6[6–7]	127
42:5[6]	363
42:7[8]	88, 120, 262, 264, 280
42:9–10[10–11]	251–52
42:9[10]	304
42:10[11]	221, 278
43:2	304
43:3	312–13, 315
43:5	110
44:19[20]	226, 311, 313
44:25[26]	127, 128, 129
46:6[7]	212
49:5[6]	172
51	80
51:8[10]	226
55:3[4]	247
55:4[5]	276
55:5[6]	231
55:8[9]	267–68
55:18[19]	260–61
55:21[22]	258
56:1–2[2–3]	274–75
56:13[14]	129, 312–13, 316
57:3[4]	274–75
57:4[5]	240–41
57:6[7]	119, 128, 129, 189–90
58:6[7]	242–43
59:3[4]	248
59:6[7]	169, 171, 173, 305–6
59:16[17]	147
60:3[5]	341, 342, 348
61:2[3]	159
62:3[4]	251–52
64:2–4[3–5]	254, 257
64:3[4]	278, 345–46
64:5[6]	188–89
65:13[14]	103, 153
66:11	185–86, 276
66:12	271
69:1–2[2–3]	119, 176–77
69:2[3]	116, 117, 120, 202, 263–64
69:4[5]	258–59
69:14[15]	116
69:15[16]	119, 176–177, 263–64
69:17[18]	147, 164
69:20[21]	220, 223, 278
69:21[22]	340, 342
69:23[24]	301, 315
69:26[27]	252
71	80
71:4	249, 345–46
71:10–11	246–47
71:20	117, 164
73:6	153
73:14	229
73:21	221, 336
74:12–15	174
75:8[9]	338–39, 342, 348
77:2[3]	164, 307
77:3[4]	159
77:4[5]	228
77:6[7]	306
77:10[11]	248
79:8	129
80:5[6]	341–43
82:4	249
84:11[12]	87
86:7	164

Scripture Index

Psalms (cont.)

86:13	117, 120
86:14	247–48
88	80, 358, 361
88:3[4]	121
88:4[5]	121, 124
88:6[7]	1, 99, 115, 119, 120, 191–92, 311, 313
88:7[8]	264–65, 276
88:8[9]	163–65, 198, 207
88:9[10]	302–3
88:17[18]	175
88:18[19]	309–10
89:46[47]	270
93:4	264
102:2[3]	147, 164
102:4[5]	252
102:9[10]	341–42
102:10[11]	233–34
106:33	336
107:10	195, 308, 313
107:14–16	196–97
107:14	308
107:26	272
109:2–3	171, 173, 260–61
109:22	220–21
109:23	233
109:29	305
112:10	239
113:7	131
116:3	118, 194–95, 205, 231
116:6	129
116:16	196
118:5	165–66
118:10–12	168–69
118:12	271
118:13	233, 280
119:25	128
119:28	131, 132, 272
119:61	194
119:85	119, 192
119:110	186, 188
119:143	164, 231
119:145	165
124:3–5	176–77
124:3	153, 170
124:4–5	263, 286
124:6	241
124:7	189
129:4	196
130:1	114
135:6	105
138:7	145
139:8	106–7
140:3[4]	344
140:5[6]	152
140:9[10]	168, 170
141:9–10	186, 188–89
142:3[4]	159–160, 188–89
142:6[7]	129
142:7[8]	197–98
143:3	2, 130, 226, 280, 311, 313
143:4	153, 159–60
143:7	123, 191–92
143:11	158
144:7	123
144:11	258
145:14	131
146:8	131
147:3	223
147:6	131

Proverbs

4:17	349
4:12	147
5:3–4	339, 347
5:22	152
9:17	327
10:26	327
14:19	110
15:30	316
16:18	280
20:20	295
26:8	146
27:7	328
30:4	146
31:6	335–36

Proverbs (cont.)

31:15	240
31:27	349
31:29	108

Ecclesiastes

2:14	294
6:4–5	316
9:12	185

Isaiah

3:22	153
5:20	294, 328
6:6	212
8:8	176
8:16	145, 146
13:7	273
15:8	151
19:5	128
24:9	328
25:12	110
26:5	110
28:20	147
29:1	151
29:18	293
30:20–21	342, 349
38:10–20	77, 83
38:10	121, 199
38:12	307
38:13	242
38:14	123
38:15	333–34
38:17	336
42:3	302
45:7	293
49:19	147
49:20	147
58:5	110

Jeremiah

4:19	157–58
6:24	153, 199–200, 228
8:18–23	81
8:21	224, 228, 305, 320
9:15[14]	342
10:19–25	81
10:19	224
11:18–23	82
12:1–6	82
14:2—15:21	82
14:17–19	251–52
15:11	164
15:18	252
17:6–8	327
17:9–18	82
18:18–23	82
18:20	192
18:22	192
20:7–18	82
20:7	245
20:10	171
23:2	233–34
25:15–19	348
31:29	349
38:22	116
47:2	176
48:41	148
49:22	148

Lamentations

1:4	336–37
1:13	186, 188, 253, 270
1:14	275
1:15	274–75
1:20	147
2:4	255, 270
2:5	245–46
2:11	223–24
3	3, 77, 81
3:1–6	233–34
3:1	245–46
3:2	2, 311
3:3	249
3:4	224
3:5	88–89, 172–73, 181, 205, 345–46
3:6	2, 311–12

Scripture Index

Lamentations (cont.)
3:7	162, 164–65, 196, 276
3:9	87, 88, 161–62, 164
3:10	87, 88, 238
3:11	242
3:12	255–56, 279
3:13	254, 256
3:15	89–90, 322, 339–40, 342–43
3:16	130, 252–53
3:19	337
3:20	127
3:30	252–53
3:43	246–47
3:48	223–24
3:52	247, 280
3:53	191
3:54	176–78
3:55	115, 120, 191–92
3:62	260–61
4:18	247

Ezekiel
4:2	181
7:27	305
16:4	327
18:2	349
21:7[12]	273
26:16	305
27:30	317, 338

Daniel
5:6–10	320
7:28	320

Hosea
4:19	146
13:12	146

Joel
2:2	295

Amos
3:5	183

Jonah
2:2–9[3–10]	77, 82–83
2:2–5[3–6]	124–25
2:2[3]	118
2:3[4]	175, 264–65
2:4[5]	234
2:5[6]	175, 177
2:6[7]	175, 198–99
2:7[8]	159–60
2:8[9]	153
3:6	317

Micah
4:13	225

Nahum
2:10[11]	273
3:19	280

Zephaniah
1:15	295

Zechariah
11:17	302
12:10	338

~

DEAD SEA SCROLLS

1QH (Hodayot)
	83–84
7:19	158–59
10:5	251
10:12–13	262, 265, 278
10:17–18	97
10:21	120
10:25–26	181, 259
10:26	256
10:27–28	267–68

Scripture Index

1QH (Hodayot) (cont.)

10:27	120–21
10:29	190
10:34–35	250
11:6	117
11:7–18	265–66
11:7–12	153, 200
11:7	180, 182
11:17	120, 254–55
11:19–20	193
11:20	122–23
11:28	186–87
11:29–30	263–64
12:8–9	234
12:8	84
12:11	340
12:14	344
12:33	227–28, 271
12:36	229–30
13:6–7	242
13:6	193
13:8	268
13:9–10	241
13:10	344–45
13:12	158–59, 333–34
13:13–15	241–42, 257–58, 278
13:14	240, 243, 279
13:15	258
13:17	222, 226, 279
13:18–19	237, 279
13:26–29	344
13:27	347
13:29–30	161, 164–65, 227–28
13:30–31	201
13:31–32	345–46
13:31	172, 304–5
13:32	303
13:32–33	140, 157, 172
13:33–34	341–43
13:33	311, 313
13:34	172–73, 302–3
13:35–36	341
13:36–37	195–96
13:38	117, 197–98
13:39	170, 175
14:22–23	176–77, 265
14:24	121, 265
14:30–31	165–66
15:2–3	301–2
15:2	116, 202, 221, 224
15:4–5	221, 225, 267
16:14–15	263, 278
16:27–28	337
16:28–29	115, 121
16:30–31	269–70
16:31	265
16:32–33	220–22, 224–25, 272
16:34	185
16:35	195–96
17:3–4	118, 175, 265
17:6	201
17:8–9	130
17:26–28	309–10, 312
17:27–28	158–59
17:27	252
19:19–22	337–38
19:31–22	164
21:4	188–89
21:6	267–68
21:8	186, 188, 190
22:14	271–72

1QM

1:14	273
8:10	273
11:9	157
14:5–6	273
14:6–7	132

11Q5

24:5	222
24:16	223

11Q6

19:9–11	118

Subject and Author Index

Ableson, Robert, 28
Agonist and Antagonist, 93, 140–48, 171–72, 208, 210, 269
  definition, 43
Akkadian, 113–14, 155, 217–19, 249, 282–87, 299–300, 319, 328, 352–53
anger, 36, 51, 53–56, 64–65, 134, 156, 270–71, 297, 331, 335, 351
archetypes, 7, 45
associative field, 24–25, 109

Backhouse, A., 324–26, 364
Bamu, 298, 320
Barr, James, xvii, 11, 13, 18–24, 37, 48, 57–62, 68, 144, 203, 360–61
Barth, Christoph, 125–26
basic level categorisation, 27, 33, 53, 59, 63, 67, 108, 152, 236
Basson, Alec, 65, 108
bitter, 89, 97, 323–54
Bleeker, C., 298
Boas, Franz, 14–16, 31
Boman, Thorlief, 22
bow and arrow, 253–56
Brown, William, 166
Brueggemann, Walter, 7–8, 79

causation, 33, 43, 50, 118–19, 130, 164, 167, 172, 188, 204, 233, 278, 315, 357–58, 360
Cienki, Alan, 100
Clines, David, 64, 304
Cognitive Linguistics, 1, 4, 8, 9, 13, 23–24, 26–69, 70, 100, 149, 322, 362
cognitive topology, 50
coherence, 67, 97, 134–35, 203, 206, 281, 312, 316, 349, 361, 362
componential analysis, 26
conceptual integration, 44–45, 59, 132
conceptual metaphor, 8, 9–10, 30–38, 94–95
  active, 6, 25, 42, 59, 84, 96, 120, 133, 205, 316, 349, 360
  and culture, 9, 37–38, 51, 54–56, 67–68
  and emotion, 53
  biblical, 62–67
  definition, 33–34
  evidence, 36–37, 95–97, 132–36, 202–7, 277–82, 314–17, 346–51
  main meaning focus, 52, 64–65, 139
  metonymic motivation, 54, 126, 156–61, 220–22, 305

415

Subject and Author Index

conceptual metaphor (*cont.*)
    non-linguistic expression, 97, 135–36, 206–7, 317, 350–51
    productivity, 23, 42, 59, 96, 206, 300, 322
    research methodology, 52, 86–98
    scope, 52, 55, 64–65
    universality and variation, 55, 97–98, 136–38, 207–8, 282–87, 317–20, 351–54
conduit metaphor, 29
CONTAINMENT. *See* image schemas
conventional language, 2–11, 81
    degree of conventionality, 96–97
Conway, John, 110–11, 154, 296
Cornelius, Izak, 106
corpus research, 55–56
cultural prototypes, 46, 55, 97, 137, 208, 272, 284, 318, 325, 362–63

darkness. *See* primary metaphors
De Blois, Reinier, 63
Dead Sea Scrolls, 5–6
Deignan, Alice, 56–57
depression, 1, 47, 64, 101, 110–11, 114, 126–28, 134–37, 154, 207, 296–97, 301, 318, 335, 362
distress, 1–2, 69, 75–77, 89–90, 92, 95, 136, 216, 282–83, 355–60, 362
Douglas, Michael, 83–84
DOWN IS BAD, 108

Egypt, 104–5, 109–10, 115, 135, 183, 254, 292, 299, 331–32
Eidevall, Göran, 141
elaboration, 45, 55, 60, 96, 132–33, 202–3, 215, 272, 347, 360
embodied realism, 31
emotion, 53–54, 64–65, 75–77
EMOTIONS ARE FORCES, 53, 215–16

encyclopedic knowledge, 39, 61, 63, 65–67, 94–95, 178–79, 183–84, 360
entailments, 95, 111, 122–24, 129, 137, 143, 164–66, 172–73, 177–78, 182, 188–91, 196–97, 312–14
entrenchment, 42, 96–97, 132–33, 203, 214, 277–78, 301, 314, 348, 360–61
ethnopsychology, 10, 19, 59, 76–77, 138, 362
etymology, 19, 21–22, 60, 90–91, 300
event structure metaphor, 161–62, 204, 233, 313
evidence. *See* conceptual metaphor
experiential gestalt, 33, 75, 95, 118, 156, 211, 278–80, 356, 360

Fabry, Heinz-Josef, 141, 145, 149
Fauconnier, Gilles, 44–45
figurative language, 48–50, 60
Fillmore, Charles, 28
Finnish, 291, 297, 318, 330, 351
FORCE. *See* image schemas
force dynamics 141–42
    definition, 43–44
form criticism, 4–5, 75
frame, 28, 32, 66, 78–80, 115, 271
Frymer-Kemsky, Tikva, 106

Gadsup, 291
gender, 17, 20, 58
general corpus, 70–74
gestalt perception, 31–33. *See also* experiential gestalt
Gibbs, Raymond W., Jr., 4, 10, 47–51, 62, 143, 156
Goddard, Cliff, 290
Goldingay, John, 140–41, 149
Greece, 300–301
Gruber, Mayer, 134, 299–300

Guhu-Samane, 331, 351, 353–54, 362
Gunkel, Hermann, 4, 78–79, 81–82

habitual thought, 17
hand of God, 218, 229, 248–50, 285
Hausa, 330–31, 352
heat, 269–74
Hebrew
    Classical, 72–74
    emotions, 361–62
    language development, 70–74
    roots, 22–23, 24–26, 60–61, 153
    thought, 20, 57–58, 67, 203, 360–61
Helman, Cecil, 215–16, 282–83
hiding and highlighting, 34, 97, 119–20, 139, 167, 204, 233, 353, 359
historical criticism, 3–4, 10
Hodayot, 3, 6, 83–84
Holm-Nielsen, Svend, 6, 83
homonymy, 23–24, 40
    definition, 23
Humboldt, Carl Wilhelm von, 14, 67

idealized cognitive model (ICM), 34–36, 86
idiom comprehension, 50, 60, 156
image schemas, 2, 8, 31–33, 44, 59, 86, 91–98, 355–56
    and emotion, 76
    BALANCE, 91, 101
    compound / situated, 93, 95, 140–54, 209, 362
    CONSTRAINT, 92, 140–209
    CONTAINMENT, 31–32, 91, 101, 142–43
    definition, 31–32
    FORCE, 32, 91–92, 136, 141, 210–88
    NEAR-FAR, 66, 91
    psychological reality, 51
    SCALE, 101
    SOURCE-PATH-GOAL, 31, 34, 91
    STRAIGHT, 100
    universality and variation, 67, 93, 141–54
    value judgments, 101, 108, 115, 154
    VERTICALITY, 65, 66, 91–92, 99–139, 175, 209, 353
inferential structure, 36, 96, 133, 203–4, 211, 278–79, 314–15, 329, 347–48, 361
intensity, 17, 32, 52, 64–65, 95, 98, 101, 111, 120, 177, 190, 204, 218, 228, 233, 243, 249–56, 258–59, 263, 279–80, 287, 291, 294–98, 318, 330–31, 343, 347–48, 361
intertextuality, 5–6, 10

Jäkel, Olaf, 62–63.
Japanese, 58, 297–98, 318
Johnson, Mark, 9, 30–38, 100–101, 142–43, 211, 278, 290
Johnston, Philip, 125–26

Kimmel, Michael, 93, 362
Kittel, Bonnie, 84
Kotzé, Zacharias, 64–65, 68, 77
Kövecses, Zoltán, 10, 51–56, 64, 68, 97, 136, 156, 215–16, 282–86, 362
Kraus, Hans-Joachim, 4, 79
Kruger, Paul, 64, 77, 128, 136
Krzeszowski, Tomasz, 101
Kutler, Laurence, 334–35
Kutscher, Eduard, 72–73

labor and childbirth, 148, 152, 155, 199–201
Lakoff, George, 9, 30–38, 290, 362
Lamb, Sydney, 18
Lamberty-Zielinski, Hedwig, 150
lament terminology, 4, 81

Langacker, Ronald, 38–41, 60, 66
lexical semantics, 39–41, 46–47, 68
LIFE IS A JOURNEY, 62–63
linguistic relativity, 10, 13–18, 37–38, 41, 44, 67, 359
lion. See scripts
literality, 48–49
literary criticism, 5–6
Lucy, John, 18

main meaning focus. See conceptual metaphor
mappings, 35, 45, 50–51, 68, 75, 86, 94–95, 114–32, 156–202, 220–77, 301–14, 333–46
master metaphor, 53, 216
McElhanon, Ken, 66–67
McMullen, Linda, 110–11, 154, 296
melting, 271–74
mental spaces, 44–45
Merwe, Christo van der, 63–64
Mesopotamia, 102–6, 109, 217, 250, 269, 292, 299, 331–32, 359. See also Akkadian
metaphor comprehension, 49–50
metaphorical transference, 25, 58–59
metonymy, 35–36, 56, 68, 80, 86, 156–61, 220–22, 224, 284, 301–3, 305–7
Mulder, H., 295

Natural Semantic Metalanguage, 46
Newsom, Carol, 84
novel metaphor, 36, 96, 133–34, 205–6, 280–81, 316, 348–49

Papua New Guinea, xix, 7, 291, 296, 329, 363
Pedersen, Johannes, 125–26
physiology, 7, 53–54, 56, 76, 94, 95, 100–101, 141–44, 156–60, 211, 214–16, 220–22, 271, 290–91, 301–5, 323–24, 336

pits, wells, and cisterns, 103–4, 137, 191–94
poetic metaphor, 50, 91
Pohlig, James, 65
polysemy, 23–24, 40, 45, 58–59, 61–62, 68, 155
  definition, 23
  generalizations over, 36, 96, 132–33, 153, 202–3, 277–78, 314, 346–47, 360
posture, 108–10, 126–32
Price, James, 295
primary metaphors, 2, 59, 91–98
  darkness, 16, 92, 289–321, 353
  definition, 34, 289
  smell, 322
  taste, 92, 94, 322–54
  universality and variation, 94
primitive mentality, 21
priority of the concrete, 24, 25, 36, 58–59, 62, 68, 93
prison, 197–99
prototype effects, 27, 35
prototypes, 26–27, 39, 46, 61, 63, 67, 80, 86–87, 89, 148–49, 326–29. See also cultural prototypes
prototypical scenario, 53, 95, 108, 144, 151, 153, 293–94, 356–60
psycholinguistics, 47–51, 61
psychological interpretation, 6–9, 10, 79
Punjabi, 112

Rad, Gerhard von, 4
Rechenmacher, H., 63
Reddy, Michael, 29
root meanings. See Hebrew roots
Rosch, Eleanor, 27
Russian, 111–12
Ryken, Leland, 6–7

Sáenz-Badillos, Angel, 72–73

salience, 60, 67–68, 80, 94, 143, 167, 179, 211–13, 305
salt, 323–29
Sapir, Edward, 15–16, 67
Sawyer, John, 24–26, 206, 360
scenario. *See* prototypical scenario
schematic networks, 40–41, 42, 60–62, 68, 144, 148, 153
schematicity, 39, 97
Schank, Roger, 28–29
Schmoldt, H., 303
scope. *See* conceptual metaphor
scripts, 28–29, 32, 360
   human conflict, 244–62
   ingestion, 353
   lion attack, 29, 237–44
   restaurant, 28
   siege, 94–95, 182
   traps and nets, 184
semantic change, 36
semantic network, 144–49. *See also* schematic networks
semantic primitives, 45–47
Selye, Hans, 214–15
Seybold, Klaus, 79–80, 229
Sheol, 104–7, 117–18, 120–21, 125–26, 137, 193
siege. *See* scripts
sign language, 37
sour, 323–29
source and target domains, 33–34, 45, 50–51, 55, 59, 68, 84, 89–92, 95, 136–37, 282–84, 290–96, 360–61
spaciousness, 206

specific corpus, 75–85, 90
stress, 150, 214–15
structuralism, 17, 19
subjectivity, 91
Sussman, Max, 229
sweet, 323–29
Sweetser, Eve, 62, 290, 315
sword, 257–58

Talmy, Leonard, 43–44, 141–42
target domain. *See* source and target domains
Taylor, John R., 6, 41–42, 60, 66
Teacher of Righteousness, 3, 83–84
tears, 341–42
topic, 75, 87–92
transparency, 25, 55, 60
traps and nets, 183–91
Tromp, Nicholas, 125–26
Turner, Mark, 10

Ugaritic, 71–72, 174
UP-DOWN. *See* image schemas

vehicle, 87–92
VERTICALITY. *See* image schemas

water, 174–78, 213, 262–68
weight, 275–77
Whorf, Benjamin Lee, 16–18, 40, 67
Whorfian linguistics, 13
Wierzbicka, Anna, 45–47, 362
wild animals, 236–44
Wittgenstein, Ludwig, 26–27

www.ingramcontent.com/pod-product-compliance
Lightning Source LLC
Chambersburg PA
CBHW072116290426
44111CB00012B/1681